John Murray

Handbook for Travellers

In Derbyshire, Nottinghamshire, Leicestershire, and Staffordshire. Third Edition

John Murray

Handbook for Travellers
In Derbyshire, Nottinghamshire, Leicestershire, and Staffordshire. Third Edition

ISBN/EAN: 9783337209001

Printed in Europe, USA, Canada, Australia, Japan

Cover: Foto ©Lupo / pixelio.de

More available books at **www.hansebooks.com**

HANDBOOK FOR TRAVELLERS

IN

DERBYSHIRE, NOTTINGHAMSHIRE,

LEICESTERSHIRE, AND STAFFORDSHIRE.

THIRD EDITION REVISED.

WITH MAPS AND PLANS.

LONDON:
JOHN MURRAY, ALBEMARLE STREET.
1892.
WITH INDEX AND DIRECTORY FOR
1904.

LONDON:
PRINTED BY WILLIAM CLOWES AND SONS, LIMITED,
DUKE STREET, STAMFORD STREET, S.E., AND GREAT WINDMILL STREET, W.

PREFACE.

IN compiling the present edition of this Handbook, an endeavour has been made to render the work as complete and accurate as possible; and, with a view to adding to its usefulness, numerous Plans and Maps have been inserted.

The Editor has revised the book, as far as possible, by personal research; but he is greatly indebted to many clergy and others, who have rendered him valuable assistance by favouring him with particulars respecting their several localities. To Mr. W. Salt Brassington, F.S.A., and to Mr. G. H. Wallis, F.S.A., his thanks are especially due for the information they have supplied with regard to the counties of Staffordshire and Nottinghamshire respectively.

It is hoped that readers who may detect any mistatements or inaccuracies will be so good as to notify them to Mr. John Murray, 50, Albemarle Street, London.

H. M. C.

1892.

LIST OF PLANS AND MAPS.

	PAGE
Plan of Derby	to face 4
Map of Matlock, Bakewell, Chatsworth, &c.	,, 28
Plan of Haddon Hall	35
Map of Buxton and environs	to face 46
,, Peak District	,, 56
Plan of Nottingham	,, 68
Map of the Dukeries	,, 96
Plan of Leicester	,, 108
,, Stafford	,, 148
,, Lichfield Cathedral	,, 162
Map of Dovedale, Ashbourne, and Matlock	,, 200
,, the Counties	at the end.

CONTENTS.

INTRODUCTION . . . . Page [1]

ROUTES.

∗ The names of places are printed in **black** in those Routes where the places are described.

ROUTE	PAGE
1. Burton to **Derby** [Repton].	2
2. Derby to Trent Junction, by **Melbourne** and **Castle Donington**.	10
3. Trent Junction to Chesterfield, by **Ilkeston, Alfreton**, and **Clay Cross** . .	13
4. Derby to Sheffield, by **Belper** and **Chesterfield** [Wirksworth] . . .	16
5. Derby to **Bakewell**, by **Matlock** and **Rowsley** .	26
6. Bakewell to Buxton [Haddon Hall, Chatsworth, the Lathkill, Tideswell] . .	33
7. Buxton to Manchester, by **Chapel-en-le-Frith** . .	46
8. Chapel-le-Frith to Bakewell, by **Castleton, Hope, Hathersage,** and **Eyam** [The Peak].	52
9. Buxton to **Hayfield** and **Glossop**.	63
10. Derby to Nottingham, by Trent Junction . . .	64
11. Nottingham to Lincoln, by **Newark**	74
12. Nottingham to Grantham, by **Bingham** and **Bottesford** [Belvoir] . .	78
13. Nottingham to **Mansfield**, by **Newstead** [Hardwick Hall, Bolsover] . . .	82
[*Derby, &c.*]	
14. Newark to Mansfield, by **Southwell**	92
15. Mansfield to Worksop and Retford [Welbeck] . .	95
16. Newark to Worksop, by Ollerton [Thoresby, Clumber]	99
17. Newark to Doncaster, by **Tuxford, Retford**, and **Bawtry**	101
18. Worksop to Doncaster, by **Tickhill** [Blyth, Roche Abbey].	104
19. Market Harborough to Leicester	106
20. Nuneaton to Leicester, by Hinckley [Bosworth Field]	114
21. Leicester to Melton Mowbray and Oakham . .	116
22. Market Harborough to Newark	119
23. Leicester to Burton, by Ashby-de-la-Zouch . .	121
24. Ashby-de-la-Zouch to Leicester, through Charnwood Forest [St. Bernard's Monastery, Bradgate Park].	124
25. Rugby to Trent Junction, by Leicester, Mount Sorrel, and Loughborough [Lutterworth]	129
26. Birmingham to Wellington, by West Bromwich and Wolverhampton . . .	134

b

ROUTE	PAGE	ROUTE	PAGE
27. Birmingham to Crewe, by Wolverhampton, **Bushbury**, and **Stafford**	142	33. Crewe to Burton-on-Trent, by **Stoke-on-Trent, Uttoxeter**, and **Tutbury** [The Potteries]	188
28. Stourbridge to Burton-on-Trent, by **Dudley, Walsall**, and **Lichfield**	152	34. Uttoxeter to Buxton, by **Ashbourne** and **Hartington** [Dovedale]	196
29. Birmingham to Burton-on-Trent, by **Tamworth**	169	35. Uttoxeter to Macclesfield, by **Alton Towers** and **Leek** [Cheadle]	206
30. Walsall to **Rugeley**, by **Cannock** [Needwood Forest]	175	36. Stoke-on-Trent to Congleton, by **Biddulph**	213
31. Tamworth to Newport, by Rugeley, **Colwich**, and **Stafford**	179	37. Stoke-on-Trent to Market Drayton, by **Newcastle-under-Lyme**	215
32. Colwich to Stoke-on-Trent by **Sandon, Stone**, and **Trentham** [Chartley]	183		

INDEX 217

INTRODUCTION.

	PAGE
I. PHYSICAL FEATURES AND GEOLOGY	[1]
II. COMMUNICATIONS	[16]
III. INDUSTRIAL RESOURCES	[19]
IV. ANTIQUITIES	[25]
V. SKELETON TOURS	[30]

I. PHYSICAL FEATURES AND GEOLOGY.

A. **Derbyshire** lies a little to the N.E. of the centre of England, and under shelter, as it were, of the great backbone of the land, at least a third of the most northerly portion of the county being occupied by the southern outliers of that range. Indeed, there is but little flat and level ground in Derbyshire, and what there is is almost entirely in the S., in the neighbourhood of the Trent, and its feeders. The mountainous district in the W. and N.W., known as the Peak, and chiefly lying, as far as Derbyshire is concerned, in the High Peak hundred, but extending southward into that of Wirksworth, contains that beautiful scenery of the millstone-grit and mountain limestone for which the county is pre-eminent. This scenic interest, however, does not arise so much from the elevation of the hills, the most lofty of which are only about half the height of the highest summits of Wales and Scotland, as from their romantic grouping, and the bold and varied arrangement of the dales and cloughs, which offer exquisite landscape pictures. It may here be noted that, although this mountainous district is generally attributed to Derbyshire, and goes by the distinctive name of the Peak, it extends in reality over a considerable portion of North Staffordshire (in the hundred of Totmanslow), where it is known as the Moorlands. The Staffordshire section includes the W. part of the valley of the Dove (the dividing line of the counties), and the valleys of the Manifold, Hamps, and Churnet (wherein stand Alton Towers), the Weaver range of hills, the wild scenery of the Roaches near Leek, and many other points of interest. The district also impinges upon Cheshire, in which county we find the wild upland moors on the W. side of the Goyt, a few miles from Buxton, culminating, at the Cat and Fiddle, a well-known moorland inn (Rte. 7). But to return to

[2]   *Introduction.—Physical Features and Geology.*

Derbyshire: the mountain, called by some the Peak, which is the centre of this district, is an escarped plateau of millstone-grit, of about 3 m. in length, in the corner between Yorkshire and Cheshire, having for its principal points Kinderscout, 1981 ft.; Madwoman's Stones, 1880 ft.; and Edale Moor. To the N. and E. of the Kinderscout range is a continuation of the grit in open moors, extending into Yorkshire as far E. as Sheffield, under the names of Glossop Moor; Featherbed Moss, 1773 ft.; Alport Moor; Howden Edge; Derwent Edge; and Bamford Moor; the majority of which are from 1500 ft. to 1800 ft. in height, and contain scenery of a wild character, pleasantly varied by the soft luxuriance of the small river-valleys.

The Derwent is the principal river of this district, rising in the grit moors near Glossop, flowing due S., and receiving the tributary streams of the West-End, Alport, and Ashop. To the S. of the Kinderscout range is the beautiful valley of the Noe (which includes Castleton), the southern boundaries of which are Cowburn; Rushup Edge, 1816 ft.; Mam Tor, 1709 ft.; and Lose Hill, 1572 ft.; round which latter hill, and between it and Win Hill, 1532 ft., the stream winds to join the Derwent lower down. To the W. of the Peak, and above Chapel-en-le-Frith, the millstone-grit continues its course into Cheshire, forming the picturesque heights of Dympus (1633 ft.) and Chinley Churn (1493 ft.). The small streams that water these valleys, such as Otterbrook and Blackbrook, run westward into the Goyt (a head-water of the Mersey), and so find their way into the Irish Channel.

To the S. of Chapel-en-le-Frith, the Manchester and Buxton Railway may be roughly taken as the division between the millstone-grit and the limestone; the former being well seen in Comb's Moss, whence it gradually becomes of less importance. To the S.W. of Buxton, which is finely placed at the point where the limestone emerges from under the millstone-grit, is Axe Edge, 1751 ft., a long prolongation of grit, giving rise to the Goyt and the Dane, which flow into the Irish Sea, and the Wye and the Dove, that run into the German Ocean. To the S. of a line drawn from Buxton, Chapel-en-le-Frith, Castleton, Hope, and Hathersage, extends a large area of mountain limestone, as far S. as Ashbourne and Uttoxeter, and E. to Matlock, Cromford, Ambergate, and Belper; indeed almost as far as Derby itself. This district is full of interesting and beautiful valley scenery, although few hills rise above 1500 ft.; the principal of these are in the valley of the Dove (of which the western portion is in Staffordshire), such as Chrome Tor, High Wheeldon, Thorpe Cloud, Wolfscote, &c., and the ramifications of the limestone dales are most beautiful and extraordinary, some of them being watered by streams of fair size, while others are mere ravines, where the water scarcely leaves a path even for the pedestrian.

The whole course of the Wye, of the Derwent from Hathersage to Ambergate, and of the Dove in its middle portion, is through a series of precipitous and escarped rocks, in which the characteristic features of limestone districts are well seen. A common occurrence is that of "swallows" or "swallow-holes," consisting of a pit or cleft in the rock, through which a stream suddenly disappears, emerging again to the light of day a considerable distance off. Such are to be found at Doveholes, Wormhill, Perryfoot, near Castleton, and in the Staffordshire valleys of the Hamps and Manifold. "These swallow-holes, as they are justly called, often seem to mark out interruptedly for miles the lines of limestone, whose actual edges may be obscured by the sliding of other matter over them."—*Phillips*. The principal development of the limestone is to the S. of Castleton, which is also famous for its magnificent caverns and mines, at Tideswell, and in the course of the Wye through Miller's Dale and Monsal Dale to Bakewell and Matlock; at which latter place the cliffs, such as High Tor and Masson, assume noble proportions.

The movements to which the limestone has been exposed are well seen in the great chasms and rifts of these river-valleys, as are also the wasting effects of the elements, which have been sufficient to excavate vertical rents and to insulate those great rock-pinnacles that, in Dovedale especially, give the most romantic features to the valleys. "The shale and grit, or flagstone, series, above the scar-limestone, is called in Derbyshire the limestone-shale. It is about 500 ft. thick, and consists principally of black or brown durable shale, forming a very wet soil, and causing landslips of great extent beneath the millstone-grit summits. Mam Tor, or the Shivering Mountain, exhibits these characters very decidedly. The shale, however, is interstratified, to a great extent and with considerable regularity, with thick rocks of fine-grained micaceous gritstone, of excellent quality for building, and (generally at the bottom of this rock) with good durable micaceous flagstone, similar to that in the more recent coal-strata. Some less regular sandstone beds, called 'cankstone,' approach very nearly to the nature of the ganister series of the coal-strata. Mr. Farey, who considers these interpolations as anomalous, calls by the same name the very characteristic beds of black argillaceous limestone which lie in this shale at Ashford and Ashbourne, and produce lime fit for water-cement."—*Phillips*.

The carboniferous or mountain limestone of Derbyshire is a formation of great but unknown thickness, consisting for the most part of nearly pure massive limestone, with a few thin partings of shale, and at least two, probably three, interstratified beds of a doleritic rock known as *toadstone*. The toadstones represent contemporaneous submarine flows of basic lava. Probably the term is a corruption of the German *Todtstein*, given to the rock by the old miners, who supposed that it was "dead" or barren of lead-ore. The Derbyshire limestone is rich in encrinites, corals, brachiopods, and other marine fossils; and many varieties form handsome marbles. The upper part of the limestone is more or less earthy, and contains layers and nodules of *chert*, a siliceous mineral, somewhat resembling flint. The ores obtained from the limetone are chiefly those of lead and zinc; the former carrying but a small proportion of silver. The ore-deposits are known locally as rake-veins, pipes, and flats. (*See* 'Geological Survey Memoirs on North Derbyshire,' 2nd edition, 1887.)

Between Ashover and Chesterfield there is a watershed, from which the Amber flows southward to the Derwent, and the Hipper and Rother northward to join the Don.

The Amber forms the boundary-line (superficially) between the limestone and the coal-measures of the Derbyshire and Nottinghamshire fields, which doubtless, prior to the elevation of the mountain limestone, were continuous with those of Cheshire and Lancashire. A line drawn from Yorkshire (for this coal-field is geologically one with the South Yorkshire field), through Chesterfield, Dronfield, Alfreton, and Heanor to Sandiacre, will mark out its western extent. On the E. it is defined by the magnesian limestone and Lower Permian strata, which overlie the coal-field and form a picturesque ridge of tableland, known by the name of Scarsdale, and extending from Barlborough on the N. to Bolsover and Pleasley, where it enters Nottinghamshire. The Erewash valley (the natural division between the two counties) intersects the coal-basin on the S. from Sandiacre to Ilkeston and Codnor Park, leaving a portion of the field in Nottinghamshire. The coal-field consists of open valleys and wooded uplands, which, on the whole, are not so much disfigured by the appliances for iron-making and coal-getting as in most colliery districts, except, perhaps, in the neighbourhood of Clay Cross. Prof. Hull gives the following general section of the Permian and Coal strata:—

Permian Rocks.

1. Marls and sandstone .. .. 40 feet.
2. Magnesian limestone .. .. 60 „
3. Marls—sandstone .. .. 30 „

Middle Coal Measures.

Strata to top hard coal about .. .. .. 700 „
Waterloo coal
Ell
Lower hard
Furnace } .. .. 1600 „
Black shale or clay
Kilburn
Shales

Lower Coal Measures or Ganister Series.

Flagstones of Wingfield Manor, shales, and flaggy sandstones, with two coals underlaid by ganister floors .. .. 1000 „

The best coals are the Top Hard and Lower Hard, the former being identical with the celebrated Arley Mine of Lancashire. The ironstone measures are of great value, and are usually called Rakes. The most important are those known as the Brown and Black Rakes of Butterley,

Introduction.—Physical Features and Geology.

Wallis's, Dogtooth, Black Shale, and Honeycroft Rakes, the latter being principally worked at Staunton, near Ilkeston. The Dale Moor Rake, worked also at the same place, abounds in fossil fish of the genera Palæoniscus and Platysomus; and the Dogtooth Rake at Chesterfield is noted for the plentiful occurrence of the shell named Anthracosia. The geologist in exploring the carboniferous strata of Derbyshire will have no difficulty in collecting a bag of characteristic specimens, the limestone everywhere displaying typical fossils, particularly mollusca and encrinites. To the S. of the limestone and coal districts occupying the remainder of Derbyshire is the New Red sandstone, through which the lower portions of the Dove and the Derwent wind their way to join the Trent. This part of the county is generally flat, though by no means deficient in beauty, and contains the most productive land, although it is of somewhat cold soil. To the S. of the Trent, and W. of the Soar, the ground is broken and varied, particularly as it approaches Leicestershire. A considerable quantity of gypsum is worked at Chellaston, between Derby and Melbourne, for the purpose of being made into plaster of Paris. (Rte. 2.)

The Upper Keuper clays here are interesting to the geologist as yielding minute Foraminifera, Cythere, Otolites, with spines and plates of small Echinoderms.

The following summary of soils of Derbyshire, compiled by Mr. Farey, may be interesting :—

Gravelly	77,000 acres.
Red marl	81,000 ,,
Yellow limestone	21,580 ,,
Coal measures	90,000 ,,
Gritstone and shale	160,500 ,,
Limestone and sandstone ..	51,500 ,,
Lower limestone	40,500 ,,
	522,080 ,,

B. **Nottinghamshire,** which is surrounded by the counties of Derby, Leicester, Lincoln, and York, has none of the varied and hilly character for which its neighbour on the west is so famous, as it lies quite out of the influence of the great ranges which form the backbone of England. But if it is wanting in mountainous scenery, it possesses all the pleasant and picturesque characters of a thoroughly English county, in which forests and rivers, uplands and fertile dales, busy villages and manufacturing towns, alternately present themselves.

The principal interest of the county is attached to the westerly portion, the most broken ground and varied scenery being found there, and, perhaps as a natural sequence, a large number of notable seats and residences. Indeed, it is to be questioned whether any district in England is so rich in fine estates as that between Worksop and Nottingham.

The Erewash river separates Nottinghamshire from Derbyshire.

[6]   *Introduction.—Physical Features and Geology.*

To the E. of this line, as far as Worksop, runs a belt of the highest ground that Nottinghamshire contains, which, speaking broadly, may be said to be included in the Sherwood Forest district, the most lofty eminences of which, however, do not exceed 600 ft. in height. In fact, they can scarcely be called hills so much as successive plateaus of high ground.

The Forest of Sherwood is now for the greater part enclosed and under cultivation, though there is still left some agreeable woodland scenery, with a few old trees here and there that possibly may have sheltered Robin Hood and Little John, particularly in the districts known as Birkland and Bilhaugh, between Worksop and Ollerton. This plateau gives rise to several streams, which, though flowing in different directions, all belong to the same watershed as that of the Trent, in which the whole county is included. They are—the Erewash, rising to the S.W. of Mansfield and flowing S. to join the Trent at Long Eaton; the Lene, from near Newstead, to the Trent at Nottingham; the Dovor Beck, which runs a nearly parallel course, a few miles E.; the Mann or Maun, and Meden, to the N. of Mansfield; and the Rainworth, rising near Newstead. These three latter streams all flow to the N.E. through the richest portions of the Dukery, and eventually unite under the name of the Maun, which, after receiving a small stream called the Poulter, runs northward to Retford, where it takes the name of the Idle and becomes a rather important navigable river.

> " Yet Sherwood all this while, not satisfied to show
> Her love to princely Trent, as downward she doth flow,
> Her Meden and her Mann she down from Mansfield sends
> To Idle for her aid."—*Drayton.*

It then passes Bawtry, receiving the waters of the Ryton (which rises near Welbeck), and makes an abrupt turn, skirting the northern division of the county, and falling into the Trent as this river leaves Nottinghamshire for Lincolnshire. The last portion of its course is known as the Car Drain.

This northern part of the county, which is bounded on the S. by the Manchester, Sheffield, and Lincolnshire Rly., is flat and comparatively uninteresting, particularly on the eastern side of the Great Northern Rly.; it partakes very much of the Lincolnshire character of scenery and its singular intersecting dykes or drains. " Whoever will take his station upon the hills near Styrrup, Everton, or Gringley, will at once perceive that the whole of the level ground now known by the names of Gringley, Everton, Misson, and Styrrup Cars—the latter extending through the lands of Tickhill, Stancil, and Hesley, to Rossington and Doncaster—has at one time been covered with water, which, divided by the high grounds of Plumtre, Bawtry, Martin, and Shooter's Hill, has to the N.E. of Rossington Bridge formed one immense lake or estuary, covering the localities where now stand Haxey, Thorne, and Hatfield, and, as we may reasonably conjecture, communicating with the Humber or the sea. The soil of all these Cars is essentially of the same character—black bog—and is filled with trees,

Introduction.—Physical Features and Geology.

generally speaking, pine, oak, and yew, which have evidently stood very thick on the ground, and, having fallen off at the base and leaving their roots *in situ*, are buried about a foot deep, although in some instances much deeper."—*Raine.*

The district between Sherwood Forest and the Trent gradually becomes flatter and less picturesque as it recedes from Sherwood; but when the Trent is approached, the scenery offers many beautiful river views, such as Gainsborough and Constable loved to paint. The Trent —celebrated by Camden as the river which

"Triginta dat mihi piscem;"

and sung by Drayton as the river

"Which thirty doth import; by which she thus divined,
There should be found in her of fishes thirty kind;
And thirty abbeys great, in places fat and rank,
Should in succeeding time be builded on her bank;
And thirty several streams, from many a sundry way,
Unto her greatness should their watery tribute pay"—

and by Milton in a juvenile poem as

"Trent, who like some earthborn giant spreads
His thirty arms along the indented meads"—

enters Nottinghamshire just after receiving the Soar from Leicestershire, and flows in a north-easterly direction across the county past Nottingham and Newark, dividing it into two unequal portions, of which the southern forms scarcely a fourth part. This district is broken and picturesque, and is known by the name of the Wolds, of which the highest portions are the Leake Hills to the E. of Kegworth. Two or three streams, such as the Smite and Devon, " two neat and dainty rills," water these miniature dales and fall into the Trent between Nottingham and Newark.

The geology of Nottinghamshire is not so interesting as that of Derbyshire. The beds of the lias, new red sandstone, magnesian limestone, and coal, succeed each other in regular sequence from E. to W. The lias district may be defined by a line drawn from near Gainsborough to Newark, and thence to Bingham, keeping on the eastern side of the valley of the Trent. Near Bingham the lias-beds extend to the S. and enter Leicestershire, their contour being marked by the valley of the Soar. " From Gringley-on-the-Hill to West Markham extends a bold and elevated chain of hills, composed chiefly of red marl, lias, shale, and limestone, which commands a very extensive view of the counties of Lincoln and Nottingham, as well as of South Yorkshire, and from which, as the most remarkable feature of the district, the hundred of Bassetlaw, Bersetlaw, the Berset Hill, has indisputably in remote antiquity derived its name." To them succeed the red marls and Keuper sandstones of the New Red, which indeed may be said to occupy by far the greatest portion of the county—extending westward to a line drawn from Doncaster to Worksop, Mansfield, and Nottingham.

The caverns of Nottingham, Sneinton, Papplewick, and others, are

Introduction.—Physical Features and Geology.

all excavated from the New Red series. Considerable deposits of gravel are found, particularly in the district of Sherwood Forest, in many places consolidated into a breccia or conglomerate. Between the New Red and the coal-basin, occupying a thin strip of about 6 to 8 miles in breadth, is the magnesian limestone, which is interesting inasmuch as several pits have been sunk through these beds to the underlying coal. Indeed, by far the greater part of what is known as the Nottinghamshire coal-basin is in reality covered superficially by Permian beds. At the Shireoaks Colliery, near Worksop, the Upper Permian marls, magnesian limestones, and Lower Permian beds, are 196 feet in thickness, through which the sinking has been carried before arriving at the coal —the subsequent strata of the coal-measures being 1500 ft., and containing the following seams of coal, together with beds of ironstone:—

	Feet thick.
The Manor Coal	2
Shireoaks	4
Furnace	3
Hayles	3
Top Hard or Barnsley (cut at a depth of 510 yds.)	4
Dunshill	3
Waterloo	4½
Soft	3½
Lower Hard	4
	31

The Duke of Newcastle's success in this attempt to prove the coal under the Permian solved a great problem, important not only as a local fact, but to the country at large, viz. the possibility and feasibility of extending our coal-workings into districts hitherto untried. The Shireoaks experiment proves " the existence of the coal in workable seams continuously from Sheffield under the Permian rocks and New Red sandstone. The seams lie so horizontal that the eastern limit of the field cannot be determined."

c. **Leicestershire,** from its peculiar conformation, presents a number of salient angles, which consequently involves a larger proportion than usual of neighbours, viz. the counties of Nottingham, Lincoln, Rutland, Northampton, Warwick, and Derby. Leicestershire does not rank high in the estimation of tourists for scenic beauty; but, although the hills, generally speaking, are anything but lofty, they frequently have, especially in the northern portion of the county, owing to geological causes, a sharpness and irregularity of outline that is highly picturesque. The vales, too, are rich and fertile, and the more open country, if somewhat monotonous, as becomes a great grazing district, is cheerful and breezy, and irresistibly recalls to all who are fond of sport the music of the hounds as they sweep along in full cry over the finest hunting country in the world. In fact, Leicestershire is a thoroughly English county, and deserves to be better known than it is by the tourist, who will find a great deal of interest in its lanes and byways,

Introduction.—Physical Features and Geology.

its moors and commons, its villages with their suggestive Danish names, and where the inhabitants often unite frame-work knitting with the rude labour of the agriculturist.

The hilly portions of Leicestershire are rather detached and isolated groups than continuous ranges, those which could best be described under the latter head being in the Wold district, which on the N.E. border are part and parcel of the same high grounds in Nottinghamshire and Lincolnshire, stretching all the way from Belvoir Castle on the borders to Barrow-on-the-Soar, and overlooking on the S. the plains of Melton Mowbray. Towards Barrow this range thickens out, and occupies part of Nottinghamshire to the S. of Bingham. It gives rise to the Devon and Smite, which flow northward to join the Trent near Newark, and on the southern side to some small streams flowing into the Wreak. This latter is a somewhat important river in Leicestershire hydrography running E. and W. to join the Soar at the base of the Wolds. It rises under the name of the Eye near Oakham, and receives a stream from Kettleby, near Melton, after which it takes its name of Wreak. The Leicester and Peterborough Rly. traverses the same valley, and the pleasant-looking stream is seldom out of sight from the line.

Along the southern portion, corresponding to the northern Wolds, is a rather long range of hills, which separate the basin of the Soar from that of the Welland, and run round, more or less interruptedly, towards the Rutlandshire border. From this range rise the Swift, flowing past Lutterworth to join the Avon, and a few smaller streams that fall into the Welland. This portion of the county thus belongs to a different water system from the rest.

The most northerly point of the county, which projects into Derbyshire, is separated on the E. from Nottinghamshire by the Soar, and is a continuation of the high grounds near Castle Donington and Kegworth that occupy the angle between the Trent and the Soar. To the S. these are connected, though with a slight interval, with the most lofty and most picturesque of Leicestershire hills, viz. Charnwood Forest, which fills up more or less with its outliers the district embraced by the Midland main line and the Leicester and Swannington Rly. There is a boldness about these syenitic ridges that at once bespeaks their igneous origin, and which, had they been a little higher, would have given them a place among English mountains. The principal range runs N.W. to S.E. from Gracedieu to Bradgate, flinging off the eminence of Bardon Hill, which, though only 853 ft. in height, from its singular position commands a more extensive view than many hills twice its altitude.

Geologically speaking, the Charnwood Forest hills may be described as a series of syenitic rocks, protruded through overlying schistose and carboniferous deposits, and surrounded at their base by triassic strata, which are disposed horizontally and were deposited subsequently to the elevation of the forest. The old rocks of Charnwood Forest form a puzzling group, the interpretation of which has, from time to time, engaged the attention of many geologists, including Sedgwick, Jukes, Ansted, Hull, Bonney, and Hill. An upheaval along an axis stretching from N.W. to S.E. has exposed a nucleus of ancient rocks, probably in part at least of archæan or pre-cambrian age. Many of the rocks appear to be composed of ashes and other volcanic ejectamenta. Roofing slates are worked at Swithland, and hone-stones, known as "Charley Forest hones," at Whittle Hill. A hornblendic granite has long been worked on an extensive scale at Mount Sorrel; but most of the other igneous rocks, such as those quarried at Markfield and Groby, are syenites. Molybdenite, a rare mineral, has been found in the Mount Sorrel quarries. The whole district is highly interesting on account of its isolation and distance from the other igneous localities of England.

Next in order—and indeed resting on the western side of Charnwood—are the carboniferous deposits forming the coal basin of Leicestershire. This coalfield is divided by geologists into 3 districts, viz. Moira on the W., Ashby-de-la-Zouch in the centre, and Coleorton on the E. "The central district is formed of Lower Coal Measures, without workable coal, and is bounded on both sides by downcast faults which introduce the workable coalbeds of Moira and Coleorton. The coal-seams of these latter districts cannot be identified with each other, though they are probably synchronous."—*Hull.* Although bounded on the E. by the Charnwood rocks, on the S. and W. they underlie the New Red sandstone; and in the district of Coleorton (and particularly at Bagworth) there are some collieries sunk through the Keuper marls of this formation, just as at Shireoaks. Indeed, at Swannington, a valuable bed of coal was sunk to, through a great mass of trap. Only in one place—viz. the northern side of the coal basin—is the limestone seen to emerge, and even there is much interrupted and distorted.

The general thickness of the Middle Coal Measures with 20 seams, of which 10 are workable, is about 1500 ft., and, below them, 1000 ft. more of Lower and unproductive measures. In the Moira district, which is remarkable for its salt-water reservoirs (Rte. 22), is a seam of cannel coal 3 ft. 6 in. thick, beneath which is the Main coal, 12 ft. thick. The latter, however, is only half this thickness in the Coleorton district. Probably owing to its proximity to Charnwood, this field is somewhat subject to igneous complications, for Prof. Hull tells us that "at Whitwick a remarkable bed of whinstone or greenstone intervenes between the coal-measures and the New Red sandstone. In one of the shafts at Whitwick Colliery it is 60 ft. thick, and has turned to cinders a seam of coal with which it comes in contact. It has evidently been poured out as a sheet of lava over the denuded surface of the coal-measures at some period prior to that of the trias."

The geological collector will find several varieties of coal-plants amongst the shales, together with the fossil fruit known as Trigonocarpum. The Anthracosia shell is also plentiful. The whole of the western portion of Leicestershire is occupied by the triassic or New Red sandstone, the limit of which is pretty accurately defined by a line running W. of, and parallel with, the main line of the Midland Rly. The lias there covers it, being a continuation of the great band of liassic strata that sweep from S.W. to N.E. through the Midland counties. At Barrow-on-Soar there are large quarries for obtaining lias lime (Rte. 24), which the geologist should visit, many splendid specimens of fishes and reptiles having been extracted from these beds. Overlying this series again is the oolite, which is not seen to any great extent in Leicestershire, save at the N.E., where it occupies the range of hills at Belvoir.

Westward, the range of Charnwood declines, though the high and broken ground of the Leicestershire coal-field fills up the district between Coleorton, Ashby, Gresley, and Burton-on-Trent. These hills furnish two small streams, which flow S. and S.W., watering a large district, to fall into the Anker near Atherstone, this latter river joining the Tame and ultimately finding its way into the Trent. The western portion of the county is undulating, occasionally rising, as at Hinckley, into considerable eminences; it is in this district that the Soar takes its rise and flows through the centre of Leicestershire, receiving a large number of tributaries, and after a course of 50 miles joining the Trent near Trent Junction.

D. **Staffordshire**, although one of the most important English counties, derives this importance more from its pre-eminence as a manufacturing district than from its reputation for beauty. In this respect, however, it is underrated, for, though fully one-half the shire is disfigured with fire and smoke, the other half possesses its share of picturesque scenery—scenery of that peculiarly diversified character which is so common in our midland counties. Of mountains, properly so called, there are none, and the only approach to them is found in the north of the county; but, in default of these, there is an extensive surface of high plateau-like ground, possessing the usual features of lofty moorlands, the boundaries of which are marked by broken and wooded escarpments overlooking luxuriant vales, watered by broad rivers, and ornamented with beautiful parks and groves. For descriptive purposes, Staffordshire may be roughly divided into North and South by a line cutting it in half, the south portion being mainly occupied by the South Staffordshire coal-field, which, next to that of Newcastle, has been the longest worked and the most productive in England. In shape it is something like an elongated and compressed pear, with the exception that both ends are rather tapering.

From the irregularity of its boundaries it trenches somewhat on the south on the counties of Warwick and Worcester, and it may be defined pretty exactly by a line drawn from Rugeley to Cannock, Wolverhampton, Sedgley, Stourbridge, and Hagley Park on the west; thence running south of Hales Owen, and returning through Harborne, Oldbury, West Bromwich, Great Barr, and Brownhills, back to Rugeley. The surface of this district is for the most part an undulating plateau, bounded externally by ridges, such as the Bromsgrove Lickey and the Clent Hills on the south ; on the west by the broken country of Shropshire ; whilst eastwards it is surrounded by the New Red sandstone plain of Birmingham and the districts watered by the Tame. Within itself, the coal-field occasionally rises up into bold and commanding heights, such as the Rowley Hills, an enormous mass of basalt to the S. of Dudley, "forming a hill about 2 m. in length and 820 ft. in height. This basalt assumes the columnar structure, affording examples of prisms as perfect as those from the Giant's Causeway in Ireland. Mr. Jukes considers that this rock has been poured out in the form of a lava-flow during the coal period, for the beds of coal dip under the basalt, and have been followed till found charred and utterly worthless."—*Hull*.

To the N.W. of the Rowley Hills is the singular chain of Dudley Castle Hill, the Wren's Nest, and Sedgley Beacon, varying from 730 to 760 ft. in height. These eminences are of the very greatest interest to the geologist as affording examples of an uprise of Upper Silurian rocks through the coal-measures, while at the same time they are instructive illustrations of denudation. In fact, the whole of these coal-measures repose directly on the Silurian rocks without the usual intervention of carboniferous limestone and Old Red sandstone—a fact which is accounted for by Mr. Jukes by supposing that, while the carboniferous rocks were being deposited, all this district was dry land, so that the coal-beds were deposited directly on the Silurian. The strata at Dudley and Wren's Nest are of Wenlock limestone and shale, and have afforded magnificent Silurian fossils.

The next high ground of any note is that of Barr, extending from Walsall to Barr Beacon, which is also composed of Wenlock limestone and which commands a splendid panoramic view. To the Barr plateau succeed the swelling moorlands of Cannock Chase, which, brown and barren as they are on the surface, contain inexhaustible mineral riches beneath. The greater portion of this extent of country is unattractive and monotonous, but the eastern and northern escarpments which overlook on the S.E. the distant valley of the Tame, and on the N. and N.E. the more beautiful Vale of Trent, are broken and romantic, and offer in the neighbourhood of Armitage, Rugeley, and Colwich, scenery of a pleasing description. It is singular that, while this large extent of country, so full of hills and rising grounds, is environed on all sides by rivers, such as the Rea, Trent, Sow, Penk, and Smestow, scarce a single stream, and not one of any note except the Tame, rises within it.

The coal-basin proper "appears to have been upheaved bodily along two great lines of fracture, which range in approximately parallel directions from north to south," and is terribly broken up by faults. The following is the succession of strata according to Professor Jukes :—

Triassic—Bunter Sandstone .. Upper mottled sandstone,
conglomerate beds, lower
mottled sandstone .. .. 1200 ft.

Introduction.—Physical Features and Geology

Permian	Breccia of felstone, porphyry, and silurian rocks; red marls, sandstone, and calcareous conglomerate 1000 to 3000 ft.
Upper coal-measures	Red and mottled clays, red and grey sandstone, and gravels .. .. .. 800 ft.
Middle coal-measures ′.. ..	1. Brooch coal. 2. Thick coal. 3. Heathen coal. 4. New Mine coal. 5. Furlong coal. 6. Bottom coal. With ironstone and other strata .. .. 510 ft.

The workable coal in the neighbourhood is exceedingly thick, about 65 ft.; of which the well-known ten-yard or thick coal is nearly one-half. This seam has been the great source of South Staffordshire wealth, but, from overworking and excessive waste, it is in a fair way to become exhausted altogether. A good seam has, however, been found and successfully worked at Sandwell Park. At Bentley there is a great fault, to the north of which this seam becomes divided and split up into nine smaller ones, separated from each other by a considerable thickness of sandstones and shales. To the north of the Cannock districts some of the pits are worked through the New Red sandstone, the dip of the coal-beds being from east to west. To the E. of the coal-field is a large district of New Red sandstone occupied by the valley of the Tame, which rises in the high ground near Essington, and flows S.E. past Perry and Aston, when it enters Warwickshire, and receives the Rea, Blyth, and Cole. Near Drayton Bassett it forms the boundary between Staffordshire and Leicestershire, and continues to do so until it joins the Trent at Alrewas, its course throughout the whole distance being through a pleasant undulating country, full of quiet English beauty. To the west of the coal-field the country is more broken as it approaches the high grounds of Shropshire. The scenery in the neighbourhood of the Smestow, and to the west of Wolverhampton, where the Penk takes its rise, is characterised by wooded chains of hills, of no great height, but of very pleasing diversity.

By far the most picturesque portion of Staffordshire lies in the northern division, although that is now greatly affected by the progress of the manufactures that have arisen in the North Staffordshire coalfield and the Potteries. Eastward of the Trent, which forms a marked line running from N.W. to S.E., the country is very pleasant, and is principally occupied by the high ground of Needwood Forest, which fills up the triangle formed by the North Staffordshire Rly. (from Stoke to Burton) and the Trent in its meandering course to the point where it enters Derbyshire. This district, though high and exposed, has been finely wooded, and several grand and famous old oaks are still standing, and, though now possessing the name only of forest, it still shows some exquisite samples of coppice, wood, and warren, alternating with fine old parks and quiet villages with venerable church-towers. To the west of the Trent, between it and the North-Western Rly., the country is more monotonous, though still somewhat elevated and undulating, and this feature continues all through the vales of the Sow and the Meese, as far as the Shropshire border, no hills of any size occurring to break the line. But between Stone and Stoke the Trent runs through one of the most pleasant parts of its career, between the wooded hills of Barlaston and Tittensor, and near the lordly gardens of Trentham. The North Staffordshire Rly. from Burton to Crewe introduces the tourist to scenery of a very different order, in which the luxuriance and beauty of the south are exchanged for the picturesque moorlands and hills of millstone grit, and the still more abrupt and romantic limestone cliffs.

The whole of the country between Newcastle and Macclesfield shows those gradations from the ridges of the North Staffordshire coal-basin to the more wild and rugged district between New Chapel and Biddulph which culminate in the ridge of Mow Cop, and in Axe Edge, which here forms the watershed of England. The district between Biddulph and the Churnet valley, where the coal-measure grits give place to the limestone, is broken and characteristic, though it is not equal to the romantic scenery of the Churnet valley, such as at Alton Towers and Cheddleton. Farther northwards, beyond Leek, the county becomes almost mountainous; and the Roaches, running from N. to S., are some of the most picturesque hills in England. Eastward of these rises a vast moorland plateau, its long westward escarpment being known as Morridge (*i.e.* Moor Edge), while to the S. it terminates in Cauldon Low and the Weaver range. This plateau is deeply indented by the gullies and waterways of some of the most beautiful streams in England, such as the Hamps, Manifold, and Dove, which give to the district a picturesque character fully rivalling Derbyshire itself.

The North Staffordshire coal-field, though much smaller than that of South Staffordshire, possesses more resources, the combined thickness of the seams being about twice as great, and it not being affected by many of those faults which interfere so seriously with the coals of the latter basin, and frequently extinguish them altogether. In addition to many valuable beds of ironstone, the workable coal-seams are 22 in number, making 100 ft. of coal. "This coal-field has the shape of a triangle, with its apex to the north at the base of Congleton Edge. The eastern side is formed of millstone grit, and the western of New Red sandstone or Permian strata."

The following brief table of geological localities in the four counties, and their produce, may be of use to the brethren of the hammer.

Derbyshire.

ASHFORD.—Carb. limestone: Phillipsia, Actinocrinus, Pinna, Spirifera acuta, Syringopora, Lithostrotion, &c.
BAKEWELL.—Carb. limestone: Platycrinus, Strombodes, Productus aculeatus, Pentremites, Cyathophyllum, &c.
DOVEDALE.—Carb. limestone.
MATLOCK.—Carb. limestone: rocks very full of typical fossils.
KINDERSCOUT.—Travertine deposit on millstone-grit.
CASTLETON and CAVEDALE abound in Phillipsia and Pleurorhynchus.
TRAYCLIFF.—Blue John mines. The beds here contain Phillipsia pustulata and Spirifera.
MAM TOR.—Goniatites expansa, Bellerophon.
DERWENT VALLEY.—Rock basins, Salt-cellars, Cakes of Bread.
STAVELEY.—Coal-fishes; Platysomus, Palæoniscus.
CLAY-CROSS.—Coal-measures, Plants, and Anthracosia.
BUTTERLEY.—Ditto.
BOLSOVER.—Magnesian limestone-quarries.
CHELLASTON.—Plaster-pits, in Keuper marl, contain Foraminifera, Cythere,&c.

Nottinghamshire.

New Red Sandstone caves at NOTTINGHAM, SNEINTON, and PAPPLEWICK.
New Red Sandstone cliffs, overhanging the TRENT between NOTTINGHAM and NEWARK.
Magnesian limestone quarries at MANSFIELD WOODHOUSE.
SHIREOAKS COLLIERY.—Permian beds.
MUSKHAM, near Newark, where human remains have been found in the valley of the Trent.

Leicestershire.

CHARNWOOD FOREST.—Slates, hone-stones, granites, and syenites.
COLEORTON Coal-field.—Whitwick greenstone.
MOIRA Coal-field.—Bath Colliery.
Lias of BARROW-ON-SOAR, where the following Fish and Saurians have been found: Cosmolepis Egertoni, Lepidotus serrulatus, Pholidophorus, Ptycholepis minor, Ichthyosaurus communis, I. intermedius, I. tenuirostris.
REDMILE, near Croxton.—Lias fossils.

Staffordshire.

DUDLEY.—Upper Silurian—an inexhaustible supply of typical fossils, including Terebratula, Euomphalus, Orthoceras, Bellerophon, Phacops, Calymene Blumenbachii, Cyathocrinus, Cyathophyllum, &c.
ROWLEY HILLS.—Columnar basalt of Rowley Rag.
WETTON HILL.—Ditto.
THE POTTERIES.—Coal-measures. Plants and Anthracosia abundant; fishes less so, but found at Fenton and Longton.
APEDALE.—Coal-measures. Fish abundant. Palæoniscus, Amblypterus, Rhizodus, &c.
NEEDWOOD.—Drift. Chalk flints and Ananchytes are common. Alabaster is found.

FROGHALL.—Hæmatite in limestone.
AXE EDGE and MOW COP.—Millstone-grit.
WATERHOUSES.—Limestone quarries. Mammoth remains.
SOUTH STAFFORDSHIRE.—Coal-measures, abounding in fish and plants.
CAULDON LOW.—Limestone quarries, abounding in Productus, Bellerophon, Euomphalus, &c.
CANNOCK CHASE.—Bunter Conglomerate in railway cutting between Rugeley and Hednesford. Characteristic Silurian and Mountain Limestone fossils.

II. COMMUNICATIONS.

A. **Derbyshire** is well supplied with railways and canals. A great artery of the Midland Railway runs through it from Trent to Manchester, passing Derby, Matlock, and Bakewell, with branches at Derby to Burton; at Duffield to Winksworth; at Ambergate to Clay Cross and Chesterfield; and at Miller's Dale to Buxton. Whilst the main line to the north, running along the Erewash Valley, to Sheffield, passes through the mineral districts of Clay Cross and Codnor Park, on the eastern border of the county, and through Chesterfield, with branches to Ambergate and Mansfield; and a line is in the course of construction through the Peak district. The London and North Western Railway has a line from Buxton to Manchester. The Great Northern Railway runs along the southern part of the county, from Nottingham to Uttoxeter, passing through the town of Derby, and having a branch line along the colliery district to Pinxton. The S.W. portion of Derbyshire is traversed by the North Staffordshire Railway; a branch line from Uttoxeter runs to Ashbourne. The Manchester, Sheffield and Lincolnshire line skirts the northern boundary, and has a branch to Glossop. A new company, the Lancashire, Derbyshire, and East Coast Railway, are making a line from the Manchester Ship Canal at Warrington, to the east coast at Sutton-on-the-Sea. This line will cut through the county transversely, passing Buxton and Chesterfield. In addition to the passenger railways, the colliery and ironworks districts are amply supplied with local lines for the accommodation of their traffic. Among these, the only one calling for attention is the High Peak Railway, which, as lately as the time of George IV., was the only means of inland traffic in Derbyshire. It commences at the Cromford Canal, near Cromford, takes a most circuitous route, near, though not close to, Wirksworth and Hartington, and passes Buxton to Whaley Bridge.

The principal canals are—

1. The Grand Trunk, which commences at Wilne Ferry, at the junction of the Derwent with the Trent, and runs thence into Staffordshire and Cheshire to connect the Trent with the Mersey.

2. The Derby Canal, which runs in a tolerably direct line from Derby to the Grand Trunk at Swarkestone, with a branch to the Erewash Canal at Sandiacre.

3. The Cromford Canal, which commences at Codnor and (sending off a branch to Pinxton) flows to Ambergate and Cromford.

4. The Erewash Canal runs from the Trent up the Erewash Valley and joins the Cromford Canal. It has a branch, called the Nutbrook Canal.

5. The Chesterfield Canal, beginning at Chesterfield, follows up the valley of the Rother, passes through East Retford, and eventually joins the Trent at Gainsborough.

B. The Communications of **Nottinghamshire** are principally supplied by the Midland Railway Co. The main line from the south enters the county from Leicester at Trent junction, and continues up the Erewash valley, on the borders of Derbyshire, to Sheffield, whilst a loop line from Kettering passes through the town of Nottingham and rejoins the main line at Ilkeston. The line from Derby to Nottingham, Newark, and Lincoln follows the valley of the Trent the whole way, sending off two branches to Mansfield. In addition to these, the Great Northern Rly. runs through the county from Grantham to Bawtry, passing Newark and Retford, with another line from Grantham to Nottingham and Derby, with a branch to Newstead Abbey and Annesley, whilst a joint line of the London and North-Western Railway and Great Northern Railway skirts the S.E. border, from Melton Mowbray to Newark. The northern districts, which are agricultural and comparatively thinly populated, are traversed by the Manchester, Sheffield and Lincolnshire Rly. from Sheffield to Retford; and a line is in course of construction by this company which will connect Sheffield with Nottingham and the south. The new line, being made by the Lancashire, Derbyshire, and East Coast Rly. Company, which is to connect the east and west coasts, will go transversely across the northern part of the county, passing through the Dukeries and Tuxford.

The water navigation, owing to the breadth and depth of the rivers, is well developed; the Trent being navigable for river craft all through the county, and the Idle from East Retford. The Grantham Canal, commencing at Nottingham, connects the Trent with the Witham at Grantham, sending off a branch to Bingham.

These two rivers are again connected near Retford by means of a canal called the Foss Dyke, thus giving water-way to Lincoln and the Wash.

The Chesterfield Canal crosses the county on the N., passing Worksop and Retford, and also joins the Trent. The Nottingham Canal connects that town with the Erewash Canal at Langley Bridge. Thus by means of the Trent, Nottingham is brought into immediate connection with the whole of the canal systems of England.

C. **Leicestershire** is furnished with railway communications chiefly by the Midland Company. Its main line from London runs through the centre of the county and the town of Leicester, entering it at Market Harborough and leaving it near Loughborough, although it skirts the Nottinghamshire border for some distance farther; whilst a loop line from Kettering enters from Rutlandshire, and passes through Melton Mowbray to Nottingham. The Rugby branch enters near Lutterworth and joins the main line at South Wigston. Through the north-east portion of the county a branch line from Syston Junction runs through Melton Mowbray to Oakham. The colliery districts to the N.W. of Leicestershire are traversed by the Leicester line to Burton. The London and North-Western Company has a joint line with the Midland Rly. from Nuneaton to Burton, passing Market Bosworth, with a branch to Loughborough (the Charnwood Forest Line); and a line from Nuneaton by Hinckley to Leicester. Another line belonging to this company runs along the S.E. border of the county, from Rugby to Peterborough, with a joint line with the Great Northern Rly., going off from Market Harborough by Melton Mowbray to Newark, with a branch to Leicester.

Two canals furnish the principal water-way: the one, the Union and Grand Union, goes S. from Leicester to join the Grand Junction Canal; the other from Ashby-de-la-Zouch to Hinckley, where it soon enters Warwickshire and joins the Coventry Canal. By these means the Soar and Trent, which are made navigable in the northern parts of the county, are connected with the water-system in the south.

D. **Staffordshire.**—The communications of this county are more numerous than in any county in England except Lancashire, owing to the large extent occupied by iron-works and collieries, and the enormous population dependent thereupon.

The main line of the London and North-Western Rly. runs through the county, entering it at Tamworth, and after passing by Lichfield, Rugeley, and Stafford, quits it shortly after leaving Madeley. It throws off numerous branches: (1) from Lichfield (Trent Valley Station) a line goes N.E. to Burton, and S.W. to Walsall and Dudley, passing Lichfield (Town Station), and another line to Birmingham *via* Sutton Coldfield; (2) from Rugeley a line runs to Walsall, by Cannock; (3) from Stafford to Wolverhampton, Dudley, and Birmingham, also to Wellington and Shrewsbury.

The North Staffordshire Rly. has lines from Crewe, passing Stoke and Uttoxeter to Derby; from Macclesfield to Burton, by Leek; and through the Potteries to Stone, with connections with the London and North-Western Rly. at Norton Bridge and Colwich.

The Great Northern Rly. has a branch line from Uttoxeter to Stafford.

The Midland Rly. runs from Derby, by Burton and Tamworth, to Birmingham, with a branch to Wolverhampton.

The Great Western Rly. has two lines running through the southern part of the county, one from Birmingham, passing Handsworth, Wednesbury, and Wolverhampton to Shrewsbury, and the other from Stourbridge, by Dudley and Bilston, to Wolverhampton.

Staffordshire is well off for water-way, being traversed throughout the whole of its length by the Grand Trunk Canal, which unites the Mersey and the Trent, and was one of Brindley's favourite undertakings. It enters the county near Harecastle, and accompanies the Trent more or less closely throughout the whole of its course. At Etruria it is joined by the Caldon Canal, which takes a very winding route through Endon to Cheddleton and Froghall, so as to bring the Churnet valley limestones and hæmatites to the iron-works of North Stafford'shire. The Coventry Canal enters at Fazeley, and joins the Grand Trunk near Alrewas, as does also the Wyrley and Essington Canal. The last is carried past Lichfield into the Cannock Chase district, where it meets with sundry others, such as the Daw End and the Fazeley Canals. These, together with the Birmingham and the Stafford-hire and Worcestershire, interlace with each other, and send off branches to every iron-work of importance, a very large proportion of the Staffordshire coal-trade being carried on by barges. The western parts of the county are accommodated by the latter canal, and that of the Liverpool and Birmingham Company.

III. INDUSTRIAL RESOURCES.

A. *Agriculture.*—The tourist cannot be long in **Derbyshire** without seeing that agricultural labour is not its chief mainstay. In fact, nearly seven-tenths of the county is occupied by mineral districts or hills, many of which, on the limestone, however, possess good herbage for pasture, while those of the millstone-grit are coarse and heathery. "A large proportion of the land is in permanent pastures, of which some are very rich. To the north of the enclosed land a traveller may proceed for miles without seeing an acre of arable land, there being nothing but a continuation of pasture both upon the hills and in the valleys. In this district scarcely any of the farms have more than 3 or 4 acres of arable land attached to them, and many have none whatever. Derbyshire cheese is noted as of a good quality, and the best is often sold for Cheshire or Gloucester, when made of the shape and colour of these cheeses. The common Derbyshire cheese is not generally coloured; it resembles some kinds of Dutch cheese and keeps well."—*Knight.*

The most productive districts are naturally the alluvial valleys of the rivers, as the Trent and the lower portion of the Dove, which occasionally overflow their banks and exercise a fertilizing influence. About the latter river there is a local saying :—

"In April Dove's flood
Is worth a king's good." (*i.e.* ransom).

"This river will swell so much in twelve hours' time that, to the great terrour of the inhabitants thereabouts, it will wash off sheep and cattel, and carry them along with it; yet falls again within the same time and returns to its old bounds; whereas the Trent being once over the banks, keeps the fields in float four or five days together."—*Camden.*

Minerals are plentiful in the county, and furnish employment to a very large number of the inhabitants. They consist of—

Lead, which is found abundantly in the mountain-limestone districts, and occasionally in the toadstone between the limestone layers. "The veins which contain lead have generally a direction E. and W.; some of them approach the perpendicular (rake-veins), others are nearly horizontal (pipe-veins), and are rather beds of spar and ore, lying between the limestone strata, and in most cases connected with the surface by a like vein."—*Knight*. The term "rake" is applied to beds of iron-ore as well as lead. Castleton (Rte. 8) is the great centre of the lead-mining districts, as are also Matlock and Wirksworth farther S. (Rtes. 4, 5). The former place is also celebrated for the "Blue John," or fluor spar, which is found in one particular cavern associated with the lead-mining, and is greatly sought after for the purpose of being made into vases and other ornaments. In the year 1891 the amount of lead-ore raised in Derbyshire, from the mines, was 4510 tons, producing 3157 tons of lead. Zinc-ore was also raised to the amount of 160 tons. Five mines, including Blue John at Castleton, produced 108 tons of fluor spar; from twelve mines 812 tons of barytes were raised; and 38,656 tons of fire-clay, 71 tons of manganese ore, 506 tons of ochre and umber, and 100 tons of petroleum were obtained.

Coal and Ironstone.—From the collieries in the county of Derby 11,039,536 tons of coals were raised in 1891. There were 32 furnaces in blast, principally at Codnor Park, Butterley, Staveley, and Clay Cross, which in 1891 made 387,127 tons of pig-iron, for which 1,115,291 tons of iron-ore were used. The amount of iron-ore raised from the coal-measures was 20,810 tons, almost entirely consisting of argillaceous carbonates and peroxide of iron.

Textile Manufactures.—It is a singular fact that the first silk-mill ever erected in England was at Derby, and the first cotton-mill at Cromford. "Whatever may be the long-existing claims of Spitalfields upon our attention; whatever Macclesfield, Leek, and Congleton may present to us as the centre of a district where the silk manufacture prevails; whatever Manchester, with her mighty engines and factories, can exhibit in relation to the modern mode of conducting this branch of industry; Derby is the place where the responsibility, anxiety, and risk of originally establishing the manufacture was felt."—*Land we Live in*. The circumstances connected with the foundation of the silk-trade are detailed in Rte. 1. At Darley, near Derby, are the "Boar's Head" mills of Messrs. Evans, where the cotton thread bearing that appellation is made in very large quantities. The town of Derby is also noted for the manufacture of porcelain. The works, now known as the Royal Derby Crown Porcelain Works, were first established about the year 1750.

The manufacture of silk hosiery is extensively carried on at Belper; and most of the surrounding villages, particularly to the N., and on the E. towards Nottinghamshire, resound with the clack of the weaver's shuttle.

Introduction.—Industrial Resources.

B. Although a large proportion of **Nottinghamshire** is devoted to farming, the county is better known for its manufactures than for its agriculture. A good deal of the land is poor and clayey, especially on the eastern portion, although there are some rich valleys particularly along the Soar, which are devoted to dairies. A considerable portion of the population finds employment in the quarries, of which there are many in Nottinghamshire. Those of Mansfield and Mansfield Woodhouse, in particular, are celebrated as having supplied the stone from which the frontage of the Houses of Parliament was built, also the terrace in Trafalgar-square, a portion of Southwell Minster, the Martyrs' Memorial at Oxford, &c. To the immediate north-west of Nottingham a very large coal-mining district has been developed in the Lean Valley.

Nottingham has from very ancient times been a thriving focus of industry, but until within a recent period the town was surrounded by Lammas land, which restricted its building space within a confined area. In consequence, the trade extended considerably to the adjoining villages and hamlets. But half a century ago, when the Enclosure Act gave the Lammas fields up to the enterprising builder, the aspect of affairs underwent a remarkable change. Large factories were erected near the town, and improved dwellings for the working classes were built. In 1873 the Borough boundary was considerably extended, embracing such populous manufacturing districts as Radford, Sneinton, Lenton, Basford, Bulwell, &c., thus increasing the population of the town to upwards of a quarter of a million. When the Castle, now a Museum of Art, was the frequent abode of Royalty, the town was already in the hands of weavers, who made large quantities of woollen cloth; but it has lost its cloth manufacture, and acquired two others, the *hosiery* and the *machine lace* industries. With regard to the latter, in 1768, a stocking-frame knitter, named Hammond, succeeded in making a net upon his stocking frame. Two years later, Else introduced the "pin" or point-net machine, so named because made on sharp pins or points. "Point-net" was afterwards improved, and the "barleycorn" introduced; this was soon succeeded by "square" and "spider" net. But with all these improvements machinery had not yet arrived at producing a solid net: it was still only knitting, a single thread passing from one end of the frame to another, and if a thread broke the work was unravelled. The threads, therefore, required to be gummed together to give stiffness and solidity to the net. To remedy this evil the "warp" or "chain" machine was invented, linking the weaving and knitting mechanism. But lace making by machinery practically dates from 1809, when John Heathcote, who did not see any reason to prevent what was being made with pins and bobbins on a cushion, being equally well done by machinery, invented his traverse bobbin-net machine.

In 1813 a new conformation of the Heathcote machine was made by John Levers, which realized the idea Heathcote originally entertained of placing all the "carriages and bobbins in one tier."

The trade, however, received a serious check from the Luddites, who destroyed Heathcote's machinery to the value of 8000*l*., which so disgusted him that he retired forthwith to Tiverton, in Devonshire. The quality of bobbin-nets depends on the smallness of the meshes, their equality in size, and the regularity of the hexagons. Up to 1831 scarcely anything more than plain net and quilling was obtained by the bobbin-net machine. But about that time many improvements were introduced, such as spotting lace whilst being made on the circular machine; this was succeeded by spotting it on the traverse warp machine. The great revolution, however, was effected in 1835, when the Jacquard system was applied to the Levers' bobbin-net machine.

One of the earliest pioneers of this great advance was Samuel Draper, who in 1834-35 took out two patents. It is alleged, however, that the first really successful application of the Jacquard was due to Hooten Deverill in 1841; but to the skill and perseverance of Richard Birkin the large and successful development of machinery and trade generally may be principally attributed.

Probably no branch of textile manufacture passes through so many processes as net; for after it is actually made it has to be "gassed," by which it is passed over gas-flames, so as to divest it, without singeing, of the little hairy filaments.

The manufacture of lace curtains is an important trade of itself, and gives employment to many thousands of hands. It has an advantage over fancy lace, as it is not so liable to the fluctuations of trade, through the constant changes in fashion. The earliest attempts in the manufacture of lace curtains were made by Hardwick about 1849-50, and they were first brought to the notice of the public at the Great Exhibition of 1851.

The machinery employed in the hosiery and lace industries has within the last few years improved remarkably in its mechanical construction and producing power. Work, formerly executed by hand at home in the villages, is now rapidly being transferred to the factories in the towns and made entirely by machinery; and manufacturers have introduced machines, which not only finish the lace, formerly done by hand, but also make up all kinds of fancy articles for ladies' adornment.

Coal.—The collieries of Nottinghamshire yielded in 1891, 7,221,017 tons.

c. The agricultural resources of **Leicestershire** are far greater than those of the two former counties, the larger portion of it being devoted to grazing—the breed of cattle and sheep known by the name of Leicesters having a wide-spread reputation. As might be expected, too, from its pre-eminence as a hunting county, a great number of valuable horses are bred. The river valleys are noted for their cheese-dairies, the neighbourhood of Melton taking the first place with its Stiltons. Of arable land there is a fair share. The county was at one time famous for its supplies of beans, as may be seen in the names of some of its villages, such as Barton-in-the-Beans, &c.; and it used to be an old saying amongst the neighbouring counties, "Shake a

Leicestershire man by the collar, and you shall hear the beans rattle in his inside."

A large number of the inhabitants in the north-west of the county are employed in collieries, which in 1891 yielded 1,528,589 tons. Others find employment in the lias lime-works of Barrow-on-the-Soar, and the mountain limestone works at Breedon, and in the granite quarries in the neighbourhood of Charnwood Forest, particularly those of Mount Sorrel. Large quantities of granite are annually sent to London for use in paving and in macadamizing roads.

Iron-ore is found in the neighbourhood of Melton Mowbray, and in 1891, 646,125 tons were obtained from nine open workings. About 80,000 tons of Fire Clay and Potter's Clay were extracted in the same year from mines and open works.

Mingled with the agricultural is the manufacturing element to a very large extent, and there are few villages within a radius of twenty miles of Leicester, Harborough, Loughborough, Hinckley, and Lutterworth that are not mainly occupied with knitting. The medium of communication generally between the knitters in the villages and the masters in Leicester is the bagman, who very often trades on his own account, and takes the produce of the knitters into Leicester on market-day. There is at present less of the factory system in Leicestershire than in Nottinghamshire—the workpeople disliking to change their old routine, and the system of doing business not requiring it. But here, like everywhere else, machinery is gradually bringing the manufacturing industries from the villages into the towns. The bulk of seamed stockings and socks are now made in factories by patent machines driven by motive power. Seamless goods, however, are still made in the cottages with the "Griswold knitter," worked by hand. It is a great improvement on the old hand frame, which it is rapidly supplanting. If Derbyshire is famous for its silk, and Nottinghamshire for its lace, Leicestershire is not less celebrated for its hosiery generally, and its stockings in particular—the stocking-loom having been invented by the Rev. William Lee (Rte. 11). After his failure and retreat abroad the stocking-making was commenced in Leicester in 1680 by one Alsop, and since that time it has firmly taken root here. In addition to hosiery, the elastic webbing and boot and shoe manufactures are largely carried on at Leicester.

D. The industrial resources of **Staffordshire** are principally centred in iron and coal, and in all those numerous branches of manufactures, which are sure to be congregated together, where those minerals abound.

a. Coal.—According to the last report on mineral statistics, 14,325,267 tons of coal were raised in Staffordshire during the year 1891, of which 5,111,498 tons were raised in the north district, and 9,213,769 tons in the south district.

b. Iron.—For very many years Staffordshire held the pre-eminence in the iron trade, and dictated prices to all the world. But of late this pre-eminence has given way to the superior advantages of other iron-making districts, such as Cleveland and South Wales. This arises partly from the comparative exhaustion of Staffordshire iron-ores and the necessary dependence upon the importation of foreign ores, partly from the wasteful working of the coal, which is becoming much more scanty and difficult to get, and partly from the ruinous system of strikes and trade unions, which have become so associated with the Staffordshire iron trade.

In North Staffordshire, in 1891, 1,071,121 tons of iron-ore were extracted from the mines, of which 1,023,885 tons were from the north, and 47,236 tons from the south district. It is estimated that 30 per cent. of metal was obtained from the ores. In North Staffordshire there were, in 1891, eight works with 37 blast furnaces, whilst in South Staffordshire there were fourteen works with 74 blast furnaces. These depend principally upon the native iron-ores, which consist of the argillaceous carbonates or coal-measure clay iron ores, and are found in alternate strata associated with the coal-beds. But of late years North Staffordshire has largely contributed iron-ores from the Churnet valley at Froghall, which consist of hydrated oxides. The remainder of the supplies is furnished from Whitehaven, Cleveland, and Northamptonshire. The characteristics of the iron districts, inasmuch as they affect the tourist, are described under the various localities of the Black country, which he will be probably at least as anxious to leave as he was to enter it. For miles it is nothing but a repetition of smoke, dirt, and flame, which require certain conditions to make them at all bearable.

c. Regarding manufactures, upon which nearly the whole of Staffordshire depends, it would be out of place in a Handbook to attempt to detail all the numerous trades and subdivisions of trades entailed by manufactures of iron, copper, tinned, and japanned goods of all descriptions. Each town has a speciality for a certain class of goods, such as—

    Wolverhampton, for locks and japanned articles.
    Willenhall, locks.
    Wednesfield, keys.
    Walsall, awls, spurs, bits, and saddlery.
    Cradley, nails.
    Tipton, anchors.
    Smethwick, glass.
    Oldbury, railway carriages.

d. *Pottery.*—The North Staffordshire coal-field, or at all events a good portion of it, is almost entirely given up to the Potteries. " Few industrial localities present a more vivid example of this rapid transformation than the Potteries, the scene of Wedgwood's splendid triumphs, and the home of wedded art and handicraft. In this instance the ware of the Potteries has been a transforming spell, and by its power a district which 100 years ago was described by the old chroniclers as 'a bleak and rugged landscape, very sparse of inhabitants,' now teems with active life, and occupies an honourable place among the world's great workshops." It was not till 1760 that porcelain-making was commenced in this district, although brown earthenware was made at Burslem (Rte. 33) about the end of the 16th century. The year 1715 saw a very great improvement by the introduction of purer clays from Devonshire and Cornwall, but it was reserved for Wedgwood to discover and make known to the world those beautiful earthenwares and porcelains which made Etruria world-famous. More than 35,000 people are employed in the 300 pottery establishments at present existing, in addition to which there is a vast amount and minute subdivision of labour in the shape of accessory manufactures, as in South Staffordshire, such as clay-grinding, colour-grinding, bone-grinding, flint-grinding, charcoal-blacking making, &c. Not the least curious fact about the Potteries is, that not one of the requirements for the trade save coal and the marl used for the making of saggars (the large vessels in which the ware is fired), is found there, but they are brought together from different parts of the country.

e. There are, in addition to the above staple resources of Staffordshire, several others of minor importance. The limestone district near Wetton and Ecton once furnished copper; the neighbourhood of Tutbury supplies alabaster or gypsum on a large scale, a good specimen of which can be seen in the shape of a "*patera*" in the Geological Museum in Jermyn-street; the Rowley Hills yield basalt, which when fused has been found to make a beautiful ornamental building material. Stourbridge yields large beds of fire-clay. In the vicinity of Sandon are some extensive salt works placed on the strata of the triassic or saliferous beds. Stafford and Stone are famous for their shoemakers, tanners, and curriers; while Uttoxeter possesses a large agricultural implement works and two breweries; Leek, sewing silk factories, and Cheadle, tape and silk mills. Nor must we forget Burton-on-Trent, with its welcome and inexhaustible supplies of bitter beer—another instance of a self-established trade, without any peculiar inducements save those of very clear and pure wells of water, which are charged with sulphate of lime. Indeed, on the whole we may say that Staffordshire is a miniature of England, and that she comprises in her voluminous resources examples of nearly all our most important trades. Drayton thus quaintly sums up the characteristics of the four counties included in this Handbook:—

> "Then Staffordshire bids 'Stay, and I will heet the fire,
> And nothing will I ask but good-will for my hire;'
> 'Bean belly' Leicestershire her attribute doth bear;
> To Derby is assigned the name of 'wool and lead,'
> As Nottingham's of old is common 'ale and bread.'"

IV. ANTIQUITIES.

A. *a. Celtic.*—This class of monuments abounds in **Derbyshire** more than any other, and they are to be seen crowning many a high ground in the shape of a tumulus, or, as it is locally called, "low." They are generally of simple character, enclosing a stone vault, chamber, or chest, usually called a kistvaen, but "in other cases a grave cut more or less below the natural surfaces, and lined, if need be, with stone slabs, in which the body was placed in a perfect state, or reduced to ashes by fire. When the latter method has been adopted the fragments of bones have been carefully collected, and in many instances placed in an earthenware vessel, which was then deposited in the vault. These stone chambers vary in their dimensions from the size of a small room to that of a receptacle suited to contain only a few calcined bones. They are constructed in many ways, sometimes by walling, but more frequently by four or more large stones being placed on one end, and covered in with a fifth stone of greater size. When vaults constructed in this manner are denuded of the earth which in most cases originally covered them, they are very conspicuous objects, and as such used formerly to be considered as Druidical altars."—*Bateman.* They are not always, however, so simple in their construction, the one at Five Wells, near Taddington, being built with galleries leading to the principal chamber.

These Celtic barrows usually contained urns of baked clay, with calcined bones, drinking-cups, ornaments, weapons of flint, stone, and bronze, lying beside the skeleton.

"In barrows of the Romano-British and Saxon periods, the construction approaches more nearly to that now in use, viz. a small mound raised over a grave of some depth beneath the surface, so that they are, strictly speaking, grave-hills. There are certainly some large barrows of this era, but they are exceptions; and, indeed, in many localities the elevation is so slight as to be scarcely perceptible."

Later on, during the Saxon period, interment was carried on in nearly the same way, the Saxons very probably making use of the Celtic barrows, and burying their dead at a small distance from the surface. In these are found a more advanced style of ornament and weapon than in the Celtic.

The following is a list of the principal "lows," a name derived from the Saxon "hlæw,"—anything that covers; hence, a grave.

Route			
5.	Arbor Low, in the parish of Youlgreave.		
5.	Bee Low	,,	Youlgreave.
34.	Benty Grange	,,	Monyash.
6.	Blake Low	,,	Longstone.
6.	Brushfield	,,	Ashford.
5.	Gib Hill	,,	Middleton-by-Youlgreave.
6.	Hay Top	,,	Ashford.
34.	Hind Low	,,	Church Sterndale.
5.	Kenslow	,,	Middleton-by-Youlgreave.
6.	Nether Low	,,	Chelmorton.
5.	Parcelly Hay	,,	Hartington.
34.	Sharp Low	,,	Tissington.
2.	The Ferns	,,	Foremark.

Of the same period possibly as the barrows are the stone circles on Eyam Moor, the singular arrangement of rocks on Higgar Tor, and the defensive position of the Carl's Work above Hathersage; the Rocking Stones, and "Nine Ladies" Circle on Stanton Moor, Robin Hood's Mark on Ashover Moor, and perhaps the earthworks at Staddon Moor; although, considering their proximity to the Roman station of Aquis, it is just as likely that these are of later date.

β. *Roman.*—Derbyshire, which was included in the district of the Coritavi, is traversed from S. to N. by the Ryknield, or Yr Icknield Street, which enters Derbyshire near Egginton, there crossing the Dove, and running to the station of Derventio (Little Chester, near Derby). At Breadsall it diverges a little to the rt., through Horsley and Denby. It is again seen at South Wingfield, where it may be traced to Chesterfield, supposed to be the ancient Lutudarum.

A second great road probably ran from Derventio N.W. to Buxton, believed by Gale to have been the Aquis of Ravennas, and thence was continued in the same direction to Mancunium (Manchester). Traces of it are discernible in the old turnpike road between Hartington and Buxton.

A cross-road intersected this at Buxton in its course from Congleton to the Roman camp at Brough, which in the interval between Buxton and Brough is called the Batham Gate, and is easily traced across the moors at the back of Tideswell. From Brough there was evidently a connection with Melandra Station (Glossop), by a road called the Doctor's Gate. In addition to these remains are the camp on Comb's Moss and the Rhedagua near Whaley Bridge. On the whole, however, Roman remains in Derbyshire are not plentiful, though in some places a number of coins, together with a few altars and some pigs of lead, have been discovered in the vicinity of roads or stations.

γ. In the Saxon period Derbyshire formed an important portion of the Heptarchy, Repton (Repandunum) being the capital of Mercia and the burial-place of the Mercian kings. To this date accordingly is attributed by some antiquaries the crypt in Repton church. Bakewell also was well known as a Mercian town, although there are now no Saxon remains. The Danes have left some traces behind them, as in the name of Derby; some works at Eckington, known as the Danes' Balk; a doubtful camp at Hathersage; and the cemetery at Knowl Hill, near Foremark, which latter, however, is ascribed to them on only slight tradition.

δ. *Mediæval.*—Of the castles that Derbyshire once possessed, only three, viz. Codnor, Bolsover, and the Castle of the Peak, remain, and even they are not of considerable extent: the last owes its celebrity partly to the situation and partly to its association with the writings of Sir Walter Scott. Of Gresley, Horsley, and Chesterfield Castles, there are very few traces. There are, however, some very fine specimens of domestic architecture, chiefly of the 15th and 16th centuries. These are—

Introduction.—Antiquities.

Route
- 4. Barlborough Hall .. .. Elizabethan.
- 13. Bolsover Castle .. .. 16th centy.
- 7. Bradshaw Hall .. .. 17th centy.
- 6. Haddon Hall .. .. 15th centy.
- 13. Hardwick Hall .. .. Elizabethan.
- 13. Old Hardwick .. .. Henry VII.
- 34. Tissington Hall .. .. Elizabethan.
- 4. Wingerworth Hall .. .. 17th centy.
- 4. Wingfield Manor-house .. .. .. 15th centy.

The remains of ecclesiastical establishments are still more scanty, and are limited to three, viz., Dale Abbey, some remains of the Priory at Repton, and Beauchief Abbey: a window or a few arches are the only remnants even of these, except in the latter case, which retains, though modernized, a considerable portion of the old building.

The churches however, will afford more scope for the ecclesiologist, many of them being of considerable size and beauty, and rich in monumental remains. "No other part of the country of the same size has anything like the same extensive variety of styles and excellent specimens of every period, both in the ecclesiastical fabrics themselves, and in the monumental remains and other details that they shelter."—*Cox.* The following is a table of those most worth attention:—

Route
- 34. Ashbourne .. .. E. E.: Dec. spire: monuments: brasses.
- 3. Alfreton .. .. Monuments.
- 6. Ashford .. .. Effigy on wall.
- 4. Ashover .. .. Mon. brasses, 16th centy.
- 4. Allestree .. .. Norm. doorway.
- 6. Bakewell .. .. Monuments, spire, cross: remnant of Norm. nave.
- 13. Bolsover .. .. Monuments.
- 4. Brampton .. .. Monuments.
- 4. Breadsall .. .. Monuments. Pieta.
- 2. Breedon .. .. The Shirley pew and monuments.
- 10. Chaddesden .. .. Monuments.
- 6. Chelmorton .. .. Dwarf stone chancel-screen.
- 5. Cromford .. .. Monument by Chantrey.
- 4. Chesterfield .. .. Perp.: crooked spire, screen, monuments, brasses.
- 5. Crich .. .. .. Monuments.
- 10. Dale .. .. .. Singing gallery.
- 4. Darley .. .. .. Monuments.
- 4. Duffield .. .. Monuments.
- 4. Denby .. .. .. Monuments.
- 1. Derby, All Saints .. Perp. Tower, monuments, screen, stained glass.
- „ St. Alkmund's Dec. monument.
- „ St. Andrew's Modern.
- „ St. Peter's .. Perp.
- 5. Dethick .. .. Perp.
- 4. Dronfield .. .. Dec.: stalls, monuments, brasses.
- 10. Elvaston .. .. Screen, monuments.
- 1. Etwall .. .. .. Monuments and brasses, 16th centy.

Introduction.—Antiquities.

Route		
8.	Eyam	Cross in churchyard, gravestones.
34.	Fenny Bentley	Screen.
1.	Findern	Modern: Norm. tympanum preserved.
34.	Hartington	Cruciform ch., interesting, though small.
8.	Hathersage	Dec.: stained glass, monuments, brasses.
3.	Heanor	Monuments.
8.	Hope	Chamber over porch, gurgoyles.
3.	Ilkeston	Screen, stained glass.
1.	Kedleston	Monuments, brass, 15th centy.
33.	Marston Montgomery	Saxon arch.
5.	Matlock	Roof.
4.	Morley	Stained glass, monuments, brasses.
2.	Melbourne	Norm. (restored): monuments.
7.	Mellor	Font and Pulpit.
34.	Norbury	Stained glass, monuments, brasses, screen, & stalls.
1.	Normanton	Norm.: corbel-table.
4.	Norton	Monuments.
5.	Rowsley	Monuments.
1.	Repton	Saxon crypt, Dec. nave.
3.	Sandiacre	Dec.: large chancel, E. window.
10.	Sawley	Saxon arch: 15th-centy. brasses.
4.	Shirland	Perp.: monuments.
2.	Stanton-by-Bridge	Monuments, 16th centy.
3.	Stapleford	Monuments.
4.	Staveley	Monuments, brasses.
13.	Sutton in Ashfield	Monuments.
2.	Swarkeston	Norm.: monuments.
13.	Teversall	Monuments.
6.	Tideswell	Dec. tower: monuments, brasses: general dignity.
1.	Willington	Norm.: doorway.
10.	Wilne	Saxon font.
4.	Wirksworth	Perp.: chapels, monuments, brasses, bas-relief.
5.	Youlgreave	Font: Perp. tower.

Holy Well. King's Newton, near Melbourne.
Crosses. Bakewell. Blackwell. Eyam. Hope. Taddington. Wheston.

B. The antiquities of **Nottinghamshire** will not bear comparison in interest or number with those of Derbyshire, there being indeed none of Celtic origin, and only one early remain considered by Mr. Bateman to be of Saxon date, viz. the burying-place at Cotgrave, to the S. of Bingham. Nottingham, however, though containing now no actual Saxon remains, was yet famous in those days for its caves in the sandstone, from which it derived its name of Snottengham. Roman remains are limited mainly to the Fosse Way, which entered the county near Willoughby-in-the-Wold in its course from Leicester (Ratæ) to Lincoln. A tradition at Willoughby that the ruins of a great city lie buried near it, and the discovery of coins, would seem to corroborate the notion that it had been a Roman station. Thence it runs N.E. through East Bridgeford, near Bingham, where are remains of a camp which is thought by some antiquaries to have been the station of Vernometum. From Bridgeford it proceeded to Newark, finally leaving the county at Collingham. The greater part of its course is now a turnpike-road. There is also a tesselated pavement, together with some remains of ancient fortifications, at Barton-in-Fabis (*i.e.* Barton-in-the-Beans), near Trent Junction.

Mediæval remains are not very numerous, considering the size and importance of the county. Newark is the only castle worth mentioning, as that of Nottingham was reduced to a ruin in the 17th century. It was rebuilt after the Reformation, and again destroyed during the Reform riots in 1831. It has since been converted into a Museum and Art Gallery. Of Cuckney and Gresley Castles there are but slight traces. Of abbeys and monastic remains Newstead is the most important and the most beautiful, though its adaption to residential purposes has put it out of the pale of mediæval buildings, the west front of the church excepted.

Next in preservation are the conventual remains at Radford, a suburb of Worksop; of Mattersey and Beauvale there are very small remains; and of the Priory of Thurgarton, none except a bay of the present church. Worksop church is the nave of the ancient Abbey. Newark church has the dignity of a Minster, and is of great beauty. Retford church is also very fine. In two cases, viz. at Scrooby and Southwell, we have ancient domestic buildings still in use as residences; the only other domestic remains (and those of the rudest character) left are those of King John's palace near Ollerton, and, of a later date, the still inhabited halls of Carcolston, Shelford, and Kingshaugh, as well as the noble Elizabethan mansion of Wollaton. In modernized mansions, however, Nottinghamshire is very rich, probably containing more than any county in England for its size; of these the principal are Newstead, Clumber, Thoresby, Welbeck, Rufford, and Serlby, all of them within the area of Sherwood Forest, that old familiar resort

"Of Robin Hood and Little John;
Of Scarlock, George a Green, and Much the Miller's Son;
Of Tuck the merry friar, which many a sermon made
In praise of Robin Hood, his outlaws, and their trade."
—*Drayton.*

It may at first sight appear singular that this district affords so few traces of the bold outlaw and his men, with whom the history of Nottinghamshire is identified; but when we reflect on the roving and sylvan character of Robin Hood, it is evident that he was not likely, from the nature of his habits and pursuits, to leave behind him much except tradition.

The attempts to elucidate the history of Robin Hood have been various; some writers maintaining his identity with an Earl of Huntingdon, the mainstay of which theory is the inscription at Kirklees, in Yorkshire. This, however, is now known to be a fabrication. Thierry, in his 'English History,' speaks of him as the chief of a body of Saxons collected together in hostility to the Normans. Others again consider him as a myth altogether, a mere peg whereon to hang the national love of sylvan lore. It would seem, however, that he was a veritable personage living in the time of Henry III., probably an

Introduction.—Antiquities.

adherent of Simon de Montfort, who, after the disastrous battle of Evesham, retired into the forest, and there made war on his own account upon his majesty's lieges. Mr. Hunter, in his short treatise upon Robin Hood, endeavours to show from public records that, during the King's progress in Lancashire and Nottinghamshire, Robin Hood was pardoned and received into the royal household. "The outlaw's was eminently a life which fitted him to be the hero of a song; in its most obvious features poetical, spent in the open country or in the depths of forests, there was nothing in nature which the poet might not summon up for the embellishment of his story; full also of adventure, some tragic occurrences, and some partaking of that good humour and disposition to merriment which are distinguishable features of his character."—*Hunter.*

The following is a list of the most interesting Nottinghamshire churches, which, however, are scarcely equal in size or beauty to those of Derbyshire or Leicestershire:—

Route
- 12. Aslacton .. .. .. Monuments.
- 10. Attenborough .. .. Monuments.
- 11. Averham .. .. .. Monuments.
- 17. Bawtry .. .. .. Norm.
- 12. Bingham .. .. .. E. E. and Dec.
- 18. Blyth .. .. .. Conventual Ch., monuments, screen.
- 10. Clifton .. .. .. Monuments and brasses.
- 10. Colwick .. .. .. Monuments.
- 11. Hawton .. .. .. Founder's sepulchre, stained glass.
- 17. Holme .. .. .. Monuments and chamber porch.
- 12. Holme Pierrepont .. Monuments.
- 13. Hucknall Torkard .. Byron's monument.
- 16. Kelham .. .. .. Monuments.
- 13. Mansfield .. .. Monuments.
- 15. Mansfield Woodhouse Sanctus bell.
- 17. East Markham .. Monuments.
- 11. Newark .. .. .. Dec.: steeple and spire, stained glass, brasses: general size and dignity.
- 10. Nottingham, St. Mary's Perp. windows, Norm. porch.
- " St. Barnabas Modern R. C. Cathedral, E. E.
- 17. Retford .. .. .. Size and dignity.
- 14. Southwell Minster .. Norm. and E. E.
- 11. Thurgarton .. .. Portion of old abbey Ch.
- 17. Tuxford .. .. .. Monuments.
- 12. Whatton .. .. .. Monuments.
- 10. Wollaton .. .. Monuments.
- 15. Worksop .. .. .. Norm. monuments, nave of abbey.

c. **Leicestershire** is an interesting county to the antiquary and the ecclesiologist, particularly in remains of mediæval date.

Of *Early Remains* there are but few; viz. an encampment on Beacon Hill, near Mount Sorrel, where a number of celts and armlets have been found; and the tumuli and earthworks on Saltby Heath, near Croxton Park.

[*Derby, &c.*] *d*

Introduction.—Antiquities.

Roman.—There are two Roman roads in Leicestershire. The Watling Street, which enters the county on the S.W. near Lutterworth, and leaves it near Mancetter (Manvessedunum), in Warwickshire. About midway between the two places is High Cross, the ancient Bennones or Vennones, where the Fosse Way enters Leicestershire and runs through the county to Rataæ (Leicester), and on to Willoughby and Bridgeford (Vernometum) in Nottinghamshire. Camden, and Burton the Leicestershire antiquary, both testify to the finding of coins near High Cross, where the tradition of a ruined city at Claybrooke, close adjoining, is still extant.

For other Roman remains Leicester can point to its Jewry Wall, one of the finest relics of the kind in England; its milestone, which clearly points to its identity with Rataæ; and the Rawdykes, the old Rhedagua of the charioteers. There are also several camps, particularly in the E. part of the county—at Burrow and Billesdon. The termination of the names of the villages in this district, and the fact that Medbourne, near Market Harborough, is said to have been a Roman station and to have yielded a number of coins, makes it probable that a road led from hence through Melton to join the Fosse Way.

Danish.—Although no remains can be pointed out, which can be attributed to the Danes, it is well known that Leicestershire was part of the Danelagh, and this is corroborated by the names of the villages, many terminating in "by," such as Ashby, Brooksby, Frisby, &c., which is so common as to be almost the rule.

In *Mediæval* remains and churches Leicestershire is tolerably rich. Of its castles, Ashby-de-la-Zouch, Castle Donington and Kirkby Muxloe (with its brick courses), still show traces of their former importance (the former in particular), whilst at Earl Shilton, Groby, Hinckley, and Whitwick little more than the site remains. Of religious houses there are the ruins of Gracedieu, the Priory of Ulverscroft, the boundary wall of Leicester Abbey, and some slight traces of Lubbesthorpe Abbey. Of old mansions, the most noticeable are Laund Abbey, Nevill Holt, Noseley, Quenby, and Withcote, all Elizabethan; Beaumanor, Coleorton, Garendon, and Rocclifle are all very fine modern houses. Of churches, Leicester contains several of much interest, which, together with Melton, are sufficient to attract the antiquary. There are, however, a considerable number of village churches containing many curious points; and the county has to thank the Leicestershire Archæological Society for directing public attention to their preservation and restoration.

The following list includes the churches best worth seeing:—

Route
23. Ashby .. .. Monuments; finger pillory.
24. Belton .. .. Monuments.
12. Bottesford .. .. .. Perp.: monuments.
21. Brooksby .. .. .. Monuments.
21. Burton Lazars .. .. Bell-tower.
19. Burton Overy .. .. Sculpture.
19. Carlton-Curlieu .. .. Monuments.

Route		
24.	Coleorton	Stained glass.
25.	Cortlingstock or Costock	Monument outside the ch.
20.	Earl Shilton	Modern frescoes.
25.	Frolesworth	Monuments.
24.	Gracedieu	R. C. chapel; stained glass.
23.	Gresley	Monuments.
20.	Hinckley	Monuments.
25.	Kegworth	Stained glass.
25.	Leake	Monuments.
25.	Lockington	Chantry chapel.
19.	Leicester, St. Nicholas	Norm.; portion of Roman materials.
	,, St. Mary's	Norm. and E. E.
	,, All Saints'	Norm.
	,, St. Martin's	Mixed styles.
	,, St. Margaret's	Perp.
25.	Loughborough	Cruciform ch., brasses.
25.	Lutterworth	Wycliffe's reputed relics.
20.	Market Bosworth	Monuments.
19.	Market Harborough	14th centy.
21.	Melton Mowbray	E. E.; Perp.
23.	Nether Seal	Monuments (15th centy.).
19.	Nevill Holt	Dec. and Perp.; monuments.
25.	Prestwold	Monuments.
24.	Whitwick	Monuments.
19.	Wistow	Monuments.
25.	Woodhouse	Miserere seats.
25.	Wymeswold	Well restored.
25.	Wysall	Stained glass.

D. The antiquities of **Staffordshire** are of more importance than those of either Notts or Leicestershire.

a. Early British remains are tolerably numerous, and much was done, particularly in the northern part of the county, by the labours of Messrs. Bateman, Carrington, and Garner, to elucidate them. In the neighbourhood of Wetton no less than 23 barrows were opened, two-thirds of which appeared to belong to the early Stone period. Some of them contained human bones, generally calcined, together with vessels, urns, stags' horns, fibulæ, &c. The Borough, near Wetton, seems to have been an important British village, containing traces of the round pits generally seen in those localities, and yielding remains of celts, stone hammers, and human bones. On the floor of Thor's Cave were many articles of the later Celtic period, such as bronze armlets, fibulæ, and rings, implements of iron, perforated pins and tools of bone, fragments of querns, and some articles of Samian ware. Mr. Garner mentions the discovery of several British ornaments, such as torques, one of which was found in Needwood Forest. Among the most interesting barrows opened in Staffordshire are—

    Saxon Low, near Tittensor;
    Bury Bank, ditto;
    Moat-in-Ribden, at the foot of Weaver;
    Mayfield;

Introduction.—Antiquities.

and a great number in the parishes of Wetton, Cauldron, Alstonefield, Stanton, Waterfall, and Ilam. In fact, the whole of the moorland grit and limestone district is covered with barrows and burial-places of more or less size, evincing the former presence of a large population.

β. *Roman.*—There are several camps in the county, probably British, but, as was often the case, afterwards utilized by the Romans. Of these were the camps near Whitmore, and at Beaudesert, and Knave's Castle, in the neighbourhood of Etocetum (now Wall, near Lichfield). This was the great stronghold of the Romans in Staffordshire, to which converged the main lines of road, viz. Yr Icknield or Ryknield Street, which entered the county at Birmingham, and took a north-easterly course through Etocetum to Burton-on-Trent, thence to Derby (Derventio); and the Watling Street, which entered at Fazeley and ran right across on its way from Etocetum to Uriconium (Wroxeter). The names of places and hamlets on the line of these roads sufficiently betoken their relationship to them. Penkridge was thought by some antiquaries to have been the old Pennocrocium, while others place it on the site of one of the numerous "Strettons."

γ. Of *Mediæval Remains*, especially in the matter of churches, there is ample store. Staffordshire was famous then, even as it is now, for its fine mansions, beautiful plates of which are given in Plot's Natural History of that county; and if it cannot boast of the largest or finest, it possesses the most graceful cathedral in England, which in itself would be sufficient to attract the archæologist.

The following is a list of the principal ancient mansions and domestic remains:—

Route
31. Aqualate.
31. Beaudesert.
27. Bentley Hall.
36. Biddulph.
33. Caverswall.
32. Chartley Castle.
26. Chillington.
28. Dudley Castle.
28. Enville Hall.
32. Gayton.
30. Hamstall Ridware.
28. Holbeach.

Route
28. Prestwood.
31. Ranton Abbey.
28. Rushall.
28. Stourton Castle.
29. Tamworth Castle.
34. Throwley Hall.
31. Tixall; Tudor Gateway; house modern.
33. Tutbury Castle.
26. Wrottesley Hall.
30. Wyrley.*

Of churches, the following are the best worth the attention of the tourist:—

Route
30. Abbot's Bromley .. Monuments; deerheads.
28. Aldridge .. .. Monuments; windows.
31. Armitage .. .. Norm. doorway.
27. Ashley .. .. .. Monuments.

* Beside these, Staffordshire abounds in fine estates, with modern houses, which are in various ways deserving of notice, such as Ilam Hall, Alton Towers, Shugborough, Patteshull, Keele Hall, Trentham, Ingestre, &c.

Introduction.—Antiquities.

Route		
28.	Alrewas	Monuments.
34.	Alstonefield	Carvings.
27.	Audley	Tombs and brass.
27.	Brewood	Monuments.
29.	Burton	Altarpiece.
35.	Cheadle	Oak carving.
„	R. C. Cathedral	By Pugin; fine spire and internal decorations.
33.	Checkley	Monuments; ancient churchyard cross.
31.	Colton	Sedilia; font.
31.	Colwich	Monuments.
29.	Croxall	Monuments.
33.	Draycott	Monuments.
26.	Eccleshall	Restored.
28.	Elford	Monuments.
33.	Ellastone	Monuments.
30.	Ellenhall	Pulpit-cloth.
27.	Enville	Monuments.
30.	Farwell	Windows; stalls.
30.	Gnosall	Monuments.
25.	Handsworth	Monuments.
29.	Hamstall Ridware	Stalls; screen; glass.
32.	Hanbury	Monuments; brasses.
30.	High Offley	Monuments.
34.	Horton	Glass; monuments.
33.	Ilam	Beautifully restored; mon. by Chantrey; mortuary chapel.
27.	Kinver	Monuments, brass.
34.	Leek	Rose window: fine (rebuilt) chancel; ancient churchyard cross.
32.	Leigh	Monuments.
27.	Lichfield Cathedral.	
„	St. Mary's	Modern.
„	St. Michael's	Restored.
30.	Longdon	Monuments.
26.	Madeley	Sedilia, monuments.
29.	Mavesyn-Ridware	Monuments.
32.	Marchington	Monuments.
36.	Newcastle	Tower ancient; body modern.
30.	Norbury	Monuments; brass.
26.	Penkridge	Monuments.
31.	Ranton Abbey	Fine tower.
32.	Rolleston	Norm. doorway; monuments.
34.	Rushton Spencer	Mainly timber.
31.	Sandon	Monuments; glass.
26.	Shareshill	Monuments.
33.	Sheen	Good modern ch., with stone roof to chancel.
26.	Stafford, St. Mary's	Monuments; general grandeur.
„	St. Chad's	Norm.
31.	Stone	Monuments.
31.	Stowe	Monuments; brass.
28.	Tamworth	Staircase; crypt; general dignity.
25.	Tettenhall	Monuments.

Route
31. Trentham .. .. Monuments; Jacobæan screen, brasses.
32. Tutbury .. .. Norm. door.
25. Wednesbury .. Monuments.
25. West Bromwich .. Monuments.
25. Wolverhampton .. Monuments; pulpit: ancient churchyard cross.
32. Wolstanton .. .. Spire: restoration.
29. Yoxall .. .. Monuments; brass.

Of ecclesiastical remains there are only:—
Route
28. Burton .. .. Some arches of abbey.
34. Croxden .. .. Very fine ruins.
34. Dieulacresse .. Scattered details.
34. Rocester .. .. Very slight.

V. SKELETON TOURS.

A.—TOUR OF ONE MONTH THROUGH DERBYSHIRE, NOTTS, AND LEICESTERSHIRE.

1. By rail from Crewe or Burton to Ashbourne. Excursion up Dovedale.
2. To Hartington, by Fenny Bentley and Tissington.
3. See Arborlow, Gib Hill, Rock Scenery at Staunton and Youlgreave; thence to Rowsley.
4. See Chatsworth, Haddon Hall, and sleep at Bakewell.
5. Excursion to the Lathkill and Parson's Tor. Drive to Ashford and Miller's Dale; thence by rail to Buxton.
6. See Buxton. Poole's Hole. Excursion to Axe Edge, and back by Staddon Moor.
7. Buxton to Chapel-en-le-Frith; whence excursion to Hayfield and Kinderfall. On to Castleton.
8. See Peak Cavern, the Speedwell Cavern, and Winnatts. See Odin's Cave, Blue John Mine, Mam Tor.
9. Hope; Brough; Hathersage; Higgar Tor; Carl's Work.
10. Eyam; Stoney Middleton; Baslow. Drive to Sheffield by Beauchief and Norton.
11. Sheffield; by rail to Chesterfield. See Bolsover and Hardwick Hall.
12. By rail to Wingfield. See Wingfield Manor House. Drive from Alfreton through Crich to Matlock.
13. See Matlock, Caves, &c. Excursion to Bonsall and Wirksworth, Cromford and Willersley.
14. Excursion to Matlock Bank and Darley Dale. By rail to Ambergate and Belper. If time, walk to Depth o' Lumb and proceed by rail to Derby.
15. See Derby and (if open) Kedleston.
16. Excursion to Melbourne, King's Newton, Repton, and Burton; returning by rail to Derby.
17. Derby to Ilkeston, Dale Abbey, and Mansfield.
18. Mansfield to Clipstone, Birkland Forest, and Worksop.
19. Worksop to Blyth, Roche Abbey, and Bawtry; then by rail to Retford.
20. Retford by rail to Newark. See Hawton and Southwell.
21. Newark to Nottingham. See Nottingham.

Introduction.—Skeleton Tours. [37]

22. See Wollaton. By rail to Bottesford, and drive to Belvoir. Sleep at Belvoir Inn.
23. Drive over the Wolds to Melton. See Melton and Burton Lazars.
24. By rail to Syston and Loughborough. Excursion to Costock Ch. and some of the neighbouring churches. By rail to Leicester.
25. See Leicester.
26. By rail to Market Harborough; drive to Lutterworth, and rejoin rly. at Ullesthorpe stat. for Hinckley.
27. See Hinckley and Bosworth Field.
28. Excursion to Kirby Muxloe, Groby, Bradgate, and Ulverscroft.
29. By rail to Bardon Hill. See Monastery. By rail from Coalville to Ashby-de-la-Zouch.
30. Ashby-de-la-Zouch. Excursion to Gracedieu, Staunton Harold, and Whitwick. By rail to Burton.

B.—PEDESTRIAN TOUR IN DERBYSHIRE OF A FORTNIGHT.

1. By rail to Ashbourne. Thence to Ilam and the Izaak Walton Inn.
2. Explore the Manifold Valley with Thor's Cave.
3. Up Dovedale and Beresford Dale to Hartington.
4. To Winster, Staunton, and Rowsley.
5. See Chatsworth, Haddon, Bakewell, and proceed to Ashford.
6. To Buxton along Miller's Dale.
7. Buxton, Axe Edge, Hindlow, Staddon.
8. From Buxton by rail to Doveholes; on to Castleton. See Caverns.
9. From Castleton to the Valley of Edale, Kinderscout, and thence to Glossop.
10. Glossop to Ashopton. Excursion up the Derwent to Cakes of Bread.
11. From Ashopton along the Moors to Hathersage.
12. From Hathersage over the Moors to Eyam, Middleton Dale, Baslow, and Rowsley; by rail to Matlock.
13. See Matlock. Walk to Ashover, catching train at Stretton for Chesterfield; or for Wingfield, and next morning to Chesterfield.
14. Chesterfield to Hardwick and Bolsover.
15. From Bolsover through Markland Grips to Worksop.

C.—TOUR OF ONE MONTH THROUGH STAFFORDSHIRE AND DERBYSHIRE.

1. Handsworth Old Parish Ch. St. Michael's Ch., Soho. Smethwick Glassworks. Wednesbury. Sleep at Wolverhampton.
2. Wolverhampton Ch. Japanning Manufactory. Excursion to Tettenhall and Wrottesley.
3. To Dudley. See Castle. Wren's Nest. Excursion to Holbeach and Enville, returning by Kinver to Stourbridge, and back by rail.
4. Walsall. Rushall. Aldridge Ch. Shenstone. Lichfield.
5. At Lichfield. Excursion to Wall, Weeford, &c.
6. Excursion to Tamworth; see Elford, and return by Alrewas.
7. Lichfield to Armitage. Excursion to Beaudesert, Mavesyn-Ridware and Abbot's Bromley. Sleep at Rugeley.
8. Colwich. Shugborough. Stafford.
9. Excursion by rail to Four Ashes, for Brewood and Chillington.
10. To Stone, Sandon, and Chartley. Sleep at Stoke-on-Trent.

11. Excursion to Harecastle, Burslem, and Wolstanton. See Minton and Copeland's Show-rooms.
12. Excursion to Trentham; then on to Etruria and Newcastle-under-Lyme.
13. Excursion to Biddulph. Ascend Mow Cop. Sleep at Congleton.
14. By rail from Congleton to Leek, and down the Churnet Valley to Alton Towers. Sleep at Uttoxeter.
15. Excursion to Tutbury and Burton. Sleep at Ashbourne.
16. Excursion up Dovedale; return to Ilam.
17. Excursion to Thor's Cave and the Manifold; return to Ilam.
18. Drive by Fenny Bentley, to Hartington. Then as in A, days 3 to 15.

D.—PEDESTRIAN TOUR THROUGH NORTH STAFFORDSHIRE.

1. Rail from Colwich to Weston or Sandon. Walk by Chartley to Uttoxeter.
2. Rail to Alton. Then walk by Wootton and the Weaver Hills to Ilam.
3. To Ashbourne by Okeover, returning by Fenny Bentley and Thorpe.
4. Up the Manifold to Grindon and Thor's Cave, returning by Wetton.
5. Up Dovedale and Beresford Dale to Hartington.
6. Walk to Longnor, Earl Sterndale, and Buxton.
7. Over Axe Edge; by Flash, to Leek.
8. Rudyard. Rushton Spencer. Mow Cop. Congleton.
9. Biddulph. New Chapel. Stoke-on-Trent.

The tourist can thence proceed by rail to Derby and Matlock, or to Burton-on-Trent for Charnwood.

CORRECTIONS AND ADDITIONS, 1904.

Page 6, l. 23. *Delete* "navigable."
P. 25, col. 2, l. 9. *For* "is in progress," *read* "runs."
P. 51, col. 2, l. 10. *For* "will shortly be opened," *read* "now runs."
P. 67, col. 2, l. 3. *For* "to the liberality," *read* "at the instance."
„   „   l. 4. *Omit* "commonly."
„   „   l. 5. *For* "Sir Robert's Bridge," *read* "Wilford Bridge."
P. 68, col. 1, l. 2. *For* "Lene," *read* "Leen."
„   „   l. 27. *For* "North Parade," *read* "Long Row."
P. 70, col. 2, l. 3. *For* "arc," *read* "were."
„   „   l. 35. *For* "it is merely a serpentine road with shrubberies near the racecourse," *read* "a large Recreation Ground, with cricket fields and the old racecourse. On the S. slopes are walks running amongst shrubberies and plantations."
„   „   l. 44. *Omit* "enlarged to serve as catacombs."
P. 71, col. 1, l. 38. *Omit* "but has been very much altered and modernised."
P. 72, col. 1, l. 17. *For* "in the rear of the building," *read* "attached to the W. wing."
P. 96, col. 1, l. 10. *For* "Birkland Forest," *read* "The Birklands."
P. 108, col. 2, l. 25. *For* "Carnarvon," *read* "Cardigan."
P. 169, col. 2, l. 43. *For* "Waldyke," *read* "Waldyve."
P. 178, col. 1, l. 24. *Add* **Hoar Cross.** The Ch. of the Holy Angels (Archts., Messrs. Bodley & Garner) was erected 1872-76, at a cost of upwards of 80,000l., by the Hon. Mrs. Maynell-Ingram, in memory of her husband. It is a handsome cruciform building of red sandstone, in late 14th cent. style, with a lofty central tower and four chapels. The interior is richly decorated, and there is an elaborately carved oak screen at the entrance to the chancel. The windows have rich stained glass representing numerous saints, and there are several oil paintings.

The Great Central Railway (hitherto known as the Manchester, Sheffield and Lincolnshire Railway) has a line from Manchester to London. This line enters Derbyshire at Beighton and runs to Nottingham, having stations at Killamarsh, Eckington and Renishaw, Staveley Town, Heath, Pilsley, Tibshelf Town, in Derbyshire; Kirkby and Pinxton, Hucknall Town, Bulwell Common, New Basford, and Carrington, in Nottinghamshire.

From Nottingham, Great Central Station, Mansfield Road, the line proceeds to Leicester, with stations at Arkwright Street (Nottingham), Ruddington, East Leake, in Nottinghamshire, and Loughborough, Quorn and Woodhouse, Rothley, Belgrave and Birstall, in Leicestershire.

From Leicester, Central Station, the line continues through Whetstone, Ashby Magna and Lutterworth, at which places there are stations, and quits Leicestershire just before reaching Rugby.

HANDBOOK

FOR

DERBY, NOTTS, LEICESTER, AND STAFFORD.

ROUTES.

⁎ The names of places are printed in **black** in those Routes where the places are described.
Those of which the hotels, conveyances, &c., are noted in the Index are distinguished by the mark ð.

ROUTE	PAGE	ROUTE	PAGE
1. Burton to **Derby** [Repton] .	2	13. Nottingham to **Mansfield**, by Newstead [Hardwick Hall, Bolsover] . . .	82
2. Derby to Trent Junction, by **Melbourne** and **Castle Donington**	10	14. Newark to **Mansfield**, by **Southwell**	92
3. Trent Junction to Chesterfield, by **Ilkeston**, **Alfreton**, and **Clay Cross** . .	13	15. Mansfield to **Worksop** and **Retford** [Welbeck] . .	95
4. Derby to **Sheffield**, by **Belper** and **Chesterfield** [Wirksworth]	16	16. Newark to **Worksop**, by **Ollerton** [Thoresby, Clumber]	99
5. Derby to **Bakewell**, by **Matlock** and **Rowsley** .	26	17. Newark to **Doncaster**, by **Tuxford**, **Retford**, and **Bawtry**	101
6. Bakewell to **Buxton** [Haddon Hall, Chatsworth, the Lathkill, Tideswell] . .	33	18. Worksop to Doncaster, by **Tickhill** [Blyth, Roche Abbey]	104
7. Buxton to **Manchester**, by **Chapel-en-le-Frith** . .	46	19. Market Harborough to **Leicester**	106
8. Chapel-en-le-Frith to Bakewell, by **Castleton**, **Hope**, **Hathersage**, and **Eyam** [The Peak]	52	20. Nuneaton to **Leicester**, by **Hinckley** [Bosworth Field]	114
9. Buxton to **Hayfield** and **Glossop**	63	21. Leicester to **Melton Mowbray** and **Oakham** . .	116
10. Derby to **Nottingham**, by Trent Junction . . .	64	22. Market Harborough to **Newark**	119
11. Nottingham to **Lincoln**, by **Newark**	74	23. Leicester to **Burton**, by **Ashby-de-la-Zouch** . .	121
12. Nottingham to **Grantham**, by **Bingham** and **Bottesford** [Belvoir]	78	24. Ashby-de-la-Zouch to **Leicester**, through **Charnwood Forest** [St. Bernard's Monastry, Bradgate Park] .	124

[*Derby, &c.*]

B

ROUTE	PAGE	ROUTE	PAGE
25. Rugby to Trent Junction, by Leicester, Mount Sorrel, and Loughborough [Lutterworth]	129	32. Colwich to Stoke-on-Trent, by Sandon, Stone, and Trentham [Chartley]	183
26. Birmingham to Wellington, by West Bromwich and Wolverhampton	134	33. Crewe to Burton-on-Trent, by Stoke-on-Trent, Uttoxeter, and Tutbury [The Potteries]	188
27. Birmingham to Crewe, by Wolverhampton, Bushbury, and Stafford	142	34. Uttoxeter to Buxton, by Ashbourne and Hartington [Dovedale]	196
28. Stourbridge to Burton-on-Trent, by Dudley, Walsall, and Lichfield	152	35. Uttoxeter to Macclesfield, by Alton Towers and Leek [Cheadle]	206
29. Birmingham to Burton-on-Trent, by Tamworth	169	36. Stoke-on-Trent to Congleton, by Biddulph	213
30 Walsall to Rugeley, by Cannock [Needwood Forest]	175	37. Stoke-on-Trent to Market Drayton, by Newcastle-under-Lyme	215
31 Tamworth to Newport, by Rugeley, Colwich, and Stafford	179		

ROUTE 1.

BURTON TO DERBY [REPTON].
MIDLAND RAILWAY. 11 m.

For **Burton**, see Rte. 29. Less than 1 m. from Burton Stat. the North Staffordshire line branches off on N. at Horninglow (Stat.) for Tutbury, the Potteries, &c. (see Rte. 33). The Midland line runs parallel for some distance with the ancient Icknield Street, and overlooks the broad meadows, through which the clear deep waters of the Trent flow. At **3 m.** the Dove is crossed, which shortly after flows into the Trent. Opposite the junction is the village of **Newton Solney**, with an E. E. and Perp. *Ch.* (restored 1884), which contains three remarkable effigies of members of the De Sulncy family; one, clad in banded mail (c. 1300), is engraved in Hewitt's 'Ancient Arms and Armour,' vol. i. Newton Hall (R. Ratcliff, Esq.) has fine grounds stretching down to the river, and is seen from the rly.

4½ m. Willington and **Repton** (Stat.). The village of Willington is very small, but the Norm. doorway of the *Ch.* is worth notice; there is also a handsome modern toll-bridge over the Trent.

1 m. W. is **Egginton** (Junct. Stat. Great Northern and N. Staff. Rlys.). The *Ch.*, dedicated to St. Wilfred, is a small building near one of the branches of the Dove. Egginton Hall (Sir H. F. Every, Bart.) is a modern mansion, in a handsome park.

1 m. S. is **Repton**, the Hreopandun of the Anglo-Saxon Chronicle, and the capital of Mercia. Here Ethelbald, slain by Offa, was buried in 755; and here the Northmen established themselves in the latter part

of the 9th centy. Repton possesses a richly endowed **Grammar School,** founded by Sir John Porte, in 1557, which now numbers 300 boys. The school precincts are entered through an ancient arch, formerly the *gateway of the Priory* of Black Canons, portions of which are still preserved. The Cellarer's buildings are now used as a schoolroom, and a master's boarding-house. The head-master's house, with a fine brick tower of Henry VI.'s reign, was of old the prior's residence. In levelling the cricket field, which is bounded on three sides by the Priory wall, a mediæval tile oven was discovered, consisting of two small chambers side by side, 5 ft. in length by 2 ft. in width. This has been boarded over and is carefully preserved. At least 20 different patterns of 14th-centy. tiles were found within, and are now arranged about the fireplace in the schoolroom. The new buildings in the Perp. style were erected in 1886, by Sir A. W. Blomfield, A.R.A., as a memorial to the late Dr. Pears, on the site of the old Priory Church, of which a portion of the foundations remains carefully preserved. Additional class rooms adjoining the ancient slype, which still exists, were added in 1888.

The **Church,** conspicuous for its lofty spire of peculiar elegance 210 ft. high, is dedicated to St. Wystan. The nave is chiefly of Dec. character, but the fabric exhibits specimens of other styles. The chancel, excepting the E. window, belongs to the Anglo-Saxon period, probably 958-975. Beneath the chancel is a most remarkable crypt, 17 ft. square, supposed to have been a portion of the old Saxon Abbey founded here in the 7th cent., and destroyed by the Danes in 874. The vaulted roof of stone is supported by four round pillars, spirally wreathed, with square capitals. The entrance to this crypt from the Ch. is by means of two Saxon stairways at the W. angles. There are some monuments to the family of Thacker; and in the crypt is an alabaster effigy of a knight in plate armour of the early part of the 15th cent. The Ch. was partially restored in 1886.

1½ m. E. of Repton is **Foremark Hall,** belonging to the Burdett family. The mansion was erected about 1760, and contains a very fine collection of family pictures. The estates descended to the Burdetts from a female ancestor of the name of Francis. The park and grounds are very pretty, especially near the river, a tributary of the Trent, where are some caverned rocks called *Anchor Church,* from the story of a hermit having made them his retreat. The Ch. of **Foremark,** built in 1662, is very small and plain. At **Ingleby,** 1 m. E., is an elm-tree, believed to be 600 years old, but still vigorous.

3 m. N. of Willington is the village of **Etwall** (Stat. G. N. Rly.), once a possession of Welbeck Abbey, in Notts, but given in 1540 by Henry VIII. to Sir John Porte, one of the justices of the King's Bench. His son, also named John, was the founder of the well-endowed Almshouses at Etwall, and the Grammar School at Repton. He is buried in Etwall Ch., which contains a fine altar-tomb for himself, his two wives and five children: there is also the tomb of his grandfather and grandmother (1512), the female effigy from which is engraved in Fairholt's 'Costume.'

Etwall Hall (Mrs. Rowland H. Cotton,) is a 17th-centy. mansion of brick, faced with stone taken from the ruins of Tutbury Castle; some portions are much earlier. It contains several family portraits, together with the identical suits of clothing which those members wore

B 2

when they sat for their portraits. There is a fine Queen Anne garden.

Dalbury Ch., 1¼ m. to the N., has some stained glass with the arms of Sir John Porte and Sir Samuel Sleigh. 3 m. to the N.E. of Etwall is **Radbourne** Ch., which has an ancient font, brought from Dale Abbey. The **Hall** is the property of R. W. Chandos Pole, Esq., the representative of the ancient families of De la Pole and Chandos. Sir John Chandos of Radbourne distinguished himself greatly in Edward III.'s war with France, and his brave deeds are chronicled by Froissart. Leland says, "The old house of Radbourne is no great thing, but the last Chandois began in the same lordshippe a mighty large house of stone, with a wonderfull coste."

5½ m. A line branches off to Trent Junction. A little to the N. is the village of **Findern**. The manor formerly belonged to the Abbots of Burton, who often held their courts in the village, when their tenants were troublesome, as mentioned in the recently-discovered Burton Chartulary. Much of the property was held under them by the Fyndernes, a family now extinct. There are no remains of their residence, but some faint traces of a terraced garden may be noticed in a field, in which formerly "garden flowers grew wild," to which a legend was attached, terming them "Fyndern's flowers, brought by Sir Geoffrey from the Holy Land." The popular belief was, that they would "never die;" but they have now entirely disappeared from the field itself, but are still to be found in some of the village gardens. The flower is the *Narcissus poeticus*. The old Norm. Ch. of Findern was in 1862 replaced by a modern Dec. building, which has, built into the N. wall, the tympanum of the ancient Norm. doorway, flanked by 2 singular figures. Findern was long the seat of a Presbyterian Academy, founded in 1693, at which many dissenters of eminence were educated. A large chapel was built by them here in 1768; it is now the property of the Trustees of Allsop's charity, and used as a schoolroom.

9 m. **Normanton** (Stat.). The village is on N. The *Ch.*, restored in 1862, has a good corbel table. The barracks, built in 1878, are the depôt of the 45th Regiment, the Sherwood Foresters (Derbyshire Regiment). To the rt. is *Osmaston Hall*, a heavy brick and stone edifice of the time of William III.

2 m. W. is **Mickleover** (Stat. G. N. Rly.), where is the County Lunatic Asylum.

11 m. ⚑ **DERBY** (Stat.), the county town, and "the Gateway to the Peak," although presenting no very striking features to the traveller, is pleasantly situated in a plain on the banks of the Derwent, from which rise gently undulating hills, particularly towards the W. But this river, according to some, did not give name to the town, which they say was anciently called *Deoraby*, a shelter for deer, a derivation adopted by the granter of its arms, a buck couchant in a park. The fact, however, that it is close to the Roman station of *Derventio*, at Little Chester, through which the Ryknield Street ran from Etocetum, disproves the "deer" theory, and points to the British word for water, "dwr" (represented by Derwent), as the origin. Derby was one of the Five Burghs of the Danes, and prior to the Norman Conquest it is stated to have held 243 burgesses, which number had declined to 100 at the time of the Domesday Survey. But its principal historical interest lies in later times, when in 1745 Prince Charles Edward occupied the town for a few days during his expedition

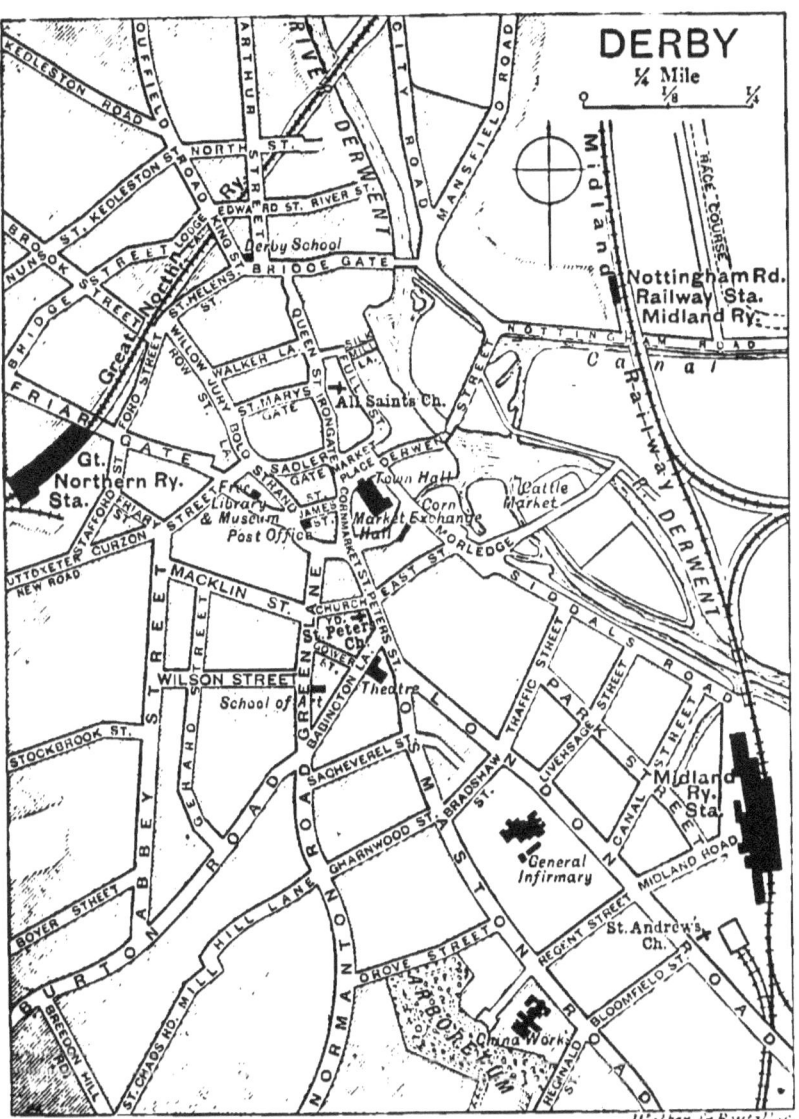

To face page 4.

Route 1.—Derby: Almshouses.

to England. His force of about 5000 men arrived from Ashbourne on the 4th Dec., and he took up his quarters at Exeter House, a fine mansion near the river, pulled down in 1854. He moved no farther S., though his advanced guard occupied Swarkestone-bridge over the Trent (Rte. 2). A stormy council of war was held, lasting all through the 5th, and at length he was induced, much against his own will, to retreat on the 6th. Surrounded as he was by 3 armies, there would have been little chance of his succeeding in a general engagement. He levied a contribution of about 3000*l*. on the town, but his followers behaved in other respects with great forbearance. Some of the common soldiers went to Ch. to take the Sacrament, while many thronged to the cutlers to have their swords ground. A very interesting account of Exeter House, as it existed in 1839, will be found in the second series of 'Miscellanies,' by Lord Stanhope (1872).

Derby has at different times obtained five charters, one of which, given by Richard I., contained a condition, that no Jews were to be allowed to reside within the liberties.

The antiquities of the town are remarkably few. Nothing remains of the castle, save an enclosure known as the Castle field, or of the old Roman station, save the name of Little Chester (Castra), a suburb to the N.E. between the river and the Rly., where Roman coins and pottery have occasionally been dug up. What pass for the foundations of a traditionary bridge may be sometimes observed when the river is low.

Neither is anything left of the Benedictine Nunnery founded in the 12th centy. by the Abbess of Derby, nor of the Cluniac cell founded by Waltheof.

Derby has returned 2 M.P.s from a very early period. It is a very busy town, chiefly owing to the Midland Railway Company, which has its headquarters here, with district lines to Birmingham, Bristol, and London, on the S., Nottingham and Lincoln on the E., Manchester, Sheffield, Leeds, Edinburgh, and Glasgow on the N., with many subsidiary branches.

The *Railway Station* is a very large brick building, which includes the chief offices of the Company, and adjoining are the workshops, where all the permanent way and rolling stock are made, and where 13,000 hands are employed. It is situated at the S.E. extremity of the town, from the centre of which it is fully a mile. There is also a passenger stat. on the Nottingham Road. The Great Northern Railway Stat., on a branch line from Nottingham, is in Friargate. Tram-cars run from the Midland Stat. to the Corn Market and from Victoria St. to Friargate near the Great Northern Rly.

Derby is deficient in good streets and handsome buildings, although it contains some fair specimens, such as the Infirmary (the foundation stone of the new buildings was laid by H.M. the Queen, 21st May, 1891), in the London Road; the Town-hall, with an Ionic portico, in the Marketplace; the Post Office; the Free Library, Museum, and Art Gallery; a large and handsome Market-hall, built in 1864; the Corn Exchange adjoining, opened in 1863; the Diocesan Training College; the School of Art and Technical Institution; the Grammar School; and the *Devonshire Almshouses*, a modernised building, originally founded by Elizabeth, Countess of Shrewsbury, "Bess of Hardwick," for 8 poor men and 4 women.

All Saints' Ch. (restd. in 1850), better known as Allhallows (formerly collegiate) is on high ground, and is conspicuous by its fine Perp. tower of the date of Henry VIII.

Route 1.—Derby: Churches.

It is 174 ft. in height, and of 3 stages, surmounted by battlements and crocketed pinnacles, which are 36 ft. more. A defaced inscription, of which the words "young men and maydens" form a part, has given rise to the legend that the tower was built by the bachelors and spinsters of Derby; "and in corroboration of the fact, it is stated that the bachelors used to ring the bells whenever a young woman born in the town was married."—*Knight.* It is, however, more likely that the words are part of the verse, "Young men and maidens, old men and children, praise ye the Lord." The tower is the only ancient part, the body of the Ch. having been rebuilt by *Gibbs* in 1725, in the pseudo-classic style. The interior is very heavy, but it contains a fine screen and many monuments that belonged to the old Ch. The Cavendish chapel has the tombs of many members of the family; among them, that of Henry Cavendish, the discoverer of the chemical compositions of the atmosphere (d. 1810). Against the S. wall is the tomb of "Bess of Hardwick;" it is said to have been erected during her lifetime, and under her own inspection. In the centre of the chapel is a sumptuous but heavy monument to William, Earl of Devonshire (d. 1628), and Christian his wife; they are represented by ghastly white effigies standing upright under a marble dome, while busts of their four children occupy the angles. There is also a monument by *Rysbrach* to the memory of the Countess of Bessborough (d. 1760), and another by *Nollekens*, with the medallion of the Earl of Bessborough her husband.

In the N. aisle of the chancel are monuments by *Roubiliac, Chantrey,* and *Westmacott,* to the families of Bateman, Chambers, and others. On the N. wall of the Ch. is a memorial to Richard Crosham, Master of the Goldsmiths' Company during the Plague of London, who left Derby as a poor boy, and bequeathed 4000*l.* for the relief of the poor of his native town. There is also a fine incised slab to Canon John Law, in the costume of a priest of the 16th centy. A beautiful open-work iron screen separates the chancel from the body of the Ch., and there is a painted window to the memory of the Prince Consort — subject, the Crucifixion. All Saints' Ch. should not be dismissed without mention of its indefatigable minister, Dr. Hutchinson, who procured nearly the whole of the money required for the rebuilding of the body of the Ch., by collecting it himself.

St. Peter's Ch. is a fine ivy-clad Perp. building, possessing a nave with a clerestory, chancel, aisles, and an embattled tower. The E. window of 5 lights (of stained glass) is Perp., but some of the other windows are Decorated. There are also a few Norm. details in the interior.

St. Alkmund's, rebuilt in 1845 by H. Stevens, is a Dec. Ch., conspicuous for its tower and spire 205 ft. in height: it has a nave and clerestory, N. and S. aisles, chancel, and S. porch. Notice the ancient altar-screen and the alabaster tomb of John Bullock, who is represented wearing a gown and ruff. The old Ch., which had Norm. traces, was the reputed burial-place of St. Alkmund, its founder. *St. Michael's,* situated between All Saints and St. Alkmund's, was rebuilt in 1858. The Roman Catholic Ch. of *St. Mary* (to which a convent is attached), in Bridge Gate, opposite St. Alkmund's, was built by A. W. Pugin, and enlarged by his son. It has some beautiful decorations in the interior, but fails as a whole.

St. Andrew's is a fine modern Dec. Ch. by *Scott,* built mainly at the cost of the shareholders of the Midland Rly. The breadth of the clerestory, nave, and apsidal chancel, gives it a striking and minster-like character.

St. Luke's Ch., of highly ornamental character, was erected in 1870 as a memorial to Bp. Lonsdale. The little bridge chapel, known as "St. Mary of the Brigg," is one of the oldest relics in the town.

In Babington Lane, where was formerly the town residence of the family of that name, was a house, now pulled down, in which Mary Queen of Scots slept on her way from Wingfield to Tutbury. Exeter House, in Full Street, where Prince Chas. Edward lodged in 1745, has also been demolished; but the oak panelling of a room that served as the council chamber has been preserved, and now lines the walls of an apartment in the Free Library (*post*).

The sect of Quakers established a meeting-house in Derby at a very early period, and, according to George Fox, were first called Quakers here (1650) by Justice Bennett, "because I bid him quake at the Word of the Lord."

Windmill Pit, to the S.W. of the town, was the scene of the burning of Joan Waste, a widow, one of the Marian martyrs, in 1556.

The old mill in Silk Mill Lane, is that in which John Lombe in 1717, and afterwards his cousin Sir Thomas Lombe, established the machinery for spinning or "throwing" silk, previously unknown in England; the former obtained it by visiting Piedmont in disguise, and bribing the workmen, some of whom he brought back with him. He died, however, soon afterwards, poisoned, it is said, by an Italian woman employed by the manufacturers whose secret he had obtained. Lombe certainly introduced the manufacture into England, and here on a swampy island in the Derwent the first silk-mill was built, at an expense of 30,000*l*. Hutton, the local historian, worked in this mill when a boy, and relates in consequence of his small size he was obliged to wear a kind of stilt, to be on a level with his work. There are now numerous other silk-mills. In 1773 Arkwright first set up a calico-mill in the town, and the Royal Derby Crown Porcelain Works, established about 1750, is in the Osmaston Road. Derby contains also paper-mills, some lead-works, a shot-tower, and several iron and machine works.

A Philosophical Society, one of the earliest provincial institutions of the kind, was established at Derby in 1772 by Dr. Darwin, and at first held its meetings in his house. The Society gradually formed a Library and Museum (in the Wardwick), where they collected many Roman remains from Derventio (Little Chester) and elsewhere. The whole, with many subsequent additions, including a large collection of books, given by the Duke of Devonshire, is now comprised in the Free Public Library. One of the rooms is lined with the oak panelling from Exeter House (*ante*), and contains several Stuart relics. Among them notice a letter from the Young Chevalier to his father, dated "Edinburgh, Oct. 22, 1745," just before commencing his march to England. It was given by H.M. the Queen. The present of this letter, as well as the fitting up of the room, resulted from the publication of "A Visit at Derby in 1839," in Lord Stanhope's 'Miscellanies' already referred to.

The Free Library and Museum, in the Wardwick, a red-brick Gothic building, was the gift of the late Mr. M. T. Bass, M.P. It was erected in 1879. The Art Gallery adjoining, also presented to the town by Mr. Bass, was added in 1883. Among the pictures are two admirable works by the native artist, Wright of Derby, "The Orrery," and "The Alchemist."

The *School*, founded in the 12th centy. by Walter Durdent, Bishop of Lichfield, and endowed by Queen Mary with a part of the possessions of Darley Abbey, was long held in the centre of the town, but was in 1862 removed to St. Helen's House, a fine mansion formerly belonging to the Strutt family. It was considerably enlarged in 1875. Bishop Juxon and Flamsteed the astronomer were among its pupils.

In the centre of the market-place is a bronze statue of the late Mr. M. T. Bass, M.P., who died in 1884, by the late Sir J. E. Boehm, Bart., R.A. The Town-hall, on the S. side of the market-place, is a handsome building. It contains portraits of the great benefactors to the town, namely, Mr. Joseph Strutt, Duke of Devonshire, and Mr. Bass. There are also preserved in it some interesting documents and MSS. of early date, and an old measure of the time of Elizabeth, dated 1601.

The School of Art is a spacious building on Green Hill. It was transferred to the Corporation in 1891 under the Technical Instruction Act, and the premises considerably enlarged. The Grand Theatre was erected in 1886. Two months after the opening it was burnt, but was rebuilt and opened again in the same year.

A little to the S. of the town, on the Osmaston road, is the free public garden, called the *Arboretum*, once the property of the late Joseph Strutt (kinsman of Lord Belper), who, having caused it to be laid out as a pleasure-ground, and planted with more than 1000 varieties of trees, presented it to his fellow-townsmen in 1840 for their

"common pleasures,
To walk abroad and recreate themselves."

The value of the land and the sum expended on it is estimated at 10,000*l*. At the entrance is a statue of the munificent donor. The visitor will notice the "Headless Cross," 4 steps crowned by a stone in the centre. In a hollow of which, filled with vinegar, the money was placed during the plague of 1665, so that a traffic in provisions could be maintained between the townsfolk and the country people who feared infection. There is also a public recreation-ground on the Holmes, and bounded by the Derwent, another gift of the late Mr. Bass, M.P., to the town. The racecourse is on the Nottingham road, where the cricket matches also take place.

Among eminent natives may be mentioned Samuel Richardson, the novelist; Joseph Wright, the painter; Hutton, the historian; and Fox, the machinist.

A pleasant *Excursion* may be made from Derby to **Kedleston Hall** (Lord Scarsdale). The distance is 4 m. on the Kedleston road.

The Park of 600 acres is pleasingly diversified in surface, enlivened with deer, and ornamented with old trees and a large sheet of water. The groves of oaks are remarkable for age and size. There is also a sulphur-spring, formerly held in great repute. The house (no longer shown to visitors) is of classical architecture, built by Robert Adam in 1765, consisting of a centre and two wings connected with the main building by corridors. The principal front is 360 ft. in length, and has a portico with columns 30 ft. high. On the garden front is the hospitable inscription "Amicis et sibi." The entrance hall, 67 ft. high, reaching to the roof of the building, is supported by 20 Corinthian columns of yellowish alabaster from Elvaston; and for grandeur of dimensions and splendour of its decoration is surpassed by few halls in England. It did not, however, please Dr. Johnson, who, according to Boswell, pronounced it "costly but ill-contrived. Behind the hall is a circular saloon, useless, and therefore ill-contrived; the grandeur was all below. The bed-chambers were small, low, dark, and fitter for a prison than a house of splendour. The kitchen has an opening into the gallery, by which its heat and fumes are dispersed over the house. There seems in the whole more cost than judgment."—*Boswell's Life of Johnson.*

The collection of works of art contains many paintings, including—
Guido Reni.--Bacchus and Ariadne. "Very pleasing in the characters and the bright cheerful effect, and carefully painted in a soft warm tone."—*Waagen.*
Luca Giordano.—The Triumph of Bacchus.
Annibale Carracci. — Orlando delivering Olympia from the sea monster by fixing an anchor in his jaws. "The subject is well suited to the vigorous turn of mind of the master." Also Mary Magdalene in the Desert ; a pretty little cabinet picture.
Cuyp.—A large mountain-landscape. "The tone of the distance too dull and reddish."
Josse de Momper. — A rich mountain-landscape with the story of Naaman. "Perhaps the highest work of the master, for with strange, fantastic, and singularly - formed wooded mountains and parts illumined by the sun, which constitute the principal claim of his pictures, it combines an extraordinary size and a far more graceful execution than is usual. The figures of men and animals happily put in by Velvet Breughel."
Claude de Lorrain.—The Tower on the Tiber, with a mill in a warm evening light. "A picture of fine effect of his later period. The general tone of the green pale, and the treatment broader than in his early works."

Guido Reni.—A Sleeping Cupid.
Rembrandt van Rijn (attributed to).—Daniel interpreting Nebuchadnezzar's dream ; a composition of 11 figures; most probably by Solomon de Koninck. "In size, powerful colouring, effect, and admirable execution, the most important work I have seen of this able follower of Rembrandt."
Barend van Orley. — A Holy Family with St. Elizabeth. "The delicacy and elevation of the characters, the admirable, tenderly-fused execution, render this picture one of the finest I am acquainted with by this eminent master; as is mostly the case with him, the tone is reddish in the lights and grey in the shadows."
Raphael.—Death of the Virgin. "a small picture in his early manner."
Nicolas Poussin.—Rinaldo holding his Shield to Amida as a mirror; an early work.
Niccolo dell' Abbate.—The Virgin and Child. St. John, and St. Joseph. "The influence of Correggio is very manifest in this picture of this rare master, which is painted in a warm brownish tone."
Jan Steen.—A Blind Beggar; a clear, well-executed little picture. There are two other pictures by this master.
Portraits, by *Lely*, of James Duke of Ormonde, of Henry Jermyn Earl of St. Albans (the supposed husband of Henrietta Maria), of the Duchess of Portsmouth, and of the Duchess of York.
Thirty-six Limousin enamels, copied from Albert Dürer's designs, of the Passion of Our Lord, decorate a wardrobe.
Adriaen van Utrecht.—Turkeys and other poultry ; very masterly.
Jan Fyt. — Dogs and game. "Strikingly true to nature, and painted in his own peculiar broad rich manner, and in a deep full tone."

Sir Godfrey Kneller.—Catherine, Countess of Dorchester, mistress of James II. Her father, Sir Chas. Sedley, though himself a man of most profligate character, resented her elevation to the peerage, and was one of the first to join the Prince of Orange on his landing, saying, in a bitter jest, "that as James had made his daughter a countess, the least return he could make was to assist in making James's daughter (Mary) a queen."

Van Dyck (?).—Sir Paul Rycaut, the historian of the Turks.

Janssens.—Prince Henry, eldest son of James I., 1603. "Very pleasing by truth of conception, delicacy of execution, clearness and brightness of tone."

Jan Matsys.—The Virgin kissing the Child; very carefully finished, not without grace. This picture is probably by Jan Matsys, the unequal son of Quentin.

Snyders.— Dead game, a swan, peacock, and deer. "The light colours brilliant and powerful; the execution very careful." Ducks pursued by a hawk; "masterly and dramatic."

In the private apartments occupying the E. wing of the house are also many good paintings:—

Carlo Dolci.— A Female Saint (Ursula or Christina) with an arrow through her neck. "Of a degree of beauty in form and expression, of a clearness in the colouring, and a delicacy of finish, which are not often found united in his works."

Il Bassano.—A Nativity.

Domenichino.—A Landscape. "A very beautiful composition, but more motley in the colouring, and more scattered than usual."

Guercino.—The Jews celebrating the Triumph of David over Goliath; of very powerful effect.

Wilson.—Landscape; a wood with beams of light of remarkable warmth and clearness.

The kitchen is a spacious apartment, crossed by a gallery, and bearing over the chimney the appropriate motto " Waste not, want not."

Kedleston Ch. (restd. 1884-5 by Lord Scarsdale) is of various periods, but retains a Norm. S. door, over which is a small sculpture. In the chancel are several monuments of the Curzons, one of them by *Rysbrach*.

The return to Derby may be agreeably varied by proceeding to any one of the stations on the Wirksworth Rly. (Rte. 4), the country being very pleasant. Duffield, the nearest, is little more than 2 m. distant. The other stats. are— Hazlewood, 3½ m.; Shottle, 5 m.; Idridgehay, 7 m.; and Wirksworth, 10 m.

ROUTE 2.

DERBY TO TRENT JUNCTION, BY MELBOURNE AND CASTLE DONINGTON.

MIDLAND RAILWAY. 12 m.

The first 2 m. of this route are travelled on the West branch of the line, as far as Normanton (Rte. 1), then the line turns off S.E. and reaches at

4½ m. **Chellaston** (Stat.), a place noted for its quarries of gypsum or plaster of Paris, which employ a considerable population, and where the geologist will find an interesting variety of Foraminifera (*Introd.*, p. [5].) A short distance to the W., at **Swarkestone**, the Trent is crossed by a singular bridge, the approaches across the alluvial flats being upwards of ¾ m. in length. The date is about the close of the 12th centy., and it is traditionally said to be the work of two maiden sisters, who were brought to poverty through their benevolence. The advanced guard of the Highlanders held the bridge in Dec. 1745. The Ch., restored in 1875, is partly Norm., and is worth a visit. It contains monumental effigies in alabaster of Richard Harpur, Chief Justice of the Common Pleas (d. 1577), and his wife; also of his son, Sir John Harpur, and his wife.

[1 m. beyond Chellaston a line branches off S. to Ashby-de-la-Zouch, and connects Derbyshire with the collieries of that district and Warwickshire. The tourist may well avail himself of it to visit the pleasant little town of Melbourne and its picturesque neighbourhood.

6½ m. On W. 1 m. is **Stanton-by-Bridge**, the Ch., restored 1865, contains several 16th-centy. monuments for the families of Sacheverell and Francis. It has a Saxon chancel arch.

7 m. **King's Newton**, a township of Melbourne. Near the river stood King's Newton Hall, a Jacobean building, accidentally destroyed by fire in 1859. Charles I. stayed there, and is said to have written on a pane of glass the anagram on Carolus Rex, " Cras Ero Lux." At the beginning of the 18th centy. the Hardinges, who possessed King's Newton, sold their ancient Hall to the Cokes of Melbourne. In the village are the steps of an old cross, and a Holy Well, on the arch of which is a Latin inscription to the effect that it was erected by Robert Hardinge in 1660. King's Newton is noted for having been at various times the residence of local literati.

8 m. ☖ **Melbourne** (Stat.), a thriving town which has a trade in silk and thread goods, and much of the surrounding land cultivated as market gardens. The Ch., dedicated to St. Michael, was restored in 1862 by Sir Gilbert Scott; it is a fine specimen of late Norm. architecture, consisting of nave, chancel, and aisles, which are separated from the nave by a series of circular-headed arches, ornamented with chevrons, and supported by round piers. From the centre rises a massive tower, Norm. below with a Perp. upper story, and there are two smaller ones at the W. end. Notice the W. door, which has some good Norm. mouldings. The chancel had at one time a semicircular apse, and there were also apses at the E. end of the N. and S. transepts, but these were removed before the Reformation. During the progress of the restoration several singular wall-paintings were discovered, the subject of one of which seemed to corroborate the tradition of the murder of Ethelred's queen by her Mercian nobles. Indeed, the erection of the original Ch. in the 7th centy. is ascribed to Ethelred in token of his grief. In the interior is a monumental slab with effigies of Henry and Elizabeth Hardinge, the ancient owners of the estate of King's Newton, who settled here in 1400. Lord Hardinge, of Italian celebrity, was descended from this family.

At Melbourne John, Duke of Bourbon, taken prisoner at Agincourt, was imprisoned 19 years; and here the Bishops of Carlisle had a palace, slight remains of which still exist.

Adjoining the village is Melbourne Hall, formerly the seat of Lord Melbourne (from whom it came to his sister, the late Lady Palmerston, and from her to Earl Cowper, the present owner), and now tenanted by W. D. Fane, Esq. The gardens are in the Dutch fashion, and occupy about 16 acres; admission can be obtained on Wednesdays after 2 o'clock, on application to the gardener.

At the old Melbourne Hall Baxter wrote his ' Saint's Everlasting Rest.'

2 m. W. is **Knowl Hills**, a very picturesque spot, where a mansion of the Burdetts is said to have existed. The only traces of such habitation now are in the series of terraces built upon arches, excavated in the new red sandstone, and thought to be cellars. In the plantation, called "*The Ferns*," is a very singular collection of mounds, about 50 in number, which was examined by Mr. Bateman, and calcined bones were found in every one that he opened. "The origin of this tumular cemetery is enveloped in obscurity; the absence of pottery and weapons affording no clue to the age or people to which the sepulchres should be attributed. They seem to be connected with the eventful period in which tradition affirms the place to have been the scene of a sanguinary conflict between the Saxons and their Danish enemies, of whose successful forays in the Vale of Trent we have evidence in the name of the adjacent village of Ingleby, as well as in that of the still nearer domain of Foremark."

The Rly. continues to **Tonge** (Stat.), a hamlet of Breedon, and to **Worthington** (Stat.). From the former, Breedon Bulwarks, Staunton Harold, and Calke Abbey, may be visited; the distance to Melbourne, for return by rail, being about 10 miles.

At the earthworks, called the Bulwarks, the geologist will notice blocks of millstone grit built in, which are foreign to the district, and were probably brought by the glacial drift from the grit moors to the N. The Ch. at **Breedon** (dedicated to St. Mary and St. Hardulph) is situated very picturesquely on a rocky eminence, consisting of an isolated mass of mountain limestone, yielding many good fossils, and supplying a large quantity of lime to the neighbouring districts. A priory once flourished here, but there are no traces of it now left. In the N. aisle of the Ch., called the "Ferrer's Aisle," and shut off by iron railings, are some fine early monuments of the Shirleys, and a curious oak pew, shut in at the top and sides, so as to separate the inmates from the rest of the congregation. The aisle was purchased at the Dissolution by a Shirley for 100*l.*, who reserved it for himself and descendants for ever.

2½ m. S.W. of Breedon is **Staunton Harold**, the seat of Earl Ferrers, which contains a family portrait by Van der Werf, and a beautifully painted ceiling in the ball-room. The N.E. front was designed by Inigo Jones. The visitor should notice the old gates which belonged to a former building, and which are particularly graceful. The Ch. is remarkable as being one of the very few built in the days of the Commonwealth. It was founded in 1653, by Sir Robert Shirley, a stout Cavalier, "whose singular praise it was to have done the best things in the worst of times, and to have hoped them in the most calamitous." This inscription is on the tower of the Ch., the interior of which is worth seeing. It consists of a nave, aisles, and a chancel, separated by wrought-iron gates. Notice the carved panelling, the painted ceiling, and the military relics of various members of the Ferrers family.

1½ m. N.W. is **Calke Abbey** (Sir V. Harpur Crewe, Bart.), a quadrangular building of Ionic character. The interior contains a state bed, presented by Caroline, George II.'s queen, to Lady Manners, one of her maids of honour, who married into the Harpur-Crewe family. There are also some good family portraits, including Sir George and Lady Crewe, by *Reinagle*; Earl and Countess of Huntingdon, Duke and Duchess of Rutland, and others.

The Abbey was originally an appanage of Burton Abbey, to which it was granted by an Earl of Mercia.

1¾ m. W. of Calke is the village of **Ticknall**, or **Tickenhall**, the Ch. of which (rebuilt in 1842) has a conspicuous spire. It contains two interesting monuments, one a stone effigy in a civilian's dress (1325), with his head hooded, holding a heart in his hands, and his feet resting on a dog; the other, an incised slab of a knight in armour; both are memorials of the Frances family.

From Worthington the Rly. continues to **Ashby-de-la-Zouch** (see Rte. 23).]

Returning to the main line at

7½ m. is **Weston-on-Trent** (Stat.), where the large and handsome *Ch.*, restored in 1877, has a lofty embattled tower and spire. There is also a curious Jacobean monument to the memory of a prebendary of Lincoln and his numerous family.

The line soon after crosses the Trent, and reaches at

10½ m. **Castle Donington** (Stat.). The town is a long straggling place, built on a steep sandstone hill, and containing at the N. the remains of an ancient castle, said to have been founded by John of Gaunt; also a fine Ch., with several monuments of the family of Hastings. On the restoration of the Ch. in 1877 a hagioscope was discovered. 1 m. W. is **Donington Park** (Lord Donington), formerly the seat of the Marquis of Hastings. The mansion, which has a fine library, was erected from designs by *Sir J. Wyatville*, and has a portico surmounted by a lantern-tower; a deer park of 350 acres, with some fine oaks, surrounds the house. Moore wrote some of his Irish melodies here. During the French Revolution the house afforded a refuge for Charles X. and other emigrants, it being placed at their disposal by the first Marquis.

12 m. **Trent Junction Stat.** Here the Midland lines running from E. and W. (from Newark on the one hand, and from Burton-on-Trent on the other) unite, and are continued S. through Leicester, Market Harborough, and Bedford, to London. A large educational establishment, Trent College, is seen almost adjoining the Stat., but the nearest villages, Long Eaton (N.) and Sawley (W.), are both about 1 m. off. (See Rte. 10.)

ROUTE 3.

TRENT JUNCTION TO CHESTERFIELD, BY ILKESTON, ALFRETON, AND CLAY CROSS.

EREWASH VALLEY BRANCH, MIDLAND RAILWAY. 27 m.

The line runs up the entire course of the valley of the river Erewash, which rises in the high ground to the S. of Mansfield. It accommodates a large and important coal district, and is the most direct route between Leicester and the North. Its course is very nearly the same as that of the Erewash Canal as far as Codnor Park; and, as the line frequently crosses the river, it is alternately in Derby and in Notts.

¾ m. **Long Eaton** (Stat.). This is little more than a continuation of the Junction, the space between being occupied mainly with sidings, coal depôts, a carriage-wheel factory, and the dwellings of the workmen. After crossing the main road between Derby and Nottingham, at

14   *Route 3.—Sandiacre—Langley Mill.*

2¾ m. is **Sandiacre** (Stat.). The village (properly San Diacre) has a Dec. Ch., well restored. The chancel, which is considerably longer than the nave, has a particularly beautiful E. window and a Norm. chancel arch. The visitor should notice the figure-heads of the doors and windows, together with the crockets and finials of the pinnacles, which seem to be carved after the model of the water-lily, a plant abundant in the Erewash.

1 m. W. is **Risley Hall** (F. W. Parsons, Esq.), which occupies the site of an Elizabethan mansion of the Willoughbys. Some remains exist of the terraced garden of the old Hall. 1 m. N.E. of Sandiacre is **Stapleford**, in Notts. The *Ch.* contains a monument to the only son of Admiral Sir John Borlase Warren, who was killed at the battle of Alexandria. At the turning of the lane to the churchyard is the shaft of a cross ornamented with rude interlaced work, probably of the 9th centy. Stapleford Hall (Lt.-Col. C. I. Wright) is a large mansion. A rugged pinnacle of rock, springing from the shoulder of Stapleford Hill, called the *Hemlock Stone*, 31 ft. high, once passed for a pagan relic. It is in reality a decided needle of Lower Keupen sandstone.

On the high ground behind Stapleford, E., is the village of **Bramcote**, with a restored Ch.

3¾ m. **Stanton Gate** (Stat.). Near here are the vast ironworks of the Stanton Iron Co. Stanton-by-Dale *Ch.* (2 m. S.) has some painted windows, a good altar-piece, and monuments. Dale Abbey (Rte. 10) is 1½ m. W.

5 m. **Trowell** (Stat.). Here is a branch line to Nottingham.

6½ m. ⚡ **Ilkeston** (Stat.) is on a short branch from Ilkeston Junction on the main line (also a Stat. G. N. Rly., with branch line to Heanor). It is an ancient market town, with some lace and hosiery factories, but is mainly dependant on the neighbouring collieries. It stands on a hill, commanding extensive views, and the Ch. of St. Mary, with its lofty pinnacled tower, is a very conspicuous object; the interior is handsome, having a painted window, a Dec. screen, and a chantry chapel. There were mineral springs and baths here, in high repute throughout the district, and particularly serviceable in rheumatic and scrofulous cases, but they are now closed. A charter of incorporation was granted to the town in 1887.

8¼ m. **Shipley-Gate** (Stat.) serves the collieries in the neighbourhood, which are very extensive. Shipley Hall (A. E. M. Mundy, Esq.) stands on an eminence in finely kept grounds.

9¾ m. **Langley Mill** (Stat.). Very near, on W., is the Ch. of **Heanor** (Stat. G. N. Rly. It is also connected with Ripley and Butterley by a branch of the Midland Rly.), a fine E. E. restored edifice, consisting of a nave, chancel, S. aisle, and tower, rising from the W. end. In the interior are monuments to the family of Mundy of Shipley, and one, with rather an Hibernian inscription, to Watson, the Derbyshire artist, who assisted Gibbons at Chatsworth.

"Watson has gone, whose skilful art displayed,
To the very life, whatever nature made:
View but his wondrous works in Chatsworth Hall,
Which are so gazed at and admired by all;
You'll say 'tis pity he should hidden be,
And nothing said to revive his memory.
My mournful friends, forbear your tears,
For I shall rise when Christ appears."

Heanor Hall is the property of A. E. M. Mundy, Esq.

Route 3.—Codnor Park—Alfreton.

1 m. E. (in Notts) is **Eastwood** (Stat. G. N. Rly.), a busy colliery village, with mechanics' institute, &c., to the establishment of which the late Lord Palmerston contributed, he having had property in the neighbourhood. The *Ch.*, which replaced a very old structure in 1858, is a handsome building.

12½ m. **Codnor Park** (Stat., also Stat. on G. N. Rly.). The ironworks here stand in what was once the park of Codnor, an ancient seat of the family of Zouche, to whom it came through the Lords Grey of Groby. The ruins of their castle overlook the vale of the Erewash, and consist of some of the round towers of the courtyard, and a few walls, with windows and doorways of the 13th centy. There is also a remarkable old dovecote, the walls of which are of great thickness. The castle was formerly moated, and there is also a large pond, believed never to fail, which gave rise to an old local saying—

"When Codenor's pond runs dry, The lordes may say good-bye."

The fulfilment of this prophecy would have less effect on its present owners, the Butterley Iron Co. (see Rte. 4, Ripley), than on the ancient residents, as they have the much larger Butterley reservoir at hand. The town which has grown up about their works is known as **Ironville**, where a *Ch.* has been built by the Company for the inhabitants, most of whom being in their employ. A hill rises behind the park, which the visitor should ascend. It is laid out in walks, and has a lofty column, erected to the memory of the late Mr. Jessop, one of the lords of the manor. It was struck by lightning in 1854. From this spot is obtained a curious view over the busy iron district. Butterley Hall (H. L. Wright, Esq.) was the birthplace of Sir Jas. Outram of Indian celebrity, whose father was an engineer here.

13½ m. **Pye-bridge Junct. Stat.** [Hence a line branches off W. to Ambergate, with a Stat. at Butterley; and another branch of 5¾ m. runs E. to Kirkby, where it joins the Nottingham and Mansfield line (Rte. 13), with a Stat. at **Pinxton** and **Selston**, both colliery villages, near the former is Brookhill Hall (W. S. Coke, Esq.).] ½ m. W. of the Stat. is **Riddings**, a colliery village, with a handsome E. E. Ch., built in 1832.

[The Great Northern Rly. from Nottingham has a line branching from **Kimberley** to **Pinxton**, running parallel with this portion of the Midland Rly., and having stations at Newthorpe and Greasley, Eastwood, Codnor Park, Pye Hill.]

16 m. ✠**Alfreton** (Stat.). The town, traditionally said to have been founded by Alfred, is pleasantly situated on the brow of a hill. It belonged, at the making of the Domesday Survey, to Roger de Bush, the lord of Tickhill (Rte. 18), and afterwards to Fitzranulf, the founder of Beauchief Abbey.

The *Ch.*, which is mainly Dec., stands on rather high ground. It consists of a nave with aisles and clerestory, chancel with a good Perp. 5-light window, and a battlemented tower of 3 stages at the W. end. The bays of the nave are formed by pointed arches with circular piers. Notice the heads that form the termination of the moulding of the arch over the S. porch, and also of the windows. In the interior are monuments of the family of Morewood, and a brass genealogical tablet to John Ormond and his wife, daughter of Sir William Chaworth, 1507. Adjoining the town is Alfreton Park, the seat of C. R. Palmer-Morewood, Esq.; the house contains some good pic-

Route 4.—Derby to Sheffield.

tures, and commands beautiful views over Normanton and Shirland. The grounds are celebrated for their fine timber.

17½ m. **Westhouses** (Stat.). Here the Alfreton and Mansfield line branches off E. and has Stats. at Tibshelf, Woodend, Teversall, Pleasley, and Mansfield Woodhouse (see Rte. 13).

In the Ch.-yd. at **Blackwell** (¾ m.) are the remains of a Runic cross and a remarkable yew-tree.

18½ m. **Doe Hill** (Stat.), a colliery village. Hardwick Hall lies about 5 m. N.E., but the way to it from Mansfield is much to be preferred (Rte. 13).

23 m. **Clay Cross Junct. Stat.** The line here joins the Derby and Sheffield line (Rte. 4).

27 m. **Chesterfield** (Stat.) (Rte. 4).

ROUTE 4.

DERBY TO SHEFFIELD, BY BELPER AND CHESTERFIELD.

MIDLAND RAILWAY. 37½ m.

The Rly., on emerging from Derby Stat., and passing Nottingham Road Stat., crosses the canal, whence a good view is obtained of the town, with the tall and graceful towers and spires of All Saints and St. Alkmund's on W. From the banks of the Derwent, between which and the line is Little Chester (the ancient Derventio), rise low hills clothed to the top with hanging woods and verdant lawns, forming a charming foreground.

At 1 m., on the W., is **Darley Abbey**, with its modernised Abbey (Walter Evans, Esq.), occupying the site of an Augustinian Friary, founded temp. Hen. I. by Robert Ferrars, afterwards Earl of Derby. The Ch. peeps prettily out from the woods. There is a large cotton-mill here belonging to the family of Evans.

At 2 m. is **Allestree Hall**, the seat of Sir T. W. Evans, Bart. Allestree Ch. has a good Norm. doorway and moulding; in the interior are monuments to the Mundys. From the opposite side of the line rises the spire of **Breadsall** Ch. (Stat. G. N. Rly.), near which, at the Priory, resided Dr. Darwin, "physician, poet, and philosopher" (d. 1802), whose monument is in the Ch. Breadsall Lodge was the residence of Lady Darwin, the relict of his kinsman, Sir F. S. Darwin. The Ch. was restored in 1877, when a beautifully carved *Pieta* was found beneath the pavement of the chancel. It has been restored to its original position in the N. aisle.

[At 3 m. a *Branch Rly.* goes E. to Ripley. The first stat. is at **Little Eaton** (3½ m. from Derby), where are some paper-mills and stone quarries.

2 m. E. is **Morley**, with a fine Perp. Ch., having a lofty spire, and containing some stained glass, brought from Dale Abbey (Rte. 10). There are several 15th-centy. *brasses* for the Stathams, and one for John Sacheverell, killed at Bosworth; 17th-centy. monumental effigies of Hyacinth and Elizabeth Sacheverell; and in the chancel a curious inscription, giving a list of the prayers ordained by John Statham (d. 1453) to be said for the souls of himself and family.

5 m. **Coxbench** (Stat.) proper is in the parish of **Holbrooke**, and the old name for that part of Coxbench, which is now in the parish of Horsley, was, according to the registers, called "Tantin's" or "St.

Route 4.—Kilburn—Duffield.

Anthony's Cross." *Holbrooke Hall* was the residence of the Rev. W. Leeke, who carried the colours of the 52nd Foot at Waterloo, and who published several works, claiming the honour of the decisive charge on that day for his regiment. At **Horsley**, 1 m. N. of the stat., are some slight remains of a castle built in the 13th centy. and called Horistan Castle. It is mentioned by Bryon in 'On leaving Newstead Abbey'—

"Near Askalon's towers
John of Horistan slumbers."

The *Ch.* is a fine E. E. edifice, well restored; one of the very singular gurgoyles and fine spire are engraved in Parker's 'Gloss. Architecture.'

7 m. **Kilburn** (Stat.), a colliery village. Kilburn Hall (Col. C. D. Pedder) has in its garden several ancient yew-trees cut so as to represent birds.

7½ m. **Denby** (Stat.), with collieries and pottery works. The Icknield Street here crosses the rly. The E. E. Ch. of St. Mary the Virgin has a remarkable and costly monument to Patrick Lowe and his wife. Flamsteed the astronomer (b. 1646, d. 1719) was a native of this parish.

9½ m. ⚔Ripley (Stat.). This was a market-town in the time of Henry III., but fell into decay, from which it was raised about the beginning of the present century by the opening of numerous collieries in its neighbourhood, to which the Butterley ironworks have since been added. It is now a flourishing town, and has many good houses; there are also extensive schools, &c., the Butterley Company contributing handsomely to their support.

Codnor Park (Stat.), on the Erc-[*Derby*, &c.]

wash Valley line, is 2½ m. E. (Rte. 3).]

Crossing the Derwent, and passing Duffield Hall (R. Smith, Esq.), the line reaches

5½ m. **Duffield** (Stat.), a pretty village, on the rt. bank of the river. The *Ch.*, which has a lofty tower and spire, lies between the rly. and river, some little distance before the station is reached. It is marked by features of the debased Perp. style, and contains a fine monument to Sir Roger Mynors and his lady, 1536, with their recumbent effigies; around the sides are niches with kneeling figures. There is also a tomb for Anthony Bradshaw, great-uncle of President Bradshaw. Concerning Anthony "there is a singular circumstance attending the history of this monument (which was put up by himself in the year 1600, and which gives, beside, the figures of himself and his two wives, the names and figures of their 20 children), viz., that when he had not very unreasonably concluded he should have no further addition to his olive-branches, he had three more children by the second wife, whose names and figures, consequently, do not appear on the monument with their 20 brothers and sisters." An absurd tradition prevails, that this Ch. was commenced on another spot, but, as fast as the workmen laid the foundations, they were removed by the devil to where the building now stands. Vicissitude Giffard died here in 1807. The foundations of Duffield Castle, an important stronghold of the Ferrars family, were discovered on Castle Hill in 1886.

[From Duffield a *Branch Rly.* runs N.W. to Wirksworth, up the valley of the Ecclesbourn. The stats. are at Hazlewood (7 m.), Shottle (8½ m.), Idridgehay (10 m.),

c

and **Wirksworth** (13½ m.), all, except the last, mere villages, without any especial interest.

§ **Wirksworth** (Stat.) occupies a very beautiful position in the bottom of a deep valley, and, when viewed from the wooded hills around, presents a perfect scene of repose. The town itself, however, which was long the head-quarters of the Derbyshire lead-mining interest, has nothing but its situation to recommend it. The Ch., restored in 1876 by Sir G. G. Scott, is a fine cruciform building of Perp. date, consisting of a nave with side aisles, N. and S. transepts, and a chancel, with a square but rather low tower. There are memorial chapels of the Vernons and Blackwalls, some *brasses* of uncertain ascription, and monuments of the family of Gell of Hopton, viz. Anthony Gell, the founder of the school and almshouses (d. 1583), and Sir John Gell, the Parliamentarian officer (d. 1671); also of the families of Lowe and Blackwell. Notice, too, in the N. aisle a singular rude antique bas-relief of the principal events in our Saviour's life. There is a curious epitaph on the exterior wall (W. end), commemorating the good qualities of one Philip Shallcross, "once an eminent quill-driver to the attorneys of the town" (d. 1787), as evinced by his affection for animals. Adjoining the Ch. is the Grammar School, founded in 1576, and rebuilt in 1828. In the Wesleyan Chapel is a tablet erected to the memory of Elizabeth Evans (d. 1849) and to her husband Samuel Evans (d. 1858), both of whom fervently preached Methodism, and are known to the world by the writings of their niece, George Eliot, under the names of "Dinah" and "Seth Bede." The novelist used to stay with her relatives, who lived at Millhouses just outside the town.

The produce of the lead-mines in the neighbourhood of Wirksworth has of late years very much decreased; it was at one time the staple trade, for the accommodation of which the **Moot-hall** was erected by the Duchy of Lancaster in 1814. Here a Court Leet is held annually, and the Barmote Courts, when required, for the regulation of the trade. These courts are of very great antiquity. "The principal part of the county where lead-ore is found in any considerable quantity is called 'The King's Field,' and comprehends nearly all the wapentake of Wirksworth, and a considerable part of the High Peak Headland. The King's Field has been from time immemorial let on lease. The lessees (of whom, when Pilkington wrote his account of Derbyshire in 1789, there were only two) have each in his respective district a steward and barmaster. The steward presides as judge in the Barmote Courts, and with 24 jurymen, chosen every half-year, determines all disputes which arise respecting the working of the mines. Debts incurred in working the mines are cognizable in these courts, which meet twice a year, or oftener if need be. The office of the barmaster is principally to put miners into the possession of veins that they have discovered, and to collect the proportion of ore to which the lessee of the crown or the lord of the manor has a claim. When a miner has discovered a new vein of ore in the 'King's Field' he may acquire a title to the exclusive possession of it, provided it be not in a garden, orchard, or high road, by a proper application to the barmaster of the liberty. Should the miner neglect to work the vein, the barmaster may, after a certain time, dispose of it to any one who is willing to buy it."—*Knight*. Here is preserved the brass dish made in the reign of Henry VIII. to serve as the legal standard measure of lead-ore in this district. The hills all around are scattered over with half-ruined huts (here called "coes") covering the mouths of abandoned mines, and forming a singular and charasteristic feature in the scenery. The veins of lead are found in forms called in Derbyshire "Rakes," and a curious old poem on the Liberties and Customs of Wirksworth is still extant, date 1653 :—

"By custom old in Wirksworth wapentake,
If any of this nation find a Rake,
Or sign or leading to the same, may set
In any ground, and there lead-ore may get;
They may make crosses, holes, and set their stowes,
Sink shafts, build lodges, cottages, or coes."

The mines in this neighbourhood are drained by adits, here called "soughs," driven for a very considerable length from the level of the Derwent, through the solid rock. One, called *Cromford Sough*, extends to that town from Wirksworth, and cost 30,000l.; it is of less value in relieving the Wirksworth mines of water, than for turning the cotton-mills at Cromford. The Wirksworth Meer Sough, E. of the town, drains a large district, and is nearly 3 m. long. The mines of this district were worked by the Romans, as is shown by the discovery, on Cromford Moor, of a pig of lead inscribed with the name of the Emperor Hadrian, now in the British Museum. Bones of a rhinoceros were found in 1882 in a lead-mine in the neighbourhood.

At Wirksworth there is an old custom called "Tap-dressing," and on Whit-Wednesday the taps and pipes of the water-supply to the town are decorated with flowers.

About 2 m. N.W. is **Hopton Hall** (H. Chandos Pole Gell, Esq.), the ancient seat of the famous Parliamentary leader, Sir John Gell, where are preserved his colours, leather doublet, and some small artillery.]

At 6¼ m. there is a very charming view on E. of the line (previous to rushing into a tunnel) at **Milford**, where the waters of the river are dammed into lakelets for the use of the cotton-mills belonging to the Strutts, which are connected by an arch thrown across the road. Makeney House is the residence of G. H. Strutt, Esq., and Milford House of Hon. F. Strutt. On emerging into light the same pretty view is continued as far as

7½ m. ⚥ **Belper** (Stat.), a long straggling town, reaching for a considerable distance on both sides the Derwent, and extending on the l. bank to the top of the wooded hill. It owes its present consequence to the cotton-mills established here 1776 by Messrs. Strutt, who have converted it from an inconsiderable village to a market-town second only to Derby in the county. Their mills, which are at the north end of the town, give work to about 1200 persons, whose employers have provided for them decent dwellings at a moderate cost. The Derwent is used in working the machinery, and for this purpose is dammed up by a large weir near the bridge. The hosiery-mills of Messrs. Ward and Co., and those of Messrs. Brettle and Co., are nearly the largest in the kingdom. In addition to silk and cotton hosiery, nails used to be made here to a great extent, also pottery, but owing to strikes the nail trade has been reduced to a low ebb; all these manufactures being due to the coal which is worked in the neighbourhood to the E. The situation of the town, the chief part of which is on the rt. of the rly., is charming. It has two modern churches, one of which— Christ Ch.—has been recently decorated after designs by Mr. E. H. Corbould, but very little is seen in passing, for the rly. is carried through Belper in a deep cutting,

c 2

with massive retaining walls, and crossed by 11 bridges in the space of little more than a mile. The annals of Belper are associated with the memory of John of Gaunt, who was a great benefactor to the town, and built a chapel, now incorporated with a modern school-house. From the discovery of foundations of a large massive building, it is believed that he had a residence here. On the ascending ground to W. of the town is Bridge Hill, the charming seat of G. H. Strutt, Esq., a member of the family to which Belper owes its prosperity, and the merits of which were recognised by a peerage.

The country to the W. is full of beautiful scenery, the outskirts of the more romantic districts of central Derbyshire. It is a delightful walk of 1½ m. to Depth o' Lumb, a romantic glen watered by a small stream. The return may be made by a détour through Hazlewood to Milford, making a ramble of about 6 m. Another pretty walk is to Wirksworth, 6 m., keeping along the high ground W. of Alderwasley, from whence the pedestrian will obtain wide views over the Nottinghamshire border.

On emerging from the rly. cuttings, and passing the cemetery on E., the valley of the Derwent becomes more contracted, its sides steeper, and all its beauties increased. The serpentine course of the river, which renders it necessary for the rly. to cross it 3 times and to traverse 2 or 3 short tunnels within 2 m. N. of Belper; the beautiful trees which fringe it, feathering down to the water's edge; and the lawn-like meadows and luxuriant woods on the hill-sides, give this valley the appearance of a park.

"In famed Attica, such lovely dales
Are rarely seen; nor can fair Tempe boast
A charm they know not"—

sings a poet of these counties—no less an one than Lord Byron. After crossing the Derwent a 4th time the line quits the neighbourhood of the stream, and reaches at

10½ m. ✠AMBERGATE JUNCT. STAT. The main line to Manchester here branches off N. through Matlock (Rte. 5), and a branch line goes off E. to Pye-Bridge (see Rte. 3). The surrounding country is very beautiful, with the little river Amber flowing W. to join the Derwent, and in that same direction are the woods of Alderwasley and the bold eminence called Crich Hill, on the top of which is a tower called Crich Stand (Rte. 5). The immediate neighbourhood, however, is much disfigured by the long range of lime kilns erected by Geo. Stephenson; the limestone being brought from the quarries at Crich by an inclined plane.

At 11 m., crossing the Cromford Canal, there is a pretty peep on E. at Buckland Hollow.

14 m. Wingfield (Stat.). On W. is the Ch. of Wingfield, restored in 1885. 2 m. E. is the town of Alfreton (Rte. 3), and 1 m. S.W., extending along a wooded hill, the village of South Wingfield; at the extreme end of which, most picturesquely situated on a knoll, and separated by a deep dingle from the adjoining high ground, is Wingfield Manorhouse.

Wingfield (more correctly spelt Whinfield or Winfield) *Manor House*, a picturesque ruin, is a good specimen of domestic architecture of the latter part of the 15th centy., prior to which time it is not easy to find an entire house of any size all of one date of architecture. It consists of 2 enclosed courts, the largest of which looking towards the N. was devoted to state and dwelling apartments, while the other was principally used for offices. There are some beautiful details in the N. court, particularly an octagon window, and a gateway which com-

Route 4.—Shirland—Stretton.

municated with the S. court. The Great Hall is 72 by 36 ft., and underneath it is a crypt with good pillars and groined roof, the centres of the groins being decorated with armorial bearings. "One-half of the range of building to the right of the entrance into the N. court seems originally to have been used as a hall, which received light through an octagon window, and through a range of Gothic windows to the S., now broken away, and a corresponding range to the N. In the other part of this range are the portal, and the remains of the chapel, and of the great state apartments, lighted through another rich Gothic window."—*Blore*.

The builder of Wingfield was Ralph Lord Cromwell, High Treasurer to Henry VI. (d. 1455). It derives its principal interest from having been at different times during 9 years the prison dwelling-house of Mary Queen of Scots under the custody of the Earl of Shrewsbury, husband of "Bess of Hardwick." "Her suite of apartments, it is generally believed, was on the W. side of the N. court, and communicating with the great tower, from which she could sometimes see the approach of her friends, with whom she carried on a secret correspondence, that got many of them into trouble, and often aroused Elizabeth's jealousy and ire."—*Hall*. During the Civil war Wingfield was held for the Royalists by Col. Dalby, but after a stubborn resistance was carried in an attack by Sir John Gell, whereupon the house was ordered to be dismantled. A large portion of the building, however, remained until 1774, when much was pulled down for the sake of the materials; what was then left is now occupied as a farmhouse.

The village of Wingfield is prettily situated on a long ridge overlooking the vale of the Amber, and it is a very charming walk of about 3 m. from hence to Crich Stand (Rte. 5), which should be visited for the sake of the wide view that it commands.

16 m. 1 m. E. is the village of **Shirland**, where are some collieries situated on the western outcrop of the Nottinghamshire coalfield. The *Ch.* is a good Perp. building, and contains an alabaster monument to the Revells, a powerful family in this neighbourhood during the 16th cent.

Continuing up the valley, the line passes W. *Ogston Hall* (W. G. Turbutt, Esq.), formerly the seat of the Revells of Shirland. The Turbutt family obtained it by marriage with the sister and coheiress of William Revell. An old legend states that the arms of the Revells—a dexter arm grasping a lion's gamb—were obtained through a contest in the Holy Land between Hugh de Revell and a lioness.

The little river Amber, which bounds Ogston Park, has its rise about 6 m. N.W. in Upper End. It flows through a very picturesque valley, past the village of ☥**Ashover**, and Stubben Edge Hall (J. Jackson, Esq.). The *Ch.* at Ashover is Perp., with square tower and spire. It contains a curious stone font with twenty leaden figures, a *brass* in memory of James Rolleston of Lea (d. 1507), and his wife, the daughter of John Babington of Dethick; and monuments to the families of Dakeyn and Babington. On the opposite bank is Overton Hall (W. de Burgh Jessop, Esq.), a former residence of Sir Joseph Banks the naturalist. A little to the E. of the village are remains of the old Hall at Eastwood.

17½ m. **Stretton** (Stat.), a hamlet of North Wingfield, one of the great centres of the coal, ironstone, and limestone trades. The scenery in the neighbourhood abounds in romantic cliffs, the bases of which are covered with wood, and the pedestrian will find it worth his while to quit the line at Stretton Stat., and explore the vale, ascending near Ashover to Darley Moor, and descending to Matlock, a walk of 7 or 8 m.

A long tunnel occupies a considerable part of the distance to

20 m. CLAY CROSS JUNCT. STAT. where the line joins the Erewash Valley Rly. (Rte. 3). The Ch. of North Wingfield, a Perp. structure, with a square tower, almost adjoins the stat. A modern Ch., built 1852, mainly for the use of the Clay Cross Company's workmen, is at some distance S., and has adjoining an Institute and Reading Room, with schools for their children. The coalmines here were once leased by Geo. Stephenson. The numerous colliery appliances, together with the smoke from the furnaces of the Clay Cross Company, leave no doubt in the mind of the traveller that he has at length reached the manufacturing districts of North Derbyshire, which extend from here with but little intermission to the Yorkshire border. The appearance of the country, however, is not so effectually spoilt as in Staffordshire and the North, as the collieries and works are a good deal scattered, allowing intervals in which the real beauty of the district is fully seen. Hardwick Hall (Rte. 13) lies 4 m. E., the road crossing a pleasant moorland district, with the Nottinghamshire hills in view. The line now descends the valley of the Rother, and at

22 m. passes on E. *Wingerworth Hall* (Hon. Mrs. Hunloke), a handsome stone building of the time of George I. The estate was purchased from the Curzons by Nicholas Hunloke in Henry VIII.'s reign, and his grandson, while attending as High Sheriff on James I. in his progress through Derbyshire, fell dead at the king's feet, on 17th August, 1623, at a very advanced age. The old Hall was garrisoned for the Parliament in 1643. The grounds extend for a considerable distance up the slopes of the hills, commanding very wide views.

24 m. ⚹ Chesterfield (Stat.). It is a town of considerable business, with engineering works, tanneries, and iron foundries, and is in the centre of a large colliery district, but, with the exception of the parish church, it has little to detain the tourist. Some antiquaries identify it (or rather, the neighbouring hamlet of Tapton) with the Roman station Lutudarum, a kind of emporium, to which the metals from the Peak were brought. It is mentioned in Domesday, as a dependency of Newbold (now one of its townships), and it was given by John to his favourite, William Briwere, to whom is ascribed the building of the castle. The town is irregularly built, but has many good houses, and a spacious market-place.

The *Ch.* of St. Mary and All Saints replaced, in the 13th centy., one that William Rufus gave to the see of Lincoln. It is a very fine cruciform building of Dec. date (1350) in its principal parts, and E. E. and Perp. in others, consisting of nave, aisles, choir, and transepts, from the intersection of which rises a square tower with octagonal pinnacles surmounted by a lofty timber spire, covered with lead, which is 230 ft. in height, and is remarkable for its crookedness. There seems no good reason for doubting that this spire was erected at or about the time when the tower and principal portions of the Ch. were built (1350-70), and the more probable and now generally accepted reasons for its crookedness are—firstly, the clinging pressure of the lead, which might cause an irregular subsidence of the timber framework, and secondly, the action of the sun causing the timbers to warp; the sun is the most powerful when at or about 2 o'clock P.M., and it is precisely in this direction where the spire leans the most. By careful measurements recently made by Messrs. Rollinson & Son, the local architects, the rod of the vane is 7 ft. 11 in. out of the centre of the spire towards the S.W., 6 ft. 11 in. to the S., and 3 ft. 11 in. to the W.

The E. (Dec.) window, the W. (Perp.) window, the S. transept (Dec.) window, and two windows in the (Dec.) baptistry are very fine examples of modern painted glass. The Oak Screen on the east of the S. transept is a fine specimen of (Perp.) carving, and the carving under the E. window, and to the west of the Chapel of the Holy Cross, are well worthy of note. The visitor should notice the timber roof of the nave and the armorial bearings of the sovereigns in whose reigns the Ch. was built or added to, and of those in authority in the county who were interested in the restoration in 1843. In the S. transept is an apsidal Dec. chapel. The extreme length of the church is 170 ft. There are among others some monuments elaborately carved, to the family of Foljambe, of the dates of the 15th and 16th cents., and a modern font with beautifully sculptured figures of angels. The gem of the Ch., however, in point of design, is the Flamboyant window, N. of the chapel of the Holy Cross, which has been recently restored.

The Grammar School, founded by Queen Elizabeth, was restored in 1815.

1 m. N. of the town is *Tapton House*, at one time the residence of George Stephenson, the "father of Railways," who took great delight in his pineries and greenhouses. Indeed, his death is ascribed to a cold caught by his eagerness to eclipse the pines of Chatsworth, which induced him to remain too long in his forcing-houses. He died in 1848 at Tapton House, and was buried in Trinity District Ch. (¼ m. from the Stat.) under the altar, where is a stained glass window to his memory, erected by his only son Robert.

The Stephenson Memorial Hall, standing near the Parish Ch., was erected in 1879 by public subscription as a tribute to the great railway engineer. The building, which cost about 14,000*l*., is in the Gothic style, and in addition to the large hall contains the Free Library and class rooms for the advancement of science and art.

The town is noted for being the birthplace of several local scholars and poets, and among others Pegge the antiquary; and gives the title of Earl to a branch of the noble family of Stanhope.

A new line is in the course of construction by the Lancashire, Derbyshire, and East Coast Railway Company to connect the east and west coasts. It will go from the Manchester Ship Canal at Warrington through Buxton, Chesterfield, the Dukeries, Tuxford, and Lincoln to Sutton-on-the-Sea.

[A pleasant trip of about 12 m. may be made W. across the moors to Bakewell (Rte. 6). The way is through **Brampton** (4 m.), the Ch. of which has a remarkable monument, to Matilda de Caus, who died in 1224, and was probably the heiress of the Barony, and Baslow, 9 m. (Rte. 8), where the Derwent is crossed. Before reaching Baslow, notice on N. the Nelson pillar on ⚔ East Moor (1010 ft.), from which there is a fine view over Chatsworth Park.]

The line after leaving Chesterfield diverges, and there are two routes to Sheffield: (1) by the Chesterfield and Masbro' branch (14½ m.) and (2) the direct line through Dronfield (12 m.).

(1) On the Masbro' branch

At 26½ m. is **Whittington** (Stat.). The villages of Whittington and New Whittington lie N. of the stat. The collieries, ironworks. and brickworks render the place a scene of great activity. The Ch. was rebuilt in 1863. Pegge, the antiquary, was the rector of this parish. He died here, 1796, and was buried in the chancel of the old Ch. In the village is the cottage, known as "Revolution House," formerly an inn with the sign of the Cock and Pynot (local for Magpie), where the 4th Earl of Devonshire and other members of the Whig party first met to concert measures for the Revolution of 1688.

28½ m. **Staveley** (Stat.), the seat of vast ironworks, at which upwards of 4000 men are employed. A suburb, called Barrow Hill, is almost entirely inhabited by the workmen. The parish is of considerable extent, embracing the hamlets of Netherthorpe, Woodthorpe, and Handley. In consequence of the extension of the M. S. & L. Rly. Staveley is likely to become a trade centre of considerable importance. The ironwork for the Exhibition of 1862 was cast here. The old hall at Staveley, now the rectory, although greatly altered and modernised, is still in existence. It was formerly the seat of the Frescheviles, one of whom defended it against the Parliament, and was in 1664 made Lord Frescheville, but his title died with him. The Ch. contains 2 *brasses* for Peter Frescheville (esquire to Henry VI.) and his family, beside other monuments, and a fine stained glass window put up by Lord Frescheville in 1676.

[A branch line of the Midland Rly. here goes off S.E. to Mansfield (see Rte. 13), with Stats. at Netherthorpe, Clown (see below), Elmton, Langwith, Shirebrook, and Mansfield Woodhouse. From Netherthorpe the Doe Lea line branches off S. to Bolsover, Palterton, Rowthorn and Hardwick (see Rte. 13), and Pleasley.]

30½ m. **Eckington** (Stat.). Near to it is *Renishaw*, the beautiful seat of Sir G. R. Sitwell, Bart., whose hanging woods cover the hills on W. The town of Eckington, about 1 m. to the W. of the stat., is very prettily situated, and contains a Norm. Ch. (restored 1878), with a tower and spire. Of the ancient castle only the site remains, and there is a slight trace of an earthwork, known as the Dane's Balk, to the N. of the town. Spink Hill, 1 m. E. of the rly., is conspicuous for its Roman Catholic college and Ch., with a lofty spire. Eckington is a busy place, with some foundries for making scythes and sickles, and with collieries in the neighbourhood. The Renshaw Iron Works are close to the stat.

[A pleasant excursion may be made from Eckington to Worksop (Rte. 15), diverging to the S. for the purpose of visiting Markland Grips. 2½ m. **Barlborough**, a colliery village, with a large Perp. Ch. Barlborough Hall is a fine Jacobean house, built by Sir John De Rodes, and is remarkable for the beautiful avenue of trees by which it is approached. One of the apartments contains a magnificent stone chimney-piece, covered with figures and armorial bearings of the Rodes family. At 3½ m. rt. is the village of **Clown** (Stat.), where the Ch. has Norm. portions. 1 m. S. is **Elmton** and **Creswell** (Stat.), the birth and burial-place of Jedediah Buxton, the calculator. At 4½ m. the tourist enters the romantic dell of *Markland Grips*, than which, though on a small scale, there is nothing prettier in the county. Follow the course of the dell to Creswell Crags, through which a road leads about 1 m. to **Welbeck Abbey** (see Rte. 15). Then turn N. to **Whitwell** (Stat.), from whence to Worksop, skirting the demesne of Worksop Manor, it is a little over 6 m. Whitwell Ch. is a large cruciform building, with Norm. tower. Whitwell Hall, adjoining the village, was the seat of Sir Roger Manners. A little to the l. of Firbeck Gate, between Whitwell and Worksop, in the hamlet of **Steetley**, is a small but perfect Norm. Ch. The arches of the chancel and apse are round headed and elaborately moulded; the stone vaulting and three small windows of the apse are all intact. It was formerly a ruin, but has now been thoroughly restored, and is used as a Chapel of ease to Whitwell. The whole of this excursion from Eckington Stat. to Worksop will be about 13 m.]

35½ m. **Woodhouse Junction Stat.** The Midland line runs N. to Rotherham (6 m.), but proceeding by the Manchester, Sheffield, and Lincolnshire Rly. N.W., and passing **Darnall** (Stat.),

40 m. **Sheffield** (Victoria Stat.) is reached. See *Handbook for Yorkshire*.

(2) By the direct line at

25¼ m. is **Sheepbridge** (Stat.).

27½ m. **Unston** (Stat.); and at

29 m. ⚥ **Dronfield** (Stat.). All are in a busy colliery district, and there are several iron-foundries, agricultural implement works, and edge-tool factories. Dronfield, once a market-town, stands on the small river Drone, an affluent of the Rother, and has a fine Dec. Ch., with lofty spire, standing on a hill S. of the town. It contains a brass

(1399) to two priests, brothers, named Gomfrey, and some tombs of the Fanshawes, one of whom founded the Grammar School, temp. Eliz., and was the great grandfather of Sir Richard Fanshawe, the well-known ambassador to Spain.

32½ m. **Dore** and **Totley** (Stat.). Here a branch line is in progress through the Peak District to Chinley (see Rte. 8).

33½ m. **Beauchief Abbey** (Stat.). The village is very small, and is only remarkable for its Ch., which is a fragment of the ancient abbey (de Bello Capite, founded (1172–1176), by Robert Fitzranulph. The remains consist of a noble Trans. Norm. tower, and a portion of the nave, now somewhat modernized and adapted to the Reformed service. There are three beautiful archways of Norm. date, one of which leads into the Ch.

2 m. E. is the village of **Norton**, where an obelisk of Cheesewring granite, together with a monument in the Ch., have been raised to the memory of Sir Francis Chantrey, R.A., the sculptor, who was born in 1781, at a house, which has been modernized and spoilt, at Jordansthorpe, to the l. of the village, whence Chantrey, in his early days, used to carry milk to Sheffield. The Ch. also contains some interesting monuments to the Blythes, two members of which family were respectively bishops of Lichfield and Salisbury (1493, 1503), and whose old timbered residence still remains at Norton Lees, between Norton and Sheffield. Adjoining the village are Norton Hall, the beautiful seat of Bernard Cammell, Esq., and the Oaks (F. W. Bagshawe, Esq.).

Passing **Ecclesall** and **Heeley** (Stats.), both in Yorkshire, at

37½ m. is **Sheffield** (Victoria Stat.). See *Handbook for Yorkshire*.

ROUTE 5.

DERBY TO BAKEWELL, BY MATLOCK AND ROWSLEY.

MIDLAND RAILWAY. 25½ m.

For description of the country from Derby to Ambergate Junction, 10¼ m., see Rte. 4. The route hence to Bakewell and Buxton lies through a succession of the finest valleys of Derbyshire, in which the characteristic features of the county are fully displayed. As far as Rowsley the rly. follows the course of the Derwent, and from that point to Buxton accompanies the Wye during the whole of its career, from the confluence to near its source. Quitting the stat., and passing the limekilns at Ambergate, the line enters a narrow valley, bounded on W. by the hanging woods of Alderwasley Park (A. F. Hurt, Esq.), famous for its oak timber, and on E. by those of Crich Chase. By ascending the hill for a little distance, a singular and impressive view is gained.

Alderwasley (locally Arrowslea) was once a part of the ancient park of Belper, and belonged successively to the Ferrars, the Earls of Lancaster, and the Lowes, a descendant of whom married the ancestor of the present owner. A portion of the estate, called "Shyning Cliff," was granted by Edward I., according to tradition, in the following quaint rhyme:—

"I and myne
  Give thee and thyne
Milnes Hay and Shyning Cliff,
While grass is green and berys ryffe"
                                [plentiful].

A short distance N.W. of Alderwasley is **Wigwell Grange**, given in the reign of Henry III. to the convent of Darley, and said to have been a favourite resort of the abbots.

13 m. ⚒ **Whatstandwell** (locally, Walsall) **Bridge** (Stat.). The neighbourhood is a busy one, stone quarries, lead mines, stocking factories, and a gunpowder magazine, being scattered around.

The pedestrian should take the road on E. to the summit of **Crich Hill**, 950 ft. The views during the ascent are lovely, embracing, to the W., the valley of the Derwent, the woods and park of Alderwasley, and Lea Hurst, while to the E. opens out the extensive district of Scarsdale, backed up by the Nottinghamshire hills.

The hill is the western boundary of the carboniferous limestone that forms the belt of the Nottinghamshire coalfield, and extends through the largest portion of Derbyshire. It is rich not only in limestone, which is quarried and sent down the incline to Ambergate, but in lead-ore. The summit is capped by a look-out tower, known far and wide as **Crich Stand**, which, erected 1788, commands a splendid view, extending on a clear day as far as Lincoln Cathedral. The *Ch.* at **Crich** contains several monuments of the Dixie family, and a curious *brass* for a child (1639). In the village is a stone cross (restored 1871), with a representation of St. Michael and the Dragon. The tourist, instead of returning by the same road, should follow one that runs along the brow of the hill, passing E. of **Lea Hurst**, the occasional residence of Miss Florence Nightingale, and emerging into the high road to Cromford or Matlock by a lane leading from Lea and Dethick.

The rly. now crosses the Derwent, and, passing through a tunnel, arrives, after a very romantic course, at

15½ m. ⚒ **Cromford** (Stat.), where the boldest scenery may be said to commence. Matlock Dale, as this portion of the vale of the Derwent is called, is a narrow, winding, and very striking defile, one of the grandest of the numerous ruptures of the mountain limestone occurring in Derbyshire, and but little inferior to Dovedale.

From Cromford bridge there is a good view of **Willersley**, the extensive mansion of F. C. Arkwright, Esq., J.P., situated on a platform on the hillside, backed by woods and with a sloping lawn, sprinkled with beautiful forest-trees, sweeping down to the water's edge. The house contains, among other paintings, some by Wright of Derby. The gardens and grounds, extending up to the rocks of Wild Cat Tor, and facing Scarthin Tor, form one of the chief sights of Matlock, and are open to the public on Mondays.

Close to the bridge is Cromford Ch., founded and partly endowed by the late Sir Richard Arkwright, and containing his grave, together with a monument by *Chantrey* to the memory of Mrs. Arkwright and her children. A little farther on are the mills of the Arkwrights, and the town of Cromford. This place, the cradle of the cotton manufacture, was a crown manor at the Domesday Survey, and only rose to notice about 1771, when Sir R. Arkwright built a cotton-mill, the first in Derbyshire, which, with two others subsequently erected, still employs a large number of hands. As late as 1836 Arkwright's original water-frames were in existence. The machinery is turned by the stream of an adit for draining mines, called Cromford Meer Sough, whence also is derived the chief supply of water for the Cromford Canal, which begins near here. In addition to this, Bonsall Brook, which rises W. of Matlock, sets in motion several mills for grinding mineral colours, a considerable quantity of which is made here. At the entrance of the town the road to Matlock Bath turns sharply to the rt. through a cleft in the rock, 200 ft. deep, called Scarthin Nick. In an instant the tourist finds himself in Matlock Dale, with Cromford shut out from view. The old bridle-road made a considerable ascent and descent, and a wide circuit, to reach Matlock Bath.

The hill called **Cromford Moor** (now brought into cultivation), S. of the town, was naturally a barren tract. Though poor above, it was once rich in mineral wealth, and commands from its upper part a most extensive view over the rich and well-wooded valley of the Derwent. One of the finest prospects in this neighbourhood is obtained from the top of **Stonnis**, called also "The Black Rocks," a lofty projecting promontory of gritstone, which here overlies the limestone. Its ascent is a favourite excursion from Matlock. It is conspicuous from its tuft of black firs, and is skirted at its base by the *High Peak Railway*, a mineral line, which runs from the Cromford Canal to the Peak Forest Canal at Whaley Bridge in Cheshire (Rte. 7). The undertaking cost nearly 200,000*l.* and did not answer as a commercial speculation, but it is now leased in perpetuity to the London and North-Western Railway Company. It is carried by a long inclined plane from Lea, up the high hills behind Cromford, passes near Hartington, Church Sterndale, and Buxton, and has a total length of 34 m.

16 ½ m. ⚒ **Matlock Bath** (Stat.) is well situated above the river Derwent, which here flows through a narrow gorge, "walled in by stupendous crags and lofty eminences, overgrown with tangled brushwood and shrubs." It consists chiefly of hotels, numerous lodging-houses, and so-called museums, *alias* shops for the sale of minerals and petrifactions, the latter being largely made here, together with articles

Route 5.—Matlock Bath.

of various kinds cut out of Derbyshire spars and marbles, the staple produce of the place. The modern Gothic church, built 1841, is in a very picturesque situation.

Matlock Bath and its neighbourhood present some of the most striking scenery in the county, of which Lord Bryon says, "I can assure you there are things in Derbyshire as noble as Greece or Switzerland." He was a frequent visitor here, particularly during the time of his attachment to Mary Chaworth, the heiress of Annesley.

The place first came into notoriety about 1698 when the warm springs were discovered, and a primitive bath erected. "This bath," wrote Daniel Defoe in 1724, "would be much more frequented than it is, if a bad stony road which leads to it, and no good accommodation when you are there, did not hinder." The water, abundantly charged with carbonic acid gas, has a temperature of 68° Fahr., and is efficacious for bilious and rheumatic complaints. The same mineral water also supplies the *petrifying* or *encrusting wells*, in which fruits, plants, and birds' nests, &c., are subjected to the spray from the water as it falls in driblets over them, and in passing deposits upon them a portion of its superabundant lime, dissolved by agency of the carbonic acid with which the water is impregnated. The calcareous matter is derived from the limestone rocks through which the waters pass, and out of which the springs issue, at the height of about 100 ft. above the level of the river. As soon as the acid is dissipated by coming in contact with the atmosphere, a part of the lime falls down, and thus the Matlock Bath springs have in the course of ages deposited a vast mass of porous tufa rock, enveloping plants, mosses, leaves, and shells. This deposit has accumulated into a sort of terrace extending along the rt. bank of the Derwent, especially near the old baths.

Among the sights of Matlock are its *Caverns*, which every stranger is expected to visit, and for which the usual charge is 1s. A toilsome walk mainly in dirt and darkness, and a pain in the back from stooping, are in general the principal results of such an expedition. The chief of them are the Cumberland Cavern, the Rutland, the New Speedwell, the High Tor Grotto, and the Devonshire Cave, none of which are anything more than worked-out mines. When properly lighted up, however, as they occasionally are, the effects are uncommonly fine.

"In the cavern at the base of the High Tor a bed of toadstone is seen on the floor, beneath the limestone strata of which the cliff is composed, and may be traced across the river to the opposite escarpment of Masson's Hill, where it is exposed on the roadside."—*Mantell*.

The gorge of Matlock Bath runs between the limestone hills in a direction nearly due N. and S. The rocky cliffs on the E. side are the most precipitous, but are beautifully clothed with foliage at their base. The grounds between the road and the river are laid out as a public garden, and on the other side of the stream is what is known as the Lovers' Walk, with zigzag paths striking up the hillside. Access may be gained to it by a footbridge.

Every isolated eminence is distinguished by a name, to which is usually appended the common appelation of Tor; thus above Willersley rises Wild Cat Tor. The Dungeon Tor, or Romantic Rocks, near the Cumberland Cavern, are on the Masson or W. side, while rising from the opposite bank is High Tor, the noblest of all, and remarkably rich in fossils and shells of the carboniferous formation. Agreeable walks have been carried up the steep

Matlock is a good point from | 17½ m. ⚡Matlock Bridge (Stat.).

heights on both sides of the valley; but, being for the most part private property and leased out, they are accessible only on paying toll. Indeed, the tourist will soon find with what ingenuity the people of Matlock manage to make him pay "bachsheesh," enough to exhaust a good amount of small change, for the privilege of beholding their charming landscapes. Nevertheless, he should on no account omit to ascend the **Heights of Abraham** (admission 6d.), on the top of which is the Victoria Tower, and the still loftier summit of **Masson**, 900 ft. above the Derwent, and 1100 ft. above the sealevel. The view is wondrously fine from the summit, embracing the whole of the dale with the long broken line of Tors opposite, backed up by the more regular outlines of Riber, Tansley, and Darley Moors.

"Proud Masson rises rude and bleak,
And with misshapen turrets crests the Peak;
Old Matlock gapes with marble jaws beneath,
And o'er scared Derwent bends her flinty teeth."—*Darwin.*

The descent may be varied by going round by Bonsall (*post*), and following the course of its little stream, studded with mills which it sets in motion, to Cromford, and thence through Scarthin Nick back to the Wells. The round will be about 7 m.

The Pavilion and Gardens opened in 1884 on the hillside, occupy about fifteen acres. The pavilion is a handsome music hall, with 228 ft. frontage, and the grounds have been attractively laid out in terraces which command picturesque views.

The limestone districts of Derbyshire abound in ferns, among which are Cystopteris fragilis, Polypodium calcareum, the Beech and Oak ferns, Moonwort, Maidenhair, Asplenium adiantum nigrum and viride, &c.

Matlock is a good point from whence to make *Excursions*, whether long or short.

Among the latter may be particularly mentioned—

(1.) To **Dethick** and Lea, the road to which turns up the hill at Cromford Stat., leading up a very steep ascent to the high table-land of Dethick Moor. There is here a fine old Perp. Ch., on the S. wall of which are sculptured the arms of the Babingtons, whose hall was adjoining, and some slight portions of which are still incorporated in a farmhouse. Anthony Babington, of Dethick, was executed at Lincoln's Inn for high treason in 1586. From hence the return may be over Riber, descending near the rly. stat.

(2.) To Wirksworth by Bonsall and Middleton, returning by Cromford. A charming pathway leads by the side of Harp Edge to **Bonsall**, a very pretty and primitive village, with a small inn, betokening by its sign, "The Pig of Lead," the calling of the inhabitants. The old marketcross, of the date 1678, still remains. The *Ch.* (restored) consists of nave, aisles, and chancel, with a tower and spire, the latter singularly ornamented. Up Bonsall Dale runs the road to Via Gellia, one of the prettiest rides in the neighbourhood of Matlock. From its name the visitor would conclude it to be a Roman road, but it was so called in compliment to the family of Gell of Hopton, through whose estate it passes. From hence follow the road up Middleton Wood, and ascend by Sally Edge to the mining village of Middleton, soon after passing which Wirksworth is reached (Rte. 4). Hence to Cromford is 3 m.

Quitting Matlock Bath, the rly. burrows under the High Tor, and, crossing the Derwent, arrives at

17½ m. ⚑**Matlock Bridge** (Stat.).

The scenery here will probably be preferred by many to that of Matlock Bath, from its more open character, the old village of Matlock, as primitive as the other is fashionable, being situated at the convergence of two valleys descending from Tansley Moor to join the widening dale of Derwent. Five roads meet at the bridge, viz. to Bakewell, Ambergate, Stretton, Winster, and Chesterfield.

The Ch. of St. Giles, which has a fine pinnacled tower, is placed on a cliff of curiously striated limestone, called Church Tor. In the vestry are some old funeral garlands, at one time common in Derbyshire, but now out of use. Some are also preserved in the Ch. of Ashford, near Bakewell (Rte. 6). These chaplets, made of paper, in imitation of flowers, and having inside a pair of white gloves, were formerly borne before the corpse of a young maiden, and afterwards hung up in the church. This custom is alluded to by Washington Irving in his 'Sketch Book.'

☥ **Matlock Bank**, which lies to the N. of and opposite to the village, has of late years obtained a notoriety for its hydropathic establishments, a better situation for which could not be obtained. **Riber Castle**, built by the late Mr. Smedley, is a landmark for miles round.

After leaving Matlock Dale, the scenery of the valley of the Derwent becomes comparatively tame, though the country is rich in pasture-land and timber.

18 m. the rly. passes at some distance W. the isolated **Oker Hill**, surmounted by two sycamore-trees; respecting which the following tradition exists—

"'Tis said that on the brow of yon fair hill
Two brothers clomb, and, turning face
   from face,
Nor one more look exchanging, grief to
   still
Or feed, each planted on that lofty place

A chosen tree. Then, eager to fulfil
Their courses, like two new-born rivers,
   they
In opposite directions urged their way
Down from the far-seen mount. No blast
   might kill
Or blight that fond memorial. The trees
   grew,
And now entwine their arms; but ne'er
   again
Embraced those brothers upon earth's
   wide plain,
Nor aught of mutual joy or sorrow knew,
Until their spirits mingled in the sea
That to itself takes all—Eternity!"
                   Wordsworth.

19½ m. **Darley** (Stat.), a very pretty village. On E. is **Stancliffe Hall**, formerly the residence of the late Sir Joseph Whitworth, Bart., in the grounds of which are some remarkably picturesque gardens laid out in an old quarry, which supplied the stone for the building of St. George's Hall, Liverpool. The Ch.-yard of Darley contains the world-famed yew-tree 33 ft. in girth, and supposed to be at least 2000 years old. It is without doubt the largest and oldest in the United Kingdom. "Whatever may be the age of this tree, there can be little doubt that it has given shelter to the early Britons when planning the construction of the dwellings which they erected not many yards to the west of its trunk; to the Romans who built up the funeral pyre to their slain comrades just clear of its branches; to the Saxons, converted perchance, to the true faith by Bishop Diuma beneath its pleasant shade; to the Norman masons chiselling their quaint sculptures to form the first stone-house of prayer erected in its vicinity; and to the host of Christian worshippers, who from that day to this, have been borne under its hoary limbs in woman's arms to the baptismal font, and then on men's shoulders to their last resting-place in soil that gave it birth."—*Cox*. In the Ch. (restored in 1877), which is of mixed styles, is a monument to Sir John de Darley, a crusader.

Route 5.—Winster—Rowsley.

There are also interesting monuments of the Rollesley, Collumbell, and Milward families, and in the porch a collection of incised coffin lids.

The Whitworth Institute and the Whitworth Hospital have recently been erected.

2½ m. S.W. is ☨ **Winster**, a small market town, with a population of miners. The Ch. mainly E. E., with a Norm. tower, contains a fine old font. The custom of ringing the curfew bell is still observed here. In the neighbourhood are the picturesque Rowtor rocks (*post*).

A pretty glen joins Darley Dale, a little to the right of the stat., at the entrance to which is a hamlet, with the euphonious name of *Toadholes*. This, however, is really a corruption of Two-dales.

22 m. ☨ **Rowsley** (Stat.). Here the Wye falls into the Derwent. The Peacock Inn is a very comfortable and pretty house, with gables and mullions of the 16th and early part of the 17th century; the Peacock is the crest of the Duke of Rutland, to whom it belongs. It is a convenient point for reaching Chatsworth, 3½ m. N., by passing the pretty Ch. (restored 1884) and parsonage of Beeley, close to Chatsworth Lodge and also to Haddon Hall, 2 m. in the opposite direction, which stands on an eminence near the main road to Bakewell (see Rte. 6). It is a good house for fishing quarters, and by staying here the angler can obtain permission to fish a considerable stretch of the Wye and Derwent, which abound in grayling and trout, about 1 lb. in weight. The waters of these rivers are very clear, and he should bear in mind the necessity of having very fine tackle and a short line.

Rowsley Ch. (modern) contains a recumbent effigy by Calder Marshall, in Chellaston stone, of Lady John Manners, first wife of the present Duke of Rutland, and her child. A chapel on the N. side of the Ch. was added for this monument, the whole conception of which is very beautiful. The old Haddon Hall Chapel *bell* is now in use in this Ch.

[The antiquary should make Rowsley his point of departure for **Stanton-in-the-Peak**, 1½ m. S.W., and the interesting early remains in the neighbourhood. The village lies on exceedingly high ground, overlooking the valley of the Wye, and adjoining it is Stanton Park (Major M. McCreagh-Thornhill). The whole of the district known as Stanton Moor (now, however, planted), lying between Stanton and Winster, together with the elevated tract of country extending westward to Youlgreave, Middleton, and Hartington, is remarkable for the number of early rock remains and tumuli, together with singular and fantastic groups of rocks heaped one above the other. Immediately to the S. of Stanton are the King's Stone: the **Nine Ladies**, a circle of upright stones, about 35 ft. in diameter; the Heart Stone; the Gorse Stone; the Cork Stone; and a little to the W., separated by a thick wood, the **Andle Stone**, which is 15 ft. in height. About ½ m. to the S. of this last are the **Rowtor Rocks**, a very remarkable group of fragments of millstone grit, worn away by the weather into fantastic shapes, with caves and passages between them. On the summit of Bradley Rocks is a rocking stone, mentioned by Camden. "In those parts also, near a village called Byrch-over, is a large rock, and upon it are two tottering stones; the one is 4 yards in height and 12 yards about, and yet rests on a point so equally poised that one may move it with a finger." At Cratcliff, or *Carcliff Tor*, on the other side of the turnpike-road, is a small cave called the Hermitage, containing a crucifix carved in relief in a recess of the rock (probably early part of the 14th centy.). Close to it is Robin Hood's Stride, or Graned Tor, on Hartle Moor; this is also called **Mock Beggars' Hall**, and is a rocky mass, surmounted on either side by two projecting knobs, which have been compared to chimneys.

⚥ **Youlgreave**, 5 m. W. from Rowsley, is a pretty village, overlooking the little river Bradford, and has an interesting *Ch.*, dedicated to All Saints (restored 1870, by R. Norman Shaw, R.A.), with a very fine tower. The round pillars of the nave are early Norm., of the 12th cent., as are also the arches on the S. side, whilst those on the N. are transition between E. E. and Dec. The chancel is Perp., with the E. window filled with modern stained glass from a design by E. Burne Jones, A.R.A. There is a very ancient font with a small projecting stoup, supported by the jaws of a dragon. In the centre of the chancel is an altar-tomb in alabaster, with the beautiful small effigy of a knight in armour, Thomas Cokayne (d. 1488). It has been well restored. In the N. aisle is a 15th-cent. mural monument, with numerous small figures to Robert Gilbert. There are also other monuments to the Gilbert family. In the vicinity is Lomberdale, formerly the seat of Mr. Bateman, the Derbyshire antiquary. Proceeding westward, the tourist will pass Bee Low, and in about 4 m. will arrive at

Arbelows, or *Arborlow*, a very large and perfect circle of prostrate stones surrounded by a ditch and a high rampart, and connected by a serpentine ridge of earth with a large barrow 350 yards distant, called Bunker's Hill, or Gib Hill. This was opened in 1848, by the late Mr. Bateman, who found in it a rectangular cist, containing an urn and burnt bones. Previous to this discovery, celts, a javelin-point, and a fibula of iron had been dug out of this barrow. Rather singularly, the place of interment at Gib Hill was found to be at the top of the mound, and was only revealed by accident, in consequence of its falling in, owing to excavations at the base. At **Kenslow**, between this and Hartington, excavations revealed a skeleton, some Kimmeridge coal, and some iron knives. In **Parcelly Hay Barrow** a skeleton was found in a sitting posture, and in unusually good preservation. The very common appellation of "Low," such as Arbor Low, Bee Low, Hadlow, &c., is derived from the Saxon word Hlæw, or Hlaw, defined by Bosworth as anything that covers—hence a small hill or barrow. Most of the tumuli in this district were opened at various times by Mr. Bateman, who always found traces of interment. A valuable collection of articles discovered in these barrows were preserved at Lomberdale, but have now been removed to the Weston Park Museum, Sheffield. In the neighbourhood of Youlgreave are the scanty remains of **Fulwood's Castle**, a mansion of the 17th centy., which belonged to the Fulwoods, a family remarkable for its sufferings in the royal cause in the time of Charles I. From them Fulwood's Rents in Holborn took their name. A rock overlooking Bradford Dale is still pointed out as Fulwood's Rock, where the then head of the family was shot by Gell, the Parliamentarian.]

The vale of the Derwent is now left by the rly., which takes a rather abrupt turn to the N.W., and follows the bank of the Wye to

25½ m. **Bakewell** (Rte. 6).

ROUTE 6.

BAKEWELL TO BUXTON [HADDON HALL, CHATSWORTH, THE LATHKILL, TIDESWELL].

MIDLAND RAILWAY. 11¾ m.

ƀ **Bakewell**, a small town, is chiefly remarkable for its charming situation, on a slope descending to the margin of the Wye, in a beautiful district of rich pastures and wood. It was called by the Saxons "Badecanwylla," and Mainwaring tells us that " Edward the Elder made a burrough of it."

The cruciform *Church*, finely placed on the height above, was extensively repaired from 1841 to 1852, and its octagonal tower and spire rebuilt. The restoration of the chancel was completed in 1881. During the excavations for the restoration a number of tombs and coffin-lids, considered to be of Saxon date, were discovered. Some of them are in the S. porch, and others in the Bateman Collection at the Public Museum, Weston Park, Sheffield. The most ancient portion is the W. end, which is early Norm. with square piers, and has an interesting triple recessed doorway with figures; " and above it an arcade with zigzag work, in part cut away to admit the insertion of a sharp-pointed window, with early Perp. tracery." Previous to the restoration the whole nave was Norm., which was ruthlessly destroyed save the specimen at the W. end. The chancel and S. transept are E. E.; another portion is Perp. In the chancel is a plain altar-tomb of marble, with carved sides, to Sir John Vernon, 1477. The Vernon Chapel contains a large marble tomb to Sir George Vernon, "the King of the Peak," who died 1561, and to his two wives; monuments to his daughter and heiress Dorothy (d. 1584), and her husband, Sir John Manuers (d. 1611), with whom she eloped from Haddon; and to Sir George Manners, their son, 1623, erected by his wife. This last is a large well-preserved structure of marble, coloured and slightly gilt, with their effigies and those of their children. In the S. transept are numerous other monuments and brasses to the Manners family. Against one of the piers, originally in the chantry of the Holy Cross, is a curious small mural monument to Sir Godfrey Foljambe, 1376, and Avena his wife, 1385; his armour and the lady's head-dress deserve notice; as also does the effigy, in alabaster, of Sir Thomas Wendesley, killed at the battle of Shrewsbury, 1403; on his helmet is inscribed "I. H. C. Nazaren." There are also an elaborately sculptured font, a good memorial window, in memory of Mr. Alleard, and some stained glass in the S. end. The bells, 8 in number, are all inscribed with rhymes composed by a local poet. In the ch.-yard is a fragment of a very ancient stone cross, with sculptured figures and interlaced patterns, supposed to illustrate the principal events in the life and death of Christ. There is a similar cross in Bradbourne Ch.-yd. The curious in epitaphs will be pleased with one to the memory of the clerk—

"The vocal powers, here let us mark,
Of Philip, our late parish clerk;
In church, none ever heard a layman,
With a clearer voice say, Amen.
Oh! now with Hallelujah's sound,
Little he'll make the roof resound.
The choir lament his choral tones,
The town, so soon lie here his bones.
Sleep, undisturbed, within this peaceful shrine,
Till angels wake thee with such tones as thine."

[*Derby, &c.*]

Also an inscription in the interior of the Ch. to John Dale, barber-surgeon, who was buried here with his two wives—

"A period's come to all their toylsome lives,
The good man's quiet;—still are both his wives."

Situated in a pleasant garden in the centre of the town are the Baths, with a news-room attached. They are supplied from a tepid chalybeate spring, which has for ages been used for bathing and medicinal purposes. The town also contains a Grammar School, founded in 1637 by Lady Grace Manners, a hospital adjoining it, founded by Sir John Manners in the same century, and a cotton-mill, originally set up by Arkwright. There is fishing to be obtained in the river; and below the bridge are extensive marble works. In the neighbourhood are Burton Closes (S. Taylor Whitehead, Esq.), a Gothic mansion designed by Pugin, on a hill overlooking the Wye, with gardens laid out by Sir J. Paxton; and Castle Hill (R. W. M. Nesfield, Esq.).

The drives and walks in every direction from Bakewell as a centre are most beautiful and interesting. The roads are good, and horses and carriages can be hired at moderate rates.

Several interesting *Excursions* may be conveniently made from Bakewell.

(1.) ☧ HADDON HALL (2 m.). The road to Haddon descends the rt. bank of the Wye, but it is a pleasanter though much more circuitous route to keep close to the river in the meadows. Haddon Hall, which is open every day to the visitor, is beautifully situated, overlooking the Wye (here crossed by a picturesque bridge), and, with its towers and battlements peering out from the rich woods, has been ever a fertile subject for the painter. This venerable edifice, an ancient seat of the Dukes of Rutland, and the chief residence of that family down to the beginning of the last century, is an admirable specimen of the baronial dwellings of the nobility of England in the 15th and 16th cents., and all the more so from its not having been adapted to the exigencies of modern comfort. Though no longer inhabited, it is in perfect preservation; but much of its ancient furniture was wantonly destroyed when the house was abandoned for Belvoir (Rayner's 'Haddon Hall,' p. 51). While capable of being defended it was by no means intended for a castle or place of strength; and it is probable that no part of it (except a portion of the gateway, perhaps temp. Edward III.) is older than the time of Edward IV., at which time the nobles had ceased to build fortresses for homes.

The keys are kept at the pretty little cottage across the bridge, in the garden of which are two yews, formerly clipt to represent the crests of the Vernon and Manners families, viz. a boar's head and a peacock. The low entrance-gateway leads up steps into a paved court, on one side of which, in what is called the Chaplain's Room, which may have been a guardroom, are shown some pewter plates and dishes, with buff jerkins and jackboots of the time of the civil wars.

In the S.W. angle is the chapel, which "appears to have been a small parish church, long before the castle was built" (Parker's 'Domestic Architecture,' iii. 220). It is Trans.-Norm., with an E.E. W. window, and has a nave with aisles, and a late Norm. font. The chancel, which is properly the chapel of the house, is Perp., and has an E. window, and the date 1427. The stained glass is interesting, but much of it was stolen early in this

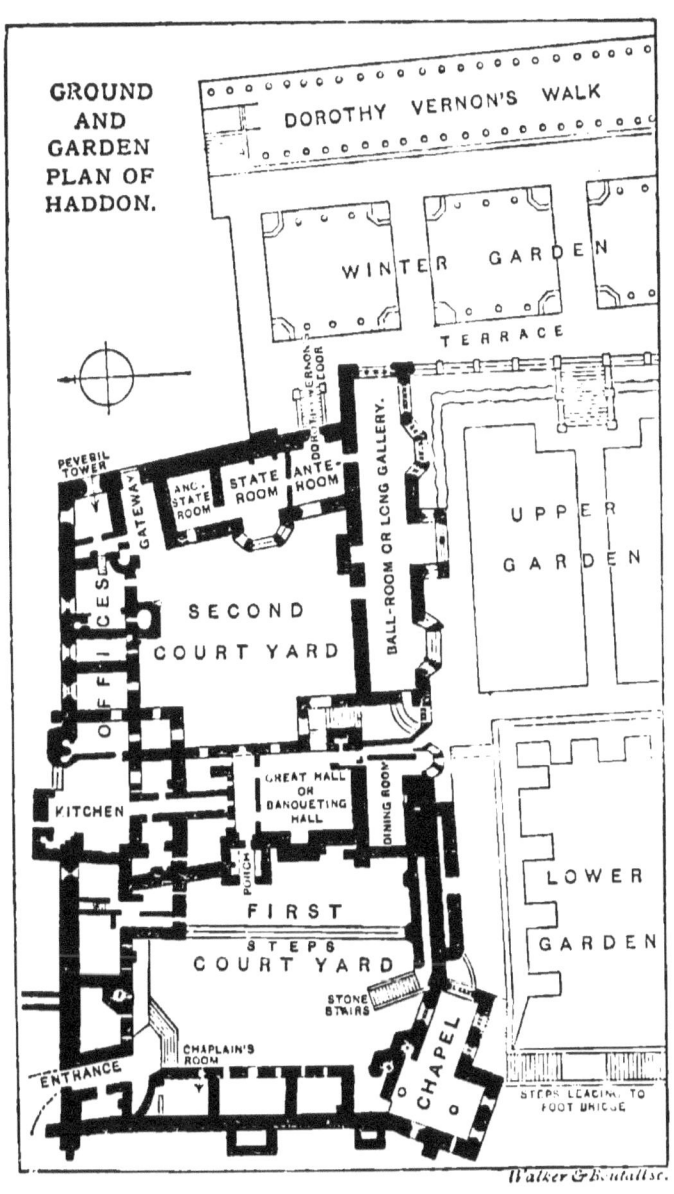

century. In the S. aisle are seats for the servants, and a large oak chest.

Across the first or lower courtyard is a porch leading to the main building. In this porch is a Roman altar, dug up in the neighbourhood, the reading of which, according to Camden, is as follows:

DEO MARTI BRACIACÆ OSITTIVS
CÆCILIAN. PRÆFECT. TEO : : : : :
V. S.

Proceeding along a passage on the rt. is the **Great Banqueting Hall**, with its daïs and old oak table, music gallery, and large fireplace between the windows; it stands between the upper and lower courts, and is interesting as the scene of baronial festivities in ancient days. Notice the fine antlers hung on the walls, and the ingenious apparatus for punishing the drinker, whose courage failed him at the toasts or the quantity of liquor prescribed. This apartment communicates directly and conveniently with the **kitchen**, in which are two hospitable-looking fireplaces, fitted for several ranges of spits, and an enormous chopping-block. The cellars and buttery are near, the doors of both being provided with hatches, through which the viands and liquors were distributed to retainers and hangers-on, and transmitted to the table of the daïs. There is also a smaller dining-room or withdrawing-room, with a coved ceiling. It is entered by a flight of steps, formed each of a solid log; it is a low room with bow windows, and interesting on account of its oak panelling; in three of the compartments are heads in relief of Henry VII.; his queen Elizabeth of York; and, it is said, Will Somers, the jester. The other carvings are coats of arms of the Peverils and Avenells (the earliest possessors of Haddon after the Conquest), and the boar's head of the Vernons, who held it from the time of Richard I. to that of Elizabeth. The last of the male line was the celebrated Sir George Vernon, called "The King of the Peak," on account of his splendour and hospitality. His arms and initials, with the date 1545, are over the fireplace. Several of the rooms retain their ancient tapestry hangings on the walls. Those of the earl's bedchamber and dressing-room, above the dining-room bear a curious representation of a boarhunt, the men in the costume of the 16th centy., and the dogs protected by a species of leather armour laced over their bodies, and ornamented with studs. The tapestries cover and conceal the doors, but, in order to prevent the necessity of lifting them up in order to pass, iron hooks are provided at the sides, by which they could be held back.

The **Long Gallery** is of the time of Elizabeth, judging from the style of its decorations, the panelled walls, and the bow window, in which are seen the Rutland shield of 25 quarterings. Round the frieze are the boar's head of Vernon, the peacock of Manners, and other animal devices. From this room is a good view of the garden divided into terraces, fenced with antique stone balustrades, but no longer kept in order. In the adjoining ante-room is the door leading to the terrace (itself one of the most picturesque sights at Haddon), by which, according to the well-known romantic story, the fair Dorothy Vernon, the heiress of these estates, eloped on a ball-night with her lover, Sir John Manners. Next is the **State Bed-room**, in which are portraits of Elizabeth, Charles I., and Prince Rupert, after Vandyck. The chimney-piece is ornamented with a grotesque representation, in stucco, of Orpheus charming the beasts. Here are a large looking-glass said to have belonged to Queen Elizabeth, and the state bed (last occupied by George IV.), the hangings of which were worked by Eleanor, daughter of Thomas Lord de Roos, and wife of Sir Robert Manners; also a rough wooden cradle, in which many of the Earls of Rutland were rocked. Adjoining this apartment is the ancient State Room containing some Gobelins tapestry, and a curious instrument, designed, it is said, for stretching and stringing crossbows. The arch of the N. gateway is the segment of a circle, or rather it is a slovenly-constructed slightly-pointed circle, and not older than the 15th centy. The **Eagle** or **Peveril's Tower**, the oldest part of the building, should be ascended for the sake of the view. A graceful little watchtower springs from the Peveril Tower.

A large part of the park was enclosed about 100 years ago, but the meadows around the hall preserve their park-like character.

(2.) ⚡**CHATSWORTH**, "the Palace of the Peak," though easily accessible from Rowsley (Rte. 5) and Hassop, is perhaps most conveniently visited from Bakewell. The carriage-road through Pilsley makes a circuit of 4 m., but there is a direct bridle or foot path, stretching up the hill called Bow Cross, a little to the rt. of the rly. stat., and through the woods, which leads to the house in a little under 3 m. The summit of Bow Cross commands a splendid view, and the road descends thence by the side of Edensor Ch. into the park.

⚡**Edensor** is one of those villages which derive, from the vicinity of a noble and generous landlord, advantages denied to those more remote from such observation. The dwellings erected by the 6th Duke are in the villa style, with gardens. The Ch. was also rebuilt by him, under the direction of Sir G. G. Scott, with a pulpit and font of Devonshire marble. In the interior is a monument to the first Earl of Devonshire, with two recumbent figures, one a skeleton (d. 1652); also a brass to John Beton (d. 1570), a confidential servant of Mary Queen of Scots. In the ch.-yard is buried the 6th Duke of Devonshire (d. 1858). He reposes under a plain uninscribed stone tomb, with a floriated cross sculptured on the top. Lord Frederick Cavendish, murdered in Phoenix Park, Dublin, on 6th May, 1882, and Sir Joseph Paxton are also buried in the ch.-yard.

Chatsworth, "a house really large, neat, and admirable," as Camden says of its predecessor, the superb seat of the Duke of Devonshire, was originally a square Palladian building with central court, erected by the 4th Earl and 1st Duke of Devonshire, in the reign of William III. To this a long wing was added by the late Duke, under the direction of *Sir Jeffrey Wyattville*. But however much this wing may add to the capacity of the house, it detracts greatly from its architectural character, which was one of dignified uniformity. It stands on a gently-sloping bank, near the margin of the "discreetly flowing Derwent," which runs through the midst of the beautiful park. A velvet lawn reaches to the water's brink, scattered over with trees sheltering the lordly mansion, yet allowing the most pleasing glimpses as you approach it, through the intervals between them, or underneath their branches. The first peep of the house seen among the trees coming from Edensor is very pleasing. The river is crossed by a stone bridge, ornamented with statues by *Cibber*, who was much employed in peopling the park and its groves with stone deities, nymphs, &c. He has recorded in his note-book, that "for

2 statues, as big as life, I had 35*l*. apiece, and all charges borne; and at this rate I shall endeavour to serve a nobleman in freestone."

Near the bridge is a small moated tower, called Queen Mary's Bower, from a tradition that the Queen of Scots passed much of her time here, and cultivated a small garden on its summit. In the courtyard, beyond the entrance gateway, the way to which is lined with tulip-trees, stands a beautiful weeping ash, transported in 1830, a full-grown tree 40 years old, from Derby, a distance of 24 m. In order to admit the passage of so huge a mass of branches and roots, with earth adhering to them, the turnpike gates on the road had to be taken down.

It would be tedious to enumerate room by room all the treasures of this superb palace, some of the windows of which have the sills of white marble, and the external frames are gilt. Its interior is distinguished by the lavish expenditure of marble, not only of the native Derbyshire varieties, of which the finest existing specimens in pillars, pedestals, slabs, and tables are to be seen here, but also of foreign marbles and porphyries. Chatsworth also displays to the fullest extent the skill of *Grinling Gibbons* and his followers, in the elaborate borders, wreaths, festoons, &c., with which the state apartments are profusely decorated. "All the wood-carving in England fades away before that of Gibbons at Chatsworth. The birds seem to live, the foliage to shoot, and the flowers to expand beneath your eye. The most marvellous work of all is a net of game; you imagine at the first glance that the gamekeeper has hung up his day's sport on the wall, and that some of the birds are still in their death flutter. There is no instance of a man before Gibbons who gave to wood the loose and airy lightness of flowers, and chained together the various productions of the elements with a free disorder natural to each species. In the great antechamber are several dead fowl over the chimney, finely executed, and, over a closet-door, a pen, not distinguishable from a real feather. When Gibbons had finished his work in this palace, he presented the Duke with a point cravat, a woodcock, and a model of his own head."—*Walpole*. He was assisted in these works by *Samuel Watson*, a Derbyshire artist of talent (see Heanor, Rte. 3), but the design and the spirit thrown into the whole probably belonged to the presiding master. Several of the apartments, including the chapel, are covered with paintings by *Verrio, Laguerre,* and *Sir James Thornhill*, in the shapes of heathen deities, allegories, apotheoses, composed of heaps of figures which seem ready to fall on your head.

"On painted ceilings you devoutly stare,
Where sprawl the saints of Verrio and
Laguerre."

The following is a brief summary of the principal objects for notice in the various apartments.

The **Sub-Hall**.—Tesselated pavement of the corridor; and painted ceiling, after *Guido's* Aurora.

The **Great Hall**.—Paintings by *Verrio* and *Laguerre*, representing scenes in the life of Julius Cæsar the ceiling being occupied by his Apotheosis. Here is an enormously large encrinital marble slab, also bronze busts from the Exhibition of 1862. From the Great Hall, a corridor containing Swiss views leads to the **Chapel**, at the S.W. of the building. The altarpiece here is *Verrio's* best work—subject 'The Incredulity of Thomas.' The statues of Faith and Hope on either side of it are by *Gabriel Cibber*, who was much employed here, and the carving by *Watson*. The side walls are adorned with paintings from the life of our Saviour. Notice two curious paintings on glass, and the altar, an oval table of malachite. Another corridor leads from the chapel, containing Egyptian sculptures, to the Sketch Gallery, the walls of which are hung with drawings by Old Masters, including many precious works; a part of this collection was once in the possession of Sir Peter Lely and Charles I. It includes 4 by *Michael Angelo* (2 sketches of figures for the Sistine Chapel); *Leonardo da Vinci*; *Raphael* (a slight sketch of the figure of Paul preaching at Athens, &c.); *Correggio*; *Titian* (his own portrait); *Holbein*, portraits of Henry VII. and VIII., half life-size; besides others, by *Julio Romano*, *Salvator Rosa*, *Pierino del Vaga*, *Andrea del Sarto*, *Albert Dürer*, and *Vandyck's* sketch-book during his travels in Italy.

In the **South Picture Gallery** are many beautiful paintings, such as a sea-piece by *Vandervelde*; *Titian*, St. John in the Wilderness; *Leonardo da Vinci* (perhaps *Luini*), the Infant Saviour with fruit, the upraised hand of which is very sweetly executed; *Jean Mabuse*, the Presentation of the Virgin in the Temple (a Gothic church), the priests in the costume of bishops of the 16th centy., with mitres; in the foreground Anna and Joachim; a curious picture somewhat damaged. *John Van Eyck*, Consecration of Thomas à Becket as Archbishop of Canterbury, in the presence of the clergy, the laity, and King Henry II.: "The proportions of the figures are rather more slender than usual in Van Eyck, heads spirited, flesh of a brownish tone. The other colours, draperies, &c., of the richest and most glowing tints, especially the dark-red robe of the bishop on the rt. hand, with golden embroidery. This picture has the oldest date (1421) of any known of Van Eyck." *Holbein*, a man with a flower in his hand; *Murillo*, a Holy Family, the Child in the cradle, St. Joseph at work; *Granet* (a modern French painter), the Convent Chapel, monks as their devotions—a wonderful effect of evening light. Others by *Albert Dürer*, *N. Poussin*; Woman taken in Adultery, *P. Veronese*.

The **State Rooms**, which extend along the S. front, and command an exquisite view, are profusely decorated with carvings by *Gibbons*, whose celebrated lace cravat hangs in the first room. The equally celebrated pen has been broken. There are also carvings by *Watson*, hardly inferior to these masterpieces. These rooms contain, among other things, the coronation chairs of George III. and William IV. and their Queens, which were perquisites of the office of Lord Chamberlain, held on these occasions by Dukes of Devoushiro. The Music-room has a collection of minerals and curious inlaid cabinets, and the State Drawing-room some copies of *Raphael's* cartoons and Gobelin tapestry. In the old State Drawing-room is a malachite clock, presented by the Emperor of Russia, and the rosary of Henry VIII. The carved game and net of Gibbons in this room are particularly beautiful. In the private Drawing-room (not shown) is a beautiful copy, by *Bartolini*, of the Venus de Medicis, and the following paintings by Old Masters:—Mary Q. of Scots, *Zucchero*; Charles I., *Jansen*; Duke of Albemarle, *Lely*; Henry VIII., *Holbein*; Philip II., *Titian*; a Venetian Admiral, *Tintoretto*; the Archbishop of Spalatro; Georgiana, Duchess of Devonshire, with her child on her lap, by *Sir Joshua Reynolds*. " Her face, which is seen in profile, is equally handsome and intelligent; the colouring remarkably warm, clear, and harmonious." There are some other portraits in the state apartments, including James Butler, 2nd Duke of Ormond, by *Kneller;* Richard Boyle, Earl of Burlington, by *Knapton;* William, 1st Duke of Devonshire, by *Kneller* (or *Riley,* 1707); George IV., by *Lawrence.*

In the **Red Velvet Room** are chiefly modern paintings by English artists. It contains a sketch of the beautiful Duchess as a child with her mother, by *Sir Joshua Reynolds,* signed by the artist; *Landseer's* celebrated Bolton Abbey; *Collins,* Boy opening the Gate; *Newton,* a Scene from Gil Blas. The ceiling was painted by *Thornhill.* Some of the apartments are called Queen Mary's, not because she actually used them, but because they contain portions of the furniture from the rooms in the old house (long since pulled down) occupied by her when Lord Shrewsbury was allowed to remove hither with his prisoner from Sheffield Manor, Wingfield, or Hardwick. These short visits occurred in 1570, 1573, 1577, 1578, and in 1581. Lord Burleigh commends Chatsworth as "a very mete howse for good preservation of his charge, having no towre of resort, wher any ambushes might lye." Hobbes, the philosopher, resided for some time in the old house, as tutor to the Earl of Devonshire, 1631. He wrote here his work 'De Mirabilibus Pecci.'

The **New Staircase,** built by *Sir J. Wyattville,* is far more striking than the old, called the Grand Stairs. The **Library** (not shown) is a noble apartment, decorated with pillars of rosewood marble, and black and grey marble, from Ashford; also with two vases of grey Siberian jasper, gifts of the Emperor Nicholas; it contains a highly valuable collection of rare books, including many from the Duke of Roxburgh's library. Here are the oldest Florentine Homer, on vellum; rare editions printed by Caxton; and many ancient MSS. with beautiful miniatures; among them a missal of King Henry VII., given by his daughter Margaret, Queen of Scotland, to the Archbishop of St. Andrew's, with paintings executed probably by Flemish artists, scholars of *Van Eyck.* There is also the "Liber Veritatis," or sketch-book of *Claude Lorrain,* in which he entered outlines, often very slight ones, of his great pictures.

The **New Dining Room,** a noble room with a coved roof, contains the following portraits by *Vandyck:* the Earl of Devonshire; "except that the position of the legs is not happy, a picture of much delicacy and elegance." His Countess, "extremely pleasing; the attitude of walking gives the figure much animation." Jane, daughter of Arthur Goodwin; "The brightness of the tone, and the delicacy of the treatment, give a great charm to this picture." Joanna of Blois, afterwards Lady Rich: "To my mind, one of the most beautiful of *Vandyck's* female portraits, and wonderfully charming: the clear, powerful colouring, the bright shining tone of the flesh, and the careful execution in all the parts, give reason to believe that it was painted rather before his settling in England." Arthur Goodwin; "The countenance is very pleasing, and the execution extremely true to nature; the colouring less forcible than usual, but in a delicate clear tone, date 1639." *Gerard Honthorst:* the Countess of Devonshire, with her two sons and daughters: "Compared with Vandyck, the arrangement is rather too inartificial, and the space not sufficiently filled; otherwise it is very spirited and carefully painted, and the colouring is fine and clear."—*Waagen.* The portals at either end of this room are adorned with pillars of African and red breccia; the two chimney-pieces, which cost 1000 guineas each, are of Carrara marble by *Westmacott*, the younger, and *Sevier*; the side-tables are made of horn-blende, porphyritic syenite, and 'Siberian jasper.

The **Sculpture Gallery**, a noble hall, lighted from above, is filled with works for the most part by modern artists of various countries, including several of the best statues by *Canova*; and foremost among them, the sitting statue of Madame Letitia, mother of Napoleon, a combination of ease and dignity, finished with the utmost care; the idea is from the antique statue of Agrippina; it is a splendid achievement of the chisel.

A colossal bust of Napoleon.
Endymion asleep, watched by his Dog : " The task of representing all the limbs dissolved in repose is peculiarly adapted to *Canova's* genius, so that this is a work of the greatest softness, and of the highest finish of the marble." Hebe pouring water from a Vase, one of *Canova's* best works.

Thorwaldsen, Venus with the Apple : " The graceful action peculiar to this artist, the natural beauty and healthful fulness of the forms, make this work very pleasing." Bust of Card. Gonsalvi : " The fine sensible features are given with great spirit, and the workmanship is highly finished."

Bas-reliefs of Morning and Night.
The Filatrice, or Spinning Girl, by *Schadow*, a Prussian, is au elegant figure.

Castor and Pollux, bas-relief. The Quoit Player (Discobolus), by *Kessels*, a Belgian, is true to nature, and original in conception : " Very spirited and carefully executed in all the parts, according to the model." The pedestal is inlaid with Swedish porphyry from Elfdalen.

Cupid taking a thorn from Venus's foot : carefully executed, but with little meaning in its composition. *Taddolini*, — Ganymede caressing the Eagle : a pretty and well-executed work. *Bartolini*, a Bacchante. *Gibson*, Mars and Cupid. *Westmacott* the younger, a Cymbal Player, and on the pedestal a bas-relief of a Bacchante; both very spirited. In the centre of the gallery stands a large granite basin, worked at Berlin, by *Cantian*, out of one of those remarkable boulder-stones which strew the sandy flats of Brandenburg, and worth notice from its size and finish. A vase of white marble contains the modelling-stick, chisel, pen, and glove, last used by Canova. A vase of fluor spar (called in the county "Blue John"), the largest ever made ; a table formed of slabs of Labrador felspar, found near St. Petersburg, where there is no such rock *in situ ;* a table of white marble from the columns of the temple on Cape Colonna ; and a copy of the Grand Mosaic discovered at Pompeii, of the battle of Darius, also deserve notice.

There are many rooms not shown in this vast mansion. The kitchen is an apartment of lofty dimensions, exceedingly well arranged, and the spits turned by a water-wheel. The cellars are spacious, and contain 12 ale-casks, called the Apostles, given by William III. to the first Duke. Besides the various treasures enumerated above, the Duke has one of the finest private cabinets of minerals in Great Britain, including all the most rare specimens that Derbyshire produces; and among the precious gems, an emerald purchased from Don Pedro, Emperor of Brazil, which in size and uniform depth of colour is scarcely to be surpassed.

The visitor passes out of the Sculpture Gallery into the Portland Walk, a glass covered way, leading from the house to the stables, which contains some very fine wall-plants, amongst others a remarkable rhododendron, and a fine specimen of *Camellia Reticulata*, some of the flowers of which are 8 inches across, and thence into the **Gardens**, which include 80 acres of mown lawn; they are laid out in the formal style, and ornamented with statues, vases, and pillars.

A lofty wall, heated from within, and lined with glass, is covered with delicate plants, as casuarinæ, acacias. Near the Italian Garden in front of the house is a vigorous young oak, planted by the Princess Victoria when she visited Chatsworth in 1832. Close to it are two other trees planted by the Prince Consort, and the Duchess of Kent. Passing through a curious gate formed by a single massive stone moving on a pivot, the visitor enters the grounds appropriated to azaleas and rhododendrons.

The **Arboretum**, a plantation of different kinds of trees from various parts of the globe, as far as they can be naturalised in this climate, occupies 40 acres on the slope of the hill. There are hothouses in the Kitchen Garden (for which an order is required) for forcing fruit, besides graperies, cherry and strawberry houses.

From the slope of the hill, nearly behind the house, descends a colossal flight of steps, surmounted by a Temple, from every part of which, on opening a valve, gush forth copious streams of water, so as to form, in descending the flight, a long artificial cascade, disappearing into the ground at the bottom. A more pleasing object than this is the **Emperor Fountain**, so called in honour of the visit of the Czar in 1844, a very lofty jet-d'eau, rising from the centre of a long sheet of water to a height of 267 ft., sheltered on either side by a shady screen of limes. There is also a curious contrivance, designed and executed by Mons. Guillot about 1790, in the form of a weeping willow, made of metal, every branch of which is a pipe, and which can be made to deluge the unwary trespasser. These are all supplied with water from a reservoir of 6 acres, on the hill-top, situated near the Hunting Tower, built in the time of Queen Elizabeth as a prospect for the ladies of the household; it is a tall square building with 4 turrets conspicuous far and near, and marked by a flag on the summit when the Duke is at home. These stately avenues, lawns, and waterworks, resemble, on a smaller scale, those of Versailles and St. Cloud. The waterworks belong to Old Chatsworth, but the horticulture and arboricultural achievements were carried out by the late Duke under the late Sir Joseph Paxton's superintendence.

The **Great Conservatory**, the glory of Chatsworth, is approached through an avenue of rocks, not a mere puny pile of stones, but an immense combination of huge blocks, skilfully composed to imitate a natural ravine or gorge. The carriage road—for the conservatory is so large as to be entered and traversed by carriages —is so contrived that nothing is seen till the visitor reaches the threshold and the folding gates are thrown open. This palace of glass consists of coved sides, surmounted by a semicircular arcade, supported on slender iron pillars, having arched projections at both ends. It is 276 ft. long, 123 ft. wide, and 65 ft. high, and covers nearly an acre of ground. It contains 40 m. of sash bars, made at the rate of 2000 ft. a day, by a machine designed by Sir Joseph Paxton. The framework is of wood, the arches formed of bent deal planks, applied together by iron fastenings; the panes of glass are disposed obliquely, in alternate ridges and furrows, like the folds of a fan or the plaits of a frill, so as to throw off the rain. A gallery runs round it, whence one can look down upon a forest of tropical foliage, palms and cedars, pines and ferns. In one corner a pile of artificial rock serves for the growth of ferns, orchidaceæ, and cactæ, while it conceals the staircase leading to the gallery. Eight large furnaces heat this house through pipes 7 m. long, which alone cost 1500*l*. They are supplied with fuel by a subterranean tramway, through a tunnel ½ m. in length. The whole was planned by the 6th Duke and Sir J. Paxton, under whose superintendence it was executed.

In the kitchen gardens, which are ½ m. N. of the house, and require a special order for admission, is the **New Holland House**, containing plants from the Australian colonies.
The Victoria Regia, or royal water-lily, has a peculiar house appropriated to it, containing a tank 34 ft. in diameter, the water in which is kept in motion by a wheel. Near the kitchen gardens is the pretty residence of the late Sir J. Paxton.

The **Cyclopean Aqueduct** is a vast structure of numerous lofty arches formed of rough-hewn angular gritstone masonry, destined to carry a stream of water to form a cascade 150 ft. high, after the fashion of a similar structure at Cassel.
Should the visitor be obliged to return to his head-quarters without extending his travels in Derbyshire, he may leave Chatsworth by a different route from that by which he entered, as he can rejoin the railway at either Hassop, Bakewell, or Rowsley; the distance is about the same (3 or 4 m.) in either case.

(3.) **The Lathkill.** A very pleasant excursion may be made over the moors westward to **Over Haddon** (2½ m.), a picturesque village, and thence up the Vale of Lathkill, a spot of rare beauty. It is traversed by the stream of the same name, a beautiful trout river, strictly preserved by the Duke of Rutland; pedestrians, however, may follow its course without let or hindrance. Cotton says of this river, that it is "by many degrees the purest and most transparent stream that I ever yet saw, and breeds the reddest and best trouts in England." Some 2½ or 3 m. above Over Haddon, the Lathkill issues from a cavern in the limestone opposite the romantic Parson's Tor. It was formerly called Fox Tor, but gained its present name from a fatal accident that befell the Rev. R. Lomas, the incumbent of Monyash, who, coming home from Bakewell in a tempestuous night (October 11, 1776), missed his way and fell over the Tor. The Lathkill is joined by the Bradford at Alport, and falls into the Wye at Fillyford Bridge, near Rowsley.

(4.) **To Buxton by Road** will be by many preferred to the rly.; the scenery is very agreeable, and it is well worth while to slightly lengthen the distance (12 m.) by an occasional stroll on the lovely banks of the Wye.

At 1½ m. is ☧ **Ashford**, locally known as Ashford-in-the-Water, from its standing on the Wye, which supplies water power for several marble mills. In the churchyard are some fine yew-trees. On the wall of the porch of the *Ch.* is a sculpture of a wolf and wild boar beneath a tree. In the N. aisle the visitor may see five funeral garlands still hanging, the relics of a very pretty custom at one time prevalent in Derbyshire. This custom fell into disuse, perhaps a century ago, but has of late years been revived. (See Ham, Rte. 34.)

"Now the low beams with paper garlands hung,
In memory of some village youth or maid,
Draw the soft tear, from thrill'd remembrance sprung;
How oft my childhood mark'd that tribute paid!" *Anna Seward.*

The practice of ringing the Curfew is still kept up in Ashford, and the still rarer one of the pancake-bell on Shrove Tuesday.

Close to the village is Ashford Hall, and at the W. end of the village are the marble-works for which this place is celebrated, where the various marbles found in this county are cut, polished, and turned in lathes. The best marble occurs in beds, none of which are more than 8 in. thick, alternating with chert. This neighbourhood furnishes all the finest varieties, such as the entrochal, bird's eye, and the rosewood, which are obtained from a quarry about 1 m. from the village.

The road follows the Wye to Monsal Dale, 2½ m., where the river flows in from the N. from Miller's Dale, at which is a Rly. Stat. (*post*). **Monsal Dale**, which at this point is joined by a small brook from Deep Dale, is about 2½ m. in length (commencing from Cressbrook Dale), and is a most lovely combination of rock and river scenery, as the stream flows under Fin Cop and Brushfield Hough.

"And Monsal, thou mine of Arcadian treasure,
Need we seek for Greek islands and spice-laden gales,
While a Temple like thee, of enchantment and pleasure,
May be found in our own native Derbyshire dales?" *E. Cook.*

A barrow opened at this latter spot contained a curious collection of swords and javelins. Another barrow at the same place was called the *Gospel Hillock*, "perhaps from the first Christian missionary having taken his stand thereon while exhorting the Saxons to forsake the worship of Woden and Thor."— *Bateman.*

By ascending Brushfield Hough, a very striking view is obtained. The Wye is seen at foot, winding from Monsal to Miller's Dale, and is crossed by a lofty viaduct, over which the train rushes as it emerges from the tunnel. The walk may be extended to Longstone Edge, which gives another wide view, and by passing through the picturesque villages of Little and Great Longstone to the Buxton road, which now leaves the river, and is carried up a streamless valley to Taddington, 6 m. from Bakewell.

Taddington stands on high ground, overlooking the valley of the Wye. Its small Ch. has a *brass* to one of the Blackwells, who have given name to an adjoining township. In the Ch.-yd. is the shaft of a Celtic cross. Miller's Dale (Stat.) is 1½ m. N. (*post*); and about a like distance S.W. is **Chelmorton**, with a Ch. worth a visit. It is of various styles, and has a dwarf stone chancel-screen and a carved font. There are two large barrows on the hill above the village.

The road again comes near the river and the rly. at **King's Sterndale**, 9 m. from Bakewell, and scarcely ever loses sight of either for the rest of the journey. At 10½ m. is an ascent into **Ashwood Dale**, a charming spot, through which the Wye flows, sometimes in miniature rapids, sometimes in wide glassy pools, so pleasant to the angler. Wood-clad slopes bound it on either side, rich in foliage, and surmounted by cliffs of limestone, scarped by the engineer, yet not altogether bare, for the ivy has crept over their surface, and some hardy shrubs have found root in their crannies. It must be admitted that the rly. works, however bold and vigorous in themselves, do not add to the beauty of the vale. At its northern end is the picturesque chasm called the *Lover's Leap* (Rte. 7); and 1 m. farther is Buxton.

Proceeding to Buxton by the Railway, at 2 m. is **Hassop** (Stat.). The very small village stands at the foot of a lofty hill. 1 m. N. is Hassop Hall (Chas. Stephen Leslie, Esq.), a house held by one of the Eyres for Charles I. A handsome Rom. Cath. chapel adjoins the Hall. The Eyres, for about a century, were styled Earls of Newburgh, but on the failure of their line, in 1853, the title was declared to belong to the Princess Giustiniani, the descendant of the 4th Earl, who died in 1768.

3 m. Longstone (Stat.). The villages of **Great** and **Little Longstone** lie N. of the Stat., and behind them Longstone Edge stretches toward Stoney Middleton. Longstone Hall (Rev. J. H. Bullivant) was, according to tradition, a hunting-seat of Henry VII. A tunnel succeeds, on emerging from which a glorious view breaks suddenly on the traveller as the train rushes through Monsal Dale, at a great height above the river, looking down upon the tributary *Cressbrook Dale*, with the little colony of mills at its mouth. Immediately above it is the hill called *Hay Top*, where, in a large flat-topped barrow, an exceedingly beautiful food-vessel was found, together with the skeleton of a child. And on Longstone Edge, in a barrow called *Blake Low*, were found the skeletons of a girl and a child, together with a drinking-cup and the tine of a stag's antler.

At 5½ m. notice on N. a very curious prolongation of limestone, known as *Tongue End*, which guards the entrance to Tideswell Dale.

6½ m. ☿ Miller's Dale (Stat.), a resort for anglers. The tourist should alight here for the purpose of exploring the various dales at his leisure, as well as for visiting

☿ Tideswell, a small town, 3 m. N.E., so called from an ebbing and flowing well, which is still to be seen at the entrance to the town.

" Here also is a well,
Whose waters do excel
All waters thereabout,
Both being in and out
Ebbing and flowing."
Sir A. Cockayne, 1658.

But the town is worth a visit for the sake of its magnificent *Ch.*, principally of Dec. style. It is cruciform, with an embattled and pinnacled tower at the W. end; the windows are particularly fine. In the centre of the spacious chancel is the altar-tomb of Sir Sampson Meverell (d. 1462); the marble slab has a fine *brass*, with evangelistic symbols, &c., and a long account of the deceased, who served in France under the Duke of Bedford, and was knighted by him; the slab is supported on pillars, and underneath is seen a figure of a skeleton. On the N. side is the altar-tomb of Robert Pursglove, prior of Gisburne, made snffragan bishop of Hull in the reign of Henry VIII.; his *brass* represents him in full pontifical vestments (though he survived till 1579), and is regarded as a valuable example of its class (Haines, 'Mon. Brasses'); he was a native of the town, and the Grammar School founded by him still exists. An earlier *brass* is one for John Foljambe, a great benefactor to the Ch. (d. 1358). There is another *brass* for Robert Lytton and wife (1483). The Lyttons, a family of great antiquity, intermarried with the Bulwers of Norfolk, and, by selling their estates in the time of Elizabeth, severed their connection with the Peak country. There were two chapels in the S. transept : one, now carefully restored, belonged to the Lyttons; in the other are effigies of Sir Thurstan de Bower and Margaret his wife, of the early part of 15th cent. In the N. transept is the Lady Chapel, which belonged to the guild of St. Mary. At **Wheston**, another hamlet, connected with the N. transept, and about 1½ m. distant, is an ancient stone cross. The Ch. there, recently restored, has a stone reredos standing in advance of the E. wall.

[From Tideswell a wild mountain road of 5 m. leads through the mining village of Little Hucklow to Castleton (Rte. 8).]

At 7¼ m. the Rly. passes in a tunnel under **Chee Tor**, one of the finest cliffs in the dale, at 8½ m. the line to Chapel-en-le-Frith and Manchester branches off N. (Rte. 7), and at 11½ m. **Buxton** is reached (Rte. 7). For these last 3 m. especially, the rly. works are very heavy, tunnels and bridges and viaducts succeeding each other with bewildering rapidity. To form any adequate idea of them the tourist is advised to walk from Buxton through Ashwood Dale to the Miller's Dale Stat. (5 m.), keeping in sight of the pretty little Wye the whole way. The botanist will find the beautiful *Geranium pratense*, and even rarer plants, and the geologist will be interested in the sections of the limestone.

ROUTE 7.

BUXTON TO MANCHESTER, BY CHAPEL-EN-LE-FRITH.

L. AND N.-W. RAILWAY. 24 m.

§ **BUXTON.** This celebrated inland watering-place is situated in an upland valley, 1100 ft. above the sea, surrounded on the S. by limestone rocks, and on the N. by round gritstone hills, which are gradually being covered by the dark foliage of fir plantations. It stands on the Derbyshire Wye, near its source, and to make room for the Crescent, the stream has in one part been arched over like a sewer and hid from view. The climate of this elevated region is rough, the wind stormy, and the rain frequent, with rapid changes of temperature; yet the air is clear and dry, partly owing, no doubt, to the absorbent nature of the soil, and the fame of the waters attracts yearly a large number of visitors. The resident population is scattered thinly, except in the town itself, over a large surface, much of which is used as grazing ground.

Though essentially a modern watering-place, Buxton bears evidence of great antiquity, and Gale, the antiquary, believed it to have been the Aquis of John of Ravenna. That the springs were known to the Romans is certain, as at the time of the building of the Crescent remains of a Roman bath were discovered; and that there was a town is rendered probable by the fact that two principal roads intersected each other here, viz. from Mancunium (Manchester) through Chester, and from Congleton to Brough, a village beyond Castleton; a portion of this road, called the Batham Gate, is easily traceable between Tideswell and Castleton. The springs were in high repute in the Middle Ages, and the chapel of St. Ann in Old Buxton was crowded by devotees who resorted to them. This concourse was either prohibited or fell into disuse at the Reformation, but in the reign of Elizabeth the waters again came into repute, so that the Earl and Countess of Shrewsbury brought hither their prisoner, Mary Queen of Scots, placing her in the

47

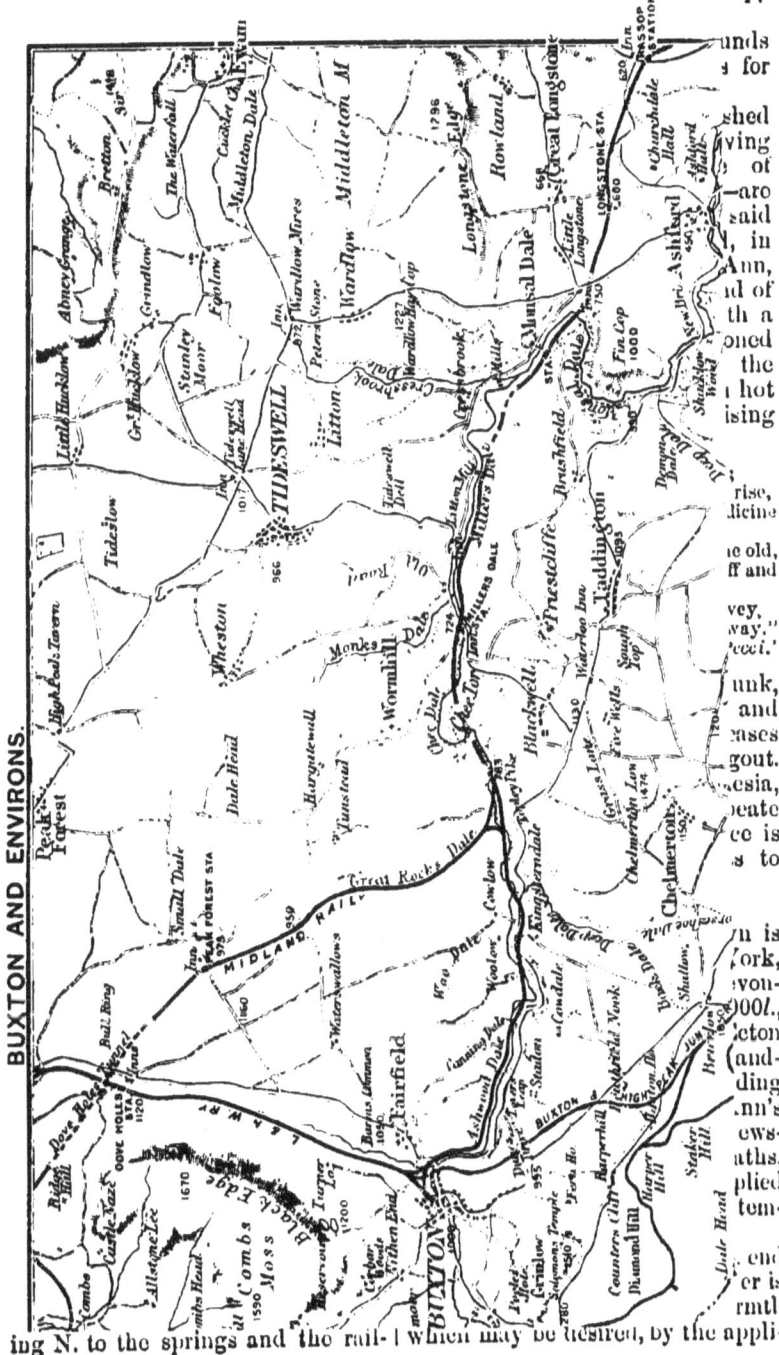

BUXTON AND ENVIRONS.

unds
for
shed
ving
of
aro-
said
, in
Ann,
d of
th a
oned
the
hot
ising

rise,
dicine

e old,
ff and

vey,
way."
ecci.'

unk,
and
ases
gout.
esin,
eate
ce is
s to

n is
ork,
von-
00l.,
eton
(and-
ding
nn's
ews-
aths,
plied
tem-

end
er is
rmth

ing N. to the springs and the rail- | which may be desired, by the appli-

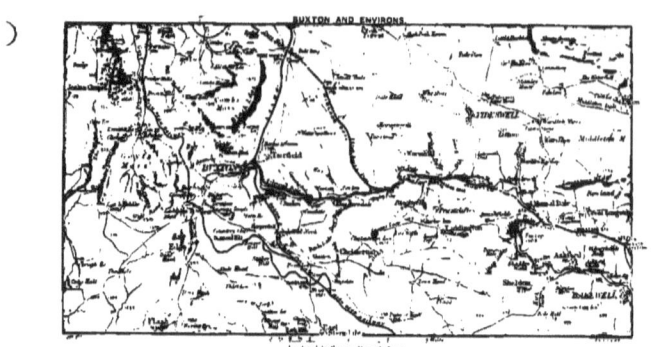

Old Hall, a part of which still exists, incorporated into the hotel of the same name. She was met here by Burghley, who also came for the benefit of the waters, and had thereby nearly excited the displeasure of his mistress, Queen Elizabeth, who feared lest the fascinations of her rival should seduce even the crafty Cecil from his duty. "At the rise of the Wye are nine springs of hot water, call'd at present Buxton Well, which being found by experience very good for the stomach, the nerves, and the whole body, the Most Honourable George Earl of Shrewsbury has lately adorn'd them with buildings, and they begin to be frequented by great numbers of the nobility and gentry, about which time the unfortunate and heroic princess, Mary Queen of Scots, took her farewell of Buxton in this distich, which is nothing but an alteration of Cæsar's verses upon Feltria:—

"'Buxtona quæ calidæ celebrabere nomine lymphæ,
Forte mihi posthac non adeunda, vale.'

But this is beside my business."— *Camden.*

The visitors, however, were very indifferently accommodated, even a century later than Camden's time, according to a 17th-centy. 'Tour in Derbyshire,' cited by Macaulay. "The gentry of Derbyshire and of the neighbouring counties repaired to Buxton, where they were crowded into low wooden sheds, and regaled with oatcake and with a viand which the hosts called mutton, but which the guests strongly suspected to be dog."—(*Hist. Eng.* vol. i.).

Buxton consists of two parts; (1) Old or High Buxton, to the S., still retaining something of its primitive appearance, with its antique chapel and remains of a market-cross; and (2) the Buxton of modern date, encircling St. Ann's cliff, and stretching N. to the springs and the rail-

way. Buxton, like Matlock, abounds in so-called museums or shops for the sale of Derbyshire spar, &c.

The mineral waters — furnished from two sources, one tepid, having a temperature at its source of 82° Fahr., and the other cold—are without taste or smell, and are said to resemble those of Wildbad, in Germany. The well of St. Ann, whence they issue, at the W. end of the lower walk, is covered with a neat stone canopy, and is reckoned one of the seven wonders of the Peak, because it furnishes both hot and cold water from springs rising not more than 12 in. apart.

"Unto St. Ann the fountain sacred is;
With waters hot and cold its sources rise,
And in its sulphur veins there medicine lies.
This cures the palsied members of the old,
And cherishes the nerves grown stiff and cold.
Crutches the lame into its brink convey,
Returning, the ingrates fling them away."
Hobbes, 'De Mirabilibus Pecci.'

These waters are sometimes drunk, but chiefly used for baths, and are considered efficacious in cases of chronic rheumatism and gout. They contain iron, lime, magnesia, potash and soda. A chalybeate spring rising at a short distance is mixed with those waters so as to form a purgative.

The chief feature of the town is the **Crescent**, by Carr, of York, erected by the 5th Duke of Devonshire in 1781, at a cost of 120,000*l.*, supplied by the profits of the Ecton copper-mine (Rte. 33). It is a handsome range of building, including an assembly-room, the St. Ann's and Crescent Hotels, and a news-room. Here are the tepid baths, both public and private, supplied with the water at its natural temperature.

The hot baths are near the E. end of the Crescent. Here the water is heated to any degree of warmth which may be desired, by the application of steam. The natural baths and the wells for drinking (including St. Ann's) are at the W. of the Crescent, with which all of them are connected by very light and elegant corridors. They have been rebuilt from designs by Mr. Currey. At the further end of the Broad Walk there is a good swimming bath.

A covered corridor leads from the Crescent to the Square, and forms a sheltered promenade. At the back of the Crescent is the **Devonshire Hospital**, formerly very extensive stables, built by the Duke in 1781. It contains 300 beds, and relieves about 3000 patients in the year. What was formerly a large open circular space, surrounded by the hospital buildings, has been covered in by a large dome, with four small ones at the corners, and a lantern tower in the centre. The diameter of the tower is no less than 154 feet, and it occupies about half an acre.

Opposite to it is the Ch. of St. John, a foundation of the 6th Duke, 1812. The old Ch., or more properly chapel of St. Ann (Buxton being a chapelry of Bakewell), is a small rude building, probably of the time of Elizabeth; it now serves as a school-church.

The Town Hall, with a Free Library, built in commemoration of the Jubilee of Her Majesty, contains a statue of Lord Frederick Cavendish. The Jubilee clock was also put up as a memorial to him.

St. Ann's Cliff, which rises immediately in front of the Crescent, was laid out in terrace walks by *Sir J. Wyattville*, and forms the chief promenade for invalids. Opposite the Old Hall Hotel is the **Park**, a large enclosure laid out in winding walks, with flower-beds and seats; the river Wye, which runs through it, is crossed by rustic bridges, and forms lakes and cascades on a very moderate scale. Attached to the gardens is a glass "Pavilion" with a room 400 ft. long, for balls and concerts, and promenades. Here there are daily concerts and recitals. Admission, 4d. and 6d., or 3s. per week.

One very pleasant feature of the S. part of Buxton is the **Duke's Drive**, a circuit of 2½ m., which leads from the Ashbourne to the Bakewell road. Part of it is a charming walk or drive, overlooking the valley of the Wye. It falls into the Bakewell road, a short distance N. of the Lover's Leap, a deep chasm in the rocks, which in some places appear almost to touch overhead; the pretty little stream that traverses it yields much to reward the botanist.

1 m. to the W. of the town, at the foot of Grinlow Hill, is **Poole's Hole** (or Cavern, as named by the showmen), which has obtained a reputation, not deserved, as one of the wonders of the Peak. It is named, according to the story, from an outlaw and robber who made it his dwelling. The entrance to it is low and narrow, but bath chairs can be taken in, for the accommodation of invalids. Its length (lighted throughout with gas) is said to exceed 600 yards, but this is an exaggeration. It contains some fine stalactites, and in this respect surpasses the Peak Cavern, to which in all other points it is inferior. To these fanciful names are given: one is called the Queen of Scots' Pillar, from a tradition that Mary actually penetrated thus far. The Wye takes its source in this cave, and flows underground for some little distance before it appears to the light of day.

" ——At length the pretty Wye
From her black mother Poole her nimble
  course doth ply
Tow'rds Darren" [Derwent].

The reputation of the Buxton

curiosities was sung by Sir Aston Cokaine in 1658:—

"The Pike to Tennariff
Au high repute doth give;
And the Coloss of brass,
Whereunder ships did pass,
Made Rhodes aspire.
Tonbridge makes Kent renown'd,
And Epsom Surrye's ground;
Poole-hole and St. Anne's Well
Makes Darbyshire excell
Many a shire."

Buxton offers to the tourist many fine walks and drives, the greater part of them depending for their beauty on their elevation. A frequent and easy walk is to **Diamond Hill**, 2 m. W.; on the summit of which are some loose stones, the remains of a tower, called Solomon's Temple, commanding a splendid view. The road to it runs through a ravine, between Grinlow and Laidman's Low, in which the so-called diamonds or quartz pebbles are found. The limestone rocks in the neighbourhood are quarried to a great extent, and burned for lime, which is conveyed away by tramroads communicating with the High Peak Rly. The hillside called **Grinlow** used to be dotted over with the singular dwellings of the workmen, excavated in the heaps of refuse limestone, which, becoming solid on the surface after exposure to the weather, were hollowed out and propped up by walls. They resembled the burrows of animals or the huts of Laplanders, and, though seldom receiving light, except from the door and chimney, contained several apartments, and were occupied by whole families of Troglodytes. Of late years, however, proper habitations have been erected for the lime-burners at the adjoining village of Burbage.

Excursions.—(1.) An interesting walk may be taken to **Chee Tor**, 5 m. E., passing by Fairfield to **Wormhill**, where is a curious old house of the Bagshaws. A little

[*Derby, &c.*]

beyond Wormhill Oh., opposite the Hall, a steep and narrow path leads into the depths of the dale, at a spot where two copious springs of water issue from beneath the rocks and rush down to join the Wye. Their previous course is curious; they are engulfed in the earth at Water Swallows, near Fairfield, and pursue a subterranean course for 3 m., until they emerge at this spot. Chee Tor is a tall bare rock of limestone, rising out of the wooded valley to a height it is said of 300 ft., nearly insulated by the river, which makes an almost circular sweep round its base, while the rocks on the opposite side are bent into the form of a crescent or amphitheatre, concave and partly overhanging their base. The rly., though close at hand, fortunately passes through a short tunnel, and except at one small spot is entirely concealed from view. Opposite the Tor are several picturesque dales, with Topley Pike in the distance. Miller's Dale (Stat.), for the return to Buxton, is about 2 m. E.

(2.) A somewhat longer excursion may be made on the W. side of Buxton, by passing through **Burbage** (1 m.), where is a modern Norm. Ch., and crossing the branch that connects the works of the Buxton Lime Company with the High Peak Rly.; these are of vast extent, employing several hundred men. At 2½ m. from Buxton the foot of **Axe Edge** is reached, it is one of the highest hills in Derbyshire, 1750 ft. above the sea, and still in its primitive condition of moss, heather, and bilberry, affording a good cover for grouse. Indeed, it is the highest, next to the Kinderscout range, between Castleton and Glossop. Here the road divides, that to the rt. going into Cheshire, and that to the l. to the Staffordshire moorlands (Rte. 35). The pedestrian should take the first, and proceed as far as

E

a little inn, called the Cat and Fiddle (5 m. from Buxton). The view from the summit of Axe Edge embraces a large extent of the high table-lands of Derbyshire, Staffordshire, and Cheshire. Four rivers have their fountain-head here, viz., the Dove and the Wye flowing eastward, and the Dane and Goyt towards the Irish Sea. The return to Buxton may be made by the Goyt Valley, leaving the Cat and Fiddle by the old Roman road, the first turning on the left enters the valley, a noted drive, which rivals on a small scale the beauty of a Swiss pass. This valley or clough ends at Goyt's bridge, whence either by walking over Goyt's Moss, or by the carriage-road which joins the Manchester Road at Long Hill, Buxton may be reached. The distance is about 6 m. A longer drive back may be made by Dale Head, whence a beautiful view of the Tors at the head of Beresford Dale is obtained. Thence to Staddon Moor, where some ancient earthworks may be noticed, and then into Buxton by the Duke's Drive. The extreme distance will be 12 m.; but the walk over the summit of Axe Edge, which is essential to the attainment of the best views, is rather rough.

(3.) An excursion to **Whaley Bridge** (6 m.), by the coach road to Stockport, leads through some fine scenery. The road rises for about 2 m. beyond Buxton, and then descends for nearly 5 m.; it is well selected and carried round the shoulder of **Comb's Moss**, through Windy Gap; at its highest point it is at least 1700 ft. above the sea. On the N.W. spur of the hill is a well-preserved Roman camp. The village of **Fernilee** presents nothing remarkable, but close adjoining is **Errwood Hall** (Mrs. Grimshawe), a modern Italian mansion, beautifully situated at the junction of two wooded dales. Above it are bold moors, but the ground to the E. is an uninteresting open district of pasture-land, destitute of trees, and intersected by stone walls. The road runs near the High Peak Rly., and passes on E. the stationary engine-house used for drawing waggons up the summit incline. Soon after, the pretty village of **Taxal** (in Cheshire) is reached, and next **Whaley Bridge**, a much more pleasant spot than the majority of factory districts. (See *Handbook for Cheshire.*) The rly. furnishes a ready means of return to Buxton, or of proceeding to Stockport or Manchester.

(4.) Several places in the vicinity of stations may yet be more agreeably visited by road. Among them are, the Peak Forest, 5 m.; Tideswell, 7 m.; Lyme Hall, 13 m.; and Chatsworth and Haddon Hall, 14 m. Eyam and Castleton are each about 12 m. from Buxton, and an omnibus runs daily to Castleton in the summer.

Leaving Buxton, the London & North-Western Rly. runs at the foot of Comb's Moss through a bleak country, the chief industry of which appears to be lime-burning, to

3 m. **Dove Holes** (Stat.). The place, which is a hamlet of Wormhill, derives its name from some of the swallow-holes so prevalent in this district, where brooks suddenly disappear to run a subterranean course. Here the line is crossed by the Midland Rly. to Manchester, in a tunnel and deep cutting.
About 1½ m. N.E., near Barmoor Clough, a little off the Castleton road, is the "*ebbing and flowing well*," used to be considered one of "the wonders of Derbyshire," though its action was readily accounted for, on the principle of the syphon. "It is," says Adams, "an intermittent spring, the frequency of its action

Route 7.—*Chapel-en-le-Frith—Roosdych.*

depending on the quantity of rain which falls, so that in dry weather the stranger may wait in vain for the manifestation of this phenomenon, but in very wet seasons it will sometimes ebb and flow twice in an hour. The action when it first commences is scarcely perceivable, but before the expiration of a minute the water issues with considerable force from 9 small apertures on the S. and W. sides. It continues to flow about 5 minutes, and in this space of time is supposed to throw out about 120 hogsheads of water. The greatest part of it runs off under the road, and part lapses back again, and the well speedily resumes its original quiet appearance." Since the rly. was constructed, however, this action has ceased, and the well is now only a drinking pond for cattle.

6 m. ⚡ **Chapel-en-le-Frith** (Stat.; also a stat. on the Midland Rly., ¾ m. N.) consists mainly of a single straight street; the *Ch.*, which is dedicated to St. Thomas à Becket, is a very plain structure. Cotton and paper mills, and print works, appear in the low grounds, evidencing approach to the manufacturing districts. All around are high hills, as Chinley Churn (for cairn, one existing on its summit), 1493 ft., and Dympus, 1633 ft. **Dympus** is the best worth ascending, as the scenery on the N. side is broken and bold, looking down on the head of Edale and the escarpment of Kinderscout. **Hayfield** is 5 m. distant, whence Kinderscout top may be reached by a 4 m. walk (Rte. 9).

[The Midland Rly. from here to Manchester keeps to the N. and E. of the London and North-Western Rly., and has four stats. in the course of its route before it quits the county. These are **Chinley** (3 m. from Chapel-en-le-Frith), **Bugsworth** (4 m.), **New Mills** (8 m.), and **Strines** (9½ m.). Chinley Churn at first

separates the two lines, and afterwards they traverse the opposite sides of the valley of the Goyt. At Mellor (2 m. E. of Marple Stat.) the Ch., has a Norm. font curiously carved and an old pulpit cut out of the solid oak. For the remainder of the route, see *Handbook for Cheshire and Lancashire*. A branch of the Midland Rly. from Chinley will shortly be opened through the Peak District, joining the Chesterfield and Sheffield line at Dore, having Stats. at Edale, Hope, Hathersage, and Grindleford.]

Soon after leaving Chapel-en-le-Frith en route for Stockport, the London and North-Western Rly. passes on N. a large reservoir supplied by streams from Comb's Moss. At the farther end, close to the rly., is the hamlet of **Tunstead**, where Brindley, the engineer, was born (1716), and where the skull of " Dicky of Tunstead " is religiously kept, and has a reputation of possessing extraordinary and ghostly powers. Above the reservoir, under Eccles Pike (1225 ft.), is **Bradshaw Hall**, once the seat of the Bradshaw family, who were seated here soon after the Conquest. John Bradshaw, who sat as President of the High Court of Justice, was either brother or cousin of the builder of the Hall, Francis Bradshaw, whose name, arms, and the date 1620, appear on the gateways. It is now occupied as a farmhouse. On one of the landings in the interior is the following inscription:—

"Love God and not gould.
He that loves not mercy,
Of mercy shall miss;
But he shall have mercy
That merciful is."

9 m. On S. is the **Roosdych**, which it is presumed served the purpose of a racecourse. " It is an artificially formed valley, averaging in width 40 paces, and 1300 paces in length. It is in a great measure cut out of

E 2

Route 8.—Chapel-en-le-Frith to Bakewell.

the side of a hill, to a depth of from 10 to 30 feet, but, where it is most so, it is enclosed on both sides with banks of earth."

The Rly. crosses the Goyt shortly after, and enters Cheshire, to

9½ m. **Whaley Bridge**. The remainder of the route to **Manchester** (14½ m.) will be found fully described in the *Handbook for Cheshire and Lancashire*.

ROUTE 8.

CHAPEL-EN-LE-FRITH TO BAKEWELL, BY CASTLETON, HOPE, HATHERSAGE, AND EYAM [THE PEAK].

BY ROAD. 23 m.

There are two roads from Chapel-en-le-Frith to Castleton. The more northerly, over Rushup Edge, is rather the shorter, but presents no feature of interest; the one by Barmoor Clough and Sparrow Pit is to be preferred. The Midland Rly. will shortly open a line through the Peak District from Chinley Stat. (3 m. from Chapel-en-le-Frith on the main line to Manchester) to Dore Stat. (on the line to Sheffield), with Stats. at Edale, Hope, Hathersage, and Grindleford. Owing to the nature of the ground the work of the construction is very heavy. There will be a tunnel 3½ m. long under Totley Moor, and another of 2½ m. under the high ground of the Peak.

[From Sparrow Pit is a road to Tideswell (6 m. S.E.) (Rte. 6), passing through the small village of **Peak Forest**, the little chapel of which was once a place of much resort for clandestine marriages. Peak Forest (Stat.) on the Midland Rly. is 3 m. S.W.]

The way to Castleton lies over pleasant breezy moors, varied only by an occasional clump of trees, a solitary farmhouse, or a wooden gin proclaiming the presence of a lead-mine.

At **Perryfoot**, 3½ m., is one of the water-swallows so characteristic of this part of Derbyshire. The interest, however, is much increased by the fact that the stream, which here disappears, has an underground course as far as the Peak Cavern at Castleton, where it again emerges. A little beyond Perryfoot the tourist should turn off to the rt. and ascend Eldon Hill, on the furthest side of which, overlooking Peak Forest, is the famous **Eldon Hole**, concerning which more absurdities have been written than about any other cave in the kingdom. It is simply a very deep perpendicular cave, "wonderful for nothing but the vast bigness, steepness, and depth of it. But that winds have their vent here is a mistake in those that have writ so; nor are those verses of Necham's, concerning the miracles of England, applicable to it:—

" 'Est specus Æoliis ventis obnoxia semper
Impetus e gemino maximus ore venit.
Cogitur injectum velamen adire supernas
Partes, descensum impedit aura potens.'"

Sir Aston Cockayne, of Ashbourne, also wrote as follows in 1658:—

"Here on an hill's side steep
Is Elden Hole, so depe,
That no man living knowes
How far it hollow goes."

At 4½ m., near Surlslow, a foot road on rt. leads to the Hazard Mine, and on to Castleton, through Cave Dale (*post*).

The road, which has been gradually rising, now zigzags down the side of Mam Tor (the Mother Hill), 1709 ft. high, and on many accounts perhaps the most interesting hill in the Peak. The tourist should pause to admire the view of the beautiful and fertile Vale of Hope, which now opens below him, framed in a setting of hills, among which may be named, beside Mam Tor, Lose Hill, and Win Hill, the range that separates the Valley of Hope from that of Edale (see *post*).

Drawing near to Castleton, the Vale of the Winnats or Windgates, once the only coach road from Buxton, is entered. It is a magnificent pass, about ½ a mile in length, the mountain limestone cliffs rising in fantastic forms to the height of about 400 ft. on either side. Very few are the days in the year in which there is not a piercing wind through the defile, which has thus obtained its name. The view of Castleton and the vale is wondrously pretty. At the bottom of the pass, which has a melancholy reputation for the foul murder of a couple on their wedding tour, is a cottage, the entrance to the Speedwell Mine (*post*).

6½ m. ☿ **Castleton**, a village in the centre of the Peak district, and the head-quarters of all that is curious in mine and cavern. It is situated in a *cul de sac*, opening into the Valley of Hope, the sides of which are formed of more or less precipitous hills, rising in the S. directly from the village in magnificent cliffs, while, on the W. and N., the more distant escarpments of Mam Tor, Bach Tor, and Lose Hill contribute to form the amphitheatre. Two or three small streams, such as the Odin Sitch and the Peak's Hole Water, issuing from the caves and mines of those names, run down the valley to join the Noe at Hope. Castleton has from the earliest times enjoyed a celebrity from its extensive and beautiful caves, which have been the foundation for many an absurd stretch of imagination, commencing with "Gervasius Tilburiensis, who, either out of downright ignorance or a lying humour, tells us a shepherd saw, in the Peak cavern, a spacious country, with small rivers running here and there in it, with vast pools of standing water."

Local antiquities have here a more persistent habitation than is generally found in Derbyshire; Castleton abounding with associations of the Peveril family, whose memory has been for ever embodied by Sir Walter Scott, although the existence of any one bearing that name in the 17th centy. is a pure fiction of the novelist.

The *Church*, which belonged to the Abbey of Vale Royal in Cheshire, has been much modernised. It is a plain building of mixed styles, with tower at the W. end, surmounted by pinnacles. Internally the visitor should notice a beautiful Norman chancel arch with billet-moulding, an old octagonal font, a modern E. window of stained glass in memory of a late vicar, and some very interesting carved oak pews of the 17th centy. There is a tablet to Mawe, the mineralogist, and a monument to an attorney (Micah Hall, d. 1804), with the churlish epitaph—

"Quid eram, nescitis,
Quid sum, nescitis,
Ubi abii, nescitis.
Vale."

The library in the vestry, a legacy from a former vicar to the parish, contains a black-letter Bible, date 1539, and a "Breeches Bible." Several old customs linger yet in Castleton, such as ringing the curfew from the 29th Sept. to Shrove Tuesday, and the placing of a garland on one of the pinnacles of the tower by the ringers on the 29th of May, and there leaving it till the following year.

The **Peak Castle** crowns the summit of the cliffs directly to the S. of the village. It was built by

William Peveril, to whom the Conqueror granted large estates in Derbyshire, "upon the principles on which an eagle selects her eyrie, and in such a fashion as if he had intended it, as an Irishman said of the Martello towers, for the sole purpose of puzzling posterity." But little is left of it save the keep, which was at the S.W. angle of the enclosure, overlooking the deep cleft above the Peak cavern, being, of course, perfectly inaccessible on this side. Two towers, now nearly destroyed, flanked the E. and W. angles, and were probably erected to command the N. passage up to the castle, which consists of a series of zigzags. The keep is a plain triangular tower, the walls of which are about 8 ft. in thickness. The ashlar work of a portion of the walls is said to have been taken away to repair the Ch. at Castleton. The castle enclosure was surrounded by a curtain wall, now dilapidated. The entrance-gate was on the E. side. The interior of the keep was occupied by 2 apartments, the lower one of which was reached by flights of steps from the outside, and the upper (according to King) by a platform attached to the outer wall. This latter contains a canopied recess. The erection of "the Castel of Peke" may be ascribed to the Norman age, though it is not impossible, from its extraordinary advantages of position, that a fortress of some sort occupied the ground previously. Although built and held for some time by the descendants of Peveril, the castle afterwards reverted to Henry II. The barons obtained possession in the reign of John, but had soon to yield it to Ferrers, Earl of Derby, who took it by assault. In the time of Edward III. it became a part of the Duchy of Lancaster. The Peverils are said by tradition to have lived in great style here, and to have held a splendid tournament in the castle-yard; but the circumscribed area, and the general want of accommodation in the buildings, forbid the notion that it was anything but a temporary residence or a convenient prison. "In the time of Henry IV. Godfrey Rowland, a poor and simple squire of the county of Derby, petitioned the Parliament against the injuries that had been inflicted on him by Thomas Wandesby, Chivaler (see Bakewell, Rte. 6) and others, who came and besieged his house at Mickel-Longsdon, and, having pillaged the same, carried him off to the Castle of the High Peak, where they kept him six days without meat or drink, and then, cutting off his right hand, sent him adrift."

The botanist will find a harvest of ferns on the surrounding rocks, the maidenhair, spleenwort, and cystopteris being all tolerably plentiful on the grassy hills over the Speedwell and other mines; while Cave Dale produces the rare green spleenwort, not yet quite extirpated by the traders in ferns, and is also rich in mosses, including the *Bryum dendroides*.

The caverns and mines at Castleton and its immediate neighbourhood consist of—1, the Peak Cavern; 2, Speedwell Level; 3, Blue John Mine; 4, Odin Mine; and, 5, Bradwell Cavern. The payments demanded for visiting most of these are extortionate, and ought to be resisted.

(1.) The largest and most important is the **Peak or Devil's Cavern**, the entrance to which is about 100 yds. from the village, and immediately under the precipice on which is the Peak Castle. From it issues a clear running stream, which has its source at Perryfoot (*ante*), and, after a long subterranean course, is found again in the Peak Cavern, many parts of which, by the way, are inaccessible after heavy rains. The entrance to the cave is in itself one of the most striking scenes. The large shelving and over-arched platform leading into the interior recesses has been used from time immemorial, as the workshop of the twine and rope spinning, which is one of the industries of the village. As seen when emerging from the inner cave, the gaunt and weird-looking machinery, the figures flitting to and fro, combined with the reverberation of their songs and exclamations, and the peculiar ghastliness of the light, have a grotesqueness and wildness peculiarly striking, although some may prefer undisturbed solitude. As the visitor cannot see the cave without the services of the guide, it will be sufficient to point out its leading features. Soon after passing through the door at the extreme end of the entrance hall, he arrives at the First Water, across which he was formerly obliged to be ferried in a little boat under a very low arch, so as to reach the great cavern. This has, however, been rendered unnecessary by blasting, and the formation of a path by the side of the river. The Great Hall is said to be 120 ft. in height, and is traversed by a pathway of steps leading to the Second Water. At the farther end of this is a series of detached rocks, the trickling of water down which has procured for it the name of Roger Rain's House. Next comes the chancel, marked by a gallery, accessible by a rough path. Here a number of lighted candles are prepared, which well show off the dimensions and general contour of this part of the cavern; and if due notice be given, a choir of singers may be stationed to add to the effect. The Devil's Cellar and the Halfway House are successively reached; and a passage thence, containing some natural groined arches, leads to the Great Tom of Lincoln or the Victoria Cavern, where a light is run up by a pulley to show the immense height and hollow of the dome. From this point the vault gradually lowers until there is only sufficient space for the stream to flow; the total length of the cave is estimated at 2300 ft. The fee is 2s. for a single person, but proportionately less for a party.

(2.) The **Speedwell Cavern** is about ½ m. from Castleton on the old Buxton road, close to the entrance of the Winnats. It is reached by what is in reality a disused mine, commenced about a century ago by some Staffordshire adventurers, who, after vainly working it for 11 years, acknowledged the uselessness of proceeding farther. The visitor descends by a flight of over 100 steps to the level or canal, along which he is taken in a boat propelled by means of pegs in the rock. This passage of 750 yds. was blasted through the solid rock, which is of great hardness, the quantity of powder used is said to have been above 50,000 lbs. The level then opens into the Great Hall, a natural cavern, the size of which is such as to make the roof and bottom invisible to the eye; indeed, rockets have been sent up to the height of 450 ft. without reaching the former. The level is carried by an arch across this chasm; but the boat is left here, and a platform ascended, from which the scene can be viewed at leisure. Water is reached at a depth of 90 ft.; and from the fact of an amazing quantity of rubbish having been apparently swallowed up, it is popularly considered to be unfathomable. The probability is, that the débris was carried away as soon as deposited by the running stream. The usual effects of blue lights and powder blastings are displayed "for a consideration."

(3.) The **Blue John Mine** is situated on the side of the Tray cliff, a little to the l. of the turnpike-road to Buxton. The mine is still worked, but the yield is decreasing every year. In this cave, which runs for about 3 m., and doubtless communicates with the rest of the system of caverns, the principal attractions are the masses of stalactite, which are to be seen in great perfection. Notice particularly the one called the Organ, near the entrance. The principal chambers here are Lord Mulgrave's Dining-room, in which that nobleman (who laboured hard to explore the mine, passing 3 days in it at one time) entertained the miners; the Variegated Cavern; and the Crystalized Cavern, the beauties of which are always shown by additional lights. Blue John or Derbyshire spar is fluoride of calcium; the blue colouring matter which distinguishes it and makes it in such request for vases and ornamental art, being oxide of manganese. The largest vase ever made of it is to be seen at Chatsworth. "Tray cliff is the only locality where Blue John is met with. It lies in 'pipe-veins,' having the same inclination as the rocks which the veins traverse. One of these veins lies in a sort of clayey stratum, and another seems to be imbedded in the nodule state in a mass of indurated débris. Besides these the whole of the limestone masses are fractured and cracked; and in addition to the pipes, the sides of the crusting are lined with beautiful sky-blue cubes of fluor and rhombic crystals of calcite."—*Taylor*. Small portions, however, of Blue John (not large enough to be worked) are found in other parts of the county.

The geologist will find in Tray cliff (lower beds) numbers of *Phillipsia*.

(4.) The **Odin Mine** is a little farther on the rt. of the same road, at the foot of Mam Tor. It is believed that lead was worked here during the Roman era, and pigs of this material, found in Derbyshire, are to be seen in the British Museum inscribed with the names of the Emperors Domitian and Hadrian. Horizontal galleries have been driven for about a mile into this mine, the lower one being for the purpose of draining it; but after inspecting the foregoing caverns it is scarcely worth exploration. It produces elastic bitumen.

(5.) **Bagshaw's Cave**, at Bradwell, lies 2 m. S.E. of Castleton, to the rt. of the road to Hope, and on the edge of Abney Moor. This is worth a visit on account of its stalactites.

Cave Dale is a remarkable cleft in the rocks to the E. of Peak Castle, something like the Winnats on a small scale. From it one of the best views of the castle is obtained. A road leads up it to the Hazard Mine, and across the moor, to join the Buxton road.

The geologist should not fail to visit **Mam Tor**. On the N. side it is easy of ascent, grassy, smiling, and tempting; whilst towards the Castleton valley it presents a precipitous escarpment of coal-measure shale and sandstone, containing much oxide of iron. Atmospheric effects, particularly after frost and rain, cause constant disintegration of the strata, the falling of which has given it the name of the Shivering Mountain. The summit is occupied by the remains of an early intrenchment. The geologist will find *Goniatites expansus* among the shales at the base, together with *Aviculopecten* and *posidonia*. The view from Mam Tor is very charming, particularly looking E. towards Hope; and on the N., over Edale, to Kinderscout. If the tourist has time, he should descend into the valley opposite Edale Chapel, and

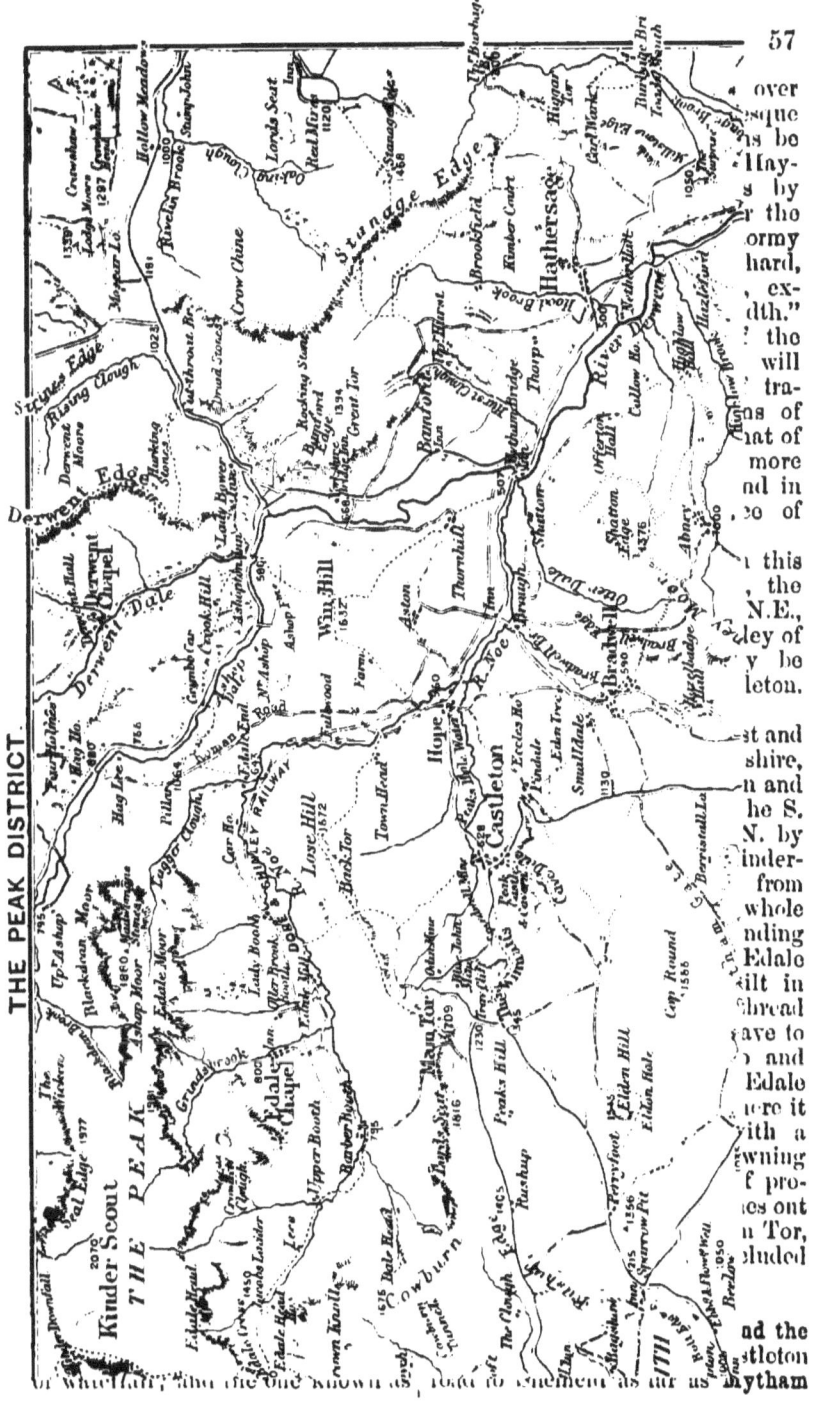

follow it down between Lose and Win Hills (properly Laws and Whin Hills) to Hope; about 6 m. If on his road northward, he should proceed up the valley, and, crossing the neck at Edale Cross, descend to Hayfield (Rte. 9).

THE PEAK.

In the country north of Castleton are situated the highest and most mountainous ridges of the county, the deepest valleys, and the wildest moorlands. It is a tract entirely of gritstone, belonging to the lower series of the carboniferous formation. Of limestone, which has so exclusive a predominance south of Castleton, there is absolutely none, and this difference of geological character produces a marked difference in the scenery. Instead of green grass, the hills are covered with purple heather. Instead of white rocks forming the basement of sloping uplands, the rocks are here quite black, and crown the summit of ridges that descend with a concave sweep into the valleys. The great block of mountain called in the Ordnance Map "the Peak," is really an extensive plateau comprising the several summits of Kinderscout, the Edge, Fairbrook Naze, Ashop Moor, Seal Edge, Madwoman's Stones, Edale Moor, &c. **Kinderscout**, 1981 ft., is the highest and most important of them all, and gives its name to the whole block. From the escarped nature of its sides, numerous romantic little ravines, or "cloughs," as they are locally called, are to be found, particularly on the S., overlooking Edale, and on the W., over Hayfield. It is the more picturesque because still in a condition of primitive moorland. Some of its rocky glens, such as Fairbrook Naze, are more like Scotland than a midland county.

Each "clough" has its brooklet, or waterfall; and the one known as Kinder Downfall, precipitated over Kinderscout, is a really picturesque fall, and should by all means be made a special excursion from Hayfield. "The water descends by leaps, from ledge to ledge, for the space of 400 or 500 ft.; and in stormy weather, when the wind blows hard, the water, blown into spray, extends a quarter of a mile in width." Following up the stream of the Kinder Water, the geologist will meet with a thick deposit of travertine, containing impressions of leaves, mosses, &c., similar to that of Matlock. This deposit is the more remarkable from its being found in millstone grit, a circumstance of some rarity.

"The great" valleys lie in this district; Edale to the N.W., the valley of the Derwent to the N.E., and between the two the valley of the Ashop. All these may be visited in a carriage from Castleton.

(1.) **Edale**, one of the loveliest and most pastoral valleys of Derbyshire, attractive from its very isolation and peacefulness, is guarded on the S. by the Mam Tor, and on the N. by the whole extent of the Kinderscout. This vale is entered from Hope, and is traversed in its whole length by the Noe, a little winding stream. To the N.E. is Edale Chapel, a small edifice rebuilt in 1810, and farther on, a lace-thread mill, the employés of which have to cross the mountain daily to and from their work. The head of Edale is its most picturesque part; here it becomes a narrow gorge, with a tumbling stream, and rocks crowning the slope, but the carriage (if provided with a good horse) comes out by a steep cart road over Mam Tor, whence a lovely view of this secluded valley is obtained.

(2.) **Valley of the Ashop and the Woodlands.** — Take the Castleton road to Sheffield as far as **Mytham**

Bridge, 4 m., then turn off to **Bamford** (where is a cotton mill, and a church built by *Butterfield*), and at ⚯**Ashopton** (7 m.) the old coach-road from Sheffield to Glossop and Manchester is joined. Here is the junction of the Derwent with the Lady Bower Brook and the Ashop, which takes its rise in the northern recesses of Kinderscout. Turning westward, for the first 2 m. the scenery has little interest; then comes the **Woodlands**, a woody glen not surpassed in picturesqueness by any in the county. After passing a small Wesleyan chapel on rt. the valley changes in character—it becomes a defile, and the mountain ranges are cleft by deep gorges and advance in precipitous promontories. All the slopes, which are not bare rocks, are covered with heather and abound in grouse. At 6½ m. from Ashopton is the **Snake Inn**, small, but very comfortable, and much resorted to by shooting parties. The view up the glen shortly before reaching the Snake is fine. From here the ascent of Kinderscout is best made. The distance is 3 m. to the top. To have a good view of the mountain the tourist should proceed about ½ m. beyond the inn. The manufacturing town of Glossop lies 6 m. W. (Rte. 9); and the whole distance from Castleton is 14 m.

(3.) The valley of the **Derwent** may be visited in conjunction with that of the Ashop. From the Inn at Ashopton, a road running N. on the E. bank of the Derwent leads to the pretty village of Derwent Chapel (1¼ m.), near which is the fine old **Hall**, formerly the seat of the Newdigates, but now belongs to the Duke of Norfolk, and has been greatly enlarged and furnished in Gothic fashion as a shooting lodge. It contains a fine collection of old oak. Permission to view the interior may be obtained from the office of the Duke's agent, Corn Exchange, Sheffield. A chapel has been added.

From Derwent Hall a footpath, commanding extensive views, leads over the old stone bridge, and crosses the hills joining the main road in the Woodlands valley near Rowlee Farm (about 1¼ m.).

The Derwent—(*Dwr-gwent*, fair water)—

"Darren, whose fount and fall are both in Derbyshire"—

from its source in Featherbed Moor, about 3 m. from Woodhead Stat. on the Manchester, Sheffield, and Lincolnshire Rly., presents many a picturesque reach, with woods, and coppices feathering down to the water's edge, and the bare moors of the Yorkshire plateau rising up more or less abruptly. From its source to Mytham Bridge the distance is some 13 m. It afterwards passes by Chatsworth, Rowsley (where it is joined by the Wye), Matlock, and Duffield, and falls into the Trent below Derby. Ashopton is a place of great resort for Sheffield excursionists, and wagonettes run between the two places daily in summer. The trip is a pleasant one (11 m.), giving good views of the Hallam moors and of the valley of the Rivelin, in which are large reservoirs for the water supply of Sheffield. Comfortable quarters may be had at the Ashopton Inn, whence to explore the neighbouring scenery, and to visit those singular rock formations known as "The Cakes of Bread," "The Saltcellar," overlooking the valley from Derwent Edge, and the rock-basins on Stanage Edge, close to the cave called "Robin Hood's."

Resuming the direct route from Castleton, the tourist enters at **8 m.** the village of **Hope**, which gives its name to a beautiful vale extending 6 m. from E. to W. and about 1 m. in breadth. The Perp.

Ch. has an E. E. tower at the W. end, surmounted by an octagonal broach spire. A parapet runs round the clerestory, aisles, and choir. The porch has a chamber in the upper part, together with a canopied niche. The gurgoyles are peculiar. In the vicarage garden is the stem of a Saxon cross with interlaced carving. The Balguys, a family of old standing, possessed large estates at Hope in the 17th centy. The parish is of large extent, some 40,000 acres, one-half of which is occupied by the tract called Hope Woodlands.

At 9 m., in the angle formed by the junction of the Bradwell Brook with the Noe, at **Brough**, is a rectangular camp, identified as the Roman station Navio, where at different times remains, such as coins, tiles, &c., have been excavated. The Batham road, which runs over Tideswell Moor to Buxton, terminates here; while another road runs in a north-westerly direction to Glossop, where was the Roman station of Meladra.

At 10½ m. **Mytham Bridge**, the Noe joins the Derwent, which flows in from the N.

At 12 m. on an eminence overlooking the valley of the Derwent, both W. and S., is the charmingly picturesque village of ♂ **Hathersage**, at the foot of the southern slopes of Bamford and Stanage Edges. Its principal feature is its Dec. *Ch.*, which has been well restored by *Butterfield*. It consists of nave, chancel, and side-aisles, with clerestory, together with a square tower of 3 stages, surmounted by an octagonal spire at the W. end. The principal attraction in the interior is the stained glass. Some of the windows were presented by the villagers, and the western one by the family of Eyre, once lords of the manor, whose old residence and decayed *Chapel* still remains at North Lees, about 1½ m. N. of Hathersage, up the valley of the Hood brook.

The altar-tomb of Robert Eyre (d. 1459), who fought at Agincourt, and his wife (Joan Padley) and 14 children is in the chancel, and there are other Eyre monuments and *brasses* both earlier and later. The old practice of hanging funeral garlands up in the Ch. was followed here until a comparatively recent date. There is a great factory in the village for needles, pins, hooks, and wire. At a short distance from this factory, a square block of stone projects from the wall, which bears the name of the Gospel-stone, "from having been, in former times, occupied by the clergymen, who stood upon it on three different days in Rogation week to pray for an abundant supply of the fruits of the earth."—*Dr. Hall.*

Hathersage, according to local traditions, was the residence and burial-place of Little John, the leal companion and trusty friend of Robin Hood. The house has been taken down, but the grave remains, marked by two stones, 13 ft. 4 in. asunder, near the Ch. porch. The first time that Little John is heard of is at the battle of Evesham, in 1265, where, say some, he shared in the defeat of the forces under Montfort, and, being outlawed, straightway, retired into the forests of Notts and Derbyshire with Robin and his merry men, in company with whom he was virtual master of the country to the N. of the Trent, and levied black mail with impunity on wealthy priors and merchants journeying to York. In addition to the popular belief that he was buried at Hathersage, the grave is said to have been opened within the last hundred years by Capt. Shuttleworth, who exhumed a gigantic thigh bone, 32 inches long. It was replaced, but again dug out, and carried away, together with Little John's green cap that hung up in the church, by some Yorkshire antiquaries.

The early remains in the neighbourhood of Hathersage are interesting, and have been explored by Sir Gardner Wilkinson. Near the Ch. is a camp, said to be Danish, but more likely British; and on Hathersage Moor, which rises to the E. of the village, there is a British fortification, known as **Carl's Wark**, "in which the eastern extremity, having on three sides a precipitous cliff, was divided from the rest of the hill by a strong vallum, extending from one side to the other, and closing the approach on the west side."— *G. W.* The vallum, about 17 ft. thick, and 150 ft. in length, has an outer facing of masonry, and a gateway on the south side. Circles and tumuli are found on most of the adjoining moors, as on Eyam Moor, to the S., and Offerton Moor, between Hathersage and Tideswell. On **Higgar Tor**, E., some very remarkable stones, of monstrous size, are piled up, but by what agency is doubtful; and there is a Rocking Stone on Booth's Edge, a little to the rt. of the road leading to Sheffield. The view from Hu-gaer or Higgar is very extensive, embracing to the N. and W. the long plateau of Kinderscout, Lose and Win Hills, Mam Tor, Tray cliff, and the Hallamshire moors; whilst to the S. are the wooded valleys of the Derwent and its tributary streams, extending as far as Chatsworth and Rowsley, beyond which, in the distance, Cromford Hill closes the view.

[From Hathersage there is a choice of roads to Sheffield, all traversing a beautiful moorland district, but varying in length from 11 to 15 m.:—1. Up the **Ridgeway** (an old Roman road to Stanage Edge), on the other side of which is Lord's Seat and the Reservoir of Redmires, a favourite excursion with Sheffield Sunday holiday-makers. 2. The road by **Higgar Tor**, which on the summit of the moors crosses the heads of the Burbage Brooks, and runs into Sheffield through Ecclesall Bierlow. 3. Over **Booth's Edge**, passing Longshaw Lodge, a shooting-box of the Duke of Rutland, and joining the road from Grindleford Bridge at Fox House Inn. This road enters Yorkshire at Whirlow Bridge, on the little river Sheaf. Here a détour of about 1 m. should be made eastward to visit the remains of Beauchief Abbey (Rte. 4). Hence it is 4 m. to Sheffield (see *Handbook for Yorkshire*).

A singular feature of these moors is in connection with the Hallamshire hunt, which scours (on foot) the whole of this wild country on the confines of Derbyshire and Yorkshire. The hounds are kept principally in the neighbourhood of Hallam, and billeted on the residents of the different villages, whose love for the chase has been proverbial ever since the days of Robin Hood. This practice, however, is not nearly so general as formerly.]

Leaving Hathersage, and following the course of the Derwent—from the bridge across it there is a charming landscape both up and down the river—and passing on E. the woods of Padley, one of the estates of the Eyres, Grindleford Bridge (14½ m.) is reached, and diverging considerably to the W., at 15 m. the road leads to the village of Eyam. There is another, and somewhat shorter road over Eyam Moor, on which will be noticed a *circle* of ten stones, all that remain of the original sixteen; it is of the class of monuments which Sir Gardner Wilkinson calls "encircled cairns." The way is by Highlow Brook (on the banks of which is the old Hall of Highlow) over the moor, crossing the road to the lofty hill called Sir William, and descending

Route 8.—*Eyam.*

into Eyam through a very picturesque dell.

§ **Eyam** (pronounced Eem) is enshrined in the memory of all, by the frightful visitation to which it was exposed, and the heroic examples of self-sacrifice there exhibited. The village was attacked by the plague in 1665 so virulently that 267 out of the 350 inhabitants fell victims to it. To limit as much as possible the spread of the pestilence in the district, the Rev. Wm. Mompesson, the rector, with the assistance of the Earl of Devonshire, established a cordon round the village, beyond which no one was allowed to pass from the world without; and so great was the respect and love with which he was regarded, that he prevailed upon his parishioners to voluntarily restrict themselves within the boundary. Mr. Mompesson had not resided above a year at Eyam when the plague broke out, and from a letter, which has been preserved, it seems he was about to relinquish the living, but he resolved not to abandon his people. The Earl supplied them with provisions; and the few other articles that they needed, being deposited just without the boundary, were paid for with money placed in troughs of running water, which are common in the district. One of these on the way to Sir William hill is still known as Mompesson's well. For more than a year did the rector and his wife (Catherine, daughter of Ralph Carr, of Cocker, co. Durham), after sending away their children, devote themselves entirely to their flock; and they were cordially assisted by the Rev. Thos. Stanley, the former rector, who had been ejected by the Act of Uniformity, but still resided in the village. A monument has recently been erected to his memory. Unfortunately, in August, 1666, the pestilence burst out more fiercely than ever, carrying off Mrs. Mompesson and the greater part of the surviving villagers. On the hillside, at some distance from the Ch., are many graves, one of which in particular, called the Riley stones, commemorates the resting-place of one family of seven of the name of Hancock, all of whom died in one week. To reduce the danger of infection, Mr. Mompesson closed the Ch., and held daily service in a natural opening in the rocks in the adjoining ravine of Cucklet Delph. The spot is still called *Cucklet Church*, and the rock whence he addressed his people, seated far apart on the grass, is known as the Pulpit Rock:—

"Here a rude arch, not form'd by mortal hands,
Th' unconsecrated church of Cucklet stands;
To this sequester'd spot, where all might seem
The sweet creation of a poet's dream,
Mompesson saw his suffering flock repair,
Daily as toll'd the sabbath bell for prayer,
When through th' afflicted village, wild with dread,
And lost to hope, the plague contagion spread:
Here from a rocky arch, with foliage hung,
Divinest precepts issue from his tongue;
To all, his kindly aid the priest affords,
They feel his love, and live upon his words." *Rhodes.*

In 1669 Mr. Mompesson was presented to the living at Eakring, near Southwell, but the people for a while refused to receive him, lest he should still have the plague about him, and he resided in a hut built for him in Rufford Park until their fears abated. He became a prebend of Southwell, but retained his living of Eakring, and died there March 7, 1709, aged 70.

The Ch. of Eyam has been added to at various times. It consists of nave, chancel, and aisles, with a tower rising from the west end. The bells, on which are inscribed, " Jesvs bee our spede," and " God save His Church," were the gift of Madame Stafford, the builder of the tower, 1619. There is a curious sundial over the S. chancel doorway. In the ch.-yard are some extraordinary epitaphs. Notice also the tomb of Mrs. Mompesson, and a fine Runic Cross of the 9th or 10th centy., said to have been found on an adjoining moor. It is curiously carved with interlacings. In the centre is a representation of the Virgin and Child, whilst on the arms of the cross are angels blowing trumpets. It owes its preservation chiefly to John Howard, the philanthropist, who, in 1788, found it lying neglected in the ch.-yard, and caused it to be erected in its present position. It was originally 10 ft. high, but 2 ft. of the shaft has been broken off. Above the village are Eyam Hall (Misses Wright) and a portion of the old mansion of the Staffords, who for several generations were proprietors of the district. Eyam has been the residence of several literary characters, as Miss Seward, the Rev. Peter Cunningham, and John Furness, a Derbyshire poet of considerable celebrity, author of the 'Rag Bag.' From this circumstance it has been dignified with the high-flown name of the Athens of the Peak. The scenery in the immediate neighbourhood of Eyam is highly romantic, two ravines descending from the village into Middleton Dale. The cliffs here rise to a great height, particularly at the entrance to Eyam Dale, where a large buttress of limestone is named the Castle Rock. In Cucklet Delph is a charming little chasm called Saltpan Rock.

The rock scenery of **Middleton Dale** is remarkably fine; particularly at the Lover's Leap (overhanging the Inn of the same name), where about a century ago a young woman, whose unrequited affection preyed upon her mind, leapt down; but, owing to her fall being broken by a tree, she was not killed, though crippled for the remainder of her life. In the dale are barytes works,

and at its extremity, 17 m., the large mining village of **Stoney Middleton**, where are tepid baths erected by the late Lord Denman, over springs supposed to have been known to the Romans. The situation of the houses, one above the other on the ledges of the rocks, make it one of the most picturesque villages in Derbyshire. The Ch. (which has been restored) is of octagonal shape, erected in 1767, but with a low square tower of ancient date. Adjoining it is Middleton Hall, the seat of Lord Denman, who has made a pleasant residence of the old farmhouse.

A short distance E. of Middleton, the Derwent is crossed by a good modern bridge, at **Calver**, where there is a large cotton factory, and the road keeps beside the river to

19 m. ☿ **Baslow**, a convenient spot from where the tourist, descending the Derwent, can explore the beauties of Chatsworth (Rte. 6). It is a neat village, with a very pretty Ch. by the waterside, under the fostering care of the Dukes of Devonshire and Rutland. Northward, the road to Sheffield, by Fox House inn, passes under Curbar Edge and Froggatt Edge, affording some striking moorland scenery. If possible the traveller should walk to the end of Froggatt's Edge, ascending the hill immediately behind Baslow to Wellington's Monument and the Eagle Rock (an isolated boulder on the moor), and from thence skirt the brow of Curbar and Froggatt Edge. There is a good path all the way. The Sheffield road is joined near the Grouse inn, about 2 m. from the Fox inn.

Passing S.W. over the high ground of **Pilsley**, with Edensor on E., at

23 m. is **Bakewell** (Rte. 6).

Route 9.—Buxton to Hayfield.

ROUTE 9.

BUXTON TO HAYFIELD AND GLOSSOP.

BY ROAD. 15 m.

Both Hayfield and Glossop can be reached from Buxton by rly., but the route, especially to the latter, is very circuitous, and the tourist is recommended to proceed only by the rly. for

6 m. to Chapel-en-le-Frith (see Rte. 7). Leaving that town by road in the course of the next 2 m. no less than 3 picturesque little streams are crossed. They rise in the mountainous region of the Peak and flow westward into the Goyt, and eventually are lost in the Mersey. A few scattered paper mills and other factories that mainly depend on water power are seen, but nothing like a connected village, until

At 11 m. is ☆Hayfield (Stat., a short branch from New Mills on Midland Rly. Main line). It stands very picturesquely on the banks of the Sett, a rapid stream that comes down from the S. face of Kinderscout, which is the proper name for the loftiest part of the Peak. Large calico-printing works give employment to most of the people, and the whole place has a very business-like aspect.

1 m. E. is the hamlet of Kinder, at which also are large print works, passing by which the ascent of Kinderscout (2-4 hrs. there and back), or the descent into Edale, may be accomplished (Rte. 8).

From Hayfield the road commands very fine prospects all the way. Outlying hamlets, as Chunal, Charlesworth, Simmondly, and Whitfield, are all busy manufacturing places. Charlesworth and Whitfield have each handsome modern churches. The road, which has hitherto been on very high ground, now begins to sink, and

At 15 m. is ☆Glossop, a thriving manufacturing town, standing in a hollow. The surrounding scenery is fine, the reservoirs for the supply of Manchester with water forming a striking feature, whilst another is found in the great railway Viaduct, which spans the Dinting valley it is 120 ft. high, and consists of 16 arches, each of 125 ft. span. Glossop Hall (Lord Howard of Glossop) is in the French chateau style, and the grounds are very fine. The Ch. has a good tower and spire, built by the Duke of Norfolk in 1855; but the building is not at all equal to the Rom. Cath. Ch., which is by far the finest edifice in the place, and has a nunnery and schools attached. There are several large cotton and print works, and the new part of the town, on the Sheffield road, is a great improvement on what still remains of the original village of Old Glossop. The Victoria Hall, with a Free Library, is a fine Gothic edifice. The Victoria Public Park, in a commanding position, contains a Hospital and also Public Swimming and other Baths, all of which were given to the town by local benefactors in commemoration of the Queen's Jubilee in 1887.

The reservoirs above-mentioned are formed by impounding a portion of the waters of the Etherow, a bright stream that descends from the moors N. of Glossop. They consist of 5 vast lakes, or "lodges" as they are termed, which have dams of amazing solidity, and in wet seasons the water descends from one to the other in a series of absolute cataracts, volume making ample amends for the moderate fall. The Arnfield and Hollingworth reservoirs contain 48 million cubic feet of water; Rhodes Wood holds 80 million; Torside covers 160 acres, and holds 240 million; and Woodhead, the uppermost, has 200 million. They are calculated to supply Manchester with 30 million of gallons a day, and the cost of construction was 1,300,000*l*. The scenery of the hills is very fine, and, together with the bold water and railway works, will well repay a visit. Near the upper reservoir is the summit tunnel of the Manchester, Sheffield, and Lincolnshire Rly., more than 3 m. in length. If the pedestrian does not wish to return to Glossop, he can make his way from Dunford Bridge Stat., at the E. end of the tunnel, down the valley of the Derwent, to the Snake inn at Ashopton. The views are very fine, but the distance is full 12 m., and the walking is difficult.

ROUTE 10.

DERBY TO NOTTINGHAM, BY TRENT JUNCTION.

MIDLAND RAILWAY. 15¾ m.

On quitting Derby Stat., this line turns S.E., passing over the alluvial ground between the Trent and the Derby canal. On N., at 2 m., is the cemetery, and near it the village of **Chaddesden**, the Ch. of which contains several monuments of the Wilmot family. Chaddesden Hall (Sir H. Wilmot, Bart.).

2¾ m. **Spondon** (Stat.). The Ch. is a handsome Dec. edifice, with lofty spire. The date of its erection is approximately fixed by an entry on the Patent Roll, of August 24, 1340, which grants a delay in the payment of a subsidy to the men of Spondon in consequence of their church, and the whole of the town except four houses, having been destroyed by fire in the preceding Lent. **Locko Park** (W. D. N. Drury-Lowe, Esq.), 1 m. N., contains some good paintings by Guercino, A. del Sarto, G. Poussin, Canaletti, Holbein, Rubens, S. del Piombo, &c. On one side of the house is a chapel of the 17th centy., with the inscription "Domus mea vocabitur domus orationis."

[Spondon is a convenient stat., whence a visit to the ruins of **Dale Abbey**, 3 m. to the N.E., may be made. The nearest stat. is West Hallam on the G. N. Rly., between Derby and Nottingham, 1 m. N.W. It was founded at the commencement of the 13th centy. by William Fitzrauf, Seneschal of Normandy, and Jeffery de Salicosa Mara, his son-in-law, for Præmonstratensian monks. An ancient legend, however, gives a different account of the origin of the foundation:—" There once lived in the street of St. Mary in Derby a baker who was particularly distinguished by his great charity and devotion. After having spent many years in acts of benevolence and piety, he was in a dream called to give a very trying proof of his good principles. He was required by the Virgin Mary to relinquish all his substance, to go to Depe Dale, and to lead a solitary life in the service of her Son and herself. He accordingly left all his possessions and departed, entirely ignorant of the place to which he should go. But directing his course to the east, and passing through the village of Stanley, he heard a woman saying to a girl, 'Take with thee our calves and drive them to Depe Dale, and return immediately.' Regarding this event as a particular interposition of Providence, he proceeded with the girl to Depe Dale, and found it a very marshy land, and distant from all human habitation. Proceeding from thence to the E., he came to a rising ground, and, under the side of the hill, cut in the rock a small dwelling, and built an altar towards the S., and there spent day and night in the Divine service, with hunger, thirst, cold, and want."— *Pilkington.* Near here he built an oratory, afterwards enlarged into a religious house by Serlo de Grendon, Lord of Badely. This establishment was filled with monks from the Abbey of Calke (Rte. 2), who, however, in course of time, preferred the pleasures of the forest to their religious duties; and a complaint having been made to the King, the liberties of the monks were curtailed, and a grant of land made to them for the purpose of support. They, however, fell into great poverty, and were succeeded by a colony of canons from Welbeck, who soon returned, disgusted with the penury of the living. The abbey was refounded at a later date by Fitzrauf; but very little of the building is left except the E. window. The Ch. near the ruins is curious and quaint, being incorporated with the ancient pilgrims' inn, from which it was once separated only by a door. The singing gallery is entered by steps from the outside of the Ch. The font has a sculpture of the Virgin and Child, and Crucifixion. A portion of the stained glass for which Dale was once celebrated is now at Morley Ch. (Rte. 4), some 3¼ m. to the W. The hermit's cell is still in existence. The story of Dale Abbey has been told by William and Mary Howitt:—

"The De'il one night, as he chanced to sail,
In a stormy wind, by the Abbey of Dale,
Suddenly stopp'd, and looked wild with surprise
That a structure so fair in that valley should rise."

From Dale the tourist may return by Ockbrook, where there is a Moravian educational settlement. The parish Ch., which has Norm. portions, has a spire and some good stained glass in the E. window.]
[*Derby, &c.*]

4¼ m. Borrowash (Stat.) in the parish of Ockbrook.

1 m. S., across the Derwent, is Elvaston Castle, the seat of the Earl of Harrington. A monotonous flat has been so treated as to produce a grand effect independent of variety of surface, which has been done by bringing together a forest of evergreens of every kind, disposed in avenues and groves. The grounds, 100 acres in extent, which on the E. side are entered by very fine iron gates, formerly belonging to the palace of Madrid, are remarkable for their evergreen glades and gardens, chiefly composed of coniferæ, and for the artificial lake and rockeries, carried out for the 5 h Earl of Harrington (1851-1862), by an eminent gardener and transplanter of trees, Mr. Barron, whose nursery is near the stat. The mansion is domestic Gothic. The drawing-room is furnished with splendid crimson hangings, presented by the King of Spain to a former Earl. There is also a small collection of pictures by Kneller, Lely, C. Jansen, Reynolds, N. Berghem, &c. The avenues by which the castle is approached from the S. and E. are all the more conspicuous, as the immediate neighbourhood is flat and uninviting. The gardens are laid out in various styles, the most remarkable being the yew-garden: many of the trees were transported full-grown from long distances. Mr. Barron's chief exploit is an artificial lake with rocky islands and shores, fringed with beautiful shrubs and trees.

At Elvaston was born Walter Blunt, created by Edward IV., in 1465, Baron of Montjoy, "whose posterity have equalled the glory of their descent and family by the ornaments of learning." In the Ch., which is Perp., with lofty tower, are a carved oak screen, and monuments of the 15th centy. to the Stanhopes, also modern ones and painted windows to the Earls of Harrington. "In 1643 Sir John Gell with the Parliamentary forces attacked and plundered Elvaston. Lady Stanhope had recently erected, at an expense of 600*l*., a rich altar-tomb to her husband, but such was the personal and political hatred of the Roundhead knight against his late stout opponent, that he proceeded to the Ch., mutilated the effigy, and then wantonly destroyed Lady Stanhope's favourite flower-garden. Nor did his revenge stop here—for he married the lady, with the express purpose of 'destroying the glory of her husband and his house.'"—*Burke.*

2 m. to the S.E. of Elvaston, where the Derby and Loughborough road crosses the Trent at Cavendish Bridge, is **Shardlow Hall** (E. Sutton, Esq.), a 16th-centy. house, modernised.

On N., 1 and 2 m., are Draycott Hall, the property of Earl of Harrington, and Hopwell Hall (E. H. Pares, Esq.).

6½ m. **Draycott** (Stat.). Here are the great cotton and lace factories of the Messrs. Towle.

7¼ m. **Sawley** (Stat.). The village is more than 1 m. to the S.E., on the bank of the Trent. The early Dec. Ch., restored in 1889, has a good Perp. tower and spire. The chancel arch and some herring-bone work are the remains of a Saxon Ch. erected prior to A.D. 822. It contains a massive oak screen of Perp. workmanship; some solid oak benches of Elizabethan date; a fine Jacobean pulpit bearing the date 1636; and a curious stone screen probably 400 years old. At **Wilne**, 1 m. E., the Ch. of St. Chad contains an old Saxon font with curious carvings. Much nearer to the stat. is the village of **Breaston**, where the great industry is warp net-making.

8¼ m. **Sawley** (Junct. Stat.).

9½ m. **TRENT JUNCTION STAT.**, where this branch joins the Midland main line (Rte. 2). The views of the Trent, as the line passes towards Nottingham, are very pleasant. The river here divides Derby from Notts, and is joined by the Soar, which separates Notts from Leicester. Thrumpton Hall, on S., is the seat of Lady Byron. From this point the line takes the vale of the Trent on its l. bank as far as Newark, thence on its rt. bank to Langford, and afterwards nearly follows the course of the old Fosse Way to Lincoln.

At 10 m. the Erewash is crossed, near its junction with the Trent.

11½ m. **Attenborough** (Stat.). On S. is the Church, with tower and spire. It contains several fine monuments to the Babingtons, Nevilles, and Leakes. In a house on one side of the churchyard was born in 1611 Henry Ireton, the regicide, and son-in-law of Cromwell. N. of the line is **Chilwell**, where is Chilwell Hall (N. J. Charlton, Esq.).

At a short distance W. is a ferry, which leads to **Barton in Fabis**, or Barton in the Beans, where a tesselated pavement can be seen in the vicarage farmyard, while some remains of fortification on Brent's Hill point to the former site of a Roman town.

2 m. S.E. of Barton is the village of **Gotham**, pleasantly situated in a valley, and with a handsome Ch. Its chief industry is mining plaster, a kind of inferior alabaster from the surrounding hills, but it is better known for its "Wise Men," the story of whom is thus told by Thoroton, the county historian; as in similar tales about other places, the simplicity was only affected. "King John, passing through the place towards Nottingham, and intending to go through the meadows, was prevented by the villagers, who apprehended that the ground over which a King had passed would for

Route 10.—Beeston—Nottingham.

ever become a public road. The King, incensed at their proceedings, sent some of his servants to inquire of them the reason of their incivility, that he might punish them by way of fine or any other way he thought proper. The villagers, hearing of the approach of the King's servants, thought of an expedient to turn away his Majesty's displeasure. When the messengers arrived, they found some of the inhabitants engaged in endeavouring to drown an eel; some were employed in dragging carts on to the top of a barn to shade the wood from the sun; others were tumbling their cheeses down the hill to find their way to Nottingham; and some were engaged in hedging in a cuckoo which had perched upon a bush: in short, they were all employed in some foolish way (or other, whence arose the old adage, 'The wise men (or fools) of Gotham.'" According to local tradition, their great exploit was the planting the hedge to keep in the cuckoo, and a spot on a neighbouring hill, supposed to have been the scene, is still called *Cuckoo Bush.*

13 m. **Beeston** (Stat.). The village, a short distance N., is a busy place, having a silk mill (its predecessor was burnt by the rioters from Nottingham in 1831), lace machines, and stocking frames. The Ch. was rebuilt in 1844, except the chancel, which has since been added. There is a fine carved stone reredos, erected in 1880. On the opposite side of the Trent, 4 m. from Nottingham, lies **Clifton.** The Hall is the ancient residence of the Cliftons, a distinguished Nottinghamshire family. The church contains some 15th and 16th-centy. monuments and *brasses* of the Cliftons. There is a fine avenue of trees, 2 m. in length, called Clifton Grove, the scene of Kirke White's poem of that name.

At **Wilford,** 1½ m. N.E., was formerly a ferry to Nottingham, now re-

placed by a bridge, which, mainly owing its completion after long delay to the liberality of the late Sir R. J. Clifton, M.P., is commonly known as "Sir Robert's Bridge." 1½ m. S.E. from Clifton is **Ruddington**, a busy village of stocking-weavers, or "stockingers," as they are locally termed. At a short distance E. is a deserted churchyard, the only vestige of a town called Flawforth, that once stood there. The Ch. having fallen into decay was pulled down in 1773, and part of the stone was used to build a bridge over the neighbouring stream, called Fairbrook.

Ruddington Grange (T. I. Birkin, Esq.).

The rly. is carried along the base of the steep rock on which stands the remains of the Castle, and reaches at

15¾ m. ☿ **NOTTINGHAM** (2 central Stats.). The county town, noted for the manufacture of lace and hosiery, is situated nearly in the centre of England, on a rocky height a little to the N. of

"The bounteous Trent ,that in herself enseams
Both thirty sorts of fish and thirty sundry streams,"

and overlooking its rich valley.

The old part of the town is a mass of mean streets, mostly crooked and narrow; and from its sloping site many of the houses rise tier upon tier one behind the other. This slope faces the S., Nottingham being sheltered from the N. by a range of high ground separating it from the district of Sherwood Forest, which in old times "supplied it with great store of wood for fire (though many burn pit-coal, the smell whereof is offensive), while on the other side, the Trent serves it with fish very plentifully." Hence this barbarous verse:—

"Limpida sylva focum, Triginta dat mihi piscem."—*Camden.*

F 2

Route 10.—Nottingham: Castle.

The lower portion is watered by the Leue, a stream from Sherwood Forest, which runs from the N., and soon joins the Trent. But of late years, since the restriction of building on the Lammas lands has been removed, the town has greatly extended, and with very great improvement in the style of building. Several of the old streets have also been widened or swept away, and the new houses in the Market-place, the Post Office, the School of Art, the High School, and the University College, and several of the more recent factories, are favourable specimens of provincial architecture.

Perhaps the most characteristic feature of Nottingham is its **Market-Place**, considered to be the largest in the kingdom. It is an open area of 5½ acres, nearly in the form of an acute-angled triangle, terminated at the E. end or base by the Exchange, a massive building, of slight architectural pretensions. There is a North and a South Parade, consisting mainly of handsome houses of early 18th-centy. date, the upper stories resting on pillars forming a covered walk. This is the spot that the "Nottingham Lambs" have rendered notorious in electioneering annals; and even now on market-days, and at the October goose-fair ("the English carnival," it has been styled) the scene is sufficiently lively. It was by a "Goose-fair mob" that Nottingham Castle was burnt in 1831. Indeed in former times the working classes here were noted for their turbulent spirit, as shown in their sympathy with the first French revolution, and their share in the Luddite outrages of 1811-12.

Nottingham was seized by the Northmen in 868, and held by them till 924, when they were dispossessed by Edward the Elder, who also built a bridge over the Trent that continued in use till late in the 17th centy.

The old **CASTLE** was built by William the Norman, who bestowed it on William Peveril. It occupied a most commanding position on a precipitous rock, 130 ft. high, overlooking the town, and having the river Lene flowing at its foot. Standing nearly in the centre of the kingdom, this Castle was for many ages one of the most important fortresses in England, and was the scene of many momentous historical events. It was assailed in vain in the wars in the time of Stephen and of King John, so as to gain the name of impregnable, and it was a frequent royal residence: as also a prison, David II. of Scotland, Owen, the son of Owen Glyndwr, young Hotham, and many others being mentioned as confined there. It was held for some years for the Parliament by Colonel Hutchinson, and at his instance in 1651 it was "slighted," or reduced to ruin, lest, as Mrs. Hutchinson informs us, it might be seized by Cromwell, whose designs of absolute power he had penetrated. After the Restoration the site was granted to the Duke of Buckingham, who soon sold it to the old Royalist general, the first Duke of Newcastle. He, though almost 80 years of age, proceeded to build a new castle on the same site, which is said to have been designed by Sir Christopher Wren, in a heavy Italian style of architecture. The building was burnt by the mob in broad day during the riots in October, 1831, because its owner, the Duke of Newcastle, had distinguished himself by his opposition to the Reform Bill. The sum of 21,000l. was paid by the Hundred to the Duke as compensation, but, from threats of further mischief, he declined to rebuild it. The remains of the old castle are very small, comprising a Norm. gatehouse, to which some injudicious modern additions have been made, and a bastion facing Castle Gate. In 1878

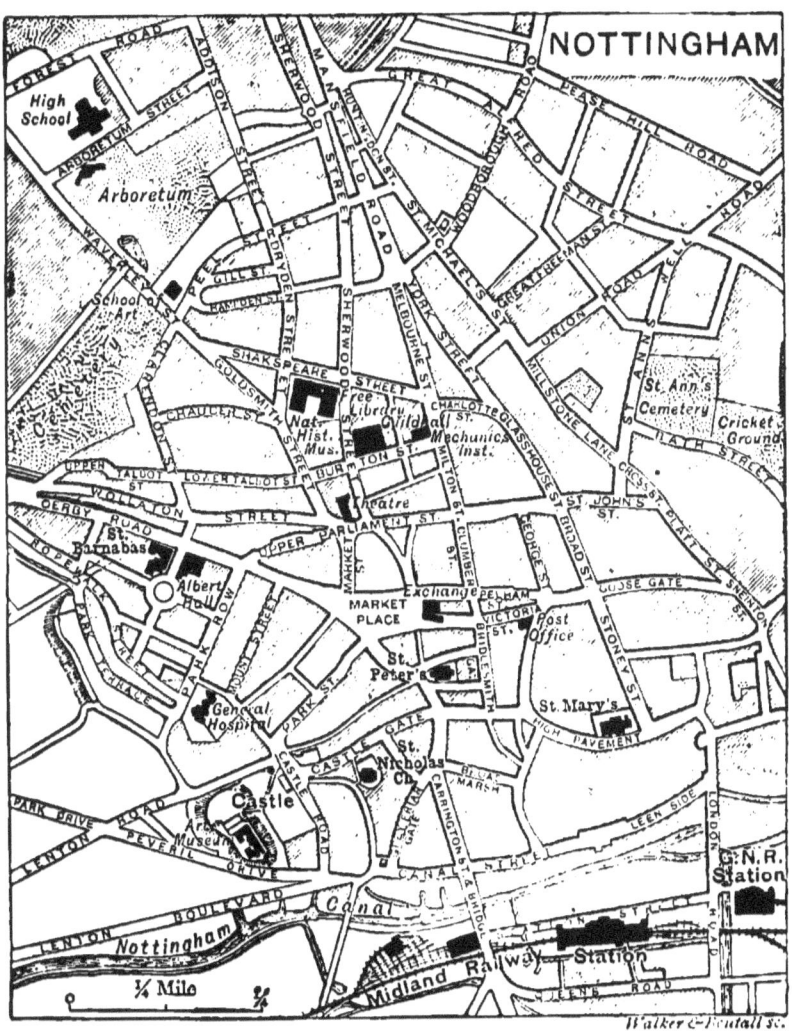

To face page 68.

the Castle was taken on a lease of 500 years from the Duke of Newcastle's Trustees by the Town Council, and fitted up as a *Museum and Art Gallery*, where there is always on view a good collection of pictures, and of objects of Art, also a valuable collection of classical antiquities presented by Lord Savile, K.C.B. They were discovered by his lordship on the site of the Temple of Diana, on the shores of Lake Nemi, during the time he was the British Ambassador at Rome. It is open daily, except Sunday, from 10 A.M. till 9 P.M. in the summer, but in the winter closes at 4 P.M. on Wednesdays and Fridays. The grounds also are well laid out, and will be found worth a visit on account of the beautiful view which the terrace commands over the plain of Trent, the town, the canal, and rlys. close at hand, the river appearing here and there in its windings, the groves of Clifton beyond it, and in the distance the Hall of Wollaton and Castle of Belvoir.

The platform on which the Castle stands is undermined with excavations extending in all directions, and it is probable that **Mortimer's Hole**, which is 107 yards in length, afforded a direct communication from the castle with the river below. It is a singular excavation, descending through the sandstone rock from the castle platform nearly to the level of the river, lighted by openings in the face of the cliff, and showing the marks of gates and stockades to bar the passage through it. It is of considerable antiquity, at least as old as the 14th centy.; and through a secret branch of it, which led to the keep, the young King Edward III., aided by Sir William Elland, Sir William Montacute and other followers, entering the castle by night, surprised Mortimer Earl of March, the paramour of the Queen his mother, on 19th October, 1330. Mortimer was seized in spite of the Queen's cries and entreaties, sent to London, and executed, " for betraying his country to the Scots for money, and for other mischiefs, out of an extravagant and vast imagination designed by him."

On the slope of the hill to the N. of the castle, between it and the old Infirmary, on the spot where is now the street called **Standard Hill**, King Charles I. first unfurled the royal standard 1612, having previously summoned all good subjects able to bear arms to attend. This important event is thus described by Clarendon:—" According to proclamation, upon the 25th day of August, the standard was erected about 6 of the clock of a very stormy and tempestuous day. The King himself, with a small train, rode to the top of the Castle Hill; Varney, the Knight Marshal, who was standard-bearer, carrying the standard, which was then erected on that place, with little other ceremony than the sound of trumpets and drums. Melancholy men observed many ill presages about that time. The standard was blown down the same night that it had been set up, by a very strong and unruly wind, and could not be fixed again in a day or two, till the tempest was allayed."

Though the Castle was in the king's hands at the beginning of the war, it had not sufficient garrison, and was soon occupied by the Parliament, when Colonel Hutchinson (whose wife's 'Memoirs' add so much interest to the story) was appointed its governor. He held the place bravely and successfully against all attacks, withstanding offers of bribery, from 1642 to 1645. Marshal Tallard and other French officers, taken prisoners at the battle of Blenheim, resided on parole in the Castle and some adjoining houses in Castle Gate, where they amused themselves with gardening.

The New Red sandstone rock on which the town and castle stand, stretching W. in the form of a low cliff along the canal through the park, is of a soft texture, easily cut, and has in consequence been perforated in very early times with caves, used as cellars and storehouses, while some till very lately served for human habitations. Such caves were probably the most ancient dwellings on this spot, and gave rise to the town. "The name of Nottingham is nothing but a soft contraction of the Saxon word Snottengaham, so called by the Saxons from the caves and passages under ground, which the ancients for their retreat and habitation mined under the steep rocks of the south parts, toward the river Lind [Lene], whence it is that assertion renders the Saxon word Snottenham, speluncarum domum, and in the British language it is 'tui ogo hanc,' which signifies the same thing, viz. 'The House of Dens.'" —*Deering*.

The **Rock Holes**, vulgarly called Papist Holes, to the W. of the Castle, in the grounds of J. W. Leavers, Esq., J.P., are a series of such cavities, undoubtedly once used as dwellings. There are traces of stairs, a chapel, of mortise-holes for timbers, designed to form what is called a "lean-to roof," and one chamber is penetrated with small pigeon-holes, in order to serve as a dovecote. Visitors are allowed to inspect these dwellings on presentation of their visiting cards.

Sneinton Hermitage, in the suburb of that name at the opposite side of Nottingham, is a low cliff of sandstone facing the Trent, pierced and excavated to form chambers for the houses built against the side of the rock. Some of them are very old, and many have neat hanging gardens on the shelves of the rock. Here are tea-gardens, much resorted to by the operatives in the summer time.

Within the last twenty years several busy suburbs to Nottingham have been erected, uniting the town to the neighbouring villages of Basford, Radford, Lenton, and Sneinton. By the 'Nottingham Borough Extension Act,' which came into force in 1877, the boundaries were extended so as to include the suburbs; and the total area of the borough is now 15½ square miles. The Lammas Lands formerly preserved an open space in every direction, and thus caused these manufacturing villages to be placed at a distance of 1 or 2 m.; but in 1845 an Act was passed, which allowed of building leases of the Lammas Lands, and now streets and factories almost cover them. As some counterpoise, various portions are laid out as recreation grounds. The Arboretum, in Waverley Street, on the N. side of the town, a tract of 19 acres, is one of these, in which is a pagoda, with its complement of Russian guns, and statue of Feargus O'Connor. The so-called Forest is another; it is merely a serpentine road with shrubberies, near the racecourse. On the S. side is the Queen's Walk, a planted avenue, ¾ m. long, leading to Wilfordbridge. The various *Cemeteries* also are ornamentally laid out, and in the Church Cemetery, on the Mansfield road, some of the cave-dwellings of old Nottingham are still to be seen, enlarged to serve as catacombs.

Nottingham possesses one very handsome cruciform Perp. **Church**, of **St. Mary**, on the High Pavement, nearly in the centre of the town. The W. end, which had been "modernized," was well restored by Scott; the S. porch, originally very rich, has lost its beauty from the corrosion of the stone by the weather. From the centre of the Ch. rises a fine tower of 2 stages, with a battlement and 8 crocketed pinnacles. The interior is lighted by a profusion of windows of fine tracery, mostly filled with stained glass. The E. window is a memorial to the Prince Consort; and that at the W. end to Thomas Adams, a lace manufacturer. A handsome reredos and screen were erected in 1885. At the extremity of the transepts under the windows are 2 monumental niches, beautifully ornamented with Perp. crockets and foliage; the one in the S. has an effigy of a warrior. The open timber roof is of good ornamental design; and there is a fine piece of groining at the intersection of nave and transepts. The chancel, beautifully restored, is ornamented by a very fine painting of the Virgin and Child by Fra Bartolommeo; it was the gift of Mr. Wright, of Upton. In a glass case of the N. wall off the chancel is a curious group of alabaster figures, found under the chancel in the course of the restoration. The Rev. John Whitelock, ejected by the Act of Uniformity, has his gravestone here (d. 1708).

St. Peter's Ch., near the Market Place, is Perp., with tower and lofty spire, but has been very much altered and modernized. It has a good altar-piece by Barber, a native artist; subject—the Agony in the Garden. It is now placed at the W. end of the Ch.

St. Nicholas Ch., in Castle Gate, is a very plain brick structure, built in 1671, in lieu of one pulled down by Colonel Hutchinson in 1643, as it commanded the platform of the Castle, "so that the men could not play the ordnance without woolpacks before them; and the bullets fell so thick into the outward castle-yard that they could not pass from one gate to the other, nor relieve the guards, but with very great hazards." — *Mem. Col. Hutchinson*, p. 177. There are numerous modern churches in Nottingham, and a large number of Dissenting chapels, but none calling for particular remark.

The handsome **Roman Catholic Cathedral** by Pugin, dedicated to St. Barnabas, is on the Derby road; it is cruciform, in the E. Eng. style, surmounted by a tower and spire 164 ft. high, and terminates at the E. end in a Lady Chapel. It contains a carved stone pulpit, and a chancel-screen of open work, flanked by figures of St. John and the Virgin. The altar is a single slab, resting on 6 pillars of Petworth marble. Behind it is the Lady Chapel, on the N. side St. Alkmund's, and on the S. the chapels of St. Thomas of Canterbury and the Venerable Bede. In the crypt is St. Peter's Chapel, set apart for masses for the dead. The windows are filled with stained glass; the centre one, at the W. end, bears the arms of John Earl of Shrewsbury, who contributed liberally towards the building.

The **General Hospital** is near the castle; it was built in 1781, the site being the joint contribution of the then Duke of Newcastle and the corporation of the town. Two wings were added in 1855, one also in 1871, and one in 1879. There are several other hospitals, and some almshouses, one of these latter, the Plumtre Hospital, being of the date of 1392. The Lunatic Asylum stands N. of the town, on a hill commanding extensive views. The **Post Office**, a handsome building, is in Victoria-street, near the Market-place.

In Shakespeare-st. is the **Univer-**

sity College, a Gothic building, the front being composed of a lofty gable surmounting three open arches, below a triplet of Dec. windows. It was erected in 1880-81 by the Corporation at a cost of 80,000l., for the promotion of higher education, and the University Extension Scheme of the Universities of Oxford and Cambridge, and was opened by the late Prince Leopold in 1881. The east wing is occupied by the Free Libraries, and in the we t wing is the Natural History Museum; whilst in the central portion are class-rooms, lecture theatre, &c., of the college; in the rear of the building are the Technical Schools. Not far from it stands the **Guildhall**, a handsome Renaissance building erected from the design of the late T. Verity in 1887 at the cost of 62,000l. The **School of Art**, a handsome stone building, is in Waverley Street. The **High School**, founded in 1513 by Dame Agnes Mellers, is a large building in Arboretum Street, and is well endowed.

At the junction of Carrington-street and Castle Gate is the **Walter Memorial**, of the Eleanor-cross order, 50 ft. high. It is a drinking-fountain, with 2 medallion portraits of John Walter, of Bearwood, who was long M.P. for Nottingham. It was erected in 1865, and presented to the town by his son.

The low-lying parts of Nottingham have often suffered from floods, particularly in 1795, to which the obstruction offered to the free course of the river by the old Trent bridge greatly contributed. It was a structure of 19 small arches, with a raised causeway and an embankment, and though usually said to have been built in 1683, contained some far older remains. In 1871 it was replaced by the New Trent Bridge, which is mainly of iron, having 3 arches over the river of 100 ft. each, beside land arches for towing-path, floods, &c. It is a very handsome structure, ornamented with polished granite pillars, and, with the approaches, is about 700 ft. in length.

The *manufactures* of Nottingham, which are greatly promoted by the existence of coal at a distance of less than 2 m., consist of hosiery, silk, cotton, woollen, and lace. The Rev. William Lee, the inventor of the stocking-frame (1589), to which Nottingham owes so much of its wealth, was a native of Calverton, in this county. What led him to take up the matter is not certainly known, authorities differing, but it appears that he thought so highly of his invention as to apply to Queen Elizabeth for a patent for a monopoly of making stockings. Such a request being justly considered unreasonable, Lee carried his process to France, where, after alternate successes and failures, he died, about 1610. He profited little by his invention in England, and not much more in France. It is not known where he is buried, and there is no memorial of him in his native place. In the town and its vicinity there are many manufactories of hosiery, machine lace, bobbins and their carriages, machinery, and warehouses for lace-dressing. The stranger at Nottingham should not neglect to see the process of making bobbin-net, "which may be said to surpass most other branches of mechanical ingenuity in the complexity of its machinery; one of Fisher's spotting-frames being as much beyond the most curious chronometer in multiplicity of device, as that is beyond a common roasting-jack."— *Dr. Ure.* A bobbin-net machine consists of perhaps 10,000 pieces, bobbins and carriages. These machines have almost entirely superseded hand-made lace.

The Jacquard machine was applied to the bobbin-net machine in 1825, but, as far as producing patterns, "progressed slowly till 1841, when a plan was discovered by Mr. Hooton Deveril for applying the Jacquard to the guide-bars; and so rapid has been the adoption of this method since that time, that at the present period there is scarcely a fancy machine at work without it, either to the bars or along the machine." The process of "gassing lace" when made, in order to burn away the loose fibres, is also well worth seeing, the lace being passed over a series of gas flames, so as to singe away the filaments without injuring the net. Many thousand young girls receive employment as lace "menders" and dressers, in starching and folding the lace. (See *Introd.*, p. [21].)

The first cotton mill was erected at Nottingham, by James Hargreaves in 1767. The building is now a dwelling-house, at the junction of Mill-street and Wollaton-street.

Nottingham was once famous for the skill of its workers in iron, who resided in Girdler Gate (now Pelhal-street) and Bridlesmith Gate; hence the jingling lines—

"The little smith of Nottingham,
Who doth the work that no man can."

In Bridlesmith's Gate are some old houses, one of them called King John's Palace. Another so-called palace of his existed in Bottle-lane, but was destroyed when the new Post Office was built. A handsome carved oak doorway (15th centy.) removed from this building is preserved in the Art Museum.

Among eminent natives of Nottingham may be named Col. Hutchinson, Dr. Jebb the physician, Thomas and Paul Sandby, R.A., Dr. Kippis, Gilbert Wakefield, and Henry Kirke White. The house in the Shambles in which the last-named was born has his portrait on its front, and his name has been given to a street in the Meadows, between the rly. and the river.

In the neighbourhood of Nottingham are several fine seats, as Holme Pierrepont, Viscount Newark (Rte. 12), Colwick Hall, J. P. Chaworth-Musters, Esq. (Rte. 11). By far the finest is Wollaton Hall (Lord Middleton), 2½ m. W., on the Derby road. This noble and most picturesque mansion is in the style of the Revival, and "a combination of regular columns, with ornaments neither Grecian nor Gothic, and half-embroidered with foliage, crammed over frontispieces, façades, and chimneys," but nevertheless highly picturesque. The architect was John Thorpe (the architect of Burghley and Longleat), assisted by Smithson. The building is simple in its plan; a square, surmounted by a massive centre, flanked at the corners by bartizan turrets, surmounted by elegant balustrades. It occupies the summit of an eminence in the midst of a noble park, abounding in aged timber, crossed by 4 stately avenues, and well stocked with deer. The grouping of the towers and turrets of the hall is in the highest degree picturesque. Other peculiarities of the exterior consist in the great extent of windows, the elegant scroll-work, and the grand porch.

It was built 1580-88, by Sir Francis Willoughby, Kt. (according to Camden, "out of ostentation to show his riches"), of stone from Ancaster, conveyed hither on horses' backs, in exchange for coals dug on the estate. The grand feature of the interior is the Hall, 60 ft. long and 60 ft. high, surmounted by a roof supported by open timber frames, elegantly carved, arranged in compartments. At one end is a richly carved screen, unfortunately disfigured by paint; the walls also have lost their panelling; yet the effect of the whole, with its pictures, stags' horns, &c., is truly baronial.

Route 11.—Nottingham to Lincoln.

In other parts of the house are some Dutch paintings: — Grace before Meat, by *Heemskerck;* a Flemish lady bargaining for provisions, figures life-size; Lions hunting Deer, attributed to *Rubens,* and three large works representing a boar hunt by *Snyders.* There are some interesting family portraits of the Willoughbys: Sir F. Willoughby, who built the house, and his Lady, by *Zucchero;* Sir Richard, Lord Chief Justice, and Sir Hugh, the navigator, who was frozen to death in the polar seas, 1553; also Francis, 2nd Lord Middleton, by *Sir Joshua Reynolds.* The view from the central tower is extensive and beautiful, reaching to Belvoir Castle. The house is not shown, but its grand exterior is well seen from the road. It narrowly escaped the fate of Nottingham Castle in 1831, the rioters being beaten off with difficulty by the Wollaton troop of yeomanry.

In Wollaton *Church* are monuments with effigies to Sir Richard Willoughby and his wife, 1471; and Sir Henry Willoughby, Knight Banneret, 1528.

Bestwood Lodge (Duke of St. Albans) is a modern Gothic mansion. It contains some fine works of art, including a Grecian statue, in a large conservatory attached to the house.

ham the rly. passes through the demesne of **Colwick Hall,** the property of J. P. Chaworth-Musters, Esq., whose ancestor obtained it from one of the Byrons early in the 17th centy., either by purchase or at the card-table. The house, by Carr of York, built 1776, occupies a very pleasing site near the Trent, backed by rocky cliffs and hanging woods. The pleasure-grounds, which have been finely laid out, are now quite neglected. Colwick Hall was attacked, pillaged, and fired, by the brutal Nottingham mob of 1831. The terror produced by this violence, committed at night, drove the lady of the mansion into a plantation for concealment, and is supposed to have caused her death Feb. 5, 1832. Such was the melancholy end of the beautiful "Mary Chaworth" of Byron's early poems, the ill-fated heiress of Annesley. The little Ch., which stands on the lawn, contains monuments to some of the Byron family; also to Sophia Musters, died 1819.

3½ m. **Carlton and Gedling** (Stat.). Here the G. N. Rly., Nottingham and Grantham line (Rte. 12), branches off to the rt. Carlton is a long straggling village, chiefly occupied in the hosiery trade. The Ch., of the Basilica type, erected by the late Lord Carnarvon, is worth visiting. ½ m. N. is Gedling. The Ch., which has a fine lofty spire, has been well restored, and is very interesting. There is a curious early monument of a deacon in his vestments. Gedling Lodge is the property of the Earl of Carnarvon, and Gedling House (J. E. Burnside, Esq.) has very beautiful grounds.

ROUTE 11.

NOTTINGHAM TO LINCOLN, BY NEWARK.

MIDLAND RAILWAY. 33¼ m.

As far as Newark the line keeps on the l. bank of the river Trent, commanding in many parts very beautiful views. Soon after quitting Notting-

5½ m. **Burton Joyce** (Stat.), properly Burton Jorz, from the family of De Georz, is close to the margin of the Trent, which in its course hither from Nottingham is characterized by a succession of weirs and osier-beds. The Ch., restored in 1879, has monuments of the Stapylton family, who held property here in the reign of Edward VI., and a fine recumbent effigy of a De Georz. The spire is of a peculiar local type. 1½ m. N. is Lambley, once the seat of the Cromwells, the builders of Tattershall Castle and Ch. (see *Handbook for Lincolnshire*). The Ch. here has been partly rebuilt by the same hand. It retains its rood-screen, and on the N. of the chancel are the remains of a building, once two-storied, apparently a sacristy with the abode of an anchorite above it.

1 m. E. across the river is **Shelford** (see Rte. 12).

7½ m. **Lowdham** (Stat.). The restored Ch. has some 14th-centy. monuments of the Lowdham family, and a remarkable incised slab of a priest. The old manor-house, now a farm, stands E. of the Ch.; and the foundations of an earlier fortified house may be traced. 1 m. N.E. is **Gonalston**, with a small E. E. Ch., of which the nave and tower have been rebuilt. It contains two altar-tombs with effigies of knights :— Richard de la Riviere, and John de Heriz, 1100, and a 14th-cent. one of a lady holding a reliquary, exquisitely sculptured. 2 m. W. is **Woodborough**, which disputes with the neighbouring village of **Calverton** the honour of being the birthplace of Lee, the inventor of the stocking-frame (see Nottingham). Woodborough Ch. has a splendid Dec. chancel, the finest in this neighbourhood. Calverton Ch. preserves in the belfry of its 18th-cent. tower some most curious sculptures, supposed to be an Anglo-Saxon calendar of the months of the year. About 1 m. E. of Lowdham the Dover-beck, a stream that rises in Sherwood Forest, falls into the Trent. At **Oxton**, 4 m. up the stream, are 3 remarkable tumuli.

10 m. **Thurgarton** (Stat.). The Priory (Bishop of Southwell), on the N., is built on the site of the Priory, founded by Walter de Aincurt in the 12th centy. The Ch. preserves one of the W. towers and 3 bays of the nave; shorn of the triforium and clerestory. It has been restored, with the addition of a chancel and N. aisle. On the S., across the Trent, Kneeton Ch. is conspicuous from its fine situation. Nearer still is **Hoveringham**. The Ch. was mercilessly destroyed in 1867. The present brick one preserves a fine Norm. tympanum of St. Michael fighting the dragon, and recumbent effigies of Sir J. Goushill and his wife, who had been Duchess of Norfolk. Two fine Dec. windows are set up as ornaments in the garden of a private house, and other remains are at the Ferry Inn.

11¼ m. **Bleasby** (Stat.). The small Ch. was restored in 1869. Bleasby Hall (R. Kelham, Esq.) is a large building with the embattled towers of the 16th centy.

13 m. **Fiskerton** (Stat.) is mainly noticeable for its well-frequented ferry across the Trent, leading to East Stoke, where took place (1487) the bloody conflict, known as the battle of Stoke or Stoke Field, the last fought between the rival Houses of York and Lancaster, in which it is computed 6000 were slain and the army of Henry VII. defeated the forces of the impostor Lambert Simnel, under the Earl of Lincoln. The Ch., which has a low ivy-clad tower, stands close to Stoke Hall (Sir H. Bromley, Bart.), a very stately mansion.

14 m. **Rolleston Junct. Stat.** Here the Southwell and Mansfield line (Rte. 14) branches off to the N.W. The village lies S. of the rly. on the bank of the Trent; it has an E. E. Ch., with a fine and peculiar Perp.

tower. 1 m. N. is **Upton** Ch. The tower has a stone roof with a fifth pinnacle rising from the centre. 1 m. N.E. is **Averham**, the Ch. of which was well restored 1865. It has a good E. window of painted glass, and several fine altar-tombs of the Sutton family. In the Rectory garden is a Perp. window removed from Southwell Minster, in mistaken zeal for the restoration of Norm. work. Between Averham and Newark is *Kelham Hall*, the seat of the ancient family of Manners Sutton. It is a Gothic building, designed by the late Sir G. Scott. The Ch., an interesting Perp. building, contains an ancient screen, and some good modern stained glass.

17 m. ♂**NEWARK - ON - TRENT** (Stat., opposite the Castle; the G. N. Stat. is 1 m. distant in Appleton Gate) was once remarkable for the number and good accommodation of its Inns, owing to the great traffic through it of travellers and goods along the North road. Among these were the Saracen's Head, which existed in the time of Edward III., and the White Hart in that of Henry IV. The former Inn has an additional interest from the writings of Sir Walter Scott, whose "Jeanie Deans" rested the night here on her way from Midlothian to London. The town (notwithstanding its name) stands some distance S. of the main branch of the Trent, but communicates therewith by a navigable cut fed by the river Devon, which is crossed by a modern 7-arched bridge.

Newark extends along the road from Nottingham to Lincoln, and from very early times was regarded as a strong post to control communication between North and South. Egbert is traditionally said to have built the first fortress here, which, after falling into the hands of the Northmen, and being again taken from them, was rebuilt by Leofric of Mercia in the time of Edward the Confessor, when it obtained the name of the "New Work." A strong Norm. Castle was built on the site of this by Alexander, Bp. of Lincoln, in 1123, but some years after he had to surrender it to Stephen. The bishop was a great castle builder, Sleaford and Banbury being also erected by him. "And because buildings of this nature seemed less agreeable to the character of a bishop, to extinguish the envy of them, and to expiate as it were for that offence, he built an equal number of monasteries, and filled them with religious societies." King John died in the Castle in 1216, but no other event of historic importance is recorded of it till the time of Henry VIII., when Wolsey occasionally occupied it. During the civil wars it was a place of great importance to the royal cause, and the townsmen were hearty royalists. It endured three sieges, in the first of which a large part of the town was burnt by the governor as a defensive measure, and it long continued a check on the country between Nottingham and Lincoln, laying all those parts, says Clarendon, under contribution. At the second siege, in 1644, it was defended by Sir Richard (afterwards Lord) Byron, until Prince Rupert relieved the town, after defeating the Parliamentarians on Beacon Hill, and capturing their cannon, ammunition, and 4000 prisoners. Towards the end of 1645 the King, "like a hunted partridge, flitting from one garrison to another," threw himself into Newark, but found the garrison in a most disorderly state, and, after a painful altercation with his nephew Prince Rupert, withdrew to Oxford. The Scottish army next besieged the castle, for the third time, but it was stoutly defended by Lord Bellasis, who performed his task with the most loyal fidelity, making several vigorous and destructive sallies, though the town was encompassed by lines and ramparts thrown up along a circuit of 2¼ m., and repelling every assault, until commanded by his master to surrender to the assailants, May 8, 1646, Charles having put himself in their hands in their camp at Kelham 3 days before. The Scots withdrew, and the Parliamentary commissioners at once set about the destruction of the Castle, reducing it to a mere shell, in which condition it still stands, a picturesque ruin, at the foot of the bridge. The walls are all Norm., and the windows Perp. insertions. The gatehouse is Norm.; as are also a crypt under the hall, the remains of the S.W. tower, and a postern-gate towards the river. The crypt is worth a visit. The long and lofty wall rising from the water-side, though Norm., has a Perp. aspect, being pierced with windows in that style. The Castle grounds on the town side have been converted into public gardens, and contain a Free Library, founded by Sir W. Gilstrap, Bart., a native of the town. Some of the fortified works thrown up in the civil war may still be traced; but Beacon Hill is now surmounted by the reservoir of the waterworks.

Newark is now a place of considerable trade, its corn-market being one of the largest in the kingdom. Malthouses, agricultural implement works, gypsum mills, and breweries furnish the chief employment of the people. In the Market-place some few of the houses with ornamented fronts remain, and at the junction of Carter Gate and Lombard-st. is **Beaumond** (or *Beaumont*) **Cross**, a handsome monolith shaft with figures in canopied niches, on the knop whence doubtless formerly sprung the cross; it is now surmounted by a modern cap of stone with a vane.

The **Grammar School**, founded in 1529 by Thomas Magnus, Arch-deacon of the East Riding of Yorkshire, has been rebuilt. Among its scholars are named Bps. White and Warburton, and Stukeley the antiquary. Warburton was a native of the town, and practised as an attorney there before he entered the Church.

The Ch. of **St. Mary Magdalene**, restored by *Scott*, one of the largest and most beautiful parish churches in the kingdom, is the grand ornament of Newark; it consists of nave with aisles, transepts, choir, and chantry chapels. The tower—a grand feature of the building—is E. Eng., surmounted by a Dec. spire, adorned with statues of the 12 Apostles, but the rest of the building is mainly Perp., temp. Henry VII. The S. aisle is Dec.; two late Norm. piers are standing in the nave, and the base of the tower seems also to be Norm.

The building is of remarkable length and height, and has a very graceful interior. The columns of the nave and chancel are slender and lofty, and the walls of the chancel are pierced with many large windows, giving the effect of a large lantern. The chancel is separated from the nave and chancel aisles by a grand canopied and pierced oak screen, finished in 1521, and which is in excellent preservation.

A former altar-piece, Christ raising Lazarus, by Hilton, is over the N. porch. In the S. transept is one of the finest and largest *brasses* known, measuring 9 ft. 4 in. by 5 ft. 7 in. It is to the memory of Alan Fleming (d. 1361), said to be the restorer of the Ch., and is elaborately engraved with his effigy, in a civic dress, under a rich Gothic canopy, environed by saints and angels. It is supposed to be of the same date and by the same artist as the Lynn brasses. There are several other smaller brasses, and an altar-tomb of

Robert Browne (1532), constable of the castle, and receiver to Cardinal Wolsey. The E. window is filled with stained glass, erected at a cost of 1000*l.* to the memory of the Prince Consort, the subjects taken from the history of our Lord. The organ, enlarged in 1865, is one of the finest in the county. In a chamber over the S. porch is a theological library, bequeathed by Bp. White, of Peterborough.

The Newark Stock Library of 18,000 volumes, and the Middleton News-room, are in a building in the Market-place, erected by Lord Middleton.

Christ Ch., on the S. side of the town, is a modern E. E. building.

The ecclesiologist should not leave the neighbourhood of Newark without visiting the Ch. at **Hawton**, 1½ m. S., the Dec. chancel of which contains a beautiful 7-light window, and an Easter sepulchre with carved figures. The subjects represent the Soldiers sleeping at the Tomb, the Rising of our Saviour, His Ascension, and the three Maries bringing ointment. The Ch. also contains a piscina, and sedilia with most elaborately decorated canopies. Some of these are engraved in Parker's 'Gloss. of Architecture.' The Perp. tower (c. 1483) is fine, but not equal to the rest of the building. The Ch. of **Balderton** (1½ m. E.) is also worth a visit.

19 m. Proceeding E. the line passes *Winthorpe Hall* (Major G. T. Peirse-Duncombe), with fine grounds bordering the Trent on N., and 1 m. further, an ancient brick house, the remains of the old Hall of Langford. The picturesque Ch. is close to the line. 1 m. W. is Holme (see Rte. 17).

22½ m. **Collingham** (Stat.). The village is mainly one long street, running N. from the line, but is divided into N. and S. Collingham (each having a good restored Ch.), and is remarkable for its clean and pleasant appearance. N. Collingham is said to be the birthplace of Dr. John Blow, the organist (b. 1648, d. 1708). There is the lower part of a fine wayside cross. At Potter's Hill, 2 m. E. of S. Collingham, is a large tumulus; and Brough and Coneygree, Roman stations on the Fosse Way, lie S. of Potter's Hill.

At 24 m. is **South Scarle**, with a large Perp. Ch.; soon after passing which the line enters Lincolnshire, and at

33½ m. is **Lincoln** (Stat.). See *Handbook for Lincolnshire*.

ROUTE 12.

NOTTINGHAM, TO GRANTHAM, BY BINGHAM AND BOTTESFORD. [BELVOIR.]

G. N. RAILWAY. 22¾ m.

Shortly after leaving Nottingham across the Trent are seen the grounds of Holme Pierrepont and the lofty spire of the Ch. The scenery here is very picturesque, the S. bank overhung by precipitous cliffs of New Red sandstone. The river is spanned by a fine bridge, and at

5½ m. is **Radcliffe** (Stat.). The village stands on high ground, ¾ m. rt., and is a busy place, stocking-weaving, malting, and basket-making being the chief employments. The Ch. was rebuilt in 1879, in the E. E. Gothic style, and has several good stained-glass windows.

1 m. W. is the village of **Holme Pierrepont**, with a noble *Hall* (a seat of Earl Manvers), inherited by the Pierreponts from the Manvers family about the reign of Edward I. The house is a large irregular building, parts of it being of considerable age. In the *Ch.* are several tombs of the Pierreponts—one with the effigy of Sir Henry Pierrepont, 1615, and a very good Corinthian structure commemorating a Countess of Kingston, of the Talbot blood. The Dukes of Kingston were buried here, though Thoresby was their principal residence.

2 m. to the N. of Radcliffe, under the shelter of the high ground overlooking the Trent, is **Shelford**, once the seat of the Earls of Chesterfield, whose mansion is now occupied by a farmer. It was garrisoned for the king by Col. Stanhope, in the civil war, and burnt by the Parliamentary troops. Before the Reformation it was a Priory of Austin Canons. Some of the family, including the celebrated Earl, are buried in the *Ch.*, which has a massive tower, once crowned with 8 pinnacles. The Stanhope monuments are interesting.

9 m. ⚘**Bingham** (Stat.), also a Stat. at Bingham Road on the L. & N. W. and G. N. Rlys. joint line (see Rte. 22). This small market town stands in a low situation, in a flat, well-cultivated district, the Vale of Belvoir, of which it is considered the capital. It is a neat thriving place, with a market-cross on the site of an older one; it was evidently once larger than it is at present. Numerous foundations of ancient buildings are found extending far beyond the present limits, even to the hamlet of Saxondale, 1½ m. W. *St. Mary and All Saints' Ch.*, once a collegiate establishment, is a large and very fine cruciform structure, the E. E. tower and Dec. spire being its main features. The chancel and transepts are Dec., but much of the tracery has been destroyed, or replaced by Perp. work. " Of the aisles arcades the northern is the earliest, as indicated by the severity of its pillar capitals and mouldings generally. The former are well worthy of careful examination, containing some beautiful specimens of carved animals. The S. arcade is for the most part built of a different kind of stone. Its pillar-shafts are octagonal; these spring from bases, some of which have bold water-mouldings; all the capitals are foliated, and the manner in which the acanthus-like leaves in one instance exhibit their nerves as they bend round the bell behind is pleasing, as well as the flow of those upon the westernmost one, as though it was yielding to the wind."—*Rev. E. Trollope.* In the S. aisle is an effigy of a knight, supposed to be that of Richard de Bingham, of the time of Edward I. Some modern stained glass is the work of an amateur. Bingham boasts of having had as three successive rectors in the 17th centy., Abbot, Archbishop of Canterbury, Wren, Bishop of Ely, and Hanmer, Bishop of St. Asaph, also of having given birth to Archbishop Secker, Admiral Lord Howe, and Robert Lowe, Lord Sherbrooke. The plague of the 17th century committed great havoc in this town.

The antiquary will find the site of a *Roman Station*, supposed to have been the ancient Vernometum, about 1 m. to the N., between Bingham and East Bridgeford, on the course of the Roman Fosse Way to Newark.

2 m. N.E. of Bingham is Carcolston; the Ch. has a fine Dec. chancel, similar to that at Woodborough. Col. Hacker, who commanded the guard at the death of Charles I., resided in the old Hall; this was afterwards occupied by Thoroton, the historian of Notts, who was buried in the ch.-yard in 1678. 1 m. farther N.E. is Screveton, where Thoroton was born. The Ch. contains some handsome 16th-centy. monuments of the Whalley family. 4 m. S.E. of Bingham is Langar, with some Scrope tombs in the Ch., and the gatehouse of Wiverton Hall, once their seat.

5 m. S.W. is Owthorpe, where Col. John Hutchinson, one of the regicides, resided; there is a monument to him in the Ch., where he was buried in 1663.

11¼ m. Aslocton or Aslacton (Stat.). A farm now occupies the site of the moated *Manor House*, in which Archbishop Cranmer was born in 1489; traces exist of its pleasure-grounds, and "Cranmer's walk" is pointed out. A short distance off is the very plain but interesting *Ch.* of Whatton, dedicated to St. John of Beverley, in which Cranmer is said to have commenced his ministry. It is cruciform, mainly E. E., with Norm. traces, and a Dec. spire. There are several monuments of early date, an altar tomb of Sir Richard de Whatton, 14th cent., and another of alabaster of Sir Adam de Newmarch, 15th cent, but the most interesting is an incised slab of the 16th centy., representing a layman named Cranmer, supposed to be the Archbishop's father (d. 1501). There are also the remains of an old village cross, carved with figures of saints. *Whatton Manor House* (Mrs. Dickinson Hall) is a very handsome mansion, with extensive grounds.

13 m. **Elton** (Stat.). The stat. lies midway between the villages of Orston (N.) and Elton (S.). The former has a local repute for its extensive gypsum beds, and a spring supposed to be very efficacious in scorbutic cases; and the latter is a meet for the Belvoir hounds. The Ch. of Orston has an E. E. chancel, and fine Dec. work about the nave; that of Elton is a very small, poor building. In 1780 a discovery was made in the ch.-yard of Elton of a very large number of silver coins of Henry II.

About 2 m. N.E. of Orston is **Staunton**, with an ancient manor house, the seat of the Staunton family, who have been settled here from time immemorial. The adjoining Ch. has a good screen, and many monuments. Thoroton (1 m. N. of Orston) has a Ch., badly restored, but with an exquisite tower and spire. Sibthorp, 1½ m. further, was of old the seat of the family of that name. The Ch. retains some traces of its ancient magnificence, when it was served by a large College of secular Priests.

The line now passes into Leicestershire, and reaches at

15¾ m. ☨ **Bottesford** (Stat.). The little town stands in a pleasant spot on the small river Deven, but is best known for its fine *Church*, which for several centuries was the burial-place for the De Roos and the Manners families. It is mainly early Perp., but has some slight E. E. and Dec. traces, and also some debased Perp. (Jacobean) portions; the tower and spire rise to the height of 222 ft., and are of very fine proportions. The chancel contains the superb monuments of all the Manners Earls of Rutland, and of several other members of the family; among them, one of two youths, whose death was ascribed to the magic arts of two female servants (Margaret and Philippa Flower), for which they were executed. There are also two *brasses*, for rectors of the Ch. (H. de Codyngton, 1404, and John Freman, 1440), and a very curious diminutive effigy in chainmail, once taken to represent Robert de Todenei, the reputed Norman founder of Belvoir, but believed now to be his great grandson, William de Albini (d. 1236), one of the 25 barons who swore to enforce the observance of Magna Charta. In the ch.-yard is a curious incised slab (14th centy.), with the semi-effigy of a female, respecting which there is a tradition that it represents "the fair maid of Normanton" (an adjoining hamlet in the parish), who was killed by earwigs.—*Rev. E. Trollope.*

4 m. S. of Bottesford stands the superb seat of ✠ **BELVOIR CASTLE** (Duke of Rutland), occupying the artificial mound thrown up on a spur of the Leicestershire Wolds by Robert de Todenei, to whom the surrounding district was granted by the Conqueror, as the site of his stronghold. This afterwards passed to the Albinis, the lords of Melton Mowbray, and, by marriages, first to the De Roos and then to the Manners family. It was forfeited to the Crown by the Lancastrian Lord De Roos in 1461, and was by Edward IV. granted to Lord Hastings. On the accession of Henry VII. it was restored to the son of the late lord. He, however, died without issue, and the estate fell to George Manners, the son of his sister Eleanor; it has ever since remained in the Manners' family. Among the older topographers there has been some discussion as to the foundation of Belvoir (locally "Beever"), Burton attributing it, but wrongly, to one of the Albinis. Its situation also, on the borders of Leicester and Lincoln, has caused it to be claimed for each shire, the fact being that the vast estate extends into both.

[*Derby, &c.*]

A priory was founded at the foot of the mound by de Todenei, and in it the lords of Belvoir were usually buried. On the suppression of the priory many of the monuments were removed to Bottesford Ch. (*ante*), and others to Croxton Abbey, by the 2nd Earl of Rutland.

Belvoir was a royal garrison in the civil war, and having suffered greatly from subsequent neglect, its rebuilding was commenced in 1800 by the 5th Duke of Rutland, under the direction of *Wyatt*. The works were carried on until 1816, when a fire made great havoc, but they were resumed on a still larger scale, and the Castle is now a pseudo-Gothic castellated building, with a frontage of 252 ft., occupying a grand position on the summit of an isolated hill, overgrown with beautiful timber. There is a country saying, "If Beever hath a cap, you churls of the vale look to that," alluding to the position of the castle, as affording a good prognostic of rain. At the bottom stand the stables and offices. The visitor enters by an archway on the N.W. The entrance-hall contains a number of figures in armour, and leads through a corridor lighted by stained glass to the staircase, which is lined with portraits of the Earls of Rutland by *Vandyck* and *Kneller*. The principal apartment is the Regent's Gallery, 131 ft. long, so called from the visit of the Prince Regent (afterwards George IV.) in 1814. In it is some tapestry, representing, with extraordinary vividness, scenes in 'Don Quixote'; also family portraits, of which the principal are Lady Tyrconnell, Marchioness of Granby, 9th Countess of Rutland, by *Lely*. Among other pictures is the Death of Lord Manners, by *Stothard*; there is also a bust by *Nollekens*. Adjoining is the chapel, containing a fine altarpiece by *Murillo*. The library has 2 portraits of Charles II., by *Vandyck* and *Vorster-*

man; and the ball-room, most of the family portraits. In the apartment known as the Queen's bedroom are curious paintings on Chinese silk. The drawing-room is fitted up most elaborately in the Louis Quatorze style, the ceiling painted with scenes of classic mythology, introducing, among other likenesses, the Duke of York as Jupiter; the sides of the room contain apartments in which is a series of miniatures, and among them a set representing Queen Elizabeth and some of her ministers. There is also a marble statue of a late Duchess of Rutland. In the dining-room is the table for holding the punch-bowl, in which the white cloth, sculptured by *Wyatt*, is marvellously represented. The Picture-gallery, 62 ft. long, contains paintings by Holbein, Vandyck, N. Poussin, Claude, Vandervelde, Teniers, Rubens, Murillo, Salvator Rosa, Ostade, West, Gainsborough, Stothard, Sir J. Reynolds, Lely, Kneller, and others. Notice particularly the Proverbs by *Teniers*, in which a portrait of his son occupies a prominent place; the Seven Sacraments, by *N. Poussin*; Shepherd and Shepherdess, *Rubens*; Crucifixion, *Vandyck*; portrait of Rembrandt, by himself; Virgin and Child, *Carlo Dolce*; Presentation, *Murillo*; Last Supper, *N. Poussin*. A number of valuable pictures were destroyed in 1816, when this portion of the castle was burnt down. Additional interest is conferred on these apartments by the beautiful and extensive views over the vale of Belvoir and the three counties of Leicester, Nottingham, and Lincoln, the castle and cathedral of the two latter towns being visible.

The keep of the Castle is known as the **Staunton Tower**, and is under the honorary command of the Staunton family, who hold it by an old tenure that they should raise soldiers for its defence when required.

The terrace gardens on the hill-side and the grounds generally are remarkable for their beautiful situation and the skill lavished on them. The visitor should obtain permission to see the **Mausoleum**, a stone building of Norm. architecture, in the grounds, containing a beautiful sculptured effigy of a late Duchess of Rutland.

Of the **Priory**, founded by De Todeni, there are no remains; but part of its site is occupied by a comfortable little *Inn*. Belvoir is open to visitors daily, Sunday excepted. For the country S. of Belvoir, see Rte. 21.

The line, soon after leaving Bottesford, passes into Lincolnshire, and arrives at

18½ m. **Sedgebrook** (Stat.).

22¾ m. ✠**Grantham** (Stat.). See *Handbook for Lincolnshire*.

ROUTE 13.

NOTTINGHAM TO MANSFIELD, BY NEWSTEAD. [HARDWICK HALL, BOLSOVER.]

MIDLAND RAILWAY. 17½ m.

The branch line to Mansfield branches off N. from the main line near the foot of the Castle rock, passing up the valley of the river Leen. There is a stat. at **Lenton**, where there are many fine seats, *Lenton Hall* (F. Wright, Esq.), *Lenton Firs*, and other residences. It is the nearest stat. to Wollaton Hall (Lord Middleton), see Rte. 10. [The G. N. Rly., Leen Valley branch, runs parallel with the Midland line from Daybrook as far as Newstead, having stations at Bulwell Forest, Bestwood Colliery, Butler's Hill, Hucknall Torkard, Linby, and Newstead. The Manchester, Sheffield, and Lincolnshire Rly. has a line in progress from Sheffield to the South, through Nottingham.]

At **Radford** (Stat.) a branch line goes off W. to Trowell.

4 m. **Basford** (Stat.), a great centre of the Bleaching Industry. The Ch., dedicated to St. Leodegarius (Basford being a Norman settlement), is a graceful specimen of E. E., and amongst other memorial windows, has one to the (Fifth) Duke of Newcastle, under whose fostering care the Ch. was enlarged, and a Chapel of Ease built at Cinder Hill, 1½ m. W., the headquarters of an extensive colliery. The internal decorations of both churches are deserving of notice.

New Basford, 1 m. S., now a separate parish, is one of the great seats of the hosiery and lace manufactures.

5½ m. **Bulwell** (Stat., also Stat on G.N. Rly.), named from a remarkably pure spring, rising in Bulwell Forest, employs a large population by its bleach yards. *Bulwell Hall* (T. Hardy, Esq.). 2 m. W. is **Nuthall**, with a small old Ch., and very extensive collieries. *Nuthall Temple* (John Holden, Esq.), once a seat of the Sedleys, is one of many copies of the Villa Capra of Palladio, near Vicenza, the casts representing groups from Æsop's Fables which adorn the dome are very interesting.

8½ m. **Hucknall Torkard**. (Stat., also Stat. on G. N. Rly.). The *Ch.*, a very plain building, with square tower at the W. end, has a family vault, in which Lord Byron, his mother, and his only daughter, are buried; as well as John, the first lord (d. 1652), and his six brothers, all stout Royalists of the time of Charles I. On the rt. of the altar is a tablet set up to the memory of Byron by his sister, the Hon. Augusta Leigh, and a slab of rosso-antico marble, sent by the King of Greece, has been inserted in the floor of the chancel over the spot where the coffin lies. There is another tablet erected to Ada, daughter of Lord Byron, wife of Earl Lovelace. The Ch. was rebuilt, and a S. aisle added in 1873, and enlarged in 1887. 3 m. W., situated amidst very broken and pretty scenery, are some slight remains of **Beauvale Abbey**, founded by Nicholas de Cantilupe, Lord of Ilkeston, in the reign of Edward III., for Carthusian monks. Little is known of the history of this Priory, except that it was one of the foundations to which John of Gaunt made an annual grant of a tun of wine. The ruins are incorporated with the offices of a farmhouse. 1 m. S. are also some remains of **Gresley Castle**, a stronghold of the Cantilupes, founded in 1341.

9¼ m. **Linby** (Stat., also a Stat. on G. N. Rly.), the Ch. of which contains some monuments of the Chaworths.

At 10½ m. **Newstead** (Stat.).

⚔ **Newstead Abbey** (W. F. Webb, Esq.)—

" An old, old monastery once, and now
 Still older mansion—of a rich and rare
 Mix'd Gothic, such as artists all allow
 Few specimens yet left us can compare
 Withal; it lies perhaps a little low,
 Because the monks preferr'd a hill behind
 To shelter their devotions from the wind "—

is 1¼ m. from the stat., the same distance from Newstead Stat. on the G. N. Rly., and about 11 m. N.W. of Nottingham by the Mansfield turnpike-road. The entrance from this road, which is E. of the house, is marked by a fine vigorous tree, called "The Pilgrim's Oak"

G 2

(sole survivor of the old wood, cut down by the 5th Lord Byron). A road of nearly ¾ m. leads down to the house; and an avenue of 1½ m., planted with *Wellingtonia giganteas*, extends from it to the stat. on W.

The Abbey of Newstead, called in old deeds de Novo Loco in Sherwode, was founded about 1170 by Henry II., in expiation of the murder of Thomas-à-Beckett. It was occupied by a community of Black Canons Regular, of the order of St. Augustine, and the names of 20 of its priors have been preserved. John Blake, the last of them, surrendered the house to the Crown, July 21, 1539, and had a pension of 16*l*. 13*s*. 4*d*.; the annual value is stated at 219*l*. 18*s*. 8*d*. On May 28, 1540, its possessions, and also those of the Priory of Haverholme, Lincolnshire, were sold to Sir John Byron, of Colwick (called "Little John with the great beard"), and his illegitimate son John succeeded him in possession. "He probably converted the domestic buildings of the monastery into a residence for himself. The Priory Church would form a quarry close at hand, from which materials could be procured for such alterations as he and his successors might desire. Excepting, therefore, its W. front, which evidently was once highly ornamented. its S. wall, of great strength, two sides of its S. transept, now transformed into the Orangery, and the vacant E. window, little remains of which can be traced above ground. The cloister court still retains its cloisters of the late Perp. style, in which may be observed an E. E. doorway, which led into the nave of the ch., near the W. end, and the position of the Norman lavatory on the S. side."—*J. M. G.* Sir Richard Byron garrisoned the house for Charles I., and the family suffered severely during the civil war. At the Restoration a pension of 500*l*. a year was granted to the widow of the 1st lord, and the second lord had a grant of money instead of liberty to cut down 1000 great oaks in Sherwood Forest which Charles I. had bestowed on him; but these were only slight compensations for its losses. Evelyn, who visited Newstead in 1654, says of it, "It is situated much like Fontainebleau in France, capable of being made a noble seat, accommodated as it is with brave woods and streams. It has yet remaining the front of a glorious abbey church." Those, however, were not days of restoration; and in the 4th generation the estate came into the hands of the 5th lord, who, from hatred to his heirs, seemed in his later years to take an insane pleasure in making as much havoc as possible. From him his great nephew, the poet, received the place in 1798, in a state of complete desolation. Its once noble woods presented a broken surface of mere stumps of trees. The gardens were neglected and overgrown, the lake was half-choked with mud, and the house falling to decay, with damp lichens spreading over its walls. Of the state of the place some 30 years before Horace Walpole speaks thus: "I like Newstead. It is the very abbey. The great E. window of the church remains, and connects with the house; the hall entire, the refectory entire, the cloister untouched, with the ancient cistern of the convent, and their arms on it; a private chapel quite perfect. The park, which is still charming. has not been so much unprofaned; the present Lord has lost large sums, and paid part in old oaks, 5000*l*. of which have been cut near the house. In recompense he has built two baby forts to pay his country in castles for the damage done to the navy, and planted a handful of Scotch firs, that look like ploughboys dressed in family liveries for a public day. In the hall is a very good collection of pictures, all animals; the refectory, now the great drawing-room, is full of Byrons; the vaulted roof remains, but the windows have new dresses making for them by a Venetian tailor."

The poet was a minor when he came into possession of his desolate heritage, and in after years his habits and want of means prevented his doing anything effectual to arrest its decay, though he always regarded it with affection. He fitted up a corner for himself, but even that was not altogether impervious to the rain. At last he sold it, in 1818, to his old schoolfellow, Col. Wildman, who, having given for it the sum of 95,000*l*., expended as much more in its restoration, with taste and judgment, under the direction of *Shaw*, the architect. Col. Wildman not only raised it from ruin, but was careful to preserve the antique character of the place, and to treat with respect all the associations connected with it, and under his care it reached a state of splendour never surpassed in its best days. The present beautiful and flourishing woods were planted by him, and the residence in effect rebuilt in the Jacobean style, preserving the old terraced gardens. In a line with the front of the house are the remains of the ruined Ch., whose vacant but elegant W. window forms a striking feature in all views:—

" A glorious remnant of the Gothic pile
(While yet the church was Rome's)
stood half apart
In a grand arch, which once screen'd many
an aisle.
These last had disappear'd—a loss to
art;
The first yet frown'd superbly o'er the soil,
And kindled feelings in the roughest
heart,
Which mourn'd the power of time's or
tempest's march
In gazing on that venerable arch.
Within a niche, nigh to a pinnacle,
Twelve saints had once stood sanctified
in stone;
But these had fallen—not when the friars
fell,
But in the war which struck Charles
from his throne;
When each house was a fortalice, as tell
The annals of full many a line undone—
The gallant Cavaliers, who fought in vain
For those who knew not to resign or reign.

But in a higher niche, alone, but crown'd,
The Virgin Mother of the God-born
child,
With her Son in her blessed arms, look'd
round,
Spared by some chance when all beside
was spoil'd;
She made the earth below seem holy
ground.
This may be superstition, weak or wild;
But even the faintest relics of a shrine
Of any worship wake some thoughts
divine.

A mighty window, hollow in the centre,
Shorn of its glass of thousand colourings,
Through which the deepen'd glories once
could enter,
Streaming from off the sun like seraph's
wings,
Now yawns all desolate; now loud, now
fainter,
The gale sweeps through its fretwork,
and oft sings
The owl his anthem, where the silenced
quire
Lie with their hallelujahs quench'd like
fire.

But in the noontide of the moon, and when
The wind is winged from one point of
heaven,
There moans a strange unearthly sound,
which then
Is musical—a dying accent driven
Through the huge arch, which soars and
sinks again.
Some deem it but the distant echo given
Back to the night-wind by the waterfall,
And harmonised by the old choral wall."

From a low-vaulted crypt on the ground floor, resting on pillars, the entrance lies into a noble hall, which has been well restored. The dining-room, panelled with oak, has a curious carved chimney-piece, with heads and the figure of a lady between two Moors in one compartment. A similar chimney-piece exists in one of the bedrooms, in which the female is said by tradition to be a Saracen lady, rescued by one of the Byrons, a crusader, from her infidel kinsfolk.

At the end of the building, next to the church, the poet's own bedroom remains nearly as he left it, with the bed, furniture, and portraits of Joe Murray, his old butler, and Jackson, the boxer, which he brought with him from Cambridge.

A low cloister runs around a court,

in the midst of which rises a quaint fountain:—

> "Amidst the court a Gothic fountain play'd,
> Symmetrical, but deck'd with carvings quaint—
> Strange faces, like to men in masquerade,
> And here perhaps a monster, there a saint;
> The spring gush'd through grim mouths of granite made
> And sparkled into basins, where it spent
> Its little torrent in a thousand bubbles,
> Like man's vain glory and his vainer troubles."

The Abbey contains, besides a portrait of Byron, interesting relics of Livingstone, the African Explorer, and many trophies of the chase and specimens of South African zoology, shot by Mr. Webb.

The garden is flanked by a raised terrace. In the middle is a monkish fish-pond or stone basin, above which rises a grove of trees, flanked at either end by leaden statues of Fauns, set up by a former Lord Byron, and known to the country folk as "the old Lord's Devils." Upon the bark of a beech stem, one of two springing from one root like brother and sister, Lord Byron carved his name and that of his sister Augusta during his last visit to the place in 1813. The inscription, being in danger of perishing, has been cut out, and is now preserved in a glass case in the house. On the edge of the pretty modern flower-garden rises "the young oak" which he planted and celebrated by some verses. Lord Byron caused the tombs of some of the monks to be opened, and raised several stone coffins, from one of which he selected a skull, and had it mounted in silver as a drinking-cup; this the present owner has interred in the chapter-house, now used as a private chapel.

On the lawn is the monument to "Boatswain," a favourite Newfoundland dog, whose epitaph by his master is engraved on it. Lord Byron desired in his will to be buried beside this monument — a direction very properly neglected by his relatives. In front of the Abbey expands a lake, frequently mentioned by the poet:—

> "Before the mansion lay a lucid lake,
> Broad as transparent, deep and freshly fed
> By a river, which its soften'd way did take
> In currents through the calmer waters spread
> Around; the wild fowl nestled in the brake
> And sedges, brooding in their liquid bed;
> The woods sloped downwards to its brink, and stood
> With their green faces fix'd upon the flood.
>
> I did remind thee of our own dear lake
> By the old Hall, which may be mine no more.
> Leman is fair; but think not I forsake
> The sweet remembrance of a dearer shore;
> Sad havoc time must with my memory make
> Ere that or thou can fade these eyes before."—*To Augusta.*

On the brink are the forts built by the old Lord, who also maintained a small vessel on the water. From some parts of the park, a conspicuous feature is the headland, once crowned with a tuft of trees, beautifully alluded to in Byron's poem of 'The Dream,' but wantonly cut down some years ago by the late Jack Musters, the former owner of the soil:—

> "A gentle hill,
> Green and of mild declivity, the last—
> As 't were the cape of a long ridge of such,
> Save that there was no sea to lave its base,
> But a most living landscape, and the wave
> Of wood and corn-fields, and the abodes of men
> Scatter'd at intervals, and wreaths of smoke
> Arising from such rustic roofs; the hill
> Was crown'd with a peculiar diadem
> Of trees in circular array, so fix'd
> Not by the sport of nature, but of man."

On this spot Byron took his last farewell of Miss Chaworth.

The estate, which is of about 3200 acres in extent, was purchased by the present proprietor in 1861, soon after the death of Col. Wildman. The park, of 880 acres, has been enclosed and divided into farms, except a tract near the house.

Newstead stands within the borders of

Sherwood Forest, originally occupying about one-fifth part of Nottinghamshire, extended from Nottingham to Worksop, 20 m., with a breadth of from 5 to 7 m., a tract of about 95,000 acres, of which between 60,000 and 70,000 are now cultivated, though the soil is but poor, producing little beside oats and potatoes. It belonged to the Crown from the reign of Henry II., and was often the scene of royal huntings; it was the resort of Robin Hood, and reputed traces of him are to be found all round Newstead. At 1 m. S. of the abbey, in the grounds of **Papplewick Hall** (H. F. Walter, Esq.), is **Robin Hood's Cave**, cut out of the red sandstone rock, with rude attempts at columns and arches; it is said to have served as a stable.

Robin Hood's Hill, and Chair, are to the N. of the park, and farther in the same direction, near Blidworth (where there is an excavated sandstone rock), is **Fountain Dale**, where Robin Hood encountered Friar Tuck—

" From ten o'clock that very day,
    Until four in the afternoon.
The curtal Friar kept Fountain Dale
    Seven long years and more;
There was neither lord, nor knight, nor earl
    Could make him yield before."

Not far off is Thieves' Wood, whence it is a walk of 2½ m. to Mansfield, passing on E. Berry Hill (James Lees, Esq.).

11½ m. Annesley (Stat.). Annesley Hall (J. P. Chaworth-Musters, Esq.), one of the seats of the ancient family of Chaworth, for whose heiress, the "Mary" of his poetry, Lord Byron entertained a secret attachment in his youth. It is a brick building, resembling an old French château, and stands in a beautifully wooded park. It is approached by a gatehouse. It contains "the antique oratory," mentioned in Byron's 'Dream' as the scene of his interview with the lady of his love—" her who was his destiny."

Mr. Chaworth, of this place, who was killed in a duel in 1765 by the 5th Lord Byron, an ancestor of the poet, is buried in the old Ch., which has been superseded by a modern Ch., erected in 1874 by the late Mr. J. C. Musters. It is situated on the high ground, and a populous colliery village has grown up near to it.

The ground in the neighbourhood of Annesley is elevated (about 600 ft.), and the summit level of the rly. is reached at Kirkby Forest, 12 m., where Robin Hood's Hills are pierced by a tunnel. These hills, which are still open and uncultivated, offer pleasant rambles, and wide and beautiful views in every direction. From Coxmoor, on a clear day, the towers of Lincoln Cathedral first catch the eye, while the southern horizon is bounded by the rocks of Charnwood. Nearer home are the woods of Newstead and Annesley in one direction, and those of Hardwick in the other, with the spires and villages of Kirkby and Sutton just at foot.

13 m. Kirkby Junct. Stat. Here a branch from the Erewash Valley line (Rte. 3) runs in. The restored Ch. has Norm. portions. Near it the Erewash takes its rise.

15 m. Sutton in Ashfield (Stat.) is a large village, with hosiery and silk mills and limeworks. It is picturesquely placed on the border of the Forest, and its Ch. is noticeable for its lofty octagonal spire. It contains a memorial window and monuments to the Arkwright and the Scarsdale families.

Sutton Hall (W. Arkwright, Esq.), a Corinthian edifice, on the site of an old seat of the Leakes, Earls of Scarsdale. In 1643 Sutton was gal-

Route 13.—Mansfield—Pleasley.

lantly held by Lord Deincourt for the king, but he eventually had to yield to a superior force under Col. Gell. A legend is told of one of the ancient Lords of Sutton, who went to the Holy Land, and, being very anxious to return home, fell asleep, and awoke in the porch of Sutton Ch. Here he found that his wife, whom he had left at home, had given him up for lost, and was that very day to be married again. Between Sutton and Mansfield is a large reservoir, made by the Duke of Portland in 1836, for a water supply for the irrigation of his meadows. Its extent is 70 acres.

17½ m. ↱ **Mansfield** (Stat.), a thriving market-town, of substantially built stone houses. It stands on the border of Sherwood Forest and of the "Dukeries" (see Rtes. 15, 16): it is traversed by the little river Maun, on the banks of which are several cotton mills; there are also lace-thread mills and shoe factories; but maltings, iron-foundries, and stone quarries now give the chief employment. The Parish Ch. has a Norm. and Dec. tower, surmounted by a low spire. The Market-place has a Town-hall, and a very elegant Gothic memorial for Lord George Bentinck, the well-known Parliamentary leader (d. 1848). In the W. part of the town is St. John's Ch., built 1855, with fine tower and spire.

Mansfield was from very early times a royal manor, and from its vicinity to Sherwood Forest was often the residence of the kings of England, who repaired thither for sport. The ballad of the King (said to be Henry II.) and the Miller of Mansfield commemorates such a visit:—

"When as our royal king came home from
  Nottingham,
And with his nobles at Westminster lay,
Recounting the sports and pastimes they
  had taken
In this late progress all along the way;
Of them all, great and small, he did protest
The Miller of Mansfield's sport liked he
  best."

The **King's Mill**, situated in a deep glen (1 m. S.W. of the town, close to the rly. viaduct), is said to have been the scene of the King's entertainment; but it is more likely that it obtained its name from being a royal manor. Not far off is the Miller's house; but both buildings are modern; the ruins of the old mill being supposed to be covered by the waters of a reservoir. The whole neighbourhood is full of traditions of high personages. At **Hambleton** or Hamilton Hill, to E. of Sutton Stat., Henry II. is said to have lost himself while hunting, and at **Low Hardwick**, on W. of the line before reaching Sutton, Cardinal Wolsey rested before his arrival at Leicester. Dodsley, the bookseller and author of 'The Toy-shop,' was born at Mansfield in 1703. The Duke's Flood Dyke between Mansfield and Ollerton is a work interesting to the agriculturist (Rte. 15). It has been conjectured by some antiquaries that Mansfield was a Roman station, from the discovery of coins, &c., and of a very perfect foundation of a villa near Pleasley, in the year 1786.

From Mansfield a very pleasant *Excursion* may be made into Derbyshire, to Hardwick Hall, and Bolsover, the whole distance being about 16 m. Both these places can be visited by Rly. by taking the Alfreton line as far as Pleasley, and changing on to the Doe Lea line.

Quitting the town by the Chesterfield road, at 1 m. is a road on N., leading to Mansfield Woodhouse (Stat.) (see Rte. 15). At 3 m. the little river Meden is crossed, and Derbyshire is entered at **Pleasley** (Stat.), a village of cotton-mills, with an ancient market-cross. The scenery is very pleasing, a narrow rocky valley traversed by the stream, which at one part is dammed up, so as to form a capacious reservoir. A walk of less than 2 m. up the river bank, passing

Newbound Mill, conducts to Hardwick Hall. On S., at 1½ m. distance, is **Teversall** (Stat.), a pretty village on a hill; the Ch. has a good Norm. doorway and some monuments of the Greenhalghs and Molyneuxs. The Manor-house (J. Gething, Esq.) has very fine gardens.

♂ **HARDWICK HALL** (Duke of Devonshire) is a fine Elizabethan mansion of great extent, scarcely altered since the day it was built; still, only an example of faded splendour. It is habitable, but destitute of all comfort, and very little suited for a dwelling of the present time. It was built by Elizabeth Countess of Shrewsbury, better known as " Bess of Hardwick," who commenced it in 1576. She was born in the old Hall, in 1520, and was the daughter of John Hardwick, Esq., a man of such moderate fortune that she received only 40 marks as her marriage-portion. She was four times married: her husbands being Robert Barlow, Esq., Sir Wm. Cavendish, the founder of Chatsworth, Sir Wm. St. Lo, and George, Earl of Shrewsbury, whom she survived 17 years. Biographers agree in describing her as " a proud, selfish, and intriguing woman, a money-lender, a dealer in coals, lead, and timber, who died immensely rich, and yet without a friend." She was, indeed, a shrewd and thrifty dame, and managed her own estates, farmed her own land, and enjoyed a rent-roll of 60,000l. a year. Her greatest passion was for building, as exemplified in the noble houses that she erected: and local tradition accounts for this by a prophecy, that she should never die until she ceased to build. Hence her incessant efforts to keep the workmen busy; but at last, in 1607, so hard a frost occurred as to render masonwork an impossibility; and during this frost her death took place. The Hall stands in the midst of an extensive park, abounding in venerable oaks, now for the most part past their maturity, stagged and gone at the head. The house on the outside looks like a lantern, so great is the number of windows—

" Hardwick Hall,
More glass than wall,"

is a local rhyme. " You shall have sometimes faire houses so full of glass that one cannot tell where to become to be out of the sun."— *Bacon's Essays*. It is surmounted by a singular parapet of stone-work, perforated with the initials of its foundress, E. S., and is fronted by a walled garden. The interior is graphically described by Horace Walpole, who cites Hardwick as a characteristic specimen of the style of architecture prevailing in the reign of Elizabeth:—" Hardwick, still preserved as it was furnished for the reception and imprisonment of the Queen of Scots, is a curious picture of that age and style. Nothing can exceed the expense in the bed of state, in the hangings of the same chamber, and of the coverings for the tables. The first is cloth of gold, cloth of silver, velvets of different colours, lace, fringes, and embroidery. The hangings consist of figures, large as life, representing the Virtues and the Vices, embroidered on grounds of white and black velvet. The cloths to cast over the tables are embroidered and embossed with gold on velvets and damasks. The only moveables of any taste are the cabinets and tables themselves, carved in oak. The chimneys are wide enough for a hall or kitchen, and over the arras are friezes of many feet deep, with relievos in stucco representing huntings. Here, and in all the great mansions of that age, is a gallery, remarkable only for its extent."

The **Hall**, which is very spacious and lofty, and set round with antlers, contains a beautiful statue by Westmacott of Mary Queen of Scots,

Route 13.—Hardwick Hall.

bearing a Latin inscription on the pedestal.

In an antechamber are some curious leather hangings stamped with patterns in gold. The spacious **Council Chamber**, 65 ft. long, is hung round with unrivalled tapestry (which abounds in all parts of the house), and its walls are surmounted by a stucco frieze 10 or 12 ft. deep, representing a stag-hunt. In the **Library**, which also is hung with tapestry, are portraits of the Countess of Shrewsbury; of Lady Sandwich (Ann Boyle), by Lely; and of Geoffrey Hudson the dwarf, by Vandyck. The chimney is ornamented with a stiff relief of Apollo and the Muses. The tapestry in the **Drawing-room** is ancient and curious, representing the story of Esther and Ahasuerus. The **Chapel** also contains some exquisite specimens of tapestry and embroidered needlework. In the **Dining-room** is a mantelpiece with the inscription—" The conclusion of alle thinges is to fear God and keepe his commandementes."

The **State-Bedroom** is a very fine apartment, containing tapestry delineating the story of Ulysses, a state canopy of black velvet, and some inlaid furniture. Queen Mary's bed was brought hither from the old house, and is placed in a chamber still bearing over the door the arms of Scotland, and letters M. R. The memory of Mary Stuart is, perhaps, the chief source of interest at Hardwick. Here are preserved the furniture which she used, the cushions of her oratory, the tapestry wrought by her hands. "The bed has been rich beyond description, and now hangs in costly golden tatters; the hangings, part of which they say her Majesty worked, are composed of figures as large as life, sewed and embroidered on black velvet, white satin, &c., and represent the virtues that were necessary to her."—*Walpole.* Grey says, "One would think that Mary was just walked down with her guard into the park for half an hour." For 16 years of her captivity in England Mary was entrusted to the charge of the Earl of Shrewsbury, the lord of this mansion, but she passed only a small portion of that time here.

The **Picture Gallery** extends along the whole E. front of the building, is magnificently lighted, and covered from top to bottom with nearly 200 portraits, which have historical value, though but few deserve to be mentioned as works of art. Among the most interesting are Sir Thos. More; Lady Jane Grey; Bp. Gardiner; James V. of Scotland and Mary of Guise; Mary Queen of Scots, a wholelength in black, pale and worn with suffering, taken in the 10th year of her captivity, 1578; Queen Elizabeth. with golden hair befrizzled, with a monstrous farthingale, and a gown embroidered with serpents, birds, a sea-horse, &c.; her minister, Burghley; the Queen of Bohemia; three different portraits of "Bess of Hardwick, Countess of Shrewsbury;" also portraits of two of her husbands, Cavendish and Shrewsbury; and her grandchild, the unfortunate Lady Arabella Stuart, when only two years of age, with a doll in her hand. She was born and lived here many years under watch and ward. Hobbes, the philosopher, lived as tutor in the Cavendish family, and died at Hardwick æt. 89, 1679.

Near the house are the remains of the **Old Hall**, built probably in the reign of Henry VII., and interesting because in it Queen Mary passed a small part of her captivity It is a ruin, roofless, draped with ivy, and tottering to its fall.

A short distance N. of the park is the village of **Ault Hucknall**, in the small Ch. of which Hobbes the philosopher is buried; there are also some Cavendish tombs.

Towards the N.E. is the hamlet of **Glapwell**, once a dependency of Darley Abbey, and at 7 m. Scarcliffe; the restored Norm. and E. E. Ch. has a remarkable 13th-centy. monument to a lady and child, probably of the Frecheville family. In the parish was a spring, called Owlsditch, noted for its greater abundance of water in dry than in wet weather, and locally regarded as one of the wonders of the district.

9 m. (or 7 m. by the direct road) ‡ Bolsover (Stat.), now little more than a village, but formerly a market-town, which grew up around a castle founded by William Peveril, and seized by the crown, temp. Hen. II. The town stands on a precipitous bank, overlooking the vale of Scarsdale, and had fortifications of its own, independently of the castle; several of the watch-towers remain, of Elizabethan date apparently; and there are also earthworks, ascribed to the Danes. The *Ch.*, Norm. and E. E., has a 13th-centy. carving of the Crucifixion, and another (15th centy.) of the Nativity. In the Cavendish chapel are some elaborate monuments to the Cavendish family, and one to the 2nd Duke of Newcastle (d. 1691), which is resplendent with variegated marbles. On the monument of Sir Charles Cavendish (d. 1617), which contains the effigies of himself, his wife and 3 sons, is an inscription that deserves perusal. The Ch. was restored in 1877.

Bolsover Castle occupies the site of the Norm. edifice, which was held for King John against the barons, and was one of the possessions of Edmd. Tudor, Earl of Richmond, but had been suffered to fall into decay in the time of Leland, who speaks of it as a ruin. The manor was granted by Hen. VIII. to Thomas, Duke of Norfolk, on whose attainder it reverted to the crown; and in 1552 it was bestowed on Lord Talbot, afterwards Earl of Shrewsbury, and one of the husbands of Bess of Hardwick.

By her management, the estate was secured to her second son, Sir Charles Cavendish, in whose descendants in the female line, the Dukes of Portland, it still remains.

The grandson of the builder, William Cavendish, Earl, and afterwards Marquis and Duke, of Newcastle, twice entertained here with great magnificence King Charles I. and his court, at a cost of 4000*l.* the first time, and of 15,000*l.* the second, being, according to Clarendon, "such an excess of feasting as had scarce ever been known in England before." On one of these occasions, 1634, Ben Jonson's masque of 'Love's Welcome' was got up in the most sumptuous manner, and performed by the courtiers. Bolsover was taken by the Parliamentary forces in 1644, and was afterwards saved from destruction by a younger brother of the Earl, who bought it in. From the date of its sale its history as a fortress ceases, and it became instead one of the most splendid residences in the land.

The present castle or castellated mansion was begun by Bess of Hardwick, and finished in 1613, by Sir C. Cavendish, her son. It stands on a fine elevated and wooded terrace, from whence there is a splendid view over Scarsdale, Hardwick Hall being conspicuous to the S.W. It is a square castellated edifice, 4 stories in height, with turrets at each corner, except the N.E., where there is a high tower, on the site of Peveril's Norm. keep. The interior consists of noble rooms, with wainscoted walls, highly ornamented chimney-pieces, and ceilings carved and gilded. A flight of steps leads up to the door, which is surmounted by the Cavendish arms, and leads into a vaulted hall. Beyond is the pillar dining-room, so called from a column round which the table is arranged. A stone staircase conducts to the Star Chamber, or drawing-room, a room 40 ft. long, richly adorned, and filled with old furniture. The roof is blue, ornamented with golden stars, and the upper part of the walls is adorned with large pictures of the 12 Cæsars, copied from those that hung in the Westminster Star Chamber in the time of Charles I. An adjoining small room, most beautifully roofed with marble, was the boudoir of the literary Duchess of Newcastle.

On the terrace is the picturesque ivy and lichen-clad ruin of a superb mansion in the late Elizabethan style, begun by Sir Charles Cavendish, and added to by his son, who also erected a Riding School, so frequently mentioned in his work on Horsemanship, which contains some excellent views of Bolsover. In the reign of George I. Bolsover ceased to be a residence of the Cavendishes, eventually went by marriage into the family of the Duke of Portland. The whole of these later buildings were dismantled, but the pseudo-Norman castle has been ever since kept in repair.

In the neighbourhood of Bolsover are extensive stone *quarries*.

ROUTE 14.

NEWARK TO MANSFIELD, BY SOUTHWELL.

MIDLAND RAILWAY. 18½ m.

Shortly after leaving Newark the line crosses the Trent near Averham (Rte. 11), and runs at the foot of the range of high ground on which the large and pleasant village of **Upton** is situated; the view S. over the vale in which the river pursues its winding course is very agreeable.

3 m. **Rolleston** Junct. Stat. (Rte. 11). The line now turns N., ascends the valley of the Greet, and reaches at

6½ m. ⚡ **Southwell** (Stat.). The town consists of 5 distinct portions, with open spaces between, and thus occupies a very large space in proportion to its population, which is about 3000.

This place was fixed on by some early antiquaries as the site of the Roman station Ad Pontem, but it is now considered to be represented by Farndon, on the Trent, 4 m. S.E. Camden says, "That this [Southwell] is that city which Bede called Tio-vul-ginacester I the rather believe, because those things which he relates of Paulinus baptizing in the Trent are always said to have been done here by the private history of this church." The Minster is supposed to have been founded by Paulinus, about 630, under the auspices of **Edwin of Northumbria**, and down to the year 1841 it belonged to the diocese of York. It became a collegiate church shortly after the Norman conquest—even before, according to some writers—and many of its prebends were founded by Northern primates. In 1540 it was surrendered to the

Crown, but the chapter was shortly after re-established, and endowed with a large part of its old possessions. In 1552 it was again dissolved, and its property granted to Dudley, Duke of Northumberland. His attainder caused it to revert to the Crown. Mary re-established the chapter, and it remained substantially unchanged until it passed into the hands of the Ecclesiastical Commissioners, 1836-1841. Several eminent Churchmen have been prebends of Southwell, among whom may be named Bps. Hutton of Durham, Sanderson of Lincoln, and Denison of Salisbury; and also Mr. Mompesson of Eyam (Rte. 8).

The **Minster** (now a **Cathedral**), which is one of the finest ecclesiastical structures in the county, stands in a well-kept close, the main approach to which is by an ivy-mantled gatehouse facing the W. front. It is a cruciform Ch., 306 ft. long, with transept, 122 ft. It has a central and two western towers (between which is a noble Perp. W. window of 7 lights), and, though on a smaller scale, bears a striking resemblance to York Minster. The nave, the transepts, and the towers are Norm., of the early part of the 12th cent., but the W. towers, which are of 7 stages, show Dec. and Perp. alterations. The central tower is of but 3 stages, of which the middle is occupied by an interlacing arcade, partly blocked. The choir, its aisles, and its small E. transepts, are Early Eng., and among the best examples of the style. The E. end has two tiers of lancet-windows. The organ-screen and the stalls are later Dec., and particularly good. Notice also the brass eagle lectern, formerly belonging to Newstead Priory. It was found in a lake there and sold as old metal, but being accidentally seen in a shop at Nottingham by the Rev. S. R. Kaye, a prebend of Southwell, it was purchased by him, and presented to the church in 1805. The eagle stands on a ball, in which when opened were found concealed deeds relating to the priory.

The N. transept contains the altar-tomb, with effigy, of Abp. Sandys of York, who died at Southwell, July 10, 1588. The S. transept, which is entered by a doorway with a segmental arch, is of 3 stages, the 2 middle lighted by circular-headed windows, with dog-tooth and billet mouldings, and the upper stage by round windows, divided from the others by stringcourses. The windows are filled in with stained glass, as is also the E. window of the choir. The triforial arches are large, those of the clerestory small.

The nave has a wooden ceiling, with 5 recessed arches and elaborate moulding and interlacing arcade, and the aisles are groined in stone; they are separated from each other by 7 massive circular piers, from which spring round-headed arches with billet moulding, and from the gallery above there springs another series with square piers. The clerestory is lighted by circular, and the S. aisle by Perp. windows, above which, externally, runs a stringcourse; some very small lights are inserted between the latter and the corbel-table. Notice the Norm. stringcourse carried along the whole of the exterior, from the transepts to the western towers. The N. porch is very fine, and has a deeply-recessed Norm. doorway.

The octagonal **Chapterhouse**, N. of the choir, is Early Dec., with a fine double door and good window-tracery; it somewhat resembles that of York, being surrounded by stalls, but it has no central column. The foliage of the capitals is particularly graceful.

To the E. of the Ch. is the Residentiary House, a plain red brick building. Adjoining, on S.

are the very picturesque remains of the **Archbishop's Palace**. The Northern primates had a dwelling here at a very early period: indeed, Ælfric died at Southwell in 1050; so did Gerard, the 2nd Norm. Archbishop, in 1108. He died whilst sleeping in the garden after dinner, and as a book on astronomy was found beside him, he was denounced as a magician, and denied burial in his cathedral. Much of the site of the palace is now occupied as a market-garden. The edifice was erected by Abp. Thoresby, c. 1360, but greatly altered and added to by Wolsey. The walls are all Dec., with Perp. windows inserted; there is a good bold roll moulding, as a string along the walls, of Dec. character, and some curious closets in the walls and buttresses. There are several Perp. fireplaces and chimneys (the lower parts Dec., the upper Perp.), some of which are engraved in Parker's 'Domestic Architecture.' The archbishops had no less than 4 parks at Southwell and its neighbourhood. One of these, *Norwood* (L. R. Starkey, Esq.), 1 m. N.W., still exists, and contains a very aged tree, known as Cludd's Oak.

Beside the Minister, there is a handsome district Ch. with spire 150 ft. high, at West Thorpe. The streets of the High Town, or Southwell proper, are well paved, and very clean and quiet, the aspect of the whole being in strict accordance with its position as a small cathedral town.

The Saracen's Head is the old inn where, tradition says, Charles I. put himself in the hands of the Scots' Commissioners, and was by them led to their camp at Kelham, opposite Newark.

To the E. of Southwell, on Burgage Green, an open space with fine trees, is the *Manor House*, the residence of Lord Byron and his mother during his boyhood. Even as a youth his passion for arms exhibited itself, and the furniture of his chamber was much cut and slashed—a circumstance subsequently turned to good account by the auctioneer, who embellished the matter by asserting the havoc to have been made with "the identical sword with which a former Lord Byron killed Mr. Chaworth." 1 m. S.W. is the village of **Halloughton**. It contains a Manor farm incorporating some interesting remains of the Prebendal Manor House of the 15th centy. The little Ch. has been restored, but preserves the old E. gable with two lancets, and a good oak rood-screen.

8½ m. **Kirklington** and **Edingley** (Stat.). These are both mere villages, standing N. and S. of the line. Kirklington has a modern castellated Hall (Mrs. Boddam-Whetham), with very extensive grounds.

11 m. **Farnsfield** (Stat.). A clean, pleasant-looking village, on the verge of the so-called Forest, which from here to Mansfield is little more than an alternation of wide stretches of heath with patches of arable land. The *Ch.*, rebuilt except the tower, is a handsome Perp. structure, with a chastely-decorated interior. Hexgrave (G. Sugden, Esq.), one of the archiepiscopal parks, is in this parish.

14 m. **Rainworth** (Stat.). This is a hamlet of Blidworth, consisting of little more than the *Robin Hood Inn*, and one or two farms. It stands on the Rainworth Water, a tributary of the Maun, amid pleasant scenery, which, though not particularly striking, will well repay a few hours' ramble.

18½ m. **Mansfield** (Stat.) (Rte. 13).

ROUTE 15.

MANSFIELD TO WORKSOP AND RETFORD [WELBECK].

MIDLAND RLY. AND M. S. & L. RLY.
22 m.

To those who can spare the time the drive of 12 m. by the coach road is much preferable, as the charm of the scenery is lost by going by the Rly. The road is, in great part, through a group of noble parks, which, from their having originally belonged to former Dukes of Norfolk, Kingston, Portland, and Newcastle, have fixed upon this district the well-known name of the "**Dukeries.**" The Duke of Norfolk, however, sold Worksop, and the Dukes of Kingston now extinct, have been succeeded in the possession of Thoresby by their descendant in the female line, Earl Manvers. The Dukes of Portland and Newcastle remain at Welbeck and Clumber. This aristocratic territory occupies that part of the area of Sherwood where spacious tracts of that ancient forest are still preserved.

Leaving Mansfield by rail, and passing over a lofty viaduct,

At 1½ m. is **Mansfield Woodhouse** (Stat.), a place remarkable for its quarries of magnesian limestone, which, and not, as commonly supposed, those of Bolsover, furnished the material for Southwell Minster (Rte. 14). The E. E. Ch. is a handsome edifice, with lofty spire, which contains a sanctus bell. It was restored in 1878. There are traces of a camp, supposed to be Roman, at a short distance, where Roman remains have been often found.

[A road on E. leads by Clipstone and Edwinstowe to Ollerton (8 m.). **Clipstone** is an estate of the Duke of Portland, and the road to it runs by the side of a canal of irrigation, formed by the late Duke, at an expense of 80,000l., and called the Duke's *Flood Dyke*; by which the stream of the Maun is distributed by minor cuts, tiled drains, and sluicegates along the slopes below it; and a previously barren valley, sides of which were rabbit-warrens overgrown with heath and gorse, and its bottom a swamp producing tussocks and rushes, has been converted into a most productive tract of meadow and pasture land, yielding three crops of grass annually. The river is diverted near the vale-head and led along the hillside, and the bottom has been drained. The canal extends to near Ollerton, about 7 m. from Mansfield, the latter portion being applied to the lands of Earl Manvers.

These famous meadows have been often quoted in sanitary and agricultural discussions. The canal water, after depositing all its more valuable contents upon the land, runs off through the bottom of the valley in a stream as clear as crystal. It is full of trout, the fishing however is preserved. The domain of Clipstone exhibits a specimen of good farming, and is well worth a visit from all who are interested in agricultural improvements.

A little to the S. of Clipstone are the scanty remains, consisting of rubble walls, of **King John's Palace**, still called "The King's House," and long possessed by the Earls of Shrewsbury. Between Clipstone and the Warsop road, about a mile from each, is the **Parliament Oak**, under which John held a council in 1212. It is still flourishing, though supported by iron rods.

Midway between Clipstone and Edwinstowe a beautiful Gothic archway, called the **Duke's Folly**, serves as a sort of lodge, the upper part being used as a free school. It is in the Perp. style, the mouldings, window tracery, and sculpture well executed; while the niches are filled appropriately with statues of Robin Hood, Little John, Maid Marian, Allan à Dale, Friar Tuck, Cœur-de-Lion, and King John, with a Latin inscription from Horace. A broad turf ride leads from this lodge to Welbeck, passing through

Birkland Forest, the wildest and most natural portion of Sherwood Forest—a very paradise of picnic-holders; whose privileges, however, have been curtailed, owing to some mischief having been perpetrated by foolish holiday-makers. There are no restrictions whatever in Earl Manver's neighbouring forest of Bilhaugh. "An enclosure act has divided amongst farmers the land which till recently gave some idea of the old forest, and here and there a scanty patch of a few acres alone remains to call to the memory of older inhabitants its former condition. But if you would know what the forest may have been, you may still find a beautifully undulating range of land, rich in furze and heather, stretching away from the first milestone on the Southwell road towards Rufford Abbey, where the partridge has been hunted with the hawk within the memory of man."—*A. W. W.* Birkland (so called from the full-grown birches) has been a good deal thinned, and very few of the real old giants are left. The gaps, however, are being filled up with relays of oaks and Spanish chestnuts. The best route for the pedestrian is from Clipstone Lodge, up the ride into the forest, and thence, in a N.W. direction, to Gleadthorpe Lodge, where the Warsop and Ollerton road is crossed. Between Budby and Edwinstowe is to be found the *Major Oak*, which has a circumference of 30 ft., and that of the branches, at its greatest extent, of 240 ft.; seven people are said to have dined in it at once. *Robin Hood's Larder* is another fine example of old forest life, which will hold a dozen people inside. It is sometimes called "The Shambles," from the fact that Hooton, a noted sheep-stealer, used to hang up the carcases of the sheep inside.

At 6 m. is **Edwinstowe**, with its pretty church, a charming specimen of a forest village. 2 m. further E. is Ollerton (see Rte. 16).]

4½ m. **Shirebrook** (Stat.), in Derbyshire. To the E. is **Sookholme**, a small village, with an ancient chapel dependent on Warsop. Near by is Nettleworth Hall (Miss Alleyne), and 1½ m. N. is **Warsop**, or Market Warsop, though not now a market town, celebrated for its horse and cattle fairs. The tourist must not confound this name with Worksop, or, as commonly pronounced, Wussup. A little beyond it the road crosses the river Meden, and farther still a high mount, called Cuckney Hill, where is a fine view to N. and E. over the woods of the Dukeries.

6 m. **Langwith** (Stat.), in Derbyshire. 2 m. E. is **Cuckney** with a handsome Perp. Ch., with Norm. doorway; it once possessed a castle, of which only the site remains.

8 m. **Elmton** and **Creswell** (Junct. Stat., with a branch line to Chesterfield). On the E. are the *Creswell Crags* (see Rte. 4), through which the road leads (2¼ m. from the Stat.) to

§ **WELBECK ABBEY**, the seat of the Duke of Portland. The park is ornamented by a large lake. and is remarkable for its woods, and for some of the finest oak-trees in Great Britain—veritable survivors of Sherwood Forest. Near the entrance to the Abbey stands the *Greendale Oak*, once so large that a carriage-road ran through its trunk, but now in the extremity of vegetable age,

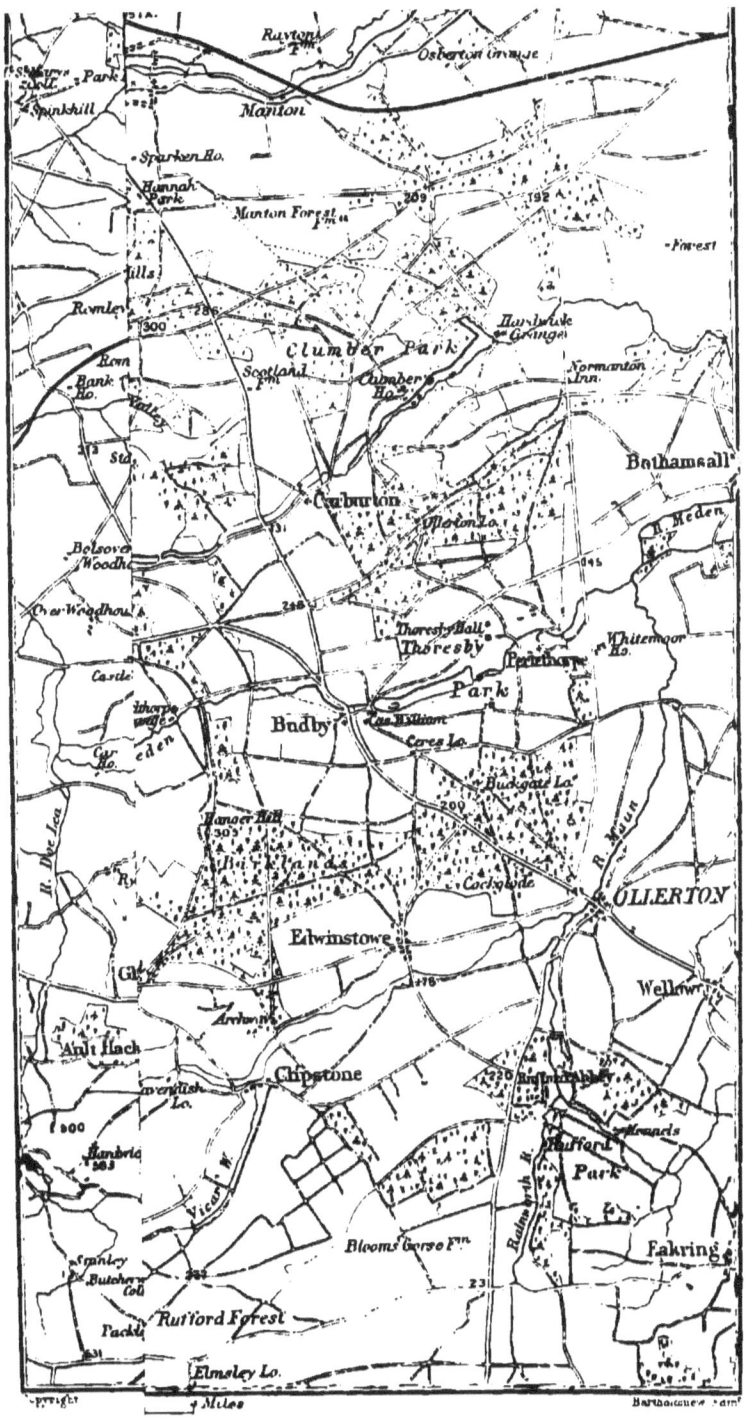

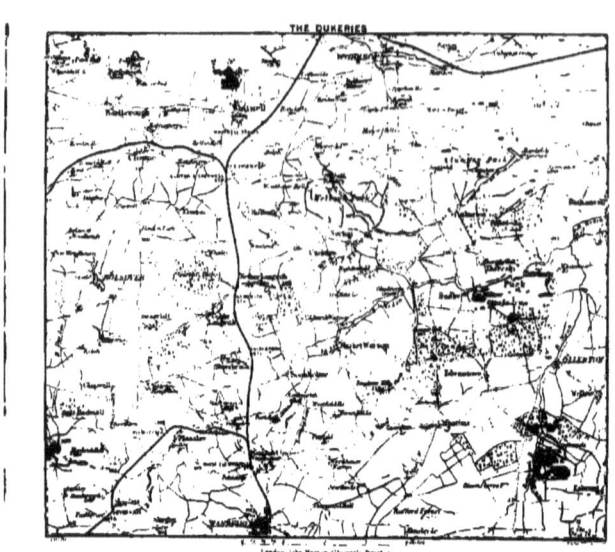

with a mere trace of vitality, and supported wholly by props; it is said to be more than 700 years old. On the side next Worksop Manor (N.) are two more vigorous stems, but stag-headed, called "The Porters," because they stand on either side a gateway. Not far off is the Duke's Walking-stick, 111 ft. high. The park has an extent of 2283 acres, and is 8 m. in circuit. The Abbey is a large battlemented house, lying in a hollow near the margin of the lake.

Welbeck Abbey, which was founded, temp. Hen. II., by Thomas de Cuckeney, was of the Premonstratensian order. At the Dissolution it was sold to the Whalleys, one of whom parted with it to the Cavendishes, who built the present house in 1604, in which parts of the old structure are incorporated. The interior is Jacobean, but badly executed, the fan tracery and pendants of some of the chief rooms being formed of stucco on basket work. (The same may be noticed in the music-room at Lullingstone, of about the same date; see *Handbook for Kent*.) Ben Jonson's interlude of 'Love's Welcome' was performed here when Charles I. was entertained by Cavendish, afterwards Duke of Newcastle.

The old stables and riding-house, now disused, were built by the same Duke. He was the author of a work on 'Horsemanship,' the staunch supporter of Charles I., and the husband of a most eccentric duchess.

The house contains some fine pictures, viz.—Thomas Wentworth, Lord Strafford, in armour, full-length and fine; Lucy Percy, Countess of Carlisle; Sir Kenelm and Lady Digby, with 2 sons, and William Cavendish, Duke of Newcastle; Archbishop Laud; Philip Herbert, Earl of Pembroke; all by *Vandyck*;—a Senator of Antwerp, and Moses in the Bulrushes, *Murillo*; St. John in the Wilderness, *Caracci*; a Holy Family, *Raphael*; Christ, and St. John with [*Derby, &c.*]

the Lamb, *Guido*. Several family portraits: Lord Rich, Cavendish, Lord Titchfield. Mr. C. Cavendish, *Sir Joshua Reynolds*: Admiral Tromp, *Corn. Jansen*. Several hunting-pieces attributed to *Snyders*, and some to *Rubens*.

The grounds were undermined by the eccentricity of the late Duke with passages and subterranean structures, among the latter a famous riding-school, now used as a ball-room and picture gallery. It is 160 ft. in length. There is an underground passage 2640 yds. in length towards Worksop, along which carriages can drive. The new riding-school, 400 ft. in length, by 106 ft. in width, and 50 ft. in height, and the tan gallop, 422 yds. long, were also erected by the late Duke. The stables, dairy, workshops, and schools for the children of the employées form quite a colony. Notice the almshouses erected by the present Duke out of his winnings on the turf. The stud stables are 1 m. distant.

Adjoining Welbeck, on N., connecting it with Worksop town, and skirted by a road on the l., is **Worksop Manor**, once the property of the Duke of Norfolk, but purchased in 1840 by the Duke of Newcastle for 350,000*l.*, and by his descendents sold in 1890 to Mr. John Robinson. The house, once a vast Italian pile, was built on the site of a former mansion, which contained 500 rooms, and was burned down in 1761, with all its gallery of paintings and statues, to the value of 100,000*l.* The Duke of Newcastle pulled it down and converted the stables into the present moderate-sized residence. The park stretched nearly up to the town of Worksop, but has been partly enclosed and ploughed up, and is let in small lots. It still retains some noble avenues. Worksop Manor is held by the tenure of providing a glove for the king's right hand at the coronation and supporting it while he holds the sceptre—a tenure shifted

H

to this place from Farnham Royal, near Windsor.

10 m. Whitwell (Stat.) (see Rte. 4).

15 m. ⚥ Worksop (Stat.), a clean country town of two principal streets at right angles, composed of redbrick houses. It has a large trade in malting, and formerly "had a great produce of liquorice." There are also some iron-foundries for agricultural implements, and many people are employed in making packing-cases for the Sheffield manufacturers.

In the suburb called *Radford*, on the E. of the town, is the parish Ch., formed out of the very interesting Norm. nave of the **Church of the Priory**, founded by William de Lovetot in 1103, with the aisles restored in the Perp. style. There are 2 W. towers, surmounted by modern battlements and pinnacles, and the E. end has a good triple lancet, with circular windows above. The S. porch has an elaborate groined roof. The Ch. contains many monuments, particularly of the Lovetots and the Furnivals, ancestors of the Talbots, Earls of Shrewsbury, from whom the house of Howard inherited their vast midland and northern estates.

A short distance E. of the present Ch. is the ruined Lady Chapel; it is very fine E. E. work, and formerly contained many of the monuments now placed in the Ch.

On the S. side is a picturesque gateway in the Dec. and Perp. styles, a relic of the Priory. Notice the figures and sculptures on the S. face.

The Roman Catholic chapel at the top of Park-street was erected by the Duke of Norfolk at a cost of 3000*l.*, and contains some good carved stallwork, a carved altar, and painted windows.

St. Cuthbert's College is a short distance on the road to Clumber, on a site given by the Duke of Newcastle.

3 m. E. of Worksop, and to the N. of the M. S. & L. Rly., is **Osberton** (F. J. S. Foljambe, Esq.). "It stands between the river Ryton and the Chesterfield Canal, and has a portico of the Ionic order. The estate contains an abundance of thriving plantations of oak, larch, and other useful timber trees ; through the whole runs a rivulet, expanding in front of the house, and losing itself among the woods, so as to appear a river of considerable magnitude.

"The surrounding scenery is sylvan, the foreground interspersed with noble oak, elm, and beech trees, occasionally standing alone, but sometimes in groups; and is backed by extensive woods that contain spruce firs of the largest dimensions, which beautifully feather to the ground."

Less than 3 m. W. of Worksop is the Duke of Newcastle's colliery at **Shireoaks**, with rly. stat. The late Duke commenced sinking in 1854, through the Permian and magnesian measures, believing that the coal would be found to be lying immediately under them. After proceeding about 200 feet, coal was found, and the top hard measure reached in 1859, at a depth of 515 yards. About 1500 tons are now raised every day from the pits, a successful attempt, founded on good geological calculation, to extend the area of our coal-producing basins. A colliery village sprung up, and for the inhabitants the late Duke erected a handsome *Ch.*, in the E. E. style, the first stone of which was laid by the Prince of Wales. The Duke died very shortly after, and the chancel was elaborately decorated, with reredos, painted windows, &c., to his memory.

From Worksop the line (M. S. & L. Rly.) continues to

22 m. **Retford** (see Rte. 17).

ROUTE 16.

NEWARK TO WORKSOP, BY OLLERTON. [THORESBY, CLUMBER.]

BY ROAD. 21 m.

Crossing the Trent by a handsome modern bridge at 2¼ m. N. of Newark, **Kelham** is reached, where the headquarters of the Scots were fixed when Charles I. placed himself in their hands. The view from the bridge is very fine. On l. are the grounds of **Kelham Park** (Col. J. H. Manners-Sutton), reaching down to the river, and the stream itself, with its many windings and broad clear flood, makes a noble appearance. The neat small village is a mere appendage to the Hall, and the most striking object in the Ch. is the monumental chapel of the Suttons, Lords Lexington. The white marble effigies of the last Lord Lexington (Robert Sutton, d. 1723) and his wife are singularly placed back to back.

The house, a fine Gothic building, was rebuilt by *Scott* (after a fire had destroyed the old house, restored by the same architect). The entrance-gateway, with pillars of polished granite, is particularly good. On W. is the road to Southwell and Mansfield (Rte. 14).

5 m. On E. is **Caunton**, on the banks of a small stream called the Willoughby. The Ch. has a good Perp. tower.

There are some old mansions in the parish, viz. Dean Hall, an Elizabethan house, Beesthorpe Hall, the property of the ancient family of Bristowe, and Caunton Manor, the residence of Dr. Hole, Dean of Rochester, the eminent florist and writer on horticulture.

Higher up the Willoughby are **Maplebeck**, a retired hamlet, and beyond it **Eakring**, with a Ch. that formerly belonged to Rufford Abbey, and of which Mompesson, of Eyam, became rector. The soil in this neighbourhood is a stiff clay, on which a coarse description of hops is abundantly grown.

8½ m. **Knesall**, once a part of the possessions of the Earls of Chester.

11 m. **Wellow**, a large village, where chair-making is extensively carried on. The Ch. is a mean building, mainly of brick. To the E. of the village is the site of **Jordan Castle** (now occupied by a farm-house), built by Jordan Foliot, temp. Hen. II.

1½ m. l., on the verge of Sherwood, is **Rufford**, a village only remarkable for its noble seat of **Rufford Abbey** (Rt. Hon. Lord Savile, G.C.B.), an extensive edifice, in which are included some portions of the Cistercian monastery founded in 1148 by Hugh Fitz-ralph and his wife. Leland visited Rufford, and says of it, "On the other side of Rume Water is a village commonly called Rufford for Rumeford, a quarter of a mile beyond which stood a late Rumford Abbey of white monks. The Earl of Shrewsbyri hath it now of the king for exchange of land of his in Ireland." The hall is Elizabethan, and contains some old paintings, chiefly family portraits.

The well-wooded park (which afforded a shelter to Mr. Mompesson of Eyam,—Rte. 8) includes an area of about 600 acres and a fine lake. The approach from the W. is by a very handsome lodge. The estate belonged to the Saviles, Baronets and Marquises of Halifax, who obtained it by an heiress from the Talbots. The heiress of the Saviles married an Earl of Scarborough and the estate has been for some time

H

Route 16.—*Ollerton—Clumber Park.*

settled on a younger branch of that family.

12 m. ⚷ Ollerton, a very small, but neat market town, pleasantly placed amid hop-grounds. The Ch. is but a chapel of ease to Edwinstowe, and is in nowise remarkable. A delightful ramble of about 8 m. may be made hence to Mansfield, passing Edwinstowe and Clipstone (Rte. 15).

Leaving Ollerton, the little river Manu is crossed, and the road hence to Worksop (9 m.) is through the midst of Sherwood Forest, or rather through that part of it where trees of most ancient growth have been preserved. This remnant of the forest, including the woods of Birkland and Bilhaugh near Edwinstowe, is estimated at 3¼ m. long by 2 broad. It is the rendezvous of all the picnic-makers of the county, and is full of the most charming forest scenery. "A thousand years, ten thousand tempests, lightnings, winds, and wintry violence, have all flung their utmost force on these trees, and there they stand, trunk after trunk, scattered, hollow, grey, gnarled, stretching out their bare, sturdy arms, or their mingled foliage and ruin—a life in death."—*Howitt.*

On the E. of the road is the noble **⚷ THORESBY PARK**, 10 m. in circuit. There is a carriage-road a mile long by the Buck Gates through the midst of a superb grove of oaks, almost all of great age, stag-headed and gnarled, and affording many fine subjects for the artist's pencil, to the **House**, the magnificent seat of Earl Manvers. The old mansion, in which Lady Mary Wortley Montagu was born, was destroyed by fire in 1745, and was rebuilt by the last Duke of Kingston. The present house has been built by Lord Manvers in the Elizabethan style, from designs by *Salvin.* The beautiful grounds are embellished with a fine lake, which is more than a mile in length, and is formed by an artificial expanse of the river Meden as it flows through the park. The bust of Pascal Paoli the Corsican, who resided here for some time, is still preserved.

For forest scenery, its grand feature, the park of Thoresby can scarcely be surpassed in England. There are some monuments to the Pierreponts and some painted glass in **Perlethorpe** (anc. Peverilthorpe) Ch. within the precincts of the park.

Opposite the park, at 1 m., is **Budby**, a model village of Gothic cottages, built by the first Earl Manvers in 1807. The inlet of Thoresby Lake is here crossed by the road.

Immediately adjoining, and to the N. of Thoresby, is **⚷ CLUMBER PARK**, the property of the Duke of Newcastle. The Park was laid out, planted, and in fact created, by the great-great-grandfather of the present Duke. The house, though of stone, is not imposing externally, from want of height: but it has comfort and splendour within. In 1879 nearly all the rooms of the older house were consumed by fire. It has been replaced by a fine Central Hall in classic style by Charles Barry, F.S.A. There is a fine Library with a good collection of books. In the State Dining-room, which will accommodate 150 guests, are 4 Market-pieces, with figures life-size, by *Snyders*; and a Game-piece, by *Weenix*. There are also good paintings, principally of the Netherlands school, dispersed about the house.

Among the most remarkable are —*Vandyck*, Rinaldo awakened by the Mermaid (Tasso); *Sir Godfrey Kneller*, George II. and Queen Caroline; *Murillo*, the Virgin in the Clouds, surrounded by Angels, standing on a half-moon; *Teniers*, the Brickmakers; *G. Poussin*, a Landscape; *Rubens*, two heads of Females, tasting and smelling; *Rembrandt*,

Portrait of a man, with a paper in his hand; *Guido*. Artemisia; *Correggio* (?). Sigismunda weeping over the heart of Tancred; *Battoni*, a Holy Family: *Van Loo*, Fruit and Flowers: small copy of *Raphael's* School of Athens: *Vandermeulen*, The Battle of the Boyne: *Vandyck*, Portrait of Charles I., ¾ size. *Titian*. Portrait of a Lady: *Holbein*, Head of a Man: *P. Neefs*. Interiors of Churches; *Ruysdael*, a Sea-piece, with breakers; *Vandyck*, Head of a Lady, in a blue dress: *A. Dürer*, Virgin and Child, between pillars, with Angels: *Domenichino*. Portrait of a Cardinal; *Gainsborough*, Two Beggar Boys. In the Hall are numerous Roman busts, and a statue by *Canova* of Napoleon 1.

The house stands on the margin of a beautiful artificial lake, 3 m. long, covering an area of 200 acres, and floating a small model frigate. Here is a fine terrace and garden, formed by the late Duke, with flights of steps leading down to the water, and decorated with vases of marble, and a fountain-basin cut out of a single block of marble 12½ ft. in diameter.

The conservatories in the kitchen garden are 1300 ft. in length; and the stud-farm is an attraction to many.

The present Duke has erected a Church beautifully decorated in the interior by E. F. Bodley, A.R.A.

About 1 m. W. of Clumber is **Welbeck Abbey** (Rte. 15), and in the space between is the small village of **Carburton**, the property of the Duke of Portland. Hence to Worksop the road has almost the character of a forest drive, with Worksop Manor on W. and on the E. a fine expanse of open country.

1 m. **Worksop** (Rte. 15).

ROUTE 17.

NEWARK TO DONCASTER, BY TUXFORD, RETFORD, AND BAWTRY.

G. N. RAILWAY. 36 m.

The Rly. keeps very nearly the same course as the old mail-coach road, which is carried from Newark across the flat meadows that occupy the space between the two branches of the Trent, upon a raised causeway, with frequent openings to give passage to the floods. This work was formed by *Smeaton* in 1770, at a cost of 12,000*l*. At **2 m.** from Newark the line crosses the Trent below Muskham Bridge, and passes the villages of S. and N. Muskham. Human remains have been found in the gravel of the river in this neighbourhood. From N. Muskham there is a ferry to **Holme**. The Ch. is most interesting, full of old woodwork, and contains a fine monument of Barton, the founder, and the tomb of two members of the family of Bellasys, who lived here in the 17th centy. Above the porch is a chamber where a woman named Nan Scott is said to have shut herself up at the time of the plague, 1666, and so escaped the disease.

5 m. On E. is the village of **Cromwell**, the original seat of a great baronial family, afterwards seated at Tattershall. (See *Handbook for Lincolnshire*.) The first Lord Cromwell was Constable of the Tower in the reign of Edward II.

6½ m. Carlton-on-Trent (Stat.). The village is a hamlet of Norwell. It had a Norm. chapel, now replaced by a small modern E. E. Ch., which has some good stained glass in the chancel. Carlton House (Lt.-Col. James Craig). 2 m. W. is Ossington Hall, the seat of the late Lord

Route 17.—Tuxford—Retford.

Ossington, who, as the Rt. Hon. J. E. Denison, was long Speaker of the House of Commons. **Ossington Ch.**, a modern Grecian building, contains some old monuments of the Cartwrights (former possessors of Ossington Park), and two statues, by *Nollekens*, of members of the Portland family, to which Lady Charlotte Denison belonged. 1 m. N. is **Moorhouse**, a hamlet with a very beautiful small Ch., built by Lord Ossington.

11¾ m. ♃ Tuxford (Stat.), a small market town, known as Tuxford-in-the-Clay (Saxon, Tuxfarne), lies ¾ m. W. The place has a modern appearance, having been almost entirely rebuilt after a fire in 1702. St. Nicholas' Ch., built in the Perp. style, contains a few ancient and mutilated monuments, possibly of the family of Longvillers, whose chief seat was here before they merged into the Stanhopes of Rampton; also a rude representation of St. Lawrence on a gridiron, one man blowing the bellows while another is turning the saint.

At *Tuxford Hall* (R. S. Wilson, Esq.) there is a fine collection of pictures, old oak furniture, china, and other art objects. Visitors are admitted.

The country around Tuxford is a pleasant agricultural district, and about a mile from Tuxford on the Great North road, there is a stone which formerly bore the inscription:—"Here lieth the Body of a Rebel, 1746."

At Darlton, 3 m. N.E., is a farmhouse, called *Kingshaugh*, traditionally said to have been a hunting seat of King John.

At **West Markham**, 1½ m. N.W., the *Ch.* was built in 1831 by the Duke of Newcastle, lord of the manor, with a burial-vault for his family beneath it. It is a Grecian edifice surmounted by a dome, the design by *Smirke*.

In **East Markam** *Ch.* (recently restored) are several monuments, one to Chief Justice Markham, "the upright judge" (d. 1408).

On Markham Moor, which was enclosed 1810, was once a celebrated posting inn.

18½ m. ♃ Retford (Stat.). The joint stat. of the G. N. Rly. and the M. S. and L. Rly. is in the parish of Ordsall, and is an important railway centre. The town, 1 m. N., is an ancient borough. In the year 1877 its boundaries were extended, and it now includes East and West Retford, with the parish of Ordsall and a considerable portion of Clareborough. The river Idle divides East from West Retford, and runs into the Trent at West Stockwith. *West Retford* has a pretty Ch., with handsome crocketed spire.

East Retford contains a noble Ch., chiefly in Perp. style, dedicated to St. Swithin. The Ch. fell down in the early part of the 17th cent., and was rebuilt on the old lines in 1667. It is of note that the brief, directing collections to be made for the rebuilding, was ordered by Oliver Cromwell, and signed by his son Richard. The building was well restored and the chancel rebuilt in 1855. The town is clean and well built, with a spacious Market-place, in which stands the Broad Stone. This was probably the base of an ancient cross, which formerly stood in a part of the town still called Dominic Cross. The Town Hall was built in 1867, and has a fine suite of public rooms. It took the place of the old Moot Hall, which was pulled down, to the great improvement of the Market-place. There is a flourishing *Grammar School*. The trade of the town and neighbourhood is of a mixed character. There are paper-mills, india-rubber works, an iron foundry, and flour-mills, which employ a considerable number of hands. The trade in hops, which has existed for centuries, has almost entirely died out.

Retford is a place of great antiquity. It is mentioned in Domesday as Redeford. The original Charter was probably granted by Richard I., and was renewed by Edward I. From the year 1571 it has been a parliamentary borough. It was at one time notorious for corrupt practices, and in 1827 a bill was brought in to transfer the franchise to Birmingham. Instead of this, the franchise was extended to the whole hundred of Bassetlaw, the area of which exactly coincides with the parliamentary division formed in 1885.

There are several fine country seats in the neighbourhood. To the S., Grove Hall (E. E. Harcourt-Vernon, Esq.). To the N.W., Babworth Hall (Lieut.-Col. H. Denison), while the Dukeries and Sherwood Forest are within a drive of a few miles (see Rtes. 15 and 16).

21½ m. **Sutton** (Stat.). The village, called Sutton-cum-Lound, lies E. ½ m. The Ch., E. E. and Perp., is large and handsome, and has been restored. W. of the line is Baruby Moor, where was one of the noted inns of the North road; it is now converted into private residences.

24½ m. **Ranskill** (Stat.), a township of Blyth, which lies 2 m. W. The name is Danish, Ravenskelf, or "Hill of the Raven," probably alluding to some battle fought in the vicinity.

1½ m. W. is **Serlby Hall** (Viscount Galway), a square modern stuccoed mansion. It contains some fine paintings, comprising portraits of Henry VIII., and of Nicholas Kreutzer, his astronomer, by *Holbein*; Charles I. and his Queen, with horses, dogs, and a dwarf, by *Daniel Mytens* (this picture was given by Queen Anne to Addison); Charles I. and his Page, by *Vandyck* (?); Lords Francis and William Russell; Lady Catherine Manners and her children, and eight views of Venice by *Canaletto*. The park is very prettily watered by the Ryton, which falls into the Idle near Bawtry.

In the country E. of Ranskill, extending to the river Idle, are several barrows, also a tumulus, called Blakow hill, and an earthwork, which is probably British. On the bank of the river, 2 m. from Ranskill, is the village of **Mattersey**, which formerly had an Abbey of Gilbertine Canons, founded 1190, by Roger de Moresay. Some remains of the buildings are worked up in a farmhouse, which bears the name of "the Abbey." The Ch. (restored 1866) is Perp., with a square embattled tower, and in it are preserved carvings representing St. Martin dividing his cloak with a beggar, and the finding of the Cross by the Empress Helena; they were found hidden under the pavement of the chancel in 1804, on occasion of digging a grave.

2 m. E. of Mattersey is **Clayworth**, in the ch.-yard of which is the following epitaph:—

"Blest be he that set this stone,
That I may not be forgotten;
And curst be he that moves this stone
Before that they be rotten."

The Ch. was restored in 1874-5. It contains a monument to a rector of 1448, and a decorated tomb to Humphrey Fitzwilliam, who became a Judge in the Court of King's Bench in 1559.

2 m. N.E. of Clayworth, on the road to Gainsborough, is the village of **Gringley**, which stands on a hill, commanding a splendid view of the country round, extending as far as Lincoln Cathedral. The Ch. is E. E., with a N. aisle added in the 18th-cent. churchwarden style. The Beacon Hill was the site of an old Roman camp, and was also occupied by Prince Rupert in 1644.

26 m. **Scrooby** (Stat.) is a neat

small hamlet, once the residence of the Archbishops of York, though of their palace only a few fragments remain, built into a farmhouse, which is still called the *Manor House*. Leland describes it " as a great manor-place withyn a moat, and builded into courts, whereof the first is very ample, and all builded of tymbre, saving the front of brick." In the garden is a mulberry-tree said to have been planted by Cardinal Wolsey. Among the tenants of Scrooby in the time of Queen Elizabeth was William Brewster, who here commenced the congregation of " Separatists," from which sprang eventually the Puritan settlements of New England. The Ch. of Scrooby is a fine E. E. edifice, with a square tower and lofty spire, which has been repeatedly damaged by lightning.

27¾ m. ⚡ **Bawtry** (Stat.). This is a small market town, on the river Idle, partly in Yorkshire. The *Ch.* is supposed to have been founded by De Busli, Lord of the Honour of Tickhill, and builder of Blyth Priory. It consists of nave and aisles, but, except a Norm. doorway on the N. side, has little of interest about it. There is an almshouse with a chapel, founded by the Morton family, who were long resident here, and who, continuing in the old religion, caused Bawtry to be regarded as " a dangerous nest of papists" when the Queen of Scots was confined at Sheffield Castle. Bawtry is on the Great North road, and it was here that the sheriff of Yorkshire anciently met royal personages, and conducted them into his county. When Henry VIII. visited Yorkshire in 1541, after the rising known as " The Pilgrimage of Grace," he was met at Bawtry by " 200 gentlemen of the county in velvet, and 4000 tall yeomen and servingmen well horsed, who on their knees made a submission by the mouth of Sir Robert Bowes, and

presented the king with 900*l*."— *Hall*.
The line now enters Yorkshire, and, passing Rossington Stat., reaches at

36 m. Doncaster (Stat.). (See *Handbook for Yorkshire*.)

ROUTE 18.

WORKSOP TO DONCASTER, BY TICKHILL. [BLYTH AND ROCHE ABBEY.]

BY ROAD. 17 m.

At 3½ m. N. of Worksop is the village of **Carlton-in-Lindrick**. It was one of the possessions of Roger de Busli at the Domesday Survey. The Ch. has some Norm. and E. E. traces, and a Norm. tympanum over the chancel doorway, also a bell prior to 1444. A small stream, which joins the river Ryton at Blyth, rises at *Wallingwells* (Sir T. W. White, Bart.), 1 m. W. of *Carlton Hall* (R. J. Ramsden, Esq.).

5 m. On E. is an arched gateway, formerly the entrance to the seat of the Cressys, and subsequently of the Cliftons, who succeeded the former in these estates about the 15th centy.

A short distance beyond this, a road leads to the decayed market-town of **Blyth** (2¼ m.), passing *Hodsock Priory*, the seat of Mrs. Mellish. A very beautiful Early Eng. chapel once existed here, to the S.W., but there are now no remains of it.
Blyth is so called, according to the venerable topographer John Norden, " a jocunditate," which, says Fuller, " I desire may be extended all over the shire, being confident that one ounce of mirth, with the same degree of grace, will serve God more than a pound of sorrow." It is well worth

a visit on account of its noble Ch., which belonged to a Benedictine priory, founded in the 11th centy. by De Busli, one of the most powerful of William the Conqueror's nobles, who held large possessions in Notts and Yorkshire. It is a fine building, consisting of a nave with a N. aisle of the original foundation, south porch (E. E.), a wide S. aisle enlarged in late 13th centy., with a ritual chancel, for the parish Ch., and a 14th-centy. W. tower; it formerly possessed, in addition, transepts, central tower, and apse, in which the choir of the monastic Ch. was included. At present the nave ends in a blank wall, cutting off one compartment to the E., once converted into an aviary by a former owner of Blyth Hall, the grounds of which adjoin the Ch. It was formerly supposed that this wall was erected and the Ch. vandalised by Edward Mellish, who rebuilt the hall at the end of the 17th centy. But at the restoration of the Ch. (carefully done by C. Hodson Fowler) in 1885, the remains of a fresco, supposed 15th centy., were discovered on this wall, together with a doorway through it, which had been before concealed by the Mellish monument, now removed into the N. aisle. This clearly showed that the monks had themselves built out the parish Ch. by turning their main chancel screen into a solid wall, as at Wymondham. The remnant of another screen, with traces of painted figures, to the W. of this wall, proves that they had an altar, or probably altars, on this side. There is a fine screen in the S. aisle, dividing off the parish chancel. with painted figures in the lower panels of St. Stephen. St. Euphemia, St. Edmund, St. Barbara, St. Ursula. The pillar and E. E. arcade, which formed the E. side of the lost S. transept, are seen in the E. wall of this parish chancel behind the altar.

The town, though small. and deprived of its market when the great North Road was made through Ret-

ford and Bawtry, is very pleasantly situated, amid fine trees, on the little river Ryton. The schoolroom contains an E. E. doorway, which originally belonged to a hospital suppressed in the 16th centy.; a small part of the endowment still remains. Blyth Hall, partly built on the site of the priory (the cellar of the refectory remains), is a fine mansion, with picturesque grounds.

Returning from Blyth to the main road

At 7 m. the tourist turns W. into Yorkshire, the object of attraction being the ruins of **Roche Abbey**. The road passes Sandbeck Park (Earl of Scarborough) on N., and at 3 m. from the main road the sheltered valley is entered in which a small colony of Cistercian monks established themselves, literally "under the shadow of a rock," some time in the reign of Stephen.

Roche Abbey (which belongs to the Earl of Scarborough) is the favourite resort of picnic-parties from the neighbouring towns; its beautiful grounds. streams, lake, and pleasant walks always kept in good order, amply repay the numerous visitors for the trouble in reaching it. There is a small house in the grounds where stabling and refreshments may be obtained. (See *Handbook for Yorkshire*.)

10 m. **Tickhill**, in Yorkshire, a small market town, noted for the remains of its old castles. And at

17 m. is **Doncaster** (Stat.). (See *Handbook for Yorkshire*.)

ROUTE 19.

MARKET HARBOROUGH TO LEICESTER.

MIDLAND RAILWAY. 16 m.

☧ **Market Harborough** (Junct. Stat.) stands on the Welland, S.S.E. from Leicester, and on the southern boundary. It has considerable business in brick and tile making, and a stay factory employs many hands.

The *Ch.*, dedicated to St. Dionysius the Areopagite, is a very handsome Perp. structure; the stone of which it is built seemingly resists all the destructive effects of time upon it. Its lofty tower and very beautiful broach spire, erected entirely on the pyramidal principle from the bottom to the apex, is a feature in the town, to which it adds a beauty of its own. An old tradition has it that the Ch. was built by John of Gaunt, but the date forbids this. He may, however, have contributed to alterations, still to be seen in the added clerestory. The building consists of two distinct portions, the chancel and tower, of the 13th centy., and the nave and aisles, a century later. In either aisle is a window of the 14th centy.; and the pitch of the old nave is still visible in the tower. There are porches on the N. and S. sides, and over each is a chamber.

Near the Ch. is the *Grammar School*, originally built in 1614, and endowed by Robert Smyth, a sub-treasurer of the city of London. The quaint-looking timber building, supported on pillars (the butter-market is held on the space beneath), has divers "godly sentences" painted on the projecting beams. It was completely restored in 1869. The School is successfully managed on a scheme approved by the Charity Commission. the Lord Mayor and Court of Aldermen of the City of London, in whom the endowment is invested, reserving the right of naming the Head-master. At a short distance is the old house in which Charles I. is said to have slept the night before the battle of Naseby; it is now divided into three separate dwellings.

Harborough is believed to have been a British settlement as well as a Roman station, and some pottery has been found to justify this belief on the site of an old camp adjoining the town, but now built upon.

The Ch. of St. Mary-in-Arden, which is preserved a Norm. arch of the 11th centy., and connected with the town by many old and distinct ties before 1662, when the building fell during a storm, was the mother Ch. of Harborough. In 1614 the Ch. of St. Mary and the chapel of St. Dionysius were united. Partly restored, it was, till 12 years ago, the chapel of the customary burial-ground. A new cemetery, however, was opened in 1879.

[The Rugby and Peterborough Rly. passes through Market Harborough, and by it the geologist should make an excursion to **Nevill Holt** (3 m. N.E. from the Ashley and Weston Stat. on that line), where there is an extensive bed of oolitic iron ore, similar to, and a continuation of, the bed in Northamptonshire. Nevill Holt Hall, an interesting old mansion, situated on a hill, is the residence of Sir Bache Cunard, Bart. The *Ch.* is Dec. with Perp. alterations, and contains some monuments to the Nevill family, who owned the Hall. 1636. The village of Holt was long celebrated for its mineral spring (chalybeate),of which a curious account was written by Dr. Short in 1792. **Medbourne** (Stat.) is conjectured to have been a Roman station

Route 19.—The Langtons—Kibworth.

on the Via Devana from Colchester to Chester, from the fact that coins are so frequently turned up in the fields by swine as to have earned the name of "hog-money," and that a good Roman tesselated pavement was some years ago discovered in the village about 5 ft. below the surface. It is one day's Roman march from Leicester. The *Ch.* is E. E., with a transept and double aisle on the S. side, also a couple of chantries. It was restored in 1880.

1 m. N W. of Nevill Hall is **Blaston St. Giles**, the Ch. of which contains an ancient chalice, supposed to be the one formerly belonging to the chapel attached to a hunting-seat of King Richard I. at Blaston.]

4½ m. **Langton** (Stat.). A group of villages called **The Langtons**, consist of E. and W. Langton, Thorpe-Langton, and Tur-Langton. In Tur-Langton is a well called King Charles's Well, from a tradition that the monarch there watered his horse in his flight from the battle-field of Naseby. The *Church* is in E. Langton, and is esteemed the finest village Ch. in the county. It was originally Dec., probably built between 1320 and 1347 by two brothers of the name of Latimer, but in the next century a noble nave and tower were erected, and it is believed that the builder was William Harwood, the designer of Fotheringhay (see *Handbook for Northamptonshire*). The place is of some celebrity in connection with the name of William Hanbury, an enthusiastic clergyman, who held the living in the early part of the reign of George III. He had great skill in planting and horticulture, and several villages in the neighbourhood are indebted to his benevolent exertions in encouraging the cultivation of fruit-trees. When he came, in his 25th year, to Langton, he was much struck by the beauty of the Ch., and, as he said, "finding so noble a room provided, made it his business to decorate it," giving to that purpose the annual profits of some plantations and fruit-gardens that he had already established at Gumley and Tur-Langton, and which were valued at 10,000*l.* His project being warmly taken up by some of the neighbouring gentry, he soon enlarged it, and devised a scheme for replacing his church by a "Minster," which was to excel all existing cathedrals, and to have a central tower 493 ft. high. He also proposed to establish a number of schools, hospitals, &c., for the benefit of the population that he expected would gather round it. His project was too vast for any one man to accomplish, but he never lost faith in it, and by indefatigable industry he collected from various sources about 4000*l.*, which at his death he left in the hands of trustees to accumulate till it reached the sum of 1000*l.* per annum: and this, in spite of the matter falling into Chancery, has of late years been done. A memorial to him has been placed in the vestry by the present vicar, his great-grandson. In 1854 the Hanbury trustees established free-schools for the Langtons, and in 1865 they accomplished the restoration of the Ch. in a most satisfactory manner, and a carved reredos in alabaster was added in 1890. The S. aisle contains an interesting monument to Sir Richard Roberts, who died in 1644.

6 m. **Kibworth** (Stat.). The handsome Dec. *Ch.*, standing on a height, has a modern embattled tower, built in 1829, the old one having fallen down whilst in the course of repair a short time before. Dr. Aikin, the editor of the 'Monthly Magazine,' was born here in 1747. 3 m. N.E. is the village of **Carlton Curlieu**, whose inhabitants, according to Camden, were unable to pronounce the letter R, and were on that account called "Carleton wharlers:" and Fuller

Route 19.—Glen Magna—Leicester.

tells us of a Fellow of Trinity College, Cambridge, a native of Carlton, who made a long speech in which not a single R occurred. The Ch. (restored in 1880) contains an alabaster tomb (date 1621) with the effigies of Sir John Bale and his wife, together with their 7 children. Adjoining the village is Carlton Hall, a fine Jacobean edifice.

8 m. **Glen Magna** (Stat.), a stocking-making village, remarkable for nothing but a reputation, according to the Leicestershire saying, of "containing more dogs than honest men." 2 m. E. is **Burton Overy**. The Dec. and Perp. Ch. has been restored, and contains a very fine altar-screen. At the rectory is a noble oak, raised from an acorn from the famous tree at Boscobel. Near the line, on S., is the village of **Wistow**, with an E. E. Ch. containing monuments of the Halford family. *Wistow Hall* (Sir H. St. John Halford, Bt.) contains many portraits of George III., his family and friends, and the saddle and stirrups of Charles I., who passed a night at Wistow just before the battle of Naseby.

12 m. **Wigston** Junct. Stat. Near here the lines from Rugby (Rte. 25) and from Nuneaton (Rte. 20) fall in. Great Wigston (so called to distinguish it from Little Wigston, a hamlet near Lutterworth) is a busy place, chiefly occupied with the hosiery trade. The modern Ch. of All Saints has a handsome tower and spire; and the Ch. of St. Wolstan, long fallen into disuse, was restored in 1853.

2 m. W. is **Oadby**, a particularly neat and clean-looking village, a meet for the Quorndon hounds. The Ch., recently thoroughly restored, has a good tower and spire; and the interior has several interesting monuments.

On the opposite side of the line,

on the river Soar, is **Aylestone**, the graceful spire of its Ch. being very conspicuous. *Aylestone Hall* (Col. J. Fryer) is an ancient building, well restored; it was a possession of the Manners' family, and the Duke of Rutland is still lord of the manor. Across the river is a farmhouse, occupying the site of *Lubbesthorpe Abbey*, of which some few fragments remain.

The country between Market Harborough and Leicester is not an inviting one as far as scenery goes; but it is celebrated for its hunting capabilities, the Pytchley, the Billesdon, and the Quorn hunts occupying all this side of Leicestershire, and it also contains several interesting village churches; as **Foxton, Saddington**, and **Mowsley** (all late E. E. or Dec.), on the W. side of the line; and Cranoe, Noseley, and Tilton, on E. **Cranoe** Ch. is a fine Perp. edifice, with memorials of the earls of Carnarvon. **Noseley** Ch. (once collegiate) has a splendid tomb for Sir Arthur Hasilrige, the regicide, and his wife and sister (*Noseley Hall*, Sir A. G. Hasilrigg, is very near).

16 m. ☿**LEICESTER** (Stat.), the County Town There can be no doubt that Leicester has claims to a very ancient history, though we may not receive the tradition of its having been the residence of King Lear and his three daughters. It seems certain, however, that it was the Roman station of Ratæ Coritanorum, various remains having been found to identify it. It was the seat of a Saxon bishopric, and was also one of the Five Burghs of the Danes; and it claims the credit of having held out for a while against William the Norman. In 1173 the town was nearly destroyed, in consequence of the disaffection of the Earl of Leicester to the Crown, and the castle, together with that of Groby (Rte. 24), was demolished. The castle was rebuilt, and remained a

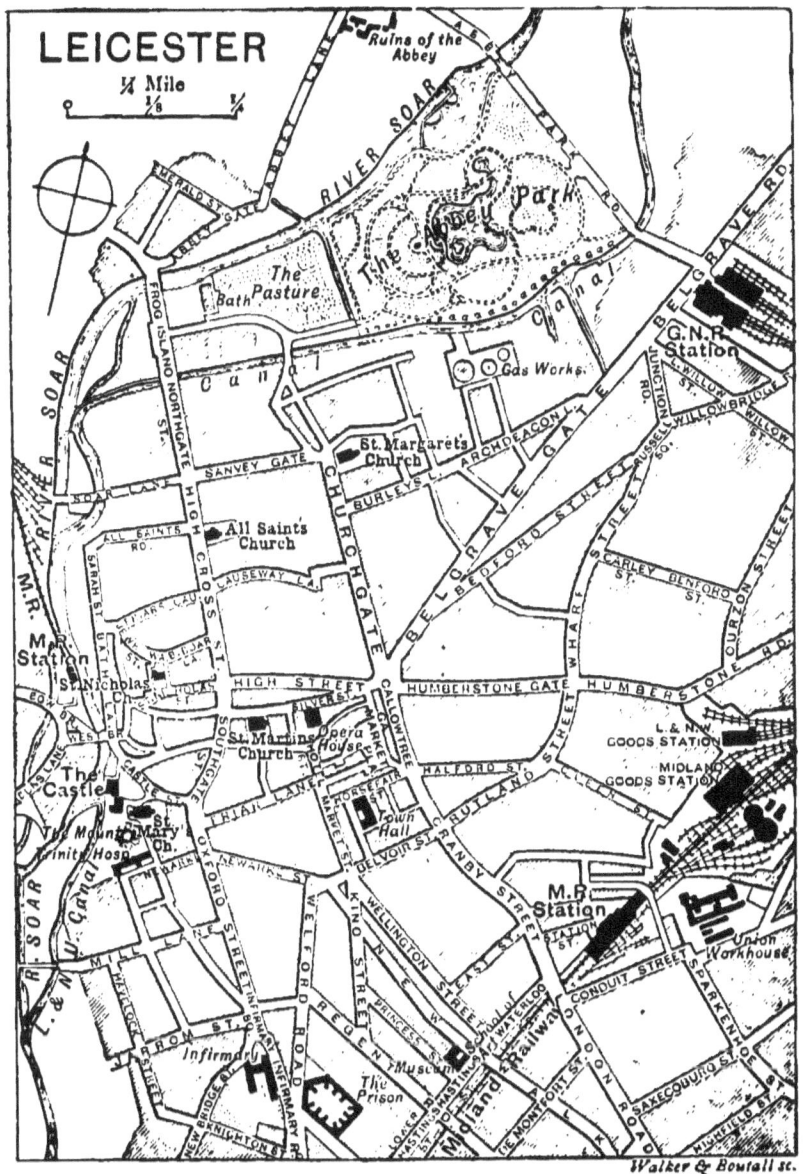

To face page 108.

Route 19.—Leicester: Jewry Wall.

place of strength until the time of the Civil war; now only the great hall and the mound remain (see below). In May, 1645, Leicester was captured by Charles I. by storm, and given up to the licence of the troops, but was abandoned in less than a week after. Since that time the town has had no history more eventful than the excesses of the machine-breaking mobs of 1816, which were followed by several executions.

The chief employment of Leicester for nearly 200 years has been stocking-making and knitting, and the town has long been noted as the centre of the hosiery trade. The trade was first commenced here in 1686, by one Alsopp, who, in the face of great difficulties and popular prejudice, erected a stocking-frame. This was nearly 100 years subsequent to the invention of the stocking-loom by Mr. Lee of Woodborough (Rte. 11). In the reign of Queen Anne there was a corporation termed the "Framework Knitters' Company," which bore for its arms a stocking-loom, supported on one side by a clergyman, and on the other by a female presenting a disused knitting-pin, in reference to the story of Lee and his wife. Other manufactories, however, are now extensively carried on, especially that of boots and shoes and of elastic fabrics.

Few even of the great manufacturing towns in the North have increased more rapidly than Leicester has done of late years, and well-built suburbs occupy what were, at a comparatively recent date, open fields. The main avenues of Gallowtree Gate, Humberstone Gate, Belgrave Gate, and High Street converge in the centre of the town, and there is an ornamental **Clock-Tower** erected by Ordish, a local architect. At its base are statues of four Leicester celebrities, viz. Simon de Montfort (1265), William Wigston (1512), Sir Thomas White (1516), and Alderman Newton

(1760). Closely adjoining is the Market-place, where are a handsome Corn Exchange and a statue of the 5th Duke of Rutland. Granby Street contains the Post Office, the Library and News-room, and the Temperance Hall—all buildings of merit. Of modern churches, that of St. Mark, the gift of the late Mr. Perry Herrick, is the most remarkable, both externally and internally. Dissenting chapels are numerous, and among them the Wesleyan chapel in Humberstone Gate, by *Ordish*, a parti-coloured brick edifice, attracts attention by its very peculiar style of architecture.

The Roman antiquities of Leicester are extremely interesting, and include the **Jewry Wall**, which is one of the most perfect remains of its kind in Britain. It closely adjoins St. Nicholas Ch. As it at present stands, it is about 25 yards in length, and 5 or 6 in height, and consists of a western side (not open to view, forming the wall of a factory) and an eastern side, "containing several arched recesses, the soffits or vaultings of which are turned with courses of large flat bricks; rows of these are likewise interspersed throughout the wall at intervals, as bonding-courses, and the Roman mode of constructing the arch with brickwork is here clearly displayed."

According to Geoffrey of Monmouth, there was in Ratæ a temple of Janus, and it may be remarked that these ruins bear a striking resemblance in many points to the ruins of one of the ancient temples of Rome. —*Bloxam*. Other antiquaries consider that the wall formed part of the gateway of the Roman city, and that the street or road led over the old Bow Bridge on to the Fosse Way. Local examiners believe that it once formed the front of a temple, having 4 entrances, and that, when it fell into decay, the western side of the town-wall was built up alongside and the portal made to correspond with its two middle arches.—*Thompson's Handbook of Leicester.* The wall has been opened through half its length by the Leicestershire Archæological Society to the original level of the Roman way; it has received some needful support, and is protected by iron railing. The footings of the piers are now visible, and it is quite evident that the building or wall never came forward in an easterly direction towards the church. These facts tend to strengthen the notion that the Jewry wall formed a portion of the western wall of Roman Leicester. No less than 11 tesselated *pavements* have been found at different times in Leicester, one of which, of considerable size, represents possibly the myth of Cyparissus and the Stag. The visitor may inspect a fine one *in situ* in the cellar of a house in Jewry Wall Street, which has been acquired by the Corporation.

" Thus, with her handmaid Sence, the Soar
    doth eas'ly slide
By Leicester, where yet her ruins show her
    pride,
Demolish'd many years, that of the great
    foundation
Of her long buried walls men hardly see
    the station;
Yet of some pieces found, so sure the
    cement locks
The stones, that they remain like perdurable rocks."—*Drayton.*

The Roman **mile-stone** which was discovered on the Fosse Way near Thurmaston, in 1771, is now in the Museum. It is about 3½ ft. high, and has an inscription to the Emperor Hadrian, with a notice that it was 2 miles from Ratæ. The **Rawdykes**, near the junction of the Burton Rly. with the Swannington line, is supposed to be a corruption of Rhedagua, and to have been the site of the Roman racecourse.

The old houses of Leicester, timber-built and picturesque, have now almost entirely disappeared. The Blue Boar Inn, where Richard III. slept on 21st Aug. 1485, the night before marching to Bosworth Field, was pulled down in 1836, and many buildings of like architecture have since been removed. The only memorial of Richard is a stone in a building close to Bow Bridge, the inscription on which asserts that he was buried near that spot. In High-street is a singular-looking domed structure (now a shoemaker's warehouse), called the **Brick Tower**. The interior is of stone, and it is a fragment of the mansion of the Earls of Huntingdon. In the time of Elizabeth it was called Lord's Place, and here Dudley, Earl of Leicester, was a frequent visitor. Mary Queen of Scots passed a night in it on her way to Fotheringhay; and here also Nonconformist preachers were sheltered after the passing of the Act of Uniformity (1662) by the puritanical Countess of Huntingdon.

Bow Bridge, over which Richard marched to Bosworth Field, was pulled down in 1862; an iron bridge of the same name has taken its place.

The old **Town Hall**, which is near St. Martin's Ch., is believed to have been the hall of a guild of Corpus Christi, but it was added to about 1586, as appears by a date on the wall. It contained portraits of Sir Thomas White and Henry, Earl of Huntingdon, both benefactors to the town. They are now placed in the Council Chamber of the Municipal Buildings. The **Mayor's Parlour**, adjoining, was built in 1636, is quaintly ornamented, and has some curious stained glass, presumed to be temp. Hen. VIII. The Library contained, among other curious matters, an early MS. of the New Testament, known as Codex Leicestrensis, and other valuable MSS., now transferred to the Municipal Buildings.

The **Municipal Buildings**, in the Queen Anne style, were commenced in 1874, and were erected at a cost of 51,000*l*.

Route 19.—Leicester: Churches.

The **Opera House**, which is capable of seating 2550 persons, was opened in 1877.

Of the Leicester churches, **St. Nicholas** is the most ancient both in style and materials, the latter having been partly supplied from the stones of the adjoining Jewry Wall. It is an example of very early rude Norman, and was once cruciform; it now consists of a nave, chancel, and north and south aisles (rebuilt), the transepts having been taken down at the end of the 17th centy. A square tower, with an intersecting arcade, rises between the nave and the chancel. There is a Norman doorway leading into the Ch. At the N. side are some blocked round-headed arches, and over them some small round-headed windows, now blocked, turned in Roman brick. The adjoining ground is called "Holy Bones," in consequence, it is presumed, of large numbers of bones (of oxen?) having being found here. On the S.E. side of the Ch.-yard is a timber-framed house with well-carved shafts and projecting spurs, which, according to a tablet affixed, afforded a night's lodging to John Bunyan and to John Wesley (1770).

The restored **Ch. of St. Mary de Castro** is of very singular interest. It consists of two naves of equal length and a narrow N. aisle; and has at the W. end a massive E. E. tower resting on noble arches and supporting a Dec. spire, built inside the S. nave, and standing independently of the walls of the ch. The N. nave was Norm., with narrow aisles, and terminated in a chancel of the same style, but without a chancel arch. The original windows exist in the chancel, and are very rich, as are the sedilia, an unusual feature in Norm. churches. The windows of the nave were built up when the S. nave was added, but may be traced in the wall. A very rich, E. E. clerestory was added in the 13th centy., but that to the S. aisle is now Perp. There is a rich Norm. N. door, and another, smaller and plainer, at the W. end, which served as an entrance from the castle. The S. porch is modern E. E. The roofs and woodwork are all rich and good, and the font, which is in the tower, is rich E. E.; the windows are filled with stained glass, and the simplicity of the arrangement of the parts and the beauty of each feature must secure the attention of the architectural student. In the S. chancel is a monument, conspicuous for its bad taste, to the Rev. Thomas Robinson (d. 1813), the author of the once popular "Scripture Characters." Closely adjoining the Ch. is the entrance to the Castle-yard (*post*).

All Saints' Ch. consists of nave, aisles, and modern chancel. The windows are of an unpleasing form of Dec. (curvilinear, with plain intersecting mullions without cusps), common in the county. At the W. end is a Norm. doorway, and at the E. end of the N. aisle is a curious clock, the hours of which are struck by figures with hammers. The tower is on the N. side, and opens to the Ch. by a narrow arch; at the angles are buttresses, which seem to have been formed of old materials from the Norm. Ch. In the interior are a Perp. roof, a carved E. E. font, and hexagonal Perp. pulpit. The Ch. was restored in 1875.

St. Martin's Ch. is a cruciform structure of great width, with a noble central tower raised on arches and supporting a fine broach spire erected in 1862 from a design by *Brandon*. A portion of the Norm. string-course of the former Ch. exists on the N. side of the N.W. tower pier. With the exception of the chancel, which is Perp., and has some rich late sedilia, the Ch. is E. E., with inserted Dec. windows; the arcades are singularly pleasing. An additional S. aisle as wide as the nave has been erected, which much enhances the beauty of the Ch., and the wooden roofs are rich and good.

The S. aisle, where the Archdeacon holds his court, once had a portrait of Charles I., painted by a native artist; but this has been removed to the Town Museum. The E. end of the aisle was called Our Lady's Chapel, and at the W. end was the Chapel of St. George. There is also a painting, once used as an altar-piece, by an artist named *Vanni* in 1563. To the N. of the chancel is Heyrick's Ch. or chapel, the burying-place of the Heyricks, an ancient Leicester family. What is now the vestry is believed to have been St. Catherine's Chapel. Abigail Swift, the mother of the Dean, was buried here in 1710. The restoration of the Church was completed in 1881.

Close adjoining the Ch. formerly stood an ancient building, called **Wyggeston Hospital**, which was erected by a Leicester alderman of that name in 1513. It has now been rebuilt on a new site at the junction of the Hinckley and Fosse Roads. A school now stands on the original site, the only vestige remaining of the old building being the sepulchral slabs from the chapel.

A *house* in High-Cross Street, near the Ch., is traditionally said to have formed part of a chantry attached to St. Martin's, called "the Chantry of the Body of Christ," and founded temp. Edward. III.

St. Margaret's Ch. occupies the site of the ancient Cathedral in the 8th centy., the bishopric having been subsequently removed to Dorchester, and then to Lincoln. Of this Ch. Leland writes, — "S. Margaret's is thereby the fairest paroch chirch of Leicester, wher ons was cathedrile chirch, and thereby the Bishop of Lincoln had a palace, whereof a little yet standeth." It is of later date than the other Leicester churches. The chancel is fine Perp., with a rich screen and stalls of the same date; but the nave arcade is E. E. The Ch. consists of nave, aisles, and chancel, with an embattled Perp. tower, more than 100 ft. high. The pillars dividing the interior has E. E. pillars dividing the nave from the aisles. Notice the Perp. E. window, also the carved niches. One of these was once occupied by a figure of the Virgin, supported by a figure said to be intended for Robert Bossu, Earl of Leicester, and founder of the Abbey; the other contained St. Margaret, the patron saint of the Ch. On the N. side of the chancel is the beautifully-vested and unmutilated alabaster effigy of John Penny, Bp. of Carlisle, and formerly abbot of Leicester (d. 1520). It is on a new pedestal.

The **Castle**, where the county business is transacted, adjoins St. Mary's Ch. (*ante*), and is said to have been founded or restored by Ethelfreda in 914, probably as the residence of the Earls of Leicester. It is but a small portion of the ancient building, concealed behind a modern brick front, and consists of the great **Assize Hall**, in which several Parliaments have been held, viz., in 1414, 1426, and 1450. At the S. end are 2 fine and lofty Norm. windows and a door of the same date. "Originally it was a large apartment, with aisles formed by two rows of oak pillars supporting the roof, 5 on each side, 30 ft. high, with carved capitals. Only one of them now remains entire." It is now divided into two courts by modern walls and passages. Close adjoining is the **Mount**, an artificial earthwork, on which stood the keep of the castle; it has been considerably lowered, and is now occupied by a bowling-green, access to which can be gained through an inn at its foot. A portion of the walls that enclosed the courtyard ran round the Mount, and may still be seen. In the 14th cent., an additional area, called the New Work, or **Newarke**, was added to this courtyard by Henry Earl of Lancaster and Leicester, the father-in-law of John of Gaunt, and was connected with the former enclosure by a turret gateway, still existing, and worth notice. The Newarke is entered from Oxford Street, by another gateway, of massive proportions, forming part of a building called the Magazine, from the circumstance that the arms of the trainbands were formerly kept in it; it is now the Militia storehouse.

Of contemporary date with the Newarke, and on the N. side of it, is **Trinity Hospital**, also founded by Henry of Lancaster, for 50 old men and 5 women as their nurses. The present front, however, is of the date of George III. At the E. end is the chapel, which contains the elaborate monument of Mary de Bohun, first wife of Henry IV. The E. window is of 4 lancets. which is very unusual. A curious wooden alms-box, with a quaint inscription, and the date 1579, may be noticed. Opposite the Hospital stood a beautiful Ch. dedicated to "our Lady of the Newarke," by the same founder, where he and his father, Constance the 2nd wife of John of Gaunt, and other noble persons, were interred; but not a vestige remains of it, above ground.

The Charities of Leicester are very numerous.

The tourist should visit the **New Walk** at the S.E. end of the town, an exceedingly pleasant promenade of half a mile in length, with an avenue of trees. Notice the statue of the Rev. Robert Hall. Here is the **Town Museum**, founded in 1849 by the joint exertions of the Leicester Literary and Philosophical Society and the Town Council. The building is in classic style, with a heavy portico. Extensive alterations and additions were made in 1891. It is open, free, every day, and is well worth a visit. In the grounds are two Russian guns. The Museum contains the Roman milestone (*ante*) and some tesselated pavements, also a good collection of fossil remains, principally from the Lias and Rhætic formations in the quarries of Barrow-on-Soar. In the Zoological Department is a well-arranged collection of birds. The School of Art, the Lecture Hall, erected 1876, and Art Gallery (1891), in which are some good pictures, adjoin the Museum.

The remains of **Leicester Abbey**, now the property of the Earl of Dysart, lie to the N. of the town, on the bank of the Soar. The walls of the precinct are all that exist, and they now enclose a nursery-ground, in which is a fragment of a mansion erected by one of the Cavendishes after the suppression of the abbey. The walls that overhang the river are rough and ivy-clad, and have a very picturesque appearance from the meadows on E.; the W. wall is of brick, in better condition, and at the S.W. angle is a very handsome niche, supposed to be part of the work of Bishop Penny.

In 1143 Robert de Bellomont, known as le Bossu, Earl of Leicester, founded here a monastic establishment of Black Canons, which was afterwards enlarged by his daughter-in-law Petronilla, of whom it was said that after her death a plait of her hair was used to suspend the chapel lamp. The abbey speedily became famous for its riches and its influence, many of its abbots sitting in Parliament. It was, however, more celebrated for its visits from royal personages, who, in their progresses northward, frequently lodged here. Here also (1530) died Cardinal Wolsey, who arrived a helpless invalid, on his way from York to London, and entered the abbey never

[*Derby, &c.*]   I

to leave it. This incident is thus related by Shakespeare:—

"At last with easy roads he came to Leicester,
Lodged in the abbey; where the reverend abbot,
With all his convent, honourably received him;
To whom he gave these words—' O Father Abbot,
An old man, broken with the storms of state,
Is come to lay his weary bones among ye;
Give him a little earth for charity!'
So went to bed, when eagerly his sickness
Pursued him still; and three nights after this,
About the hour of eight (which he himself
Foretold should be his last), full of repentance,
Continual meditations, tears, and sorrows,
He gave his honours to the world again,
His blessed part to heaven, and slept in peace."—*Henry VIII.*

The **Abbey Park** was opened in 1882 by the Prince and Princess of Wales as a public recreation ground.

The excursion to the abbey may be prolonged for 1 m. to **Beaumont Leys**, remarkable for its beautiful curved avenue.

ROUTE 20.

NUNEATON TO LEICESTER, BY HINCKLEY. [BOSWORTH FIELD.]

L. AND N.-W. RLY. 19¼ m.

The Leicester branch of this line furnishes accommodation to the loom districts to the S.W. of Leicester. From Nuneaton (*Handbook for Warwickshire*) the line runs to Hinckley, crossing about halfway the Watling Street, in its course to Manvessedunum (Mancetter), which, for a considerable distance, forms the boundary between Leicestershire and Warwickshire.

4½ m. ⚓Hinckley (Stat.), a busy manufacturing town, the chief occupation of which is coarse cotton stocking making and shoes. It is divided into two liberties, the Borough and the Bond, and has many good houses and two churches. Its situation on an elevated table-land is very fine, and the views extensive, more than 50 churches being believed to be visible. A strong castle was founded here by Hugh de Grentmesnil in the reign of William Rufus; but it was in ruin in Leland's time, and a part of the site is now occupied by the house of the steward of the Crown manor, the town being part of the possessions of the duchy of Lancaster; the castle ditch, however, may still be traced. Of the *Priory* founded in the 12th cent., by Robert Blanchemains, Earl of Leicester (" so called from the whiteness of his hands "), nothing is left. *St. Mary's Ch.*, a fine early Perp. building, has the peculiarity of being broader than it is long. It has a lofty tower and spire, and its roof of carved oak is very handsome. It was restored in 1881, when the old E. window, and many objects of interest, were ruthlessly destroyed. There is a *brass* for a lady, 15th centy.; and a monument with painted bust, which reminds the visitor of the Shakespeare bust at Stratford-on-Avon.—*M. H. Bloxam.*

" Mr. William lliffe introduced a stocking-frame, which is said to have cost 60l., into Hinckley, as early as 1640, and with this single frame, which, by the aid of an apprentice, he kept constantly working day and night, he gained a comfortable subsistance for his family; his immediate descendant, Mr. Joseph Iliffe, after having carried on the manufacture there with considerable success, died in 1795, aged 76."

[An *Excursion* may be made by road to **Bosworth Field** from Hinckley (4 m.), the way lying through the villages of **Stoke Golding** (Stat.), in which may still be seen the house which tradition says that Richmond slept on the night after the battle (notice the handsome restored Ch., mainly Dec.), and **Dadlington**, in the ch.-yd. of which many of the dead from the field of Bosworth were buried. The spot may also be reached by rly. from Nuneaton (7 m.). The field of battle, where Richard III. was defeated and killed, Aug. 22, 1485, by Richmond, is situated nearly in the centre of a lozenge-shaped area, of which the angles are Market-Bosworth, Shenton, Dadlington, and Sutton Cheney, and is traversed by the Ashby-de-la-Zouch Canal. The White Moor, where Richmond's force encamped the night before the battle, is about ¾ m. to the S. of Shenton (Stat.), while Richard encamped on Red Moor, on the banks of the little stream between Dadlington and Stapleton. The battle was fierce, but brief; its issue being determined by the defection of the Stanleys and their followers. Richard killed Brandon, his opponent's standard-bearer, unhorsed Sir John Cheyney, and was furiously seeking to encounter Richmond himself, when he was borne to the ground and slain. The vivid picture of the battle presented by Shakespeare may well be quoted. (*Richard III.* Act V. Scene 4.) Catesby exclaims to Norfolk:—

" Rescue, my lord of Norfolk, rescue, rescue!
The king enacts more wonders than a man,
Daring an opposite to every danger;
His horse is slain, and all on foot he fights,
Seeking for Richmond in the throat of death;
Rescue, fair lord, or else the day is lost!"

Richard then rushes in, exclaiming

"A horse! a horse! my kingdom for a horse!"

Catesby, thinking that he meditates flight, replies,

"Withdraw, my lord, I'll help you to a horse;"

but is silenced by the furious exclamation,

" Slave, I have set my life upon a cast,
And I will stand the hazard of the die!
I think there be six Richmonds in the field;
Five have I slain to-day, instead of him.
A horse! a horse! my kingdom for a horse!"

The loss on Richard's side was about 1000 men, including himself, the Duke of Norfolk, Lord Ferrers, Sir Richard Radcliff, and Sir Robert Brackenbury. Catesby was taken prisoner, and beheaded. Richmond's loss is said not to have been more than 100; but it must be remembered that we have only Tudor chroniclers. Richard's crown being found on the field of battle, Richmond was invested with it at once by Lord Stanley.

" Courageous Richmond, well hast thou acquit thee!
Lo, here, these long-usurped royalties,
From the dead temples of this bloody wretch,
Have I pluck'd off, to grace thy brows withal;
Wear it, enjoy it, and make much of it."

A well on the field of battle, at which it is said Richard refreshed himself, is still called King Richard's Well. It was cleared out and restored in 1812 by Dr. Parr, who wrote a Latin inscription for it. There is also a spot known as "Dickon's Nook," which is evidently connected with the same monarch:—

" Jockey of Norfolk, be not so bold,
For Dickon thy master is bought and sold."

Overlooking the field of battle is *Shenton Hall* (F. E. A. Wollaston, Esq.), built in 1629 by William Wollaston, a member of that ancient family, who acquired great wealth in London.

2 m. to the N. is the little town of **Market-Bosworth** (Stat on the Ashby and Nuneaton line). The Ch., a Perp. building with tower and lofty spire, has been restored: it contains a curious font. *Bosworth Park* (C. N. L. Tollemache Scott, Esq.) adjoins the town. Simpson the

mathematician was born here in 1710; and Salt the Abyssinian traveller was educated in the Grammar School, founded by one of the Dixies, where Dr. Johnson was once usher, but soon became disgusted with the drudgery.

4 m. N.W., and near Shackerston Stat., is **Gopsall Hall**, the seat of Earl Howe. The house, which was built by Charles Jennens, the friend of Handel, at a cost of 100,000l., has a fine Corinthian front of 180 ft. in length, with a portico in the centre. The S. front has a pediment, which bears in relief a ship in a storm, introduced to commemorate the naval victories of Lord Howe. Some original music by Handel, who during his residence here composed part of the 'Messiah' and 'Israel in Egypt,' is preserved, as also the 4 first editions and many of the quarto plays of Shakespeare. In the library is a stained-glass window, the work of the Baroness Howe, the daughter of the Admiral. The chapel is fitted up with cedar of Lebanon, except the carved legs of the altar, which are of Boscobel oak; the altarpiece is the Crucifixion, by *Vandyck*. Among the paintings are,—Infant Jesus Sleeping, *Murillo*; Landscape, *Claude*; Cattle, *P. Potter*; Views in Venice, *Canaletto*; Angel restoring sight to Tobit, *Rembrandt*; a full-length portrait of Handel, by *Hudson*. The lodge was erected by Sir J. Wyattville, after the model of the Arch of Constantine. The deer-park is 500 acres in extent, and contains 300 deer.]

7½ m. **Elmesthorpe** (Stat.). The country about here is low and marshy, traversed by the little river Nar, a tributary of the Soar; many rare aquatic plants are found here. In this place Richard III. is said to have passed the night before the battle of Bosworth, whilst other accounts make him encamp on the field. For many years the tower only of the Ch. remained, large trees growing within the ruined walls; fortunately this has been now remedied, and the edifice again fitted for divine worship. 2 m. N. is the hosiery village of **Earl Shilton**, the *Ch.* of which has been restored, and the interior decorated with frescoes by the late incumbent (Rev. F. E. Tower). The mound remains of a castle built by the Bellomont Earls of Leicester, whence the name.

9½ m. **Croft** (Stat.). A pleasant village, situated on a syenite rock, with a quarry employing a large number of hands.

12¼ m. **Narborough** (Stat.). Here is a *Ch.* of various dates, with a massive tower, E. E. sedilia and piscina. It has recently been restored, and is well worth a visit.

15 m. **Blaby** (Stat.), a busy place, the inhabitants of which are chiefly occupied in framework-knitting and boot and shoe making. Blaby Hall is the residence of Mrs. Allen.

16 m. **Wigston** (Glen Parva Stat.) (see Rte. 19). The military depôt, a large red brick building, adjoins the Rly.

19½ m. **LEICESTER** (Stat.) (Rte. 19).

ROUTE 21.

LEICESTER TO MELTON MOWBRAY AND OAKHAM.

MIDLAND RLY. 26 m.

Proceeding on the main line as far as

4½ m. **Syston** (Junct. Stat.), and then turning off on the rt. Syston is a populous village, partly occupied by stocking-makers, but having also malthouses and gypsum quarries. The Ch., restored 1881, is large, with a square 15th-cent. tower. Here the Leicester and Peterborough branch runs off on E., and ascends the valley of the Wreak, being seldom far distant from the river. Many of the villages along the route will be noticed as having their names terminating in "by," an evidence of Danish occupation. 1 m. E. is **Queniborough**, a pleasant-looking village, which has a restored Dec. Ch. with lofty spire. Prince Rupert had his head-quarters here at the siege of Leicester in 1645.

7½ m. **Rearsby** (Stat.). The village is a pretty rural-looking place, showing that the manufacturing district has been left behind. Notice the small 14th-cent. bridge leading to the Ch. 2 m. W. is **Ratcliffe on the Wreak**. Here is a Roman Catholic College, built by *Pugin*, mainly at the expense of the Duchess di Sforza, who is lady of the manor. Her grandfather, the 8th Earl Ferrers, added a tower and spire to the parish Ch. The Fosse Way traverses the parish, and there is a large barrow, called Shipley Hill, 40 ft. high.

8½ m. **Brooksby** (Stat.). This is an agricultural parish, of very small population. The Ch. contains monumental effigies of the Villiers, together with some old stained glass. *Brooksby Hall* was formerly the seat of that family, and was the birthplace of "Steenie."

1 m. N. is **Hoby**, a primitive-looking village, but with a well-cared-for Ch.; and 2 m. farther N. at **Ragdale** (properly, **Wreakdale**) is a farmhouse, once the residence of the Earls Ferrers, whose arms are to be seen carved in the dining-room.

11 m. **Frisby** (Stat.). Here are an

E. E. Ch., dedicated to St. Thomas Becket, one tolerably perfect stone cross, and the remains of another, known as the Stump. There is also an E. E. Ch. in the adjoining parish of **Rotherby**.

12 m. **Asfordby** (Stat.). The village contains nothing calling for notice; but *Asfordby Hall* (B. E. A. Cochrane, Esq.) is a handsome building in the Italian style.

4 m. N. is *Wartnaby Hall* (T. M. Turner-Farley, Esq.), where Charles II., while on a royal progress, took breakfast with Mr. Hacket, the then owner. **Kettleby** *Ch.*, a short distance E., has some interesting Norm. details, and monuments to the family of Digby.

At 13 m. is **Kirby Bellars**, where was once an Augustinian priory. The Ch. is large and handsome, with tower and lofty spire. *Kirby Park*, a hunting-seat of the Burdett family, is now a farmhouse.

15 m. ⚥**Melton Mowbray** (Stat. Also a Stat. on the L. & N.-W. and G. N. Rlys. joint line). This is the Utopia of hunting-men who will find in the accommodation for man and beast, the famous packs in the neighbourhood, and the character of the country, everything that they could wish for. Hunting is the great employment of Melton during the season, although it is celebrated in a minor degree for its Stilton cheese and pork-pies; of the latter upwards of three tons a week are sent away by rail. Melton obtained its appellation of Mowbray from the barons of that name during the Norman era. The original grantee under the Conqueror was Geoffry de Wirce, from whom the lands passed to Nigel de Albini, who took the name of Mowbray, and transmitted the estates to a line famous for ages for their states-

manship and military renown. William de Mowbray, the 4th Baron, took a very prominent part in obtaining Magna Charta from King John. A Cluniac cell once existed here, subject to the Priory of Lewes in Sussex, which at the Dissolution was granted to Dudley, Earl of Warwick, but of this there are no remains.

St. Mary's Ch. is a cathedral in miniature, consisting of nave, aisles, chancel, transepts, and a tower rising from the intersection. A great mixture of styles is apparent; the W. front, the lower stage of the tower, the four central piers and arches, and some remains of capitals, being of E. Eng. date. The S. transept is rather later, as are the nave and chancel, the latter dating about 1320. Both transepts have aisles. The upper portion of the tower and the clerestory are Perp. The visitor should particularly notice the beautiful porch at the W. end, with its doorway and 8 niches; it is of the time of Edward II. The clerestory also is extremely graceful, and contains 48 windows, each of 3 lights. The nave is separated from the aisles by 6 pointed arches with clustered columns. The W. window, of 5 lights, is particularly fine. There is a tomb in the S. aisle, with a recumbent cross-legged figure, which an inscription tells us is Lord Hamon Belers, brother of Lord Mowbray; but Mr. North, in his paper on the Mowbrays (in the 'Transactions of the Leicestershire Antiquarian Society'), has shown that this can hardly be, as Hamon died at least 100 years before the Ch. was built. Another tomb of Purbeck marble, once had a brass, and there is a curious *brass*, on which is inscribed a heart, placed by Bartholomew Gonson, vicar of the Ch., in 1543. in memory of his parents. Since 1850 the work of restoring this noble Ch. has been carried on, with satisfactory results, and some good carved stalls have been erected in the chancel. There are several modern painted windows, some of which are very fine. There are several chained books dating from the time of Elizabeth.

Opposite the Ch. is the Maison Dieu, or "Hudson's Bede-house," built 1641; it has several aged inmates, but a part of the building is used as a *Museum* and *Library*.

In the Roman Catholic chapel, a work of *Pugin*, some good stained glass may be seen.

Among natives of Melton may be named John de Kirby, a justice itinerant, temp. Hen. III.; William de Melton, Archbishop of York (d. 1340); and Orator Henley (b. 1692), who was also curate here.

Near the town is Egerton Lodge, the hunting residence of the Earl of Wilton.

1½ m. S. from Melton is the village of **Burton-Lazars**, so called from its once possessing "a rich hospital, to the master of which all the lesser lazar-houses in England were in some sort subject, as he himself was to the master of lazars in Jerusalem. It is said to have been built at first by the Normans, by a general collection throughout England, but chiefly by the assistance of the Mowbrays, about which time the leprosy (by some called Elephantiasis) did run by infection all over England. And it is believed that the disease did then first come into this island out of Egypt, which more than once had spread itself into Europe: first in the days of Pompey the Great, afterwards under Heraclius, but never before that time did it appear in England." — *Camden*. A bath famous for the cure of scrofulous diseases was opened here in 1760, but owing to the well having become dried up, is now disused. Traces of the hospital site are visible near the *Ch.*, which has a rather curious bell-turret, that appears to have been erected with the view of securing a failing western wall. The nave is Trans.-Norm., and the aisles are decorated.

Thorpe - Arnold, a small village 1½ m. N.E., had once a castle, built by Arnold de Blois, of which no trace remains. The font in the Ch. is Norm.

[The Midland line to Nottingham proceeds in a N.W. direction, passing through the charming Leicestershire and Nottingham Wolds, and has Stats. at Grimston, Old Dalby, in Leicestershire, Upper Broughton, Widmerpool, Plumtree, and Edwalton in Nottinghamshire. At **Willoughby-on-the-Wolds** (2 m. W. of Upper Broughton) are seven fine monuments to the Willoughby family.]

19 m. **Saxby** (Stat.). To the S. of the line is *Stapleford Hall* (James Hornsby, Esq.), on the banks of the river Eye. The front of the house, which is of different dates (from 1500 to 1776), has square-headed mullioned windows, and is decorated with 15 statues of ancestors of the Sherards, Earls of Harborough, among whom William the Conqueror figures. The *Ch.* is indifferent Gothic, rebuilt 1783, and has the Sherard and other arms outside. In the interior are some Sherard monuments from the old Ch., with a *brass* to Geoffrey and Joyce Sherard, with 14 children (1490).

21½ m. **Whissendine** (Stat.), in Rutland. 1½ m. N.E. is **Wymondham**, with a handsome Ch. in E. E. style. It has a fine spire. 3¼ m. further is **Buckminster**, where the Perp. Ch. (restored 1883) with a massive tower and spire deserve notice. In the ch.-yd. is the mausoleum of the Dysart family. *Buckminster Hall* (Earl of Dysart) is a classic edifice.

26 m. **Oakham** (Stat.), see *Handbook to Rutland.*

ROUTE 22.

MARKET HARBOROUGH TO NEWARK.

L. AND N.-W. AND G. N. JOINT RLY.
46¾ m.

On leaving Market Harborough (see Rte. 19) the line runs in a northerly direction to

7 m. **Hallaton** (Stat.). The Ch. of St. Michael has some early Norm. arches in the nave, an E. E. chancel, and a Perp. tower. There is an ancient cross, where the market was formerly held. Near the village are the remains of an encampment, called Hallaton Castle Hill. A branch line joins the Rugby and Peterborough Rly. (see Rte. 19).

9 m. **East Norton** (Stat.), a small village on the Rutland border and on the main road from Leicester to Uppingham. The Manor House (J. H. Heycock, Esq.) is a fine building in Tudor style. Loddington Hall, 1½ m. N., is a hunting-box of Earl of Morton.

13½ m. **Tilton** (Stat.). The village stands on a hill 1½ m. W. from the Rly. The 12th-centy. Ch., with an embattled tower and tall spire, has a tomb with effigies of Sir John Digby and his wife, dated 1269, and another to Sir Everard Digby (1509). On Howbank Hill are remains of a Roman Station.

At **Billesdon**, 2 m. S.W., there is another camp occupying several acres. The village is irregular and scattered, which has given rise to the Leicestershire proverb: "In and out like Billesdon." It is situated on a small stream, called the Billesdon Brook, celebrated in hunting annals as the scene of a tremendous leap by Assheton Smith. The village was once a market-town, and the cross remains; the Ch. has a lofty spire. There is a free school, built in 1650, in the place of one in which it is said that both Villiers, Duke of Buckingham, and George Fox, the Quaker, were educated. Near Billesdon is the Coplow (Mrs. Freer), close by which is a very noted fox-cover. Launde Abbey and Withcot Hall, both fine Elizabethan mansions, lie to the E. of the Rly., on the borders of the county. The former contains some remains of the religious house founded by Richard Bassett in 1125.

[At Marefield Junction, 1 m. N. from Tilton, a branch line of the G. N. Rly. goes off W. to Leicester.

1½ m. Loseby, or Lowesby (Stat.). The Ch., restored 1868, has a very old font, the remains of a screen, and some ancient monuments. Loseby Hall (Sir F. T. Fowke, Bart.), standing in a wooded park, was anciently a possession of the Burdett family. A legend says that William Burdett, "on his return from the Crusades, urged by the slanders of some miscreant retainer, slew his innocent and unsuspecting lady; to atone for which fatal error he founded the monastery of Arrow."—*Burke*. The Hutchinsons afterwards held Loseby, and Mrs. Hutchinson here wrote a great part of her Memoir of her husband. A portrait of Gen. Ireton still exists. Passing *Quenby Hall* (Viscount Downe), the Rly. at 5 m. reaches Ingarsby (Stat.). The old Hall, now a farm-house, contains some good carved woodwork. At 7 m. is Thurnby (Stat.), and 9 m. Humberstone (Stat.) the Rly. then reaches Leicester. 11 m]

Continuing N. the line passes

16¾ m. Twyford, with a Stat. named John O'Gaunt. The Ch., restored in 1849, is E. E. This district S. of Melton Mowbray is interesting, owing to its containing many villages which in name and remains betoken their Roman origin. The chief of these is **Burrow**, or Burrough-on-the-Hill, 1¼ m. N.E., where portions of the walls of a large encampment, 20 ft. high, still exist. The Ch., too, is interesting, and possesses some inscribed bells and a monument of the 15th centy. to Sir William Stockton and his wife. There is also a fine 12th-centy. font.

At 20 m. is **Great Dalby** (Stat.), and at

23½ m. **Melton Mowbray** is reached (see Rte. 21).

26¾ m. **Scalford** (Stat.). The village takes its name from the ford over the river Scald. The Ch. is a handsome 13th-centy. edifice, built of stone, with a square tower; there are traces of Norm. work in the chancel. 12 m. N.E. is **Goadby Marwood**. The Ch., in mixed styles, contains some good tracery in the windows. Francis Peck, the historian (d. 1743), is buried here. The *Hall* is a fine mansion. From Scalford a branch line for mineral traffic to **Waltham-on-the-Wolds**, which has a large and handsome (restored) cruciform Ch., E. E. and Dec., with lofty central tower and spire. It contains some carved stalls and a good font. The original frame of the hour-glass is still fixed to the pulpit.

Croxton Kyriel, 4 m. N.E., once famous for its house of Præmonstratensian canons, built here in the reign of Henry II. by Sir Andrew Luttrell, but at present better known for the Croxton Park Races, held annually in the park of the Duke of Rutland, who had at one time a hunting seat here, now pulled down. About 3 m. to the E. is **Saltby Heath**, on which are the remains of 2 barrows and a singular earthwork, consisting of a wide ditch, running parallel with a vallum formed of the earth excavated from it. This is called King Lud's Intrenchment, and is in all probability Danish.

Between Croxton and Grantham is Harlaxton Manor (see *Handbook to Lincolnshire*).

28½ m. **Long Clawson** (Stat.). The village lies at the foot of the Wold Hills, on the river Symte. The Ch. of St. Remigius is a fine Perp. building.

31½ m. **Harby** and **Stathern** (Junct. Stat.). Here a line branches off to Nottingham, passing Baruston (Stat.), Bingham Road (Stat.), and joining the Nottingham and Grantham Rly. before reaching Radcliffe (see Rte. 12).

35¼ m. **Redmile** (Stat.). This is the nearest Stat. to Belvoir Castle (see Rte. 12), and after crossing the Nottingham and Grantham Rly. at **Bottesford** (see Rte. 12), the line passes Cotham, and reaches at

46¾ m. **Newark** (see Rte. 11).

ROUTE 23.

LEICESTER TO BURTON, BY ASHBY-DE-LA-ZOUCH.

MIDLAND RAILWAY. 30½ m.

This route skirts the forest of Charnwood at too great a distance to give any good idea of the romantic character of that district. The tourist is therefore advised to supplement it by a walk or drive through the Forest, as hereafter indicated. (Rte. 24.)

On leaving Leicester from the main stat. the line at first runs S. for about 2 m., and turns W., passing *Braunstone House* (Capt. R. G. Pochin. R.N.). It reaches at 5½ m. **Kirby Muxloe** (Stat.), where is a small ancient Ch. The ivy-clad remains of a slightly fortified manor-house (misnamed a castle) of the time of Henry VII. or VIII., are very picturesque. It is of brick with stone dressings, and the moat remains perfect. It was built by one of the Hastings family, and was used rather as a residence than as a place of defence. The entrance was by a gateway flanked by two towers, to the rt. of which was another square tower of three stories.

8 m. **Desford** (Junct. Stat.). There is a good Perp. Ch. It is part of the possessions of the Duchy of Lancaster, and the Queen is lady of the manor. Here the old Leicester and Swannington colliery line from the West Bridge Stat., Leicester, falls in. It is used also for passenger traffic, and has stats. at **Glenfield** and **Ratby**. Near the latter place is an early entrenchment, known as Bury Camp, covering an area of more than nine acres, close to which it is probable that the Via Sevena passed in communication between Ratæ (ancient Leicester) and Deva Colona. The *Ch.*, restored 1890, was appropriated to Leicester Abbey in 1291. It is a fine Dec. building, with a massive tower. The ancient font is unique. In the chancel is a tomb with a recumbent effigy, in robes and ruff, of Henry Sachevell, 1620. 2 m. W. of Desford is the village of **Newbold Verdon**; the ancient Hall was successively the residence of Lord Crewe, Bishop of Durham (who built and endowed the school), and Lady Mary Wortley Montagu.

12½ m. **Bagworth** (Stat.). Here the Leicestershire colliery district may be said to begin. 2 m. W. is **Ibstock**, a living once held by Laud.

14½ m. **Bardon Hill** (Stat.). The

colliery village of **Hugglescote** (Stat. L. & N. W. Rly.—Charnwood Forest line) is 1 m. W. At about the same distance E. rises **Bardon Hill**, a celebrated midland eminence, covered with trees, and crowned with a summerhouse. Though only 852 ft. above the sea-level, it commands views of the Shropshire and Derbyshire hills, and even, it is said, of the Sugarloaf in Monmouthshire. To the N. may be seen the broken uplands of Charnwood Forest, at the base of which runs the road from Markfield to Ashby through Whitwick (Rte. 24). According to the old legend, a man might once have walked from Beaumanoir to Bardon without seeing the sun, so thick was the forest: but at present rocks are more plentiful than trees. Bardon Hill is on private property, but is open to the public on application.

1 m. from Bardon, at **Donnington-on-the-Heath**, is a mansion of the 13th centy., once the seat of William de Sees, but now a farm-house, consisting of an oblong square, with projecting buildings on the N. side. The details afford good examples of the domestic architecture of the time of Henry III.

16 m. **Coalville** (Stat., also Stat. at Coalville East, on the Charnwood Forest line, L. & N. W. Rly.). This is a populous village that has sprung up of late years with the extension of the collieries. It contains many good houses and shops, and the Ch. is a handsome structure.

17 m. **Swannington** (Stat.). One of several ecclesiastical districts formed out of the large parish of Whitwick. The Ch. is a very plain building, and the place is altogether black and grimy, being situated in the very heart of the collieries. Swannington was the terminus of Robert Stephenson's first railway, which is now incorporated with the Midland system.

21 m. ☿ **Ashby-de-la-Zouch** (Stat.), a well-built and thriving town, depending partly on the neighbouring coal-works and partly on its baths and waters, which have gained a high reputation for the cure of rheumatic complaints. The termination of "by" denotes its Danish origin, but it received its distinctive appellation from a certain Alan de Zouch, a Breton baron, who married the heiress of the manor in the reign of Henry III. It was granted in 1461 by Edward IV. to his chamberlain, William Lord Hastings, beheaded in the Tower, in 1483. The manor descended in the female line with Hastings' estates and baronies to the late Marquis, and are now owned by Lord Donington. The Chamberlain built (about 1474) the greater part of the castle, on the S. side of the town, now in ruins, but preserved from further decay by timely repairs. The principal portions remaining are the tower (all but the S. side), to the summit of which there is a winding staircase; the chapel; an upper room, containing a good mantelpiece: the great hall, the masonry of part of which is supposed to date from the reign of John; and the kitchen tower, with its fireplace and chimney. The visitor will scarce need to be reminded that this castle is the locale of some of the most striking scenes in Sir Walter Scott's 'Ivanhoe.' The great tower has a sculptured fireplace in the top storey, and on the outside a panel, within which are the Hastings arms. To the E. of the tower is the courtyard. The chapel, now roofless, was lighted by 4 beautiful Dec. windows on each side. To the E. of the castle is a triangular building, called the Mount-house, which was connected with the kitchen tower by a subterranean passage. Mary Queen of Scots was lodged in the castle for a night in her hasty removal to Coventry in 1569, in consequence of the Northern rebellion, and it was visited by James I. and

his Queen, who were magnificently entertained in 1603. It was garrisoned and defended for Charles during the civil war; but was taken, and dismantled by the order of Parliament.

The Ch., dedicated to St. Helen (restored and enlarged in 1880), is Perp., and consists of nave, S. aisles, and chancel, with a western tower. On the S. side of the chancel is the Hastings chapel, in which is a monument to Lady Catherine Hastings, in the dress of the 16th centy. Selina Lady Huntingdon, the friend of Whitefield and Wesley, was buried here in 1791, "in the white silk dress in which she opened the chapel in Goodman's Fields," and on the floor of the chancel is a fine brass to her memory. Here are also a monument with effigies of Francis, 2nd Earl of Huntingdon, 1561, and his lady, 1576, and to Theophilus, 9th Earl, 1746, by Rysbach; but the most remarkable of all the monuments in the Ch. is "the Pilgrim monument," as it is styled, and which is considered to be perfectly unique. It is an alabaster figure of the 15th cent.; and is in the E. end of the N. aisle under a depressed ogee arch; it represents a man clad in the sclavine, or pilgrim's robe, but evidently a person of consideration, as the collar of S. S. appears round the neck. — *M. H. Bloxam*. Notice also the alabaster slab of the Mundys on the W. wall near the tower arch, and the bust of Mrs. Margery Wright, 1623, over the S. door, remarkable for its quaintness and simplicity. Under the tower arch is a finger-pillory, an instrument for the punishment of those who were disorderly in church, consisting of a horizontal beam opening with a hinge, with grooves for inserting the fingers in it. The fine painted glass windows are modern, as is also the alabaster pulpit.

On the S. side of the town are the *Ivanhoe Baths*, a handsome building, with a pump room (used also for balls), swimming baths, &c., supplied from the Moira mines, a distance of 3 miles. The baths, arranged on the newest principle, are admirably managed, and are chiefly used for bathing, but the water possesses aperient qualities, and is useful in chronic cases of scrofula, skin diseases, dyspepia, &c. It contains muriate of soda (sea salt) and muriate of magnesia with bromine. Adjoining the baths are extensive subscription grounds, including cricket ground, tennis courts, &c., belonging to the Ashby Bath and Hotel Company. Near by is an Eleanor Cross, 70 ft. high, erected in 1879 to the memory of the Countess of Loudoun. It was designed by Sir G. G. Scott, R.A.

The Grammar School, founded in the 16th cent., is a handsome edifice rebuilt in 1880.

About 1 m. to the W. of the town is a small plain, which is supposed to have been the scene of "the gentle passage of arms," so graphically described by Sir W. Scott, in 'Ivanhoe': "An extensive meadow, of the finest and most beautiful green turf, surrounded on one side by the forest, and fringed on the other by straggling oak-trees, some of which had grown to an immense size." The Lords of Ashby were great patrons of these tournaments, and the field of Ashby was one of the most noted in England.

Ashby is situated in the centre of the Leicestershire coal-field, but there are no collieries within three miles. The whole field seems to have been thrown up by the upburst of syenitic rocks scattered over the Charnwood district.

Joseph Hall, Bishop of Exeter and Norwich, was born in 1574 at Prestop Park, in the parish of Ashby.

3½ m. N. is **Staunton Harold Hall** (Earl Ferrers). See Rte. 2.

23½ m. Over **Seal** and **Moira** (Stat.). This is a great colliery

Route 24.—Ashby-de-la-Zouch to Leicester.

stat., situated on the southern slope of the high grounds known as Ashby Wolds, whence a line runs to Nuneaton, through Market Bosworth (Rte. 20).

"In the main coal of Moira. especially in the Bath colliery, at a depth of 593 ft., salt water, beautifully clear, and of nearly the same composition as sea-water, trickles down from the fissures whence the coal is extracted. The brine is carried to Ashby-de-la Zouch in tanks, and is considered highly beneficial in scorbutic and rheumatic affections."—*Hull* (see above). In this locality there are 12 workable seams of coal averaging about 55 ft. in thickness, the main coal section being 14 ft. "A singular pathway, called *Leicester Headland*, runs across the Wolds near Moira, in a direction nearly E. and W., about 10 feet wide, and raised throughout with a clear red gravel, which must have been brought from some distance, as no such gravel is found in the neighbourhood. Tradition states that this is part of a road which originally stretched from Leicester to Stapenhill, at which latter place it is also stated that one of the earliest Christian churches was built, and that burials took place there from Leicester. It may, however, have been a passage from the abbey at Leicester to that at Burton-on-Trent."—*Mammatt*.

3 m. S.W. lies **Nether Seal**, with a good E. E. Ch., which contains a 15th-centy. monument to Roger Doughton, once rector. **Over Seal**, an adjoining hamlet, has a very handsome modern E. E. chapel of ease. *Cadborough* was perhaps an early British camp. There is a barrow near Dead Dane bottom.

The line passes into Derbyshire, before reaching at

25¾ m. Gresley (Stat.). Church Gresley is a busy place, with collieries, potteries and firebrick works.

The Ch. is Norm., with monuments to the Gresley family, one of whom founded an Augustinian priory here, temp. Henry I. 4 m. N. is **Bretby Park** (Earl of Carnarvon). The estate of Bretby formerly belonged to the Berkeley family, and came to the Stanhopes by purchase in the 16th centy. The house is a modern castellated building, not later than the beginning of the present centy., to which a handsome dining-hall was added in 1871. The park is of great extent, and many charming views are to be obtained in it.

Passing between *Drakelow Hall*, formerly the seat of Sir H. Des Vœux, Bart., on S., and **Stapenhill**, with a handsome Ch. on N., the line soon after crosses the Trent, and enters at

30½ m. Burton-on-Trent (Stat.) (Rte. 29).

ROUTE 24.

ASHBY-DE-LA-ZOUCH TO LEICESTER, THROUGH CHARNWOOD FOREST. [ST. BERNARD'S MONASTERY, BRADGATE PARK.]

BY ROAD. 18 m.

Leaving Ashby by the Loughborough road, at

2 m. is the village of **Coleorton**, on the summit of a picturesque ridge. **Coleorton Hall** (Sir G. H. Beaumont, Bart.) is a fine stone building, with classic portico. It was erected by Sir G. H. Beaumont in 1814, on the site of the old house built in 1604. This baronet was well known for his accomplishments and his liberal bequest of pictures to the national collection. The house contains some good paintings, and a sculpture of "Psyche borne by the

Zephyrs," by *Gibson*. The family of Beaumont, of which Sir George is the representative (although the barony has passed to heirs female), ranks with those of Courtenay and Fielding in descending from royal stock. Lewis Beaumont, Bishop of Durham, and his brother, ancestor of the baronet (and who obtained Whitwick and part of the adjacent estates by marriage with the heiress of Comyn, Earl of Buchan), were cousins by male descent from St. Louis the French King, and settled in England in the reigns of Edward I. and II. Several of Wordsworth's poems were written in this house, together with the inscription on a tablet in the grounds:—

" Th' embow'ring rose, the acacia, and the pine
Will not unwillingly their place resign,
If but the cedar thrive that near them stands,
Planted by Beaumont's and by Wordsworth's hands."

The gardens are very pretty, and are adorned with memorials to Sir Joshua Reynolds, and Beaumont the dramatic writer. The terrace commands views of great beauty, embracing the towers of Belvoir, some 30 miles off.

The *Ch.* contains some curious monuments of the Beaumont family, including a fine alabaster tomb, Sir H. and Lady Beaumont, 1604. It was restored and enlarged in 1851 in admirable taste. There is some stained glass in the tower brought from Rouen by a former baronet.

The scattered parish is a very clean, pleasant-looking place, with some almshouses of ornamental character. The prefix " Cole " appears to be due to the reign of Henry VIII., when the collieries in this parish were first worked. The coal-seams of this eastern district cannot be identified with those of Moira, although they are probably synchronous.

Crossing Colcorton Moor, on which is a very plain modern Ch., at

5½ m. is **Whitwick** (Stat. L. & N.W. Rly., Charnwood Forest line), "where a remarkable bed of whinstone or greenstone intervenes between the coal-measures and the New Red sandstone. In one of the shafts of Whitwick colliery it is 60 ft. thick, and has turned to cinders a seam of coal with which it comes into contact. It has evidently been poured out as a sheet of lava over the denuded surface of the coal-measures at some period prior to that of the trias."—*Hull*. The manor, which was very extensive, belonged to the Norman earls of Leicester, and was by Edward I. granted to one of his Scottish partisans, Comyn, Earl of Buchan. There are some slight traces of the castle, which was built by King John and became subsequently the property of the Earls of Lancaster and Leicester and the Lords Beaumont. The manor subsequently passed to the Hastings family. The *Ch.* (restored) is a fine building, of various dates, with a very solid-looking low square tower. On an altar-tomb in the N. aisle is a mutilated figure in armour, upwards of 7 ft. long, in memory of Sir John Talbot. He was born in 1336 and died in middle life. He appears to have been a remarkable man both for his height and other gigantic qualities and characteristics, but now, according to an old parish rhyme—

" Naught remains of Talbot's name,
But Talbot Wood and Talbot Lane."

1¼ m. to the N. of Whitwick on the Loughborough road is **Grace Dieu Manor**, a handsome modern seat (with a Rom. Cath. chapel attached) of E. M. Phillipps de Lisle, Esq. "This family is descended from Fitzazor and Jordanus de Insula or De L'Isle, who received the grant of the lordship of Wordyton in the Isle of Wight from the Conqueror in 1069. They inherited the lordships of Garendon and Grace Dieu from the Phillipps family, which became extinct in 1777, when they assumed that name."—*Walford*. The chapel contains two beautiful stained glass windows representing the legend of St. Elizabeth of Hungary, and the Lord's Supper. At a short distance from the house, and well seen from the high road, are the scanty ruins (now no longer ivied) of the old **Nunnery** of Grace Dieu, founded 1236-42 by the Lady Roesia de Verdon, and suppressed in 1539, complaints having been made of certain irregularities on the part of the inmates. Wordsworth alludes to it thus, in lines written at Coleorton:—

"Beneath yon eastern ridge, the craggy bound,
Rugged and high, of Charnwood's forest ground,
Stand yet, but, stranger, hidden from thy view,
The ivied ruins of forlorn Grace Dieu."

The boundary of the garden, made by the nuns to resemble that of Gethsemane, may yet be traced. At the Dissolution the house passed into the hands of the Beaumonts, and here the dramatist Francis Beaumont, the colleague of Fletcher, was born in 1586. In the Ch. of **Belton**, 2 m. to the N., is the tomb and recumbent effigy of the Lady Roesia. removed from Grace Dieu at the Dissolution.

1 m. E. of Whitwick is the **Abbey of Mount St. Bernard**, a Cistercian monastery, originally founded in 1835 at a short distance S., but removed to the present site in 1839. The late Mr. Ambrose Phillipps de Lisle gave the rough forest land, where six monks established themselves, gradually brought the ground into cultivation, and erected some humble buildings. In 1839 the Earl of Shrewsbury gave the sum of 2000*l.*, when the present structure was commenced; and was formerly opened on the feast of St. Bernard, August 20, 1844. It is the first abbey completed by the Roman Catholics in England since the Reformation, and one of the few spots where a monastic life may be witnessed without crossing the Channel. Fair accommodation for visitors may be obtained at an establishment styled the Forest Rock Hotel in the immediate neighbourhood.

The buildings of the Abbey occupy a lofty site in the midst of a spot formerly a desert, on the S. base of a bare rock, now converted into a Calvary, which is a conspicuous object from afar. They were designed by *Pugin* in the simple and severe style of the E. E., and consist of the conventual buildings and cloisters, with the nave of a Ch., to be extended, as funds will admit, by the addition of choir and transepts. A Gothic open screen separates the temporary choir from that part of the Ch. to which the public are admitted. The Abbey is occupied by about 60 monks of the Cistercian Order, founded by the Englishman Stephen Harding. They observe perpetual silence, employ themselves in husbandry, and have redeemed the neighbouring waste land by their industry, and brought it into cultivation. The estate of the monastery consists of an upland platform of about 300 acres sloping gently to the N., and surrounded by a natural barrier or palisade of the granite peaks of Charnwood Forest, through which a breach has been cut for entrance. The approach is through well-kept grounds, open to all, and here, in advance of the Ch., stand the gate-house and guest-chambers; the former serves also as an Hospice, where the poor are daily fed. Ladies are not allowed to penetrate beyond these out-buildings, but male visitors, on application at the porter's lodge, are most courteously received by the guest-master, and are conducted through the cloisters to the Ch., the chapter-house (in which is a *brass* for the first abbot), the library, museum, refectory, &c. The cemetery is a very beautiful flower-decked spot. Several useful trades are carried on in the precincts of the monastery, even to tailoring and gas-making.

At a short distance was the Reformatory, which occupied the site of the former abbey, but is now disused and fallen into decay.

1 m. E. of the Monastery is **Oaks.** Its *Ch.* was the first built after the enclosure of Charnwood Forest. It was consecrated on the 18th June, 1815, and is hence commonly known as " Waterloo Church." 1½ m. S.E. is *Charley Hall,* which occupies the site of a small religious house, united to Ulverscroft Priory in 1495.

Returning to the main road, is passed, at

7½ m. *Abbot's Oak,* a modern mansion, which preserves the memory of one of the old forest-trees; and at

9 m. is reached the cross roads, where once stood the famous **Copt Oak,** a place of assembly where the forest courts were held, and where the Parliamentarian Earl of Stamford mustered the train bands of the district in 1642. A modern Ch. (rebuilt 1889) now marks the site.

1 m. E. of Copt Oak, and remote from the high road, are the very picturesque remains of **Ulverscroft Priory,** founded by Robert Blanchmains, Earl of Leicester, in the reign of Henry II. for Augustinian hermits. It is the finest ecclesiastical ruin in Leicestershire, but little of the original structure exists, the present remains being Dec. They mainly consist of a tower, still 60 ft. high, of later date than the rest of the Ch., which communicates with the nave by a lofty pointed arch. In the interior of the tower are traces of three apartments, on different levels, apparently intended as cells for recluses of the order. The S. wall of the chancel is standing, in which 3 stone sedilia remain, and there are some traces of a chapter-house and cloisters. Several of the Lords Ferrars of Groby were interred in the Ch., but none of their monuments remain. A large part of the Prior's lodgings still exists, converted into agricultural buildings. The priors of Ulverscroft were persons of great importance ; " they kept their hounds and hawks; they employed a ranger, a huntsman, and a falconer; they had a woodhouse, and seven woodmen constantly employed in cutting firewood for the house; they brewed ten quarters of malt weekly; they kept open house for all visitors and wayfarers: they maintained all the poor in the surrounding parishes, and had at one time 300 beasts, 1000 sheep, and 300 swine on the forest."

At 10½ m. the lower road from Ashby, through Hugglescote (Rte. 22), comes in. The adjoining village of **Markfield** has extensive granite quarries. Markfield Knoll and Markfield Cliff Hill, isolated masses of syenite, though scarcely 500 ft. high, are very picturesque objects, and command extensive views.

2 m. E. is the village of **Newtown Linford,** where the Ch. has a Dec. tower, but the body is very late Perp. Hence a pathway leads beside a clear trout-stream to **Bradgate Park,** in which are the ruins of the hall, interesting as the birthplace of Lady Jane Grey, it having been built by her grandfather, Thomas Grey, 2nd Marquis of Dorset. " It is said of the wife of the Earl of Stamford who last inhabited Bradgate Hall, that she set it on fire, or caused it to be set on fire, at the instigation of her sister, who then lived in London. The story is thus told: Some time after the Earl had married he brought his lady to his seat at Bradgate. Her sister wrote to her, desiring to know

how she liked her habitation and the country she was in. The Countess wrote for answer, that 'the house was tolerable, that the country was a forest, and the inhabitants all brutes.' The sister, in consequence, by letter desired her 'to set fire to the house and run away by the light of it.' The former part of the request, it is said, she immediately put into practice."—*Throsby*. The lady of whom this story is told was Elizabeth, daughter of Sir Daniel Harvey, but its truth is very doubtful. The park stands within the ancient bounds of Charnwood Forest, which abounds still in picturesque views, though greatly altered from its former condition; "where a squirrel might hop 6 m. from tree to tree without touching the ground, and a traveller might journey from Beaumanor to Bardon on a summer day without once seeing the sun." Trees are now scanty, yet a few fine oaks survive. It seems to have formed part of the great forest of Arden, which in the time of the Romans extended from the Avon to Trent. Drayton thus writes of Charnwood:—

"O Charnwood, be thou call'd the choicest of thy kind;
The like in any place, what ford hath hope to find?
No tract in all this isle, the proudest let her be,
Could show a sylvan nymph in beauty like to thee."

Bradgate Hall was captured by Prince Rupert in 1642, the owner (Earl of Stamford) being then in arms against the king. In 1696, it was visited by William III. and early in the next century, being greatly damaged by fire, it was abandoned. It was a moated house, of brick with stone quoins, and the principal remaining features are 2 towers; the N. side is partly overgrown with ivy.

The best preserved part is the chapel, which was roofed over by the late Earl of Stamford, and the mullioned windows partially bricked up. It is the family burial-place, but the only monument is one, with recumbent effigy in armour, for Henry Grey, first Baron of Groby (d. 1614), and his wife Anne, daughter of Lord Windsor.

There are still traces of the moat, pleasaunces, and fish-ponds; and there are some very fine old oaks in the park. Adjoining the house is a beautiful avenue of aged Spanish chestnuts, under which Lady Jane Grey may reasonably be supposed to have walked. At Bradgate her preceptor, Roger Ascham, found her with astonishment reading the 'Phædo' of Plato, while all the other youthful inhabitants of the house were gone hunting. Fuller says of her, "She had the innocency of childhood, the beauty of youth, the solidity of middle, the gravity of old age, and all at 18—the birth of a princess, the learning of a clerk, the life of a saint, and the death of a malefactor for her parent's offence."

On the hill in the park, called "*Old John*" (so named from a man who was accidentally killed, in 1823, at the celebration of the 6th Earl's coming of age), is a prospect tower, which commands an extensive view of Bardon Hill, Mount Sorrel, and parts of Leicester and Nottingham. The park is open to the public on Mondays only, but there is a public footway across a portion of it.

13½ m. **Groby**, once a market town, but now a hamlet of the parish of Ratby, containing some remains of the brick and stone mansion of the Greys, Barons Ferrers of Groby. It is now occupied by a tenant of the Countess of Stamford and Warrington, and the barony court is still held in the old hall, which contains a curious inlaid table. Elizabeth Woodville, afterwards Queen of Edward IV., was first married to Sir John Grey of Groby, and passed there the few happy years of her life, until by her husband's death in the battle of

St. Albans the estate was forfeited. Near the house and the modern Ch. is the small Norman mound, almost the only remains of the ancient castle. *Bradgate House* is a modern Elizabethan residence, the seat of Col. Adrian E. Hope; it occupies the site of an old house called Steward's Hay, midway between Groby and the ruins in Bradgate Park.

On the road to Bradgate is a quarry of Charnwood syenite; also *Groby Pool*, a small but beautiful mere of 40 acres, fronting a picturesque building called Pool House. Concerning this mere there are two local proverbs: "Then I'll thatch Groby Pool with pancakes," alluding to something improbable; and "For his death there is many a wet eye in Groby Pool;" that is, no eyes are wetted by tears for him. The pool contains numbers of pike and perch, and it is also a great resort of waterfowl. Between Groby and Leicester the old Leicester and Swannington Rly. approaches the road, and is carried through a tunnel to Glenfield (Rte. 23).

Passing on rt. Braunstone Hall (Capt. R. G. Pochin, R.N.), on l. Glenfield Frith House (Mrs. Ellis), a little to the S. of which is "**The Bird's Nest**," said to have been the site of a hunting-seat of John of Gaunt, and crossing at the turnpike the old Roman Fosse Way, the tourist reaches

18 m. Leicester (Stat.). (Rte. 19.)

ROUTE 25.

RUGBY TO TRENT JUNCTION, BY LEICESTER, MOUNT SORREL, AND LOUGHBOROUGH. [LUTTERWORTH.]

MIDLAND RAILWAY. 40½ m.

The rly. runs through a pleasant country from Rugby, and crosses [*Derby, &c.*]

the Watling Street into Leicestershire, some distance S. of

7¾ m. **Ullesthorpe** (Stat.). This is a hamlet, dependant on, but larger than **Claybrooke**, 1 m. W., where there is a good Ch., chiefly Perp., with square embattled tower. The country around Claybrooke is high, and the river Soar rises in its neighbourhood. 2 m. W. of Claybrooke Ch. the Roman road of the *Fosse Way* enters Leicestershire, and runs parallel with the rly. to Leicester. *High Cross*, where it crosses the Watling Street at rt. angles,

"Where Fosse and Watling cut each other in their course,"

is supposed to have been the site of the station of Vennones. A pillar was erected to mark the spot in 1712, by Lord Fielding.

[3 m. S.E. of Ullesthorpe is the small market-town of ꝗ **Lutterworth**, pleasantly placed on a hill overlooking the Swift, a tributary of the Avon; it is a very quiet place, with hardly any manufactures, the ribbon and hosiery trades, once flourishing, being no longer carried on. The *Ch.* of *St. Mary* is a large, handsome Perp. edifice, with a lofty tower: it has been restored, when two fine frescoes were brought to light: one gives a singular representation of the Resurrection. Lutterworth is proud of its association with the memory of John Wickliffe the Reformer, who was rector of the parish from 1375 to 1384. After his death his works were condemned by the Council of Constance (1414), and himself branded as a heretic. His bones were accordingly dug up and burnt, and the ashes thrown into the river Swift, which flows past the town. The carved oak pulpit, said to be the same in which he preached, is reverently preserved, with other relics. There are also a portrait of him, and an alto-relievo, sculptured by *Westmacott*.

K

11 m. **Broughton-Astley** (Stat.). The village is 1 m. to the l., halfway between the rly. and the Roman Fosse Way. 2 m. S.W. is **Frolesworth**, the Ch. of which contains some good monuments. Notice those of Francis Staresmore, lord of the manor, and wife (d. 1657). He is represented in armour, and his lady, on a separate tomb, is enveloped in a shroud, leaving only the face visible. In the village is a fine block of buildings consisting of twenty-four almshouses for widows of the Ch. of England, founded by the Baron Smith, Chief Justice of the Scotch Exchequer, who died in 1726.

14½ m. **Countesthorpe** (Stat.). Here framework-knitting and brick-making are extensively carried on. The Ch. was rebuilt in 1842, except the tower. 3 m. S.E. is the village of **Arnsby**, the birthplace of Robert Hall, whose father was a Baptist minister here (b. 1764, d. 1831).

16½ m. **Wigston** (South Stat.). (Rte. 19.)

20 m. **LEICESTER** (Stat.). (Rte. 19.)

From Leicester the rly. runs due north to

24½ m. **Syston** (Junct. Stat.), passing on W. the villages of Belgrave and Thurmaston, and on E. that of Barkby, with Barkby Hall (Thomas Brooks, Esq.). Syston is the point of junction of the Melton and Peterborough Rly. with the main line (Rte. 21). 1½ m. W. is **Wanlip**. The Ch. is worth a visit, as it contains one of the finest *brasses* in England, to the founders, Sir Thomas Walsh and Dame Katrine his wife, 1393. Wanlip Hall is the seat of Sir A. R. Palmer, Bart.

1 m. further W. is **Thurcaston**, the birthplace of Hugh Latimer (1470), to whose memory there is a marble tablet in the Ch., of which Bp. Hurd was once rector.

At **26 m.** the line crosses the Wreake, a small stream that near this spot joins the Soar.

28 m. Sileby (Stat.). The line is carried through the village on an embankment and bridges. The Ch. is a fine Dec. and Perp. building, with a lofty embattled tower; and an elm-tree. 30 ft. in girth, stands in the ch.-yard.

1½ m. W., finely situated on rising ground above the river Soar, is the town of ✠**Mount Sorrel**. "Heretofore it was famous for its Castle, seated on a steep and craggy hill, and overhanging the river. This first belonged to the Earls of Leicester; afterwards to Saher de Quincy, Earl of Winchester, in the Barons' time. At this day there remains nothing but a heap of rubbish; for in the year 1217 the inhabitants of these parts pulled it down to the ground, as a nest of the devil, and a den of thieves and robbers."—*Camden*. The town is divided into N. and S. End, and each part has a Ch. That at North End is a Perp. structure, with heavy square tower; that at South End is modern E. E., with a spire. There was formerly a Market-cross here, which Sir John Danvers removed in 1793 to his mansion of Swithland; he erected instead a small round building with cupola, supported by 8 pillars, which is called the Market-house. Stocking-weaving is carried on, but the granite or syenite quarries close to the town give the chief employment, the stone being conveyed by a branch rly. to the Barrow Stat. (*post*). There is a Hospital on the hill, built by the Quarry Co., for the benefit of the employés in the quarries and others.

There is an old saying in this neighbourhood, "He leaps like the Bell-giant or devil of Mount Sorrel

This is founded on the legend of a giant who took three tremendous leaps, commencing at Mount Sorrel, where he mounted his sorrel horse, thence making a three-mile jump of it to Wanlip (one leap). He then leapt another mile to Birstall, where, with the force of the shock, he burst himself and his horse; but he managed even then to leap one more mile, as far as Belgrave (1 m. from Leicester), where, as the name implies, he was buried.

2 m. S. is the village of **Rothley**, adjoining which on W. is *Rothley Temple* (H. R. Parker, Esq.), where there are remains of a chapel, once a Preceptory, granted by Henry III. to the Order of Templars, and on their fall it was transferred to that of the Knights of Jerusalem. Here the author, critic, and orator, Thos. Babington Macaulay, was born, Oct. 25, 1800.†

[The country to the W. of Mount Sorrel is broken and occasionally wooded, it being the verge of Charnwood Forest (Rte. 23). 2 m. W. is **Swithland**, famous for its slate quarries. The Ch. contains monuments of the Danvers family. *Swithland Hall* (Earl of Lanesborough) has many fine portraits by *Vandyck* and *Lely*, and in the park is set up the old Market-cross from Mount Sorrel. 1 m. W. is *Rocliffe Hall* (W. U. Heygate, Esq.), a handsome mansion, surrounded by thriving plantations, the site being quite a modern reclamation from the forest.

N. of Swithland are the pleasant villages of **Woodhouse** and **Woodhouse Eaves**. The lover of stained glass should visit Woodhouse Ch., which formerly contained an elaborate series of armorial bearings of the Neville family. The late Mr. Perry-Herrick, of Beaumanor, restored some of this glass, filling the

† See 'Macaulay's Life,' vol. 1. p. 25, &c.

5-light E. window with subjects from the life of our Saviour, and the side windows with various coats of arms. The Ch. of **Woodhouse Eaves** is most picturesquely placed on a rock, under which is a cavern and spring of water, the remains of an abandoned quarry, and the village is the very perfection of neatness. *Maplewell*, a large building, is the residence of Sir W. H. Salt, Bart. The name is supposed to have been originally May-pole-well, from a spring near which 1st of May dances took place. A cluster of a few houses a short distance off, called the **Brand**, indicates one of the places where cattle were formerly marked before being turned out into the forest.

Almost adjoining Woodhouse is **Beaumanor**, the beautiful modern Elizabethan seat of Mrs. Perry-Herrick (Railton, architect), standing in a noble park. It occupies the site of two former mansions, to one of which Richard II. and his queen paid a visit. The property belonged, as early as the 12th centy., to the Despensers, but on their attainder it was conferred on Henry de Beaumont, who built the 2nd house and formed the park, which was 20 m. in circumference. It afterwards passed into the hands of the Hastings, Grey, and Essex families, from the last of whom it was purchased by Sir William Herrick, ancestor of Robert Herrick, the poet. The present house is remarkable for its noble hall and staircase, rich in fine oak carving, and it contains many good portraits. In the hall stands an enormous chair without nail or joint, being carved from an oak, 37 ft. in circumference, that grew in the park. On this chair hangs a garland of roses, annually renewed by the Farnham family as a feudal service.

In cutting a drive at **Beacon Hill**, on which there is an encampment, a number of early remains, such as celts, armlets, &c., were found.]

30 m. Barrow-on-Soar (Stat.). famous for its lime, which is held in high estimation. The geologist will find in the liassic measures here many typical fossils. Some of the fishes and reptiles of this formation afforded great matter for wonder in the early days of geological study, particularly the ichthyosaurus and plesiosaurus, several varieties of which have been found here; and some of the specimens may be seen in the Leicester Town Museum. The manor of Barrow was one of the possessions of Harold, and it was also held by Lord Hastings, beheaded in 1483 by Richard, Duke of Gloucester. The Ch. in Dec. style was restored in 1870, and the tower rebuilt. In the chancel is an interesting monument with a punning epitaph on the names of Braham and Cave. Bp. Beveridge. of St. Asaph, was a native of Barrow, and he gave the living to St. John's College, Cambridge.

1 m. W. is **Quorndon**, best known as the head-quarters of the Quorn hunt. The kennels and stables are a source of interest to many visitors. Quorndon House is the seat of W. E. J. B. Farnham, Esq., whose family have been here for many generations. In the Ch. is a monument to Sir John Farnham (d. 1587), which represents him engaged in besieging a fortress; but the figure has suffered considerable mutilation. *Quorn Hall* (E. Warner, Esq.) was formerly known as the Nether Hall, and Quorndon House as the Over Hall.

32 m. ☿ Loughborough (Stat., also Stat. on the Charnwood Forest Line of L. & N. W. Rly.). This wellbuilt, thriving town is, next to Leicester, the largest and most important place for the manufacture of hosiery in this district, and embraces, in addition to stocking weaving, that of bobbin-net, in which interest it is more associated with Nottingham. Indeed, this was one of the head-quarters of the bobbin-net trade, until the disturbances of the Luddites, when the patentee removed his factory into Devonshire. There are also a celebrated bell-foundry belonging to the Messrs. Taylor, and a large locomotive factory of the Electric Brush Light Co. The parish Ch., dedicated to All Saints, is cruciform, with a fine western tower, erected in the 15th centy. It was restored by *Scott* in 1862, and consists of nave, with single N. aisle and double S. aisle, N. and S. transepts, and chancel. In the interior "its bold and lofty piers—its still more lofty arches and their excellent proportions—are features that render it one of the finest of the parish churches of the county. Its fault is not its simplicity, but its monotony. Throughout the Ch. every pier, every window, every moulding is the same."
Loughborough was one of the possessions of the elder Despenser, and after his death was granted to Henry, Lord Beaumont. In later times it was owned for many generations by the Earls of Huntingdon, and it afterwards came into the hands of the Rawdon-Hastings family.
Dishley Grange, 1½ m. N.W. of Loughborough, was once the residence of Mr. Bakewell, the eminent breeder of stock. 2 m. further is **Garendon Park**, the seat of E. M. Phillipps de Lisle, Esq. The house of which one front is Elizabethan, and the other of Italian architecture, is built on the site of an abbey, founded in 1133, by Robert le Bossu, Earl of Leicester, for Cistercian monks. At the Dissolution it was sold to the Earl of Rutland, and became by marriage the property of the Villiers, Dukes of Buckingham, the last of whom sold it to a lawyer. Ambrose Phillipps, the ancestor of the present proprietor. The grounds are very beautiful, and have local

renown for a hawthorn tree that "miraculously" blooms at Christmas. "In the park is a temple to Venus, which formerly contained a fine statue brought from Rome, destroyed by a mob in 1811." The entrance lodges are worthy of notice. That from Sheepshead (W.) is a triumphal arch, adorned by a relief of Actæon's metamorphosis. The forest entrance has pillars of Charnwood porphyry, being the first of the sort ever made of that material. The neighbourhood of **Sheepshead** (Stat. L. & N.W. Rly.) is very picturesque, as it lies on the outskirts of Charnwood Forest, the broken ridges of which form a very charming accompaniment of the scenery.

2 m. E. of Loughborough is **Prestwold**. The Ch. (restored) contains some fine monuments to members of the Packe family. Some are ancient, as to Sir Christopher Packe, temp. Charles I., and others modern, by Bacon and Westmacott; one of these is to Major Packe, who was killed at Waterloo. Prestwold Hall, a fine Palladian building by Burn. The park contains some magnificent cedars of Lebanon. Very near Prestwold is *Burton Hall* (Duke of Somerset), where the Duchess di Sforza (the granddaughter of the 8th Earl Ferrars) was brought up by her guardian, Mr. Mundy, under rather romantic circumstances. 1½ m. N.E. is **Wymeswold**, with a fine restored Ch., well worth a visit.

Soon after leaving Loughborough the line crosses the Soar and enters Nottinghamshire.

At **34 m.** on the E. is **Stanford Park** (R. Ratcliff, Esq.), in Edward IV.'s time the residence of Sir Richard Illingworth. The elms and limes in the park are particularly fine, some of the latter having fluted stems like pillars.

35 m. Hathern (Stat.), a village in Leicestershire of framework-knitters. The adjoining village of **Normanton-on-Soar** is mainly occupied by limekilns and brickfields, and is an uninviting locality.

37 m. Kegworth (Stat.). The village in Leicestershire is picturesquely situated, overlooking the Soar, which is crossed by a bridge, the original part of which is an old and beautiful structure. The restored *Ch.* consists of a nave with aisles, transepts, and chancel, with a tower and spire. In the interior is some remarkably good stained glass, and (in the nave) a curious row of figures in wood of performers playing on musical instruments. The vestry was formerly a "domus inclusus," or anchorite's apartment.

1 m. N. is **Kingston-on-Soar**, a village remarkable for a fanciful crescent of cottages, built in the Gothic style by the late Lord Belper. *Kingston Hall* is the seat of Lord Belper, whose ancestor in the decorating of the grounds followed the system of transplanting full-grown trees. The Hall, which in style resembles a Norm. château, stands on the site of the residence of the Babingtons. The Ch., a small, poor structure, contains a beautifully sculptured tomb, decorated with the rebus of the Babington family, a babe and tun, and stated to be that of Anthony Babington, the conspirator; but this is a mistake, as the style is of the 15th cent., consequently prior to the reign of Elizabeth, in which he lived.

Eastward of Kegworth are the villages of **West** and **East Leake**, where the Ch. (restored 1886) has some remarkable monuments. In the vestry is a curious trumpet or horn 7 ft. 6 in. in length, used till about 1850 for one of the bass singers in the choir to sing through; also **Wysall**, where notice the miserere seats remaining in the chancel of the Ch. Midway between the two is **Cortlingstock** (locally, Costock), where the tourist will find a curious canopied tomb (probably that of the founder) on the outside of the chancel of the Ch. (restored 1863). Under the S.W. window in the chancel is a low side window, which still possesses the original iron transoms. 2 m. beyond Wysall is *Widmerpool*, the modern Elizabethan seat of Major G. C. Robertson.

Westward is **Lockington**, in Leicestershire, where some handsome monuments to the Story family are to be seen in the chancel of the Ch. From the situation of Lockington, at the utmost northern angle of the shire, the saying has arisen, " Put up your pipes and go to Lockington wake;" tantamount to an order to be off and not be troublesome. *Lockington Hall* (N. C. Curzon, Esq.). The adjoining township of **Hemington** has considerable remains of a Ch.; it was once a separate parish.

From Kegworth the rly. pursues a northerly course beside the pleasant stream of the Soar, passing on W. the Ch. and village of **Ratcliffe-on-Soar**, near which the latter river joins the Trent. The Ch. contains some interesting monuments of the Sacheverell family, one of whom is habited as a knight, of the time of Edward IV. The rly. then tunnels through a ridge of red sandstone hills, immediately after which it crosses the Trent, and, skirting the grounds of Thrumpton Hall l., joins the Derby and Nottingham line at

40½ m. **Trent** (Junct. Stat.), (Rte. 2.)

ROUTE 26.

BIRMINGHAM TO WELLINGTON, BY WEST BROMWICH AND WOLVERHAMPTON.

GREAT WESTERN RAILWAY. 32 m.

This line quits Birmingham from the Snow Hill Stat.

Passing Hockley (Stat.) (1 m.), the first stat. in Staffordshire is

1¼ m. **Soho**, a suburb of Birmingham. A short distance N. are the remains of the buildings which, under the name of the **Soho Works**, obtained a European celebrity, and will always be of the greatest interest, as the locality where Watt toiled for so many years, and where he demonstrated to the world the power of his steam-engines. Little less than 130 years ago Soho was a barren heath, upon which was a single rolling-mill; this was bought by Boulton in 1762, who speedily built on its site the manufactory, to which he transferred from Birmingham his already extensive trade in toys and metallic goods. Finding his water-power insufficient, he, in 1767, adopted one of Savery's engines, which he discarded two years later, on entering into partnership with James Watt, by the help of whose engineering skill he extended the original manufactory and added another for coining. They also established an engine factory, where they made engines for England and all the world. In fact, the history of Soho is the history of engineering in general; but the glory of Soho has now departed, leaving only the memory of the greatest mechanic that the world ever knew. On the death of James Watt, the son of the engineer, in 1848, the engine factory was removed to Smethwick, and the Soho works are now grass grown ruins. The Park, which was the residence of Mr. Boulton, has disappeared, and the site is now occupied by streets and terraces.

The once famous Soho Pool was closed and drained 1869; and the site is now built upon.

2½ m. **Handsworth** (Stat.). The township includes Soho, Perry Barr, and Birchfields, and has 3 stations on G. W. Rly. at Hockley, Soho, and Handsworth, and on L. & N. W. Rly. at Perry Barr and Hamstead.

Two lines of Tramways pass through the district. (1) The Cable Tramway from Colmore Row, Birmingham, to New Inns, Handsworth. (2) Steam Tramcars run from the Old Square, Birmingham, to Perry Barr, passing through Birchfields. There is a branch line from Great Hampton Row to Lozells. Tramcars also run from West Bromwich to New Inns.

In Domesday Book this place is called Horneswode, and the name "Handsworth Wood" still remains. In Norman times it was held by the Lords of Dudley Castle, who granted it to the family of Parles, from whom it passed through many hands to the Calthorpes.

The Parish Ch. of St. Mary is picturesque and well situated on a hill. There are traces of Norm. work in the tower, which is at the E. end of the S. aisle. The chancel is Dec., and the Wyrley Chapel, probably, Tudor. In recent times the Ch. has been almost rebuilt in a florid style very different from the original design. Architect, J. A. Chatwin. It was restored in 1878. There are several monuments to the old lords of the manor. An effigy of a knight in armour on an altar tomb, with an emaciated figure or *memento mori* beneath, is supposed to be Sir Wm. Stanford or Stamford, Knt., of Perry Hall (d. 1558).

In the Wyrley Chapel is an altar tomb with effigies of a knight and his lady, representing William Wyrley and his wife. Also a monument to John Fulnetly, Canon of Lichfield (d. 1636). The monument of James Watt, one of Chantrey's finest works, stands in a Chapel built for its reception on the S. side of the chancel. The bust of W. Murdock (introducer of lighting by gas) is also by Chantrey. That to the memory of Mathew Boulton, by Flaxman, is a fine work of art.

St. Paul's Ch., Lozells, consecrated 1880, is a handsome brick building. J. A. Chatwin, architect.

In the Friary Road is situated the Wesleyan Theological College, built 1880. A handsome Gothic building.

The Victoria Park is a spacious recreation ground of more than 20 acres. There is a good Free Library. At Handsworth the formerly celebrated Lunar Society used to meet, once a month when the moon was at the full. The members having far to go, preferred to travel by moonlight. Amongst its members were included James Watt, Boulton, Dr. Darwin of Lichfield, W. Murdock, Josiah Wedgwood, and many others.

At **Heathfield** is James Watt's house, now belonging to Mr. Tangye; in the upper story is Watt's workshop, with all his tools, books, apparatus, &c., still preserved in much the same condition as they were at the time of his death.

Smethwick, a hamlet of Harborne, lies to the S.W. of Handsworth, and has three stats. (Soho, Rolfe Street, and Spon Lane) on the Stour Valley line, which for several miles runs nearly parallel with the G. W. Rly. (Birmingham and Wolverhampton line). The Stourbridge Extension of the G. W. Rly. has a stat. at Smethwick Junct. There are also Steam Tramcars to Dudley and Birmingham.

It occurs in Domesday Book as Smedewick, and, though now possessing a population of more than 36,000, is still only a hamlet in the parish of Harborne. The little chapel erected in 1719 by Dorothy Parkes is now supplemented by four modern churches, the most beautiful of which is Holy Trinity Ch. The principal manufactories here are the works of Messrs. Chance, who make crown, sheet, and rolled plate-glass. They are specially noted for their lighthouse works. A large number of hands are employed, and schools have been erected for the education of the children. Other important establishments are Messrs. Tangye Brothers' Hydraulic Works, which cover a large area, and employ about 2000 men, Nettlefold's Screw Manufactory, the Patent Nut and Bolt Company, the Muntz Metal Company, the Crown Ironworks, and the Patent Rivet Company, which formerly belonged to the engineering firm of Fox, Henderson, and Co., celebrated in connection with the Great Exhibition of 1851 and the Crystal Palace. The Wolverhampton canal, which runs through Smethwick, is crossed by a fine wide bridge, Talford's work, known as the Summit Bridge.

Harborne (Stat., branch line L. & N. W. Rly. from Birmingham), a rapidly increasing suburb of Birmingham, upon the borders of Worcestershire and Warwickshire, now included within the city of Birmingham, lies 3 m. S. of Smethwick. Omnibuses to New Street, Birmingham, every quarter of an hour.

The Parish Ch. of St. Peter is in the style of 13th-centy. Gothic, and has a chancel, nave, aisles, and tower. It was rebuilt with exception of tower in 1867, and has modern stained glass windows, to David Cox and others. The celebrated artist, David Cox, is buried in the ch.-yard.

Ch. of St. Mary, Catholic, is attached to a monastery of the Passionist Fathers, in Lodge Road.

Harborne is chiefly a residential suburb of Birmingham, but there are small works where wrenches, hammers, spectacles, and steel are made.

At Metchley, on the borders of the parish, are the remains of an extensive camp near to the Roman Ickneild Street, which passes from Alcester to Wall, near Lichfield.

6 m. ☿ West Bromwich (Stat.) can boast of even a more rapid growth than Soho, the greater part of its present site having been as late as 1806 a rabbit warren, whereas it is now one of the busiest districts in the Black Country, with a Pop. of nearly 60,000. The town consists of a well-built High Street, 1½ m. long, with many others branching out. There is a steam tramway to Birmingham.

The parish *Church* stands 1 m. N.: it was given to the convent of Worcester by Henry I., and afterwards granted by them to the prior of Sandwell, who rebuilt it in the Dec. style. In 1786 it was almost rebuilt in the barbarous taste of that period, but was restored in 1872, and is now a handsome Dec. edifice, with square pinnacled tower. There is a good 16th-centy. font, some monuments to the family of Whorwood, of Sandwell Park, who flourished in the 16th century, and a stained window to the memory of the late Earl of Dartmouth. There are seven other churches in the parish. The *Oak House* is a 16th-centy. mansion of much interest, fairly preserved. William Jesse the naturalist was born at West Bromwich, and Hallam the historian resided at Charlemont Hall (1 m. N.E.), which was his property.

The Town Hall, which was opened in 1875, is a fine and complete building. There is also a Free Library, an Institute, and various clubs. Dartmouth Park, with an artificial lake, is a public recreation ground.

A celebrity of West Bromwich was Walter Parsons, a gigantic blacksmith, who became a porter in the household of James I. He could carry a yeoman of the guard under each arm, and his good temper was equal to his strength. Once, when insulted in the street, he took his revenge by hanging up his opponent on the hooks of the butchers' shambles by his waistband. (Fuller, ' Worthies,' p. 759).

Adjoining the town, S.E., is *Sandwell Park*, the property of the Earl of Dartmouth, who has given up the house as an educational establishment for (1) a school for the daughters of clergymen and others of limited means, and (2) an industrial school for boys and girls. Sandwell (Sancta Fons) was formerly a Benedictine priory, founded temp. Hen. II., by William de Ophene, or Offney, and on its suppression was purchased by the Whorwoods. The grounds and woods are exceedingly pretty, and one can scarcely realise their proximity to a busy manufacturing district.

7 m. Swan Village (Stat.), a particularly grimy place.

8½ m. ♂ Wednesbury (Stat.) (popularly Wedgebury), a place of great antiquity, a castle having been founded here in the 10th century by Ethelfleda, " Lady of the Mercians," a daughter of Alfred. The town itself is still older, as its original name was apparently **Wodensburgh**, betokening an occupation in heathen times.

It is now given up utterly to ironworks and foundries, which, together with a manufactory of railway tyres and axles, form the staple employment. There is documentary evidence to prove that the mines were worked in this parish in the 13th centy. The *Ch.* occupies a good situation on the hill, where the castle formerly stood. It is a fine Perp. building, consisting of nave, with aisles and clerestory, chancel, transepts, and a very graceful octagonal spire at the W. end. In the interior are some early 17th-cent. monuments to the Parkes family, and one (with a bust) to Mr. Addison, who was instrumental in restoring the Ch.; also an incised slab to "John Cumberfort and his wyffe," 1559. The other churches are St. John's and St. James's. An Art Gallery adjoining the Town Hall has recently been erected. In addition to the Great Western, the South Staffordshire Railway to Dudley and Burton has a stat. here, and there is a short branch to Deepfields, on the North-Western line.

Willingsworth Hall, now a farmhouse, ½ m. W. of Wednesbury, is regarded as the original seat of the Dudleys, and there Henry VII.'s " wolf " is said to have been born in 1462.

10 m. Bradley and **Moxley** (Stat.). Both outskirts of Bilston. At Bradley the first charcoal blast-furnace was erected a century ago, by John Wilkinson, a man famous in the district for first applying iron to the building of canal boats.

11 m. Bilston (Stat.), a town of great antiquity, originally called **Bilrestation**, in Domesday Book **Billestune**, and later **Bylstune**, stands on the northern portion of the great coal-field that stretches, with but short intervals, from West Bromwich to Cannock Chase. It was formerly one of the busiest towns in the district, and was almost surrounded with collieries and ironworks, the "spoil banks" of the one and the "cinder mounts" of the other (the accumulation of ages) presented huge barren hills in every direction. Owing, however, to the coal mines having been exhausted or flooded with water, the appearance of the town has of late years undergone a great change. Large tracts of mines' debris have been levelled and the land restored to cultivation. Bilston is famous for grit-stone, used for setting edged tools. The local proverb runs, " A

Route 26.—Priestfield—Wolverhampton.

Dudley man and a Bilston grindstone may be found all the world over." The town is irregularly built, but has been of late much improved. Its principal street, formerly bordered on each side by pit-mounds, has now well-built houses and a double row of trees. There is a Town Hall (in which is a free library) in the Italian style, public baths and wash-houses, a Temperance hall, an Institute, &c. The principal church is that of St.Leonard, dating from the 13th centy., rebuilt in 1827, and restored 1882: there are 3 other churches, St. Mary's. St. Luke's, and St. Martin's, all built since 1829. and without special interest. The population is chiefly composed of iron-workers, and persons employed in the japanning works, which are extensive. The story of "the boy of Bilston" (William Perry), whose imposture was detected by Bp. Morton of Lichfield, is told in full detail by Plot. Bilston gained in 1832 a painful notoriety from the dreadful ravages of the cholera, which were more disastrous here than in any other part of the kingdom. Coffins were imported daily from Birmingham, and, when the disease abated, many children were found without parents, and others ignorant of their names or relations. The clergy were most assiduous in their work all through the misery. and a cholera orphan school was subsequently founded.

The L. & N.-W. Rly. has also a stat. at **Ettingshall Road**, about 1 m. to the W. of Bilston.

"Passing onwards by rail to Wolverhampton, I felt that I was truly in the heart of the manufacturing districts of England, I could have fancied myself transported to the forges of Vulcan and Cyclops, in Lemnos, for the sight was so marvellous, and the scale of the undertaking so colossal, that to an uninitiated eye it appeared something superhuman. As far as the eye reaches you see manufactories, with chimneys rising like lofty towers, pouring forth red flames, that shine the more brightly from the sky being darkened by the eternal exhalations of smoke."—*Waagen*.

12 m. **Priestfield** (Junct. Stat.), where the line from Stourbridge and Dudley falls in (Rte. 28).

13 m. ☿ **Wolverhampton** (Low Level Stat.), commonly shortened to "Whampton," has long been famed as one of the most important centres of industrial enterprise in the county of Staffordshire. It is situated on rising ground, and being nearly 300 feet above the level of the sea, the air is somewhat harsh but salubrious. The town has the peculiarity that the water from its western side flows through the Severn into the Bristol Channel, while that from the eastern side passes through the Trent into the German Ocean. It is often described as the Metropolis of the "Black Country," owing to the Parliamentary Borough including Bilston, Willenhall, Wednesfield, and Sedgley. It is not, however, actually in the Black Country, but adjoins it, and stands upon the thick bed of new red sandstone, which meets the great coal-field on its western extremity. The aspect is consequently manufacturing on one side and agricultural on the other, and by virtue of its position it has become the chief agricultural and trading emporium of the district. In its neighbourhood, on the north, the south, and the west, are many hills of moderate height, from which the Clee hills, the Wrekin, and even the mountains of Wales are visible.

Few places in Staffordshire possess such ancient lineage as Wolverhampton (its name is a corruption of Wulfruna's ham or town), though not many memorials of its early foundation remain. As the town did not grow into very great importance till the discovery of coal and iron in its neighbourhood, its history is chiefly that which belongs to its ecclesiastical state. Wulfhere, first Christian king of Mercia. A.D. 659, established. it is believed, a monastic institution here, dedicated to St. Mary. More than 3 centuries afterwards. in the reign of Ethelred II., Wulfruna. sister of the king, and widow of Athelm. Duke of Northampton, founded the Ch. of St. Mary, afterwards rededicated to St. Peter. and endowed it with lands for the maintenance of a dean and canons. The deanery was united by Edward IV. to that of Windsor, but separated therefrom by Mary. On the death of the last dean (Dr. Lewis Hobart), in 1846, the collegiate establishment was dissolved by the Ecclesiastical Commissioners, and the Ch. was made parochial.

The fine old Church of St. Peter occupies a conspicuous situation adjoining Queen's Square. It is a stately structure consisting of a lofty nave, side aisles, transepts. and chancel, with a magnificent embattled and richly ornamented tower rising in the centre to the height of 120 ft. The edifice was begun in the reign of Edward III., but the tower and the clerestory were not completed till towards the close of the 15th centy. In the time of Edward VI. its property was granted to Dudley, and was only partially recovered in the next reign, much of it being held in spite of law by the Levesons. During the civil war. the Ch. itself was almost ruined, and the chancel was not rebuilt until 1683. The Ch. has undergone many alterations, and since 1851 has been almost entirely restored. A striking feature in the Ch. is the stone pulpit, date about 1480; it is richly sculptured in panels with boldly cut relief ornaments, and at the foot of the staircase is the figure of a grotesque animal in a sitting posture. The font is 14th-cent. work, and is carved with quaint devices and symbols. The W. window is in memory of the late Duke of Wellington: the stained glass in it is by *Wailes*, as well as the two lancet windows below with figures of St. Peter and St. Paul. The N. transept. called Lane's chancel, the windows of which are peculiar, contains an altar-tomb with effigies of Thomas Lane and his wife. 1582, and against the E. wall a monument to the loyal Col. John Lane of Bentley Hall (Rte. 26). who with his daughter aided King Charles in his escape after the battle of Worcester. In a niche near is a life-size figure of John Baptist, carved by Earp. In the S. transept is a fine statue in bronze, by Le Sueur, of Admiral Sir Richard Leveson. who served with great distinction against the Spaniards in the reign of Elizabeth. He is said to be the hero of the beautiful ballad called the ‘Spanish Ladye's Love,’ inserted in Percy's ‘Reliques.’ This transept also contains an altar-tomb, with recumbent figures, of John Leveson and Joyce his wife (1575). The chancel (the work of Dean Turner, afterwards a Nonjuror as Bp of Ely) was rebuilt in 1851. in late Dec. style, by Christian, with the addition of an apse, the 7 memorial windows of which are filled with stained glass, by O'Connor of London. The reredos beneath is a carving of the Last Supper by Forsyth. There are also several other memorial windows and numerous mural tablets of interest in the Ch.. amongst them one dated 1728 to Dr. William Gibbons, an early benefactor of the Blue Coat School. In the porch is a tablet with a singular epitaph (1732) to the memory of C. Phillips, an itinerant musician. In the ch.-yard is a time-worn column, about 20 feet high, with rude sculptures of birds, griffins. &c.. spirally arranged, commonly known as "the Dane's Cross," and supposed to commemorate the great battle between the Saxons and the Danes near Tettenhall. in 7th centy.; but the better opinion seems to be that it is an ordinary ch.-yard cross of Norm. workmanship.

St. John's Ch. is a handsome edifice, in the Grecian style, and contains a remarkably fine organ, built originally for the Temple Ch. about 1672 by Renatus Harris, rival of the celebrated Bernard Schmidt. The altarpiece is a good copy of the Descent from the Cross, by Rubens; it was painted by J. Barney, R.A., a native artist. There are at least 16 other new churches in the original parish, which was very extensive, comprising parts of what are now Bilston, Ettingshall, Wednesfield Heath and Willenhall, but none of them of any interest.

In the Market-place, now named Queen's Square, is an equestrian **Statue** of Prince Consort, by *W. H. Thornycroft*, R.A., which was unveiled by the Queen in 1866, a large Russian cannon having been removed from the spot to Snow Hill in order that the statue might be placed in the best situation that the town afforded. On Snow Hill is a marble statue of the Rt. Hon. Charles Pelham Villiers, M.P. Wolverhampton has some fine public buildings, such as the Town Hall, the Drill Hall, the Library, the Theatre, St. George's Hall, the Exchange, the Market Hall, and the Agricultural Hall, which covers a space of 1200 yards. The South Staffordshire Hospital, in Cleveland road, is a handsome building, but it is surpassed by the Orphan Asylum, which occupies a beautiful position at Goldthorn Hill, in the neighbourhood of the town. The Art Gallery and Museum. New Lichfield-street, was presented to the town by one of its inhabitants, Mr. Philip Horsman, and includes Mrs. Sydney Cartwright's bequest of pictures. It is open to the public daily. The School of Art adjoins it. The High Level Stat. (L. & N.-W. Rly.) has a fine front looking up Queen-street.

The Low Level Stat. (G. W. Rly.) is alongside of it.

"The introduction of the lock trade into South Staffordshire took place as early as the reign of Queen Elizabeth, but it did not flourish very extensively till the end of the 17th centy., when it became one of the chief staple industries of the district. In the year 1660, when hearth-money was collected, Wolverhampton paid for 84 hearths, and Willenhall for 97, most of which were used by the locksmiths of those times." The industries of the town at the present time may be said to include every description of ironmongery and hardware, including locks and keys, tools, gas fittings, iron fencing, tubes, cut nails, castings, and all kinds of iron work, from the smelting of iron to the greatest perfection of manufacture. Japanning and enamelling are also largely carried on, and of late years extensive electric light works have been erected.

Bird the painter was born in Wolverhampton, 1772; while Abernethy the surgeon, and Congreve the inventor of the rocket, were educated at the Grammar-School, which was founded by Sir Stephen Jenyns, a native of the town, in 1515. The School was removed in 1875 from its old quarters in St. John Street to the handsome buildings it now occupies in the Compton Road.

The Deanery, which was rebuilt in the reign of Charles II., was long occupied by Mr. Parke, a well-known bookseller (d. 1876). The Old Hall, once the residence of the Leveson family, is now a japan and papier-mâché factory.

The *Public Park*, opened in 1881, occupies the site of the old Race-course. It has two extensive artificial lakes, and is picturesquely laid out.

Tunstall Hall, 1 m. N.W., long the seat of the Hamptons, and a moated Elizabethan house, with a lofty square gate-house, is now a farm.

Continuing from Wolverhampton, at 1 m. is a branch to the Bushbury Junction (Rte. 27), and the line then bending N.W. passes on the N. of the village of **Tettenhall**, still pretty, though many of the famous elms on its green have now fallen into decay. Tettenhall was the scene of a great defeat of the Danes by Edward the Elder, A.D. 910. The *Ch.* (partially E. E.), which, like Wolverhampton, was once collegiate, and up to the Dissolution had a dean and 5 prebends, contains a chapel on the north aisle, in which members of the Wrottesley family are buried, and which is separated from the aisle by a carved oak screen. In the S. chancel is a fine tomb of a Leveson. The E. window has 5 lancets, with a curious representation of the Archangel trampling on the Dragon. In the spacious chancel are some sedilia and wood screen-work; there is also an octangular font. Notice the monuments to the 2 members of the Wrottesley family who were killed, one in the Caffre war, and the other at the capture of Bomarsund.

Tettenhall Towers is the fine seat of Lt.-Col. Thorneycroft. It has been arranged by its owner on the most improved sanitary principles.

The Wolverhampton Corporation have large reservoirs and waterworks at Tettenhall, conspicuous for their lofty tower. A Ch. has been built at Tettenhall Wood, and a large *Dissenting College*, in creditable Gothic, forms a conspicuous feature in Tettenhall landscapes.

At **Penderford**, 2 m. N., is a remarkable pool, mentioned by Plot, which is clear in fine weather, but becomes troubled with bubbles and covered with a yellow foam on the approach of rain.

17½ m. **Codsall**. The country here resumes its agricultural character, and becomes well wooded and picturesque. The Ch., a short distance N. of the stat., was rebuilt in 1848, but the E. E. tower, and a Norm. doorway with good mouldings, have been preserved. There is a fine altar-tomb, with a recumbent effigy in armour to Sir Walter Wrottesley, 1630. **Wrottesley Hall**, 1 m. S. of the stat. (Lord Wrottesley), is finely placed on an eminence. Sir Hugh de Wrottesley attended Edward III. at the siege of Calais, and had a licence in 1350 to make a park here. He was one of the original Knights of the Garter. The present house was built by Sir Walter Wrottesley in 1696, the former one having been much damaged in the civil war, during which it was garrisoned for Charles I. In the park some remains of early buildings were found, which Plot and other antiquaries believed to be those of Tettenhall or Theotenhall. Gough held that it was the site of Uriconium, but this has been sufficiently disproved.

1½ m. N.W. of the stat. is **Chillington Hall** (R. H. Briscoe, Esq.), formerly the seat of the old Roman Catholic family of Giffard, who held it from the time of Stephen. The present house superseded one of the time of Henry VIII., which was rendered almost uninhabitable from damage received during the Commonwealth, when the Giffards were especially obnoxious to the ruling powers as the owners of Boscobel (see *Handbook for Shropshire*), and was built by Peter Giffard, the 17th lord of Chillington, from the designs of *Sir John Soane*. The grounds, which are freely opened to the public during the summer months, are very extensive and beautifully wooded, and contain a large lake called the Pool; but the principal attraction is the main avenue, which is over 2 m. in length. There is a sulphur well, formerly in much repute for the cure of leprosy, in the grounds, and in Codsall wood, not far off, is a similar spring, which gushes out from beneath an aged oak.

20¼ m. **Albrighton** (Stat.), in Shropshire, but several of the fine adjoining seats are in Staffordshire. 4 m. N. is **Weston Park** (Earl of Bradford). The house is a plain, though large building. The ivy-clad *Ch.* stands in the park. It has a painted E. window, and some monuments of the Bridgemans; also two ancient wooden effigies supposed to represent Templars, of the Weston family, with the dates 1188 and 1304 inscribed on tablets of doubtful authority.

Patshull (or Patteshull) is 2 m. S. The *Park*, the seat of the Earl of Dartmouth, belonged to the Astleys, one of whom erected the present house, which is in the Vaubrugh style. It afterwards passed to the Pigots (one of them was Governor Pigot, the possessor of the famed Pigot diamond), from whom it was purchased by the late Lord Dartmouth. His son, the present possessor, has greatly improved the house under Burn, and has laid out beautiful gardens. The park contains some picturesque scenery, and is adorned by a serpentine sheet of water, terminating in a lake. The *Ch.*, an Italian structure of the close of the 17th centy., which stands in the Park, has 2 altar-tombs, from an older building, of Sir John Astley and his wife (temp. Henry VII.), with panels of his 7 sons and 8 daughters, and of Sir Richard Astley, recumbent between his two wives. It also contains monuments of the Pigot family. There are several stained glass windows, memorials to former Earls of Dartmouth. The building was completely restored by the present Earl in 1874. 2 m. S.E. of Patshull is **Pattingham**, with a fine old Ch. of various dates. The nave is Norm., the chancel E. E., and the S. aisle Dec.; the tower also is Dec. with modern spire. It was well restored by *Scott*.

For **Shiffnal** (25 m.), **Oakengates** (29 m.), and **Wellington** (32 m.), see *Handbook for Shropshire*.

ROUTE 27.

BIRMINGHAM TO CREWE, BY WOLVERHAMPTON, BUSHBURY, AND STAFFORD.

LONDON AND NORTH-WESTERN RAILWAY. 53½ m.

The L. & N.-W. Rly. has two independent routes from Birmingham to Wolverhampton, viz. by the Stour Valley, and by the line viâ Bescot Junction, formerly the Grand Junction Rly.

1. By **Stour Valley.** Leaving New Street Stat., and passing through a tunnel, the traveller emerges at once amongst the blackened chimneys and smutty atmosphere of manufacturing Birmingham. This is abundantly evident, not only from the physical signs of labour, but from the dense population accumulated on either side the line and the frequent stations along the route.

For some distance out of Birmingham there is a stat. at every mile or so, as at **Edgbaston, Soho, Smethwick Junct.** (whence a line goes off to Stourbridge, Rte. 28), and **Spon Lane,** the nearest stat. to Messrs. Chance's works (Rte. 26). At **5 m.** is **Oldbury** (Stat.), in Worcestershire, where are ironworks and collieries, and a large railway-carriage manufactory. At **6 m. Albion** (Stat.), adjoining ironworks of the same name, and the hamlet of **Tividale,** where is a basaltic rock called Coxe's Rough, of great interest to the geologist. At **7 m., Dudley Port** (Junct. Stat.), the South Staffordshire Rly. passes beneath the Stour Valley line, running N. to Walsall and Lichfield, and S. to Dudley (Rte. 28).

Route 27.—Tipton—Aston. 143

9 m. **Tipton** (Stat.). This place is called Tybbington in Domesday Book, but contains nothing of interest to the antiquary, except the tower of the old parish Ch. It still stands, although it has sunk some 30 ft. into the ground owing to mining operations. The Ch. itself was shattered by the same cause in 1797, when it was removed by an Act of Parliament to its present site. The town, which has a Pop. of over 30,000, spreads over a circular area about 2 m. in diameter, with coal-pits, iron-works, and dwellings, all mixed up together. In fact, every inch of available ground is covered with furnaces, Tipton being celebrated for its iron, as adapted for heavy works. It possesses a speciality for chains, cables, and anchors; and steam-engine boilers are also largely manufactured. The G. W. Rly. has also Stats. at Tipton and Great Bridge, and the two lines run nearly side by side to Wolverhampton.

Shortly beyond Tipton a branch line runs to Wednesbury (Rte. 26), with stats. at Prince's End and Ocker Hill.

10 m. **Deepfields** (Stat.), the seat of several large ironworks. On W., about 2 m., is **Sedgley**, situated on a high ridge of ground overlooking Himley and the vale of Salop. In the beginning of the 17th centy. the manor of Sedgley was purchased by Thos. Parkes, whose son Richard figures conspicuously in Dud Dudley's curious work, 'Metallum Martis.' In the upper portion of the parish is Sedgley Park, once a seat of the Dudley family, and afterwards turned into a Roman Catholic school, which was for years in high repute, but now extinct. The Ch. of All Saints, a handsome Gothic edifice, was rebuilt in 1825 by the Earl of Dudley. The ancient civil parish includes Coseley, Upper and Lower Gornal and Hurst Hill, but they are now distinct parishes. Gornal is famous for fire-bricks and nail-making.

11 m. **Ettingshall Road** (Stat.). Ettingshall and New Village are busy iron-working districts, with a Pop. of 7000. Bilston is 1 m. E. (Rte. 26).

12 m. **Monmore Green** (Stat.), a suburb of Wolverhampton, principally occupied by engineering and varnish-making works.

13 m. **Wolverhampton** (High Level Stat.) (Rte. 26).

2. By **Grand Junction Rly.** This, in early rly. times, was the main line between Birmingham and the North, and it was in fact the nucleus of the present gigantic system of the London and North-Western Company. It was projected as early as 1824, but it was not sanctioned by Parliament until 1833, and was only opened from Warrington to Birmingham in 1837; the extension to London was effected in the following year. This is by far the most agreeable route from the Midland metropolis, as it leaves the Black Country altogether to the l., and itself skirts pleasant rural districts.

Passing the surburban stat. of **Vauxhall**, at 2 m. is **Aston** (Junct. Stat.), whence a branch runs N. to Lichfield and Derby. The town was a rural village as recently as 1850, but now forms part of Birmingham. Steam trams run frequently to Corporation St. **Aston Hall**, built by Sir Thomas Holt (1618-1635), is a fine Elizabethan house. The main buildings, ranged round three sides of a square, are of red brick and stone, with gables and three towers surmounted with domes. Charles I. was entertained here in 1642, a few days before the Battle of Edgehill. The Hall was besieged and taken by the Parliamentary forces. In 1858 the

Corporation purchased the Hall, with 40 acres of the ground surrounding it, and converted them into a Museum and public park. Aston Ch. is a fine edifice, with remains of Dec. and Perp. work. It has been recently restored and enlarged (J. A. Chatwin, architect). There are monuments to the Ardens, Holts, and Edingtons, also a brass to Thomas Holt (d. 1545) and his wife. The modern stained glass is fine.

The rly. now enters Staffordshire, and at

3½ m. is **Perry Barr** (Stat.), a corruption of Parva Barr. On E. are the village of Perry and *Perry Hall*, the Elizabethan seat of Hon. A. C. Gough-Calthorpe, overlooking the Tame, which flows through the park. To the N. of the village, on the other side of the canal, the ground rises into considerable uplands, forming the Barr Common, across which the Icknield Street runs. Occupying a conspicuous position on these heights is the *Roman Catholic College* of **Oscott**, 2¼ m. from the Stat. The present building has a fine Tudor front, and has otherwise been improved, from designs by *Pugin*; it has superseded the old college, which was greatly damaged by a fire, and is now used as an orphanage. Near to Oscott is the Princess Alice Home, an orphanage established in 1882 through the munificence of Mr. S. Jevons, of Birmingham.

4¾ m. **Great Barr** (Stat.). On S., very near the stat., is *Hamstead Hall*, commanding a grand prospect. The property, from the time of Henry II. to James II., belonged to the Wyrleys, of which family was William Wyrley, the herald, who assisted Erdeswick, Burton, and other early county historians (d. 1617). On N. 2½ m. is the village of Great Barr. The Ch. has been rebuilt with the exception of the spire. The name of Barr, which signifies Head, sufficiently attests the hilly character of the district. *Barr Beacon*, 2 m. N. of the village, rises to the height of 653 ft. It was one of the stations in General Mudge's survey, and commands a view of the Lickey, the Wrekin, Castle hill in Beaudesert, Sutton, the Bardon hills.

Great Barr Hall (Lady Bateman Scott) is a fair specimen of modern Gothic, and its very fine grounds afford an extensive prospect. It formerly belonged to the Stapletons, and afterwards to the Booths. By one of the latter it was sold in 1618 to William Scott, the ancestor of the present proprietor Thomas, the grandson of William, is thus spoken of by Sir Simon Degge, the Staffordshire antiquary:—" At Barr are the seats of several families of the Scotts, whereof Thomas le Scott, the principal, is owner of a pretty gentleman's estate, but may justly be accounted the prince of the yeomanry, he continuing the old manner of housekeeping in hospitality to strangers and relieving the poor; and, as he is not sparing to himself in taking the recreation with his hounds, when his other affairs will give leave, so is he not ashamed to put his hand to the plough to encourage his servants; and in truth in these parts I know none equals his yeoman-like manner of living, but many that take upon them to be gentleman-like come far behind him both in state and manner of living."

6 m. **Newton Road** (Stat.). West Bromwich is 1 m. W. (Rte. 26).

8½ m. **Bescot** (Junct. Stat.). Here the South Staffordshire line crosses the Grand Junction, giving access on l. to Wednesbury and Dudley; and on rt. to Walsall and Lichfield (Rte. 28).

Bescot Hall (J. Slater, Esq) is a modern edifice; the old site is now a garden surrounded by a moat, crossed by an ancient bridge.

Route 27.—*Wood Green—Bushbury.* 145

9 m. Wood Green (Stat.), a small parish 1 m. N.E. of Wednesbury.

9¼ m. James Bridge and **Darlaston** (Stat.), whence a short branch leads to Wednesbury (Rte. 26). Darlaston, which belonged to the Staffords, temp. Hen. VI., is a busy iron town, midway between Bilston and Wednesbury. The old Ch. of St. Laurence (restored in 1872) was formerly famous for its stained glass, which has now disappeared.

1 m. N. of James Bridge is *Bentley Hall*, which was purchased by Richard Lane in 1426, and, having been rebuilt in the Jacobean style, was the residence of his descendant, Col. Lane, during the civil war, whence, when further concealment was too dangerous, his sister, Jane Lane, conducted Charles II. on horseback to Bristol. A good engraving of the house is given in Plot. The Hall was sold by the colonel's great-grandson in 1748, and became a farmhouse, but is now again a private residence.

11½ m. Willenhall (Stat., also a stat. on Midland Rly. on line from Walsall to Wolverhampton), where the Vanes once had a seat, is the centre of a district almost exclusively employed in making locks, the number and variety of which would puzzle the stranger, varying as they do from the intricate safe-lock at five guineas to the little padlock at 1*d.* or 2*d.* There are 4 churches; the oldest, that of St. Giles, has been rebuilt, and has a fine modern stained glass E. window. In this Ch. the celebrated Dr. Wilkes is buried. He was educated for the Church, but afterwards practised as a physician, and was a diligent investigator of the natural history and antiquities of Staffordshire (b. 1691, d. 1760).

2 m. N.W. is **Wednesfield** (Stat. on the Midland Rly.). This place is as famous for the manufacture of keys [*Derby, &c.*]

as Willenhall is for locks. The town is of ancient date, but the Ch. is modern. At Heath Town (Stat. Midland Rly.) a handsome Ch., parsonage, school, and almshouse for poor women, have been built by the munificence of the late Mr. H. Rogers, a merchant of Wolverhampton.

14 m. Wolverhampton (High Level Stat.). (Rte. 26.)

15½ m. Bushbury (Junct. Stat.). Hence access is gained to the Stour Valley line and all parts of the Great Western system. Bushbury Ch., about 1 m. N.E. of the stat., is Perp., with square tower and a Norm. S. door. Charles I. was at Bushbury in 1645, as is shown by the diary of one of his officers : — " The Prince's headquarters was at Wolverhampton, a handsome town, one fair church in it. The King lay at Bisbury, a private sweet village." Not far from the stat., on Low Hill, was a tumulus, but all traces of it have now been destroyed.

2 m. N. of Bushbury is **Moseley Old Hall**, a picturesque half-timbered mansion, one of the places where Charles II. was concealed after he left Boscobel. The Hall, which is now a farmhouse, has been rebuilt. The bedstead in which the king slept, and the hiding-place constructed under the floor of a closet where he was concealed, still remain. In Charles's day it belonged to the Whitgreaves, who have several monuments in Bushbury Ch. 1 m. N.E. is **Hilton Park**, the seat of A. L. Vernon, Esq., into whose family it came in 1547 by marriage with the heiress of the Swinnertons. In the grounds, which command beautiful views, is a tower called Portobello, to commemorate the taking of that place by Admiral Vernon. A curious custom is mentioned by Erdeswick as being observed here, viz. that the lord of the neighbouring manor of Essington was to bring to

L

Hilton Hall a goose on the 1st day of each year and drive it 3 times round the fire. He then carried it to the table, and received a dish of it for his own use. This custom was continued for 140 years, and was only abandoned when the manors came under one lord. 1 m. N. is **Shareshill**, where the Ch. has a Grecian body most incongruously added to the old Perp. tower. Here are the effigies of Humphrey Swinnerton and Cassandra his wife, former possessors of Hilton.

19 m. Four Ashes (Stat.). On E. are the great Sareden ponds, which feed the river Penk; on W. *Somerford Hall*, an old seat of the Monckton family. 2 m. W. is **Brewood** (pronounced Broode), which is well worth a visit.

Brewood Ch. (restored in 1879), like the rest of the town, is placed on very high ground, it is a fine E. E. and Perp. building, and contains a great number of monuments to old families of the neighbourhood, such as the Giffards of Chillington (including 4 altar-tombs with recumbent effigies), the Moretons of Engleton, the Fowkes of Brewood Hall and Gunstone, and the Moncktons of Somerford; Bishop Berington, the Countess of Cork and Orrery, and others. Before the repairs in 1827, an oak screen divided the chancel from the nave, but this, as well as some stalls, was taken down and soon lost. In the ch.-yard is buried Colonel Carlos, the faithful adherent of Charles II. He was born at Bromhall, in this parish. It was on his knees that the defeated king rested his head and fell into a deep sleep while concealed in the oak at Boscobel. Dr. Jeremiah Smith, a well-known High Master of the Manchester Grammar School, a native of Brewood, is also buried here. The *Grammar School* of Brewood, founded by Dr. Knightley in the reign of Edward VI., has been much celebrated, and is still in some repute.

Bp. Hurd, Dr. Beddoes, Dr. E. Burton, and many eminent men have been educated at it. But the glories of Brewood are all of the past, and but little remains beyond tradition and a few local names to show its ancient importance. It is said to have been the seat of a bishopric before the Conquest; also that King John held his court in it, and that later on it was the principal residence and property of the bishops of Lichfield, to whom it was granted by Henry III. Brewood Hall (Miss Monckton) was the seat of the Fowkes, the last member of whom was Dr. Fowke, who contributed the 'Life of Phocion' to the edition of Plutarch's 'Lives' for which his friend Dryden wrote the preface. The ancient forest of Brewood included Boscobel and White Ladies. (See *Handbook for Shropshire*.)

20½ m. **Spread Eagle** (Stat.). The line here crosses the Watling Street, which runs nearly due E. and W. About 2 m. E. the Street is carried over an extensive upland called Calf Heath, or sometimes Galley Heath, and a little further E. is the inn of the *Four Crosses*, where Swift, in his journeys to his Deanery in Ireland, once stopped for the night. But not liking his accommodation, and the lady being a notorious scold, he wrote the following distich on a window with a diamond:—

"Thou fool, to hang four crosses on thy door!
Hang up thy wife, there needs not any more."

½ m. N. of this inn is *Hatherton Hall* (Sir Charles Clifford, Bt.), whence the first Lord Hatherton took his title. 2 m. W. of the stat. is the village of **Stretton** (possibly the ancient Pennocrucium), close to which is *Stretton Hall* (F. Monckton, Esq.).

Passing towards Penkridge, on W., at **22 m.**, is **Kinvaston**, the birthplace of Dr. James, the inventor

Route 27.—Lapley—Stafford.

of the fever powders that bear his name.

[At 4 m. W. is **Lapley**, where some remains of the nunnery founded before the Conquest exist, and are built up into farm buildings. The Ch., which is large, and has Norm. portions, was almost destroyed in the civil war, but has of late years been restored. 4 m. W. is **Blymhill**, where the Ch. has been restored, in an indifferent manner; but a better fate has befallen **Sheriff Hales**, 3 m. farther W., which has been rebuilt, and has a very handsome carved oak ceiling.]

22¾ m. **Penkridge** (Stat.). This is a thriving village, placed between the Penk and the Stafford and Worcester Canal. The Ch., which is supposed to be of 14th centy., was once collegiate, it is a fine edifice, mainly Perp., but with a Dec. E. window. It was restored in 1883. There are several monuments to the family of Littleton, the former lords of the manor. One of them in particular bears the following complacent inscription:—

"Reader, 'twas thought enough upon the tomb
Of that great captain, the enemy of Rome,
To write no more but 'Here lyes Hannibal;
Let this suffice thee then instead of all:
Here lye two knights, the father and the son,
Sir Edward and Sir Edward Lyttleton."

Like Brewood, Penkridge was of more importance formerly than now, and was thought by Camden to have been the site of Pennocrucium. Others, however, like Plot and Stukely, place the Roman station at Stretton, as being close to the Roman road.

2 m. S.E. from Penkridge, on the Cannock road, is *Pilaton Hall*, formerly a seat of the Lyttletons, of which an account is given in the 'Gentleman's Mag.' for 1789.

Teddesley Park, the beautiful seat of Lord Hatherton, who succeeded

to it from the Littletons, taking their name, is 2 m. N.E. of Penkridge, and occupies the westerly slopes of the high ground known as Cannock Chase, from which it was reclaimed about 90 years ago. It is well seen from the rly.
The rly. still keeps a northerly direction, accompanied on E. by the Penk and the Stafford and Worcester Canal. 1 m. N. of Teddesley Park is the village of **Acton Trussell**. The Ch. of St. James formerly belonged to the Priory of St. Mary Stafford. It is very ancient, and has a square tower. It was restored in 1870, and is worth a visit.
At 26 m. the branch from Colwich, on the Trent Valley line (Rte. 31), falls in, and opposite the junction there is a good view of Stafford Castle, on its wooded height.

29 m. ⚔ **STAFFORD** (Junct. Stat.) stands in rather a low situation on the l. bank of the Sow, and a little before it joins with the Penk. The town is well built in the modern style, but contains many ancient houses, some of them timbered. Of the latter, most noticeable is a many gabled house well-known for a dialogue there between Charles I. and Prince Rupert (see *infra*). Amongst other ancient edifices is the "White Lion" Inn, once the Hospital of St. John the Baptist, on the Green in Forebridge; another inn, called "Noah's Ark," in Crabbery St., is associated with an early visit of Queen Elizabeth to the town.
The visitor will remark the extraordinary number of shoemakers, leather being, as at Northampton, the staple trade.
An encampment, called Bury Ring, 1 m. beyond the modern castle and 2½ m. from the town on the W., testifies to an early military occupation of the district. As does also, apparently, the mound upon which the modern castle stands. Both

L 2

strong sites are of uncertain origin, but belonged to Earl Edwin at the Conquest, and on his defection were given to Robert de Stafford, a younger brother of the head of the Norman house de Todeni. His lineal descendant, the first Earl of Stafford, erected by license, and perhaps on the ancient castle's site, in 1348, upon the hill nearer to Stafford, a baronial castle. Writers have often confounded it with the King's Castle of Stafford, in the town itself, of which Robert de S. was probably first Governor. This was called indifferently "The King's Castle or his Gaol of Stafford." Traces existed of it in the reign of Elizabeth. The present gaol is modern and more to the W. The Baron's Castle was held by Lady Stafford for a brief period against the Parliamentarians. The town received a charter from John in 1206, and has returned M.P.s from the time of Edward I.

There were, until the dissolution of the monasteries, friars at either end of the town, viz., Franciscans on the North and the Austin Friars towards the South: both had been founded by the Staffords.

St. Thomas the Martyr, below the town on the Sow, was a Priory founded in 1180 for the Black Canons, by Peche, Bishop of Lichfield, who was buried there in 1182 It was dissolved by Cardinal Wolsey, and is now entirely dismantled After various changes it became a cotton mill, and is now a corn mill.

There are two ancient churches of much interest. One of them, indeed, may be placed in the first class of English churches, not entitled to the dignity of being considered as Minsters. This is **St. Mary's**, once collegiate, having 13 canons, who are mentioned in Domesday, but included a dean perhaps from the time of King John. It is a very fine cruciform Ch. of Trans.-Norm., E. E., and Dec. architecture, and was restored by *Scott*, largely at the expense of Mr. Watts Russell, of Ilam Hall (Rte. 33). The nave is Trans.-Norm. (c. 1180), the S. transept is E. E., as is the chancel, whilst the N. transept is Dec. The noble tower, square below and octagonal above, was formerly surmounted by a spire. The fine E. window is a memorial of the late Earl Talbot (d. 1849). Notice among other monuments, one in the N. transept to Sir Edward and Jane, Lady Aston, of Tixall, with their effigies in alabaster. The font, the date and origin of which are disputed, is supported by 4 human figures, and on the rim is an inscription in Lombardic characters. The restoration of the interior involved a cost of about 30,000*l.*, and of the exterior 4000*l*. A marble bust to the memory of Izaac Walton, who was born in the parish in 1593, was placed in the Ch. in 1878. It is mentioned by Plot, in speaking of skilful marksmen, that Prince Rupert showed himself one at Stafford, "where, standing in Capt. Richard Sneyd's garden at about 60 yards' distance, he made a shot at the weathercock upon the steeple of the collegiate Ch. of St. Mary with a screwed horseman's pistol, and a single bullet, which pierced its tail, the hole plainly appearing to all that were below; which the king, then present, judging as a casualty only, the prince presently proved the contrary by a second shot to the same effect."

The other Ch. is St. Chad's, in which, however, there is but a fragment of the original edifice, dating it is said from the time of Stephen. This is the chancel and a small part of the nave, of Norm. architecture, and a square Dec. tower. The nave and aisles have been destroyed, and workshops and dwelling-houses built on the assumed site. Under one of these a dark passage once led from Greengate-st. to the Ch. A partial restoration revealed the existence of

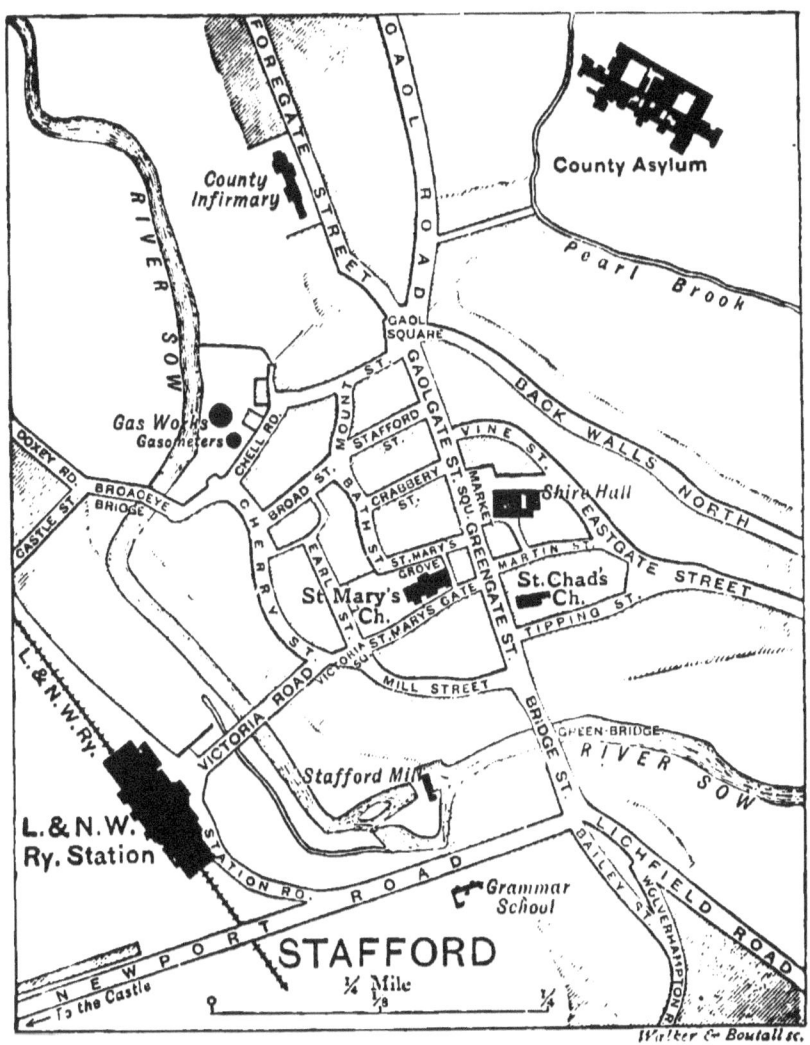

STAFFORD

To face page 148.

Route 27.—Seighford—Eccleshall.

some interlacing arcades, and the chancel-arch was brought to light; the complete restoration of the Ch. was effected in 1874-5, as a memorial of Mr. Salt, the brother of the collector of the Library, which is now the property of the county (*post*).

At the N. extremity of the town is the County Gaol, a very large edifice. Other buildings to be noticed are, the Shire Hall, in the Market Place, and the Lunatic Asylum and Infirmary, in which Frank Barber, Johnson's servant, died in 1801, after undergoing a painful operation. The *Grammar School*, remodelled, is a handsome edifice, with large playground, on the Newport road. The William Salt Library, in Market Square, was presented to the town by the widow of Mr. Salt, the antiquary; it contains a very valuable collection of books and MSS., mainly relating to Staffordshire. It is also the headquarters of the William Salt Archæological Society, which is publishing "Collections for a History of Staffordshire." A handsome Borough Hall was erected in 1876-7, in the French Gothic style of the 14th cent.; attached to it are the Free Library, the Wragge Museum, and School of Science and Art.

Izaak Walton was a native of Stafford, and he made a bequest of considerable value to the poor of the town.

A pleasant walk of 1½ m. on the Newport roads leads to the *Castle of Stafford*, which occupies a position on a wooded knoll, commanding a magnificent view of the Welsh hills, and a large tract of country to the south. It is an unfinished edifice, on the site of a former stronghold, and was erected by Sir George Jerningham, 1810-15. The N. front, having been never completed, has fallen into ruin, and part of the central area is now used as a kitchen-garden; but the S. front, which consists of 3 stories with octagonal towers, makes a very striking appearance from its following the lines of the ancient castle. It is now only inhabited by a keeper, but the interior is very well worth seeing, as well as for the view from the summit. At the foot of the hill is the pretty little Norm. Ch., restored by *Scott*, of **Castlechurch**; the parish embraces some part of Stafford borough.

From Stafford the Rly. runs in a north-westerly direction, following the course of the Sow.

At 31 m. is **Seighford**, where the very ancient Ch. of St. Chad contains a handsome altar-tomb for William Bowyer and wife (1593). Seighford Hall (F. F. Eld, Esq.) stands in a wooded park. On E. of the line is Creswell Hall (G. Meakin, Esq.), with the ruins of a chapel in the grounds.

After passing **Great Bridgeford** (Stat.) at 33½ m. is **Norton Bridge** (Junct. Stat.), whence a branch of 3¼ m. runs to Stone, to join the N. Staffordshire line (Rte. 32). The Stat. is in the parish of **Chebsey**, where there is a rude monumental pillar of early date in the ch.-yard.

3 m. W. of the Stat. is the small town of ☧ **Eccleshall**, where from the 13th centy. to the year 1867 was the usual residence of the bishops of Lichfield, called Eccleshall Castle. This was built c. 1200 by Bp. Muschamp, but greatly added to, a century after, by Bishop Walter de Langton, treasurer to Edward I. Having suffered much in the civil war, the greater part was rebuilt of brick by Bp. Lloyd in 1695, and beyond one ivy-clad tower and the bridge nothing of antiquity is left, the moat being converted into a garden. The property now is in private hands, and the bishop's residence is at Lichfield. The *Ch* is one of the finest in the county; it contains excellent stained glass,

and is mainly E. E., with a very spacious chancel; it was restored by Street, as a memorial to Bp. Lonsdale, who died in 1867, and is buried in the ch.-yard. under a cross of granite. Several other bishops have been buried here and have monuments in the Ch., as Bp. Sampson, 1554; Bentham, 1579; and Overton, 1609. The parish is a very extensive one, being divided into no less than 21 townships. One of these is Croxton, where a very fine tract of 1700 acres of woodland remains, called the Bishop's wood, a part of the ancient forest of Blore, beyond which stretches Blore Heath, the scene of the battle in 1459 between the Yorkists and Lancastrians.

[A ride or drive between Eccleshall and Market Drayton will give the tourist a glimpse of the very pleasant scenery of the Shropshire border.

Starting from Eccleshall, Pershall Park is soon passed; it is now only grazing ground, but formerly the domain of an ancient family of the same name. A short distance S. of the road is Cop Mere, a fine sheet of water. near which is Sugnall Hall (Major Walter Williams). The road continues through an open country. in which, on N.. stands the gateway of *Bromley Hall*, the seat of the noble family of Gerard of Bromley (now extinct); it was a fine Elizabethan building, with a very perfect gatehouse, and is spoken of by Plot as the "most magnificent structure in Staffordshire." The Hall is now a farmhouse. At 5 m. is **Broughton**, with a small ancient Ch.,built about 1500, and which still remains almost unaltered; it contains some good old glass in the chancel, and several 16th and 17th centy. monuments of the Bagots and the Broughtons. Broughton Hall, the property of Sir H. D. Broughton, is a most picturesque gabled edifice.

2 m N. is the village of **Ashley**. The *Ch.* (restored in 1861) was built by David Kenric, a native of the place, from his spoils of war gained as a soldier in the army of the Black Prince. In the Ch. are two handsome mortuary chapels, one of which, belonging to Mrs. Moynell Ingram of Hore Cross, contains several interesting monuments, among others to the Lords Gerard or Garrard of Bromley (underneath which is an effigy of a favourite black servant). In the other are monuments to different members of the Kinnersley family, one being by Chantrey, and another representing the angels of life. death and judgment, by Noble. A *brass*, with the following inscription, records the foundation of the Ch.:—

"In perpetuam Rei memoriam
Manubias Deo
David Kenricus Pietas ejus memoria
Hoc virtutis Præmiolum dicavit."

Dr. Lightfoot, the Hebrew scholar, was rector of this parish. The neighbourhood of Ashley is prettily broken and wooded, and rises to a considerable height.

Returning to the Drayton road, and after crossing Ashley Heath, the hamlet of Blore is reached, where **Audley's Cross** marks the scene of the death of the Lancastrian leader. The battle was fought on Sept. 23, 1459. Lord Audley, with a strong body of Shropshire and Cheshire men. had posted himself behind a brook that runs into the Tern, and his object was to prevent the Earl of Salisbury (the father of the Kingmaker) crossing it to join his brother-in-law. the Duke of York, at Ludlow. Audley's forces were much the strongest, but Salisbury was a practised commander, and having by a feigned retreat induced his opponents to quit their strong post, he fell on them whilst crossing the stream and gained a complete victory. The slaughter was particularly great among the Cheshire gentry, many of them being in each army. Drayton thus mentions their mutual slaughter:—

" There Dutton Dutton kills; a Done doth kill a Done;
A Booth a Booth—and Leigh by Leigh is overthrown;
A Venables against a Venables doth stand:
A Troutbeck fighteth with a Troutbeck hand to hand;
There Molineux doth make a Molineux to die;
And Egerton the strength of Egerton doth try."

1 m. S. is Hales Hall (Phillips Buchanan, Esq.), adjoining which is the beautiful *Ch.* of St. Mary, **Hales**, built in 1856 from designs by *Sir G. Gilbert Scott.*

2 m. N. stands **Mucklestone** Ch., from the fine Dec. tower of which (the rest of the Ch. was rebuilt in 1884) Margaret of Anjou is said to have witnessed the defeat of her friends, and with difficulty made her escape to the Bishop's palace at Eccleshall, where the king then resided, as it was in his hands through a vacancy of the see. 1 m. W. is Oakley Hall (Sir G. Chetwode, Bart.), bounded on one side by the Tern, which divides Staffordshire from Shropshire.

Passing on l. Tunstall Hall, which is almost surrounded by the Tern, at 1¼ m. is **Market Drayton** (see *Handbook for Shropshire*). The return journey can be made by the N. Staffordshire Rly., either joining the present Rte. at Madeley 8½ m. (*post*), or continuing on to the Pottery district.]

37¾ m. **Standon Bridge** (Stat.). 2 m. E. is **Swynnerton**; the Dec. Ch. stands on high ground, and has the cross-legged effigy of a Swynnerton. temp. Edward II. S. of the Ch. is Swynnerton Hall (Basil T. Fitzherbert, Esq.). The present owner is a descendant of the Judge, who wrote " Natura Brevium," and whose portrait is preserved here.

42 m. **Whitmore** (Stat.). The Ch., which was restored in 1880, has some Norm. fragments, and contains the altar tomb of " Edward Manwaryng and Alys his wyffe, ryghte heir of Whittemore and Bedulphe." Whitmore Hall (M. D. Hollins, Esq.) belongs to the Mainwaring family. 1 m. N.E. is Butterton Hall (belonging to the Pilkingtons), a modern Tudor house, built on the site of an old seat of the Swynnertons. W. of the Stat. the country rises into gentle hills, known as the Sugarloaf, Berry Hill, Camp Hill, and the Berth (anc. Brough), the latter surmounted by some earthworks, supposed by some to indicate a Roman station.

Whitmore Stat. is distant 5¼ m. from Newcastle-under-Lyme (Rte. 37), and by a cross-road, 5 m. from Trentham Park (Rte. 32).

2 m. S. is the very pretty village of **Maer**, placed between wooded hills, and with a small lake or mere, in which the river Tern has its source. The Ch. (restored in 1880) has an altar-tomb, with faint remains of painting and gilding, for Sir John Bowyer and wife (d. 1604). *Maer Hall* is the property of H. Davenport, Esq.

44¼ m. **Madeley** (Stat.; there is also a stat. at Madeley road on the Stoke and Drayton branch of the North Staffordshire line, Rte. 37). Great Madeley lies a short distance N. of the stat. The *Ch.*, which is mainly Perp., but has a Trans. Norm. N. arcade, with a small lancet window blocked up on one side of the chancel arch, was restored in 1872 by Lord Crewe, the lord of the manor. It contains monuments of the Offleys, one of whom founded the Grammar School, now an elementary school. Notice also the altar-tomb of Ralph Egerton and wife, 1525, with their effigies incised. There is a brass to one of the Egertons and his wife Elyn, 1518, and another to a scholar, Robert Hawkins, who died 1586, aged 14 years. There is a large timber house in the village (restored by Lord Crewe) which bears on its front the inscription:

"I. S. B. 1647.
Walk, knave, what lookest at?"

There are also some remains of **Madeley Manor**, a fine timber house, engraved by Plot, once the seat of the Offleys. Sir Thomas Offley was Lord Mayor of London in 1556, and kept such a hospitable table that it provoked the following distich:—

" Offley three dishes had of daily toast—
An egge, an apple, and (the third) a roast."

It was to Sir John Offley, a member of the family, that Izaak Walton dedicated his 'Complete Angler.'

The country, which from the outskirts of Stafford has had quite a rural character, suddenly changes its aspect beyond Madeley, the district of the North Staffordshire coal-field being now entered. At **47 m.** the little stream of the Wal is crossed, and the line enters Cheshire. 1½ m. further is **Betley Road** (Stat.), to the E. of which are the villages of Betley and Audley (both in Staffordshire), worth notice. **Betley**, 2 m. N. of the Wal, was once a market town. The late Perp. *Ch.* is remarkable for having the pillars and arches of wood, though the walls and tower are of stone; it contains several monuments of the Egertons and the Tolletts. **Audley**, 4 m. N.E., has a fine early Dec. Ch. (temp. Ed. II.), with many Audley tombs, some of early date (notice particularly the *brass* of Sir Thomas de Audley, 1385), and a recumbent figure in cap and gown of Edward Vernon, "Divinarum Literarum Professor" (d. 1622).

53½ m. **Crewe** (Stat.). See *Handbook for Cheshire*.

ROUTE 28.

STOURBRIDGE TO BURTON-ON-TRENT, BY DUDLEY, WALSALL, AND LICHFIELD.

G. W. RLY., L. AND N.-W. RLY., AND S. STAFF. RLY. 35¼ m.

⚜ **Stourbridge**, although, strictly speaking, in the county of Worcester, is sufficiently near the border to entitle it to mention in a description of Staffordshire, the more so as the traveller from the south here enters the mineral activity of the midland districts. It is a busy town, mainly consisting of 2 long streets, very prettily placed on the Stour, called by Erdeswick "the proud brook," and contains in its environs the last traces of broken and wooded country that the traveller will meet for some miles. Except the *Grammar School*, a handsome building, well endowed, and where Dr. Johnson received a part of his education, there is little to see in the town itself, the principal interest attaching to it being in its glass manufactures, the conical houses for which are visible westward, some little distance from the station. The cause of the pre-eminence of Stourbridge in this particular branch lies in the possession of a peculiar bed of fire-clay, for which, as early as 1566, a working lease was granted. Glass-making was established in 1557, by some French refugees from Lorraine. Plot, writing in 1686, says:—" The most preferable clay of any is that of Amblecote, of a dark blueish colour, whereof they make the best pots for the glasshouses of any in England; nay, so very good is it for this purpose, that it is sold on the place for 7d. a bushel, whereof Mr. Gray has 6d. and the workman 1d.; and so very necessary to be had that it is sent as far as London, sometimes by waggon, and sometimes by land to Bewdley, and so down the Severn to Bristol, and thence to London." The real Stourbridge clay, however, is confined to a district of not more than 2 miles radius, and is found at depths varying from 3 or 4 yards from the surface to 180 yards. In all cases it is below the thick coal, and it is generally overlaid by a shaly, friable coal known as batts.

The various products of Stourbridge have great facility of egress by the canal, which carries them into Staffordshire and to the Severn at Stourport, beside which there is abundant railway communication. A line connects Stourbridge with Birmingham (12 m.), passing through the **Lye** (Stat.), a fireclay and mining locality, which has the credit of having been the last place in England where bulls were baited. The next stat. is **Cradley** (2 m.); here nearly the whole population is employed in making chains and anchors. The next is **Rowley** (4 m.). The village of Rowley Regis stands 1 m. N., and Turner's Hill, in its neighbourhood, is the highest point in South Staffordshire. Roman silver coins, to the number of 1200, were found here in 1794. It is one of the most populous and flourishing of the smaller manufacturing centres. The inhabitants are chiefly miners, chain-makers, and nailors. Thence to Smethwick, and so on to Birmingham, the character of the country is "industrial," and unpicturesque.

[The country W. of Stourbridge is diversified, and very pretty. A round of little more than 20 m. will enable the tourist to visit Stourton, Enville, Upper Arley, and Kinver, all places of interest. At 2½ m. on the Bridgnorth road is the charming little inn called *Stewponey* (or sometimes "Foley Arms Hotel") in Kinver, where the Kidderminster and Wolverhampton roads branch off. The Stour here runs in a very picturesque valley alongside of the Stafford and Worcester Canal, and there is a beautiful view at the junction of the Kinver road, looking towards Stourton Castle.

Opposite Stewponey, and overlooking the river, is **Stourton Castle** (the property of H. J. W. Hodgetts-Foley, Esq.), a modern residence, which embodies some small portion of the 15th-centy. red-brick mansion in which Reginald Pole was born in 1500. This, about 1550, passed into the hands of the Whorwood family, who held it at the time of the civil war, during which it was garrisoned for the king. Plot gives a curious account of a rock between Stourton and Prestwood. "It lay at the foot of a hill, at which it has been observed that birds doe lye, frequently pecking and licking it, and 'tis supposed for the salt they find in it; that many birds delight in licking of salt, especially pidgeons, is very certain, but that there is any in this rock, I must confess I could not find." Higher up, and separated from Stourton by the river, which runs in a deep defile called "The Devil's Den," is **Prestwood** (H. J. W. Hodgetts-Foley, Esq.), a Jacobean house with Dutch gables, a view of which is given in Plot. It was built by Sir John Lyttleton, who bought the ground from Lord Dudley. But whilst it was occupied by Gilbert, Sir John's eldest son, Edmund Lord Dudley, the son of the vendor, alleging fraud, laid claim to it, and, not content with going to law, made a violent attack with his tenants, and succeeded in capturing a number of sheep and cattle, which he drove off to Dudley Castle, where he killed and ate them. For this little bit of Highland cattle-lifting Lord Dudley was brought before the Star Chamber in 1590.

Continuing on the main road from Stewponey, and passing Stourton Hall, the tourist arrives at

6 m. ⚥ Enville, the beautiful seat of the Countess of Stamford and Warrington. The grounds, containing a fine lake, and laid out in the most picturesque manner, were all designed by the poet Shenstone. Even before his time, the water was not only a valuable scenic accessory, but, according to Plot, was used for turning the spits in the kitchen. The fountains are remarkably beautiful, and throw up such a body of water that they are visible as far as Wolverhampton. The pleasure-grounds are open to the public on any day on application to the head gardener.

The Hall, erected temp. Hen. VIII., has 2 lofty turrets at the entrance, and rich stepped gables with ornamented chimneys on each side. The centre, which recedes from the wings, has the windows formed with Gothic pointed arches, and is flanked by 2 rectangular towers; from these the wings extend, appearing as modern additions, and round the top of the whole runs an embattlement. In the park is the Shenstonian cascade, which dashes over the rocks into a deep glen, whose rugged sides are nearly hid by the thick laurel and shrubs overhanging the edge.

The Ch. (restored by *Sir G. G. Scott*) has nave, aisles, chancel, and tower of Norm. date, though considerably modernized, and contains a number of monuments to the Grey and Hastings families; one in the N. side of the chancel, in carved alabaster, with figures of men in complete armour, to Thomas Grey (1559),

who built "the proper brick house which formed the nucleus of the present mansion; also several oak stalls. Under a well-executed zigzag arch is an ancient altar-tomb with effigy, without arms or inscription. Judge Lyttleton bequeathed a book called 'Fasciculus Morum' to this Ch. The lady chapel was built in 1333 by Philip de Lutteley, Eschestor to the king. During the restoration of the Ch. some curious carved figures, supposed to be Saxon, were found.

3 m. N.W. of Enville is **Blacklands**, the curious half-timber house of Levington, the antiquary. It is in the parish of Bobbington, on the Shropshire border.

A drive of 6 m. S.W. over a high and open country, commanding a fine view of the richly-wooded Shropshire hills and the noble park of Kinlet, brings the tourist to **Upper Arley**, which belonged to Wulfruna, the foundress of Wolverhampton. It was seized by William Rufus, and was afterwards a possession of the Mortimers. The E. E. and Dec. Ch. contains a 13th-cent. altar-tomb to Sir Walter de Balem, and several Lyttleton 16th and 17th centy. monuments. The view from the Ch.-yard is very fine, extending far over the Severn, on which the fishermen still use the coracle, a light boat of osiers covered with tarred canvas. A Roman encampment may be traced in Arley wood. The grounds of Arley Castle (R. Woodward, Esq.) are beautifully laid out, and in the arboretum is an extremely rare specimen of Sorbus Domestica.

For the return, the road lies over the bold height of Kinver Edge. 5 m. N.E. is **Kinver** or **Kinfare** (possible derivation *Ken*, head, and *Vare* (*vaer*), great). The name of this place probably is derived from the bold hill which occupies a large portion of the parish, and is called Kinver Edge. "Here the Lower

Mottled Sandstone underlies the Bunter conglomerate, and caves or 'rock-houses' have been excavated in the Edge and in a detached mass of sandstone called the Holy Austen Rock. The Bunter conglomerate forms the 'Ridge' and caps Kinver Edge, dipping east or south-east at from 5 to 8 degrees."—*Prof. E. Lapworth, LL.D., F.G.S.* The *Ch.* stands on a hill overlooking the village. It has some Norm. work. The windows are mostly Dec. The tower is of three stages. There is a monument to John Hampton (d. 1472), lord of the manor of Stourton; one to Wm. Talbot (d. 1685); and a perfect brass upon an altar-tomb in the chancel, representing Sir Edward Grey, his 2 wives, 7 sons, and 10 daughters. This brass and that at Ashbourne (see Rte. 34) c. 1545, are probably by the same engraver. The arms of Sir Edw. Gray were also in the windows, which still contain some beautiful fragments of old glass. There is an interesting crypt under the chancel, also an old oak desk within which some ancient books were formerly chained. They are now kept in an iron safe. On Kinver Edge are traces of a square earthwork, the origin of which is unknown. From Kinver a road leads to Stourbridge (3 m.).]

Leaving Stourbridge for Dudley, at 1½ m. is **Brettell Lane** (Stat.), and at 2¼ m. **Brierley Hill** (Stat.), the centre of a busy iron and colliery district, ever alight with the brilliant flames from the furnace mouths. The town lies a little to the rt., and is placed on a high ridge of ground, from which, when the atmosphere is tolerably clear, a singular and extensive view is gained. The Ch. was built in the last century, and has frequently been enlarged to suit the increasing population. Its first incumbent (1770-1800), the Rev. Thos. Moss, was the author of the well-known lines beginning

"Pity the sorrows of a poor old man,
Whose trembling limbs have borne him to your door,"

though they have been often ascribed to others. 2 m. N.W. is **King's Swinford**, the Ch. of which has a heavy square tower; and there are some rude sculptures over the S. door. *Bradley Hall*, timbered and gabled, is late Elizabethan (1596).

Very soon after leaving Brierley Hill the line enters a detached portion of Worcestershire, passing 2¾ m. **Roundoak** (Stat.), close to which are the noble ironworks and forges of the Earl of Dudley; thence 4½ m. past **Netherton** (Stat.), and through a long tunnel to

5½ m. ☩**Dudley** (Junct. Stat.). As the tourist enters the station, he sees rising above it a considerable hill, well covered with trees, and forming a most unlooked-for oasis in the desert of smoke and fire through which he has hitherto travelled. Dudley (in Worcestershire) is a flourishing town indebted for its prosperity to the mineral wealth, the coal, iron, and lime, with which the district teems. On the whole it is well built, consisting of a long main street, with a church at each end. A network of minor streets occupies the sides of the hill. Besides its importance in the iron trade, Dudley has obtained a character for science, a very prosperous geological society having fixed its Museum and headquarters here (in Wolverhampton Street), whose members can readily explore the interesting Silurian districts of the neighbourhood. The collection is particularly rich in trilobites (Homalonotus and Ogygia) and in corals. In the centre of the marketplace, on the site of the old Town Hall, is a Fountain, erected at the cost of 3000*l*. by the late Earl of Dudley from designs by Forsyth. It is a Renaissance arch, the ornamental enrichments of which represent Mining and Agriculture placed in niches under the dome. There are 2 basins, into which river horses, on rare occasions (as the Whitsuntide holidays), discharge jets of water, and the whole is surmounted by figures of Industry and Commerce. At the entrance to the castle is a fine marble statue of the late Earl of Dudley. The old *Ch.* (*St. Thomas*) was rebuilt in 1819; it has a lofty tower and spire, and, from the elevated position on which it stands, is seen from a great distance. The E. window contains a well-painted representation of the Ascension, and there is a good bas-relief of the Confession of St. Thomas. Another Ch., St. Edmund's, near the Castle, was ruined in the civil war, and was not rebuilt until 1724. There are five other churches, all modern.

The Cluniac Priory, founded by Gervase Paganell in 1155, was almost totally destroyed soon after the Dissolution. A modern house, bearing the same name, was built near its site by the late Earl of Dudley in 1828. Ruins of the chapel and some portions of the monastic residences are in the grounds. A Roman Catholic chapel, S.E. of the castle, contains a complete altar service with ornaments, a processional cross, a silver gilt chalice with enamelled foot of 13th centy., and a set of vestments.

The **Castle Hill** (in Staffordshire), a picturesque eminence, thickly wooded, varied on its surface with glens and dingles, is traversed in all directions by shady walks, kept up at the expense of the Earl of Dudley, and much appreciated by the inhabitants of the town. Dudley is supposed to take its name from Dud or Dudo, a Saxon prince, who is said to have erected a fortress here in the 8th centy. It is mentioned in the 'Domesday Book' as being in the possession of William Fitz-Ansculph, after whom it frequently changed owners, and underwent several mutations, being dis- mantled by Henry II., but again put into defensive order in Henry III.'s reign. The Suttons, a Nottinghamshire family, held possession until the time of Charles I., when Frances, the grand-daughter of the last Lord Sutton of Dudley, carried it by marriage into the family of Humble Ward, goldsmith to the queen. From this marriage is descended in the male line the present family, ennobled by the title of Dudley, who have ever been famous for uniting the industry of commerce to the dignity of family, and have been celebrated amongst the ranks of iron-masters. Indeed, there are few establishments so largely and successfully carried on as the Earl of Dudley's ironworks and collieries. The castle underwent a siege of 3 weeks during the civil war, when it was garrisoned for the king by Col. Leveson, but he had eventually to surrender to Sir W. Brereton, the Parliamentarian. It was accidentally burnt in 1750, and not restored. The ruins cover an oblong area of about an acre, the whole of which is surrounded by a wall flanked with towers, and consist of a portal leading to the great tower, the court, and portions of a tall keep, of E. Dec. style, affording excellent specimens of castellated ornamented work. Parts of the outer walls, however, are late Perp. The great attraction is the view from the summit, which embraces not only a large portion of manufacturing Staffordshire, but a grand panorama of distant ranges, in which are the Malvern, Clent, Abberley, Rowley, and Shropshire hills, the Wrekin, and in fine weather those of Wales and Derbyshire, are clearly discernible. But the characteristic view from Dudley castle is only to be obtained at night, when the whole horizon is lighted up with flame. The earth seems to belch forth fire from the furnaces, forges, and coal-pits, while the effect is enhanced by the roar of the different works, and the constant hurrying to and fro of trains. The effect due to the furnaces, however, is on the wane, as many of them are now capped over, and the total number in blast has been reduced. The neighbourhood is densely populated, and is cut up in every direction by railways.

The Dudley Canal (to Birmingham) is carried through the Castle Hill in a most remarkable series of *Caverns*, which can be seen at intervals from openings in the higher grounds. These caverns in the limestone of the Upper Silurian rocks are in part exhausted quarries, and they form a singular sight when lighted up with gas, which is done annually at the Whitsuntide Castle fêtes. The Hill is a mass of Silurian limestone pushed up like a dome from below the surrounding coal-field, and, as it forms an island of limestone in this very extensive district, it acquires great value and is largely quarried. The excavated chambers, halls, and galleries, which have been driven through the productive body of stone, are of vast extent, and are supported at intervals by massive pillars of the rock left standing. The limestone is peculiarly interesting to the geologist on account of the fossils of the Wenlock series, particularly corals and zoophytes, with which it abounds. About 1 m. to the W. is the **Wren's Nest**, "a steep headland, covered on the top with stunted wood, presenting the appearance of a truncated dome. Its summit is deeply excavated, whence its ironical name. The limestone teems with the characteristic fossils of the Silurian system, viz. terebratula, lingula, orthis, atrypa, trilobite, crinoid, coral, &c., and the truncated appearance has evidently originated from the denudation of the upper part of the dome of which it once consisted."—*Mantell*.

4 m. W. **Himley Hall** (Earl of Dudley), a modern house, with an extensive lake in front. It is the residence of the Dowager Countess of Dudley. The Ch. in the village, rebuilt in 1764, contains several good monuments.

½ m. S. of Himley is **Holbeach House** (Earl of Dudley), a picturesque old mansion, with modern additions, remarkable in history as being the place in which several of the parties to the Gunpowder Plot were taken, after a fierce conflict with the forces of the sheriff, November 8, 1605. Both the Wrights were killed, Catesby and Percy, who were standing back to back, were shot through with one bullet, Rookwood and Winter wounded, and the few who cut their way through were soon after apprehended.

½ m. N.W. is **Wombourne**, where there is a good half-timbered manor-house, Wodehouse (Hon. P. J. Stanhope), the seat of the Woodhouses from the time of Edward II. to that of William III. It has been well restored and contains a good collection of old oak furniture. 2 m. further is **Trysull**, where the Ch. (Perp., with low square tower) has the figure of a bishop in a niche in the wall of the N. aisle. On the common beyond is *Apewood Castle*, and another British camp, both of which command fine views of the valley of the Severn about Apley and Bridgnorth. (*See Handbook for Shropshire*.) 1 m. from Trysull is the hamlet of **Seisdon**. The Hall, an old house, is the seat of G. P. Aston-Pudsey, Esq.

From Dudley the route is by the L. & N.-W. Rly. to **Dudley Port** (Stat.) (Rte. 27), where the line is crossed by the Stour Valley line.

7 m. **Great Bridge** (Stat.), thickly surrounded by works of all descriptions.

9 m. **Wednesbury** (Stat.) (Rte. 26).

After crossing the main line of the L. & N.-W. Rly. from Birmingham, at

12 m. is ♂ **Walsall** (Stat.), an ancient town, once possessed by "King-making Warwick," and after him by his son-in-law Clarence, the Buckinghams, and the Dudleys, but the traces of antiquity are now altogether lost in the busy stream of manufactures which pervades it. There are several streets of new and handsome houses in the lower part of the town, and the Guildhall is a structure of considerable merit. Walsall is the chief seat of the saddlery and harness trades, where nine-tenths of the bits and stirrups used in the kingdom are made. Upwards of 80 factories are kept employed in this branch.

The oldest part of the town is built upon a long ridge terminating to the N. in a sort of cliff of limestone. Here stands the *Parish Ch.* on a platform so circumscribed that the path round it is carried on an archway below the chancel; the only ancient part remaining. It dates from 1462, is in Perp. style, and was carefully restored and relieved from plaster, bricks, galleries, &c., 1880, by Mr. E. Christian. The tower is also old. The nave was rebuilt in 1821. Nothing remains of the ancient monuments that it once possessed. A flight of 60 steps leads from the W. door down to the High-st. The other churches, 6 in number, are all modern. There is a Grammar School founded by Queen Mary, with part of Dudley's forfeited lands; it has been rebuilt in the Elizabethan style, and in it the first Lord Somers and Bp. Hough were educated.

In the cemetery rest the remains of Miss Pattison, "Sister Dora," the hospital nurse and benefactress of the poor of Walsall. There is a statue of her in the centre of the town.

The Midland Rly. has a line from here to Wolverhampton (High Level Stat.). It runs nearly parallel with the W. part of that described in Rte. 26, and has 6 stats., which accommodate the N. parts of Walsall, Willenhall, and Wednesfield. There is also a line to Birmingham, *via* Sutton Coldfield.

14 m. Rushall (Stat.). 1 m. S.E. is the old manor-house, which was the seat of the Harpur family (temp. Henry VI.), whose arms remain over the arched gateway, but now the property of the Mellish family. The house was a royal garrison during the civil war, and before that it had been a Lancastrian stronghold. It was fortified with embattled walls and moat. The latter has been filled up, but the walls remain. A modern residence (W. H. Duignan, Esq.) is incorporated with the ancient walls. The Ch., which is adjoining, was rebuilt in 1854 and enlarged in 1868. An epitaph in the Ch.-yard commemorates a local celebrity:

" Within this tomb Charles White doth lie :
He was six feet and full six inches high ;
In his proportion Nature had been kind,
His symmetry so just, no fault could find."

2¼ m. N.E. of Rushall is the village of **Aldridge**, on elevated ground. The Perp. *Ch.* with a square tower, restored in 1853, has some good modern stained glass windows. The subject of the E. window is the Crucifixion. The presumed effigy of the founder once under an arch outside, but still occupying the same position, now lies within the chancel, the wall being built so as to include it ; and that of Robert Stapleton (temp. Hen. III.) is within the tower. 1 m. E. is *Little Aston Hall* (Hon. E. S. Parker-Jervis), an early specimen of Wyatt's architecture. The original house was the seat of Sir Robert Ducie, a London alderman, who was most severely treated by the Parliament for his loyalty ; it afterwards belonged to Sir Andrew Hacket, the son of the Bishop of Lichfield, so honourably known by his exertions for the restoration of his cathedral.

15½ m. **Pelsall** (Stat.). The village, which lies a short distance N.W., is dependent on the coal and iron works in the neighbourhood. The Ch., which belonged to the canons of Wolverhampton, has been rebuilt in red brick and a new chancel added in 1889. The old structure had a rude picture on the wall of an old man holding a purse, in commemoration of one Richard Harrison, who left a dole to the poor.

17½ m. **Brownhills** (Stat.), a colliery township on the Watling Street, with **Ogley Hay** adjoining, is a populous district owing to the numerous coal mines. **Burntwood** and **Chase Town** form a joint township, where the Cannock Chase Colliery Company have their works. Near here is the County Lunatic Asylum, situated on the summit of a hill. *Castle Old Fort*, a British (?) entrenchment, occurs at Over Stonnall, a village 2 m. S.E., and another work, known as *Knave's Castle*, among the coal pits 1 m. N. of the stat., consisting of a tumulus surrounded by 3 ditches, with an entrance at the S. It is situated on the straight road running from the Watling Street to Etocetum, and was probably a castrum æstivum.

20 m. **Hammerwich** (Stat.), a colony of coal-miners and nail-makers. The Roman station at Wall is but 2 m. from Hammerwich; but as it is more conveniently visited from Lichfield, it is described hereafter.

Very soon after leaving **Hammerwich** the traveller comes in sight of the graceful spires of

23 m. ⚔ **LICHFIELD** (City Stat., St. John Street). A neat, quiet cathedral city, till recently without manufactures or trades of any consequence, but of late years the excellence of the water supply in the Trent valley, which has made Burton so famous, has led to the great development of brewing in Lichfield, and there are now two prosperous and increasing companies in the city. It is the headquarters also of the South Staffordshire Waterworks Company, which has its large pumping station in the city, for the supply of Walsall and other towns. Vegetables, which are largely grown in the neighbourhood, also supply the markets of the Black Country. The town stands in a pleasant country, and has two very picturesque lakelets. That called the Minster Pool is on the S. side of the cathedral, and contributes no little to the picturesqueness of that building, the outline of which is seen rising over a belt of trees, while its image is reflected on the surface of the water. The other is Stowe Pool, to the N.E. of the town. Both are reservoirs of the South Staffordshire waterworks. Its situation near the centre of England, on the great Holyhead and Liverpool roads, caused it formerly to be a focus of traffic, and to be much frequented by travellers of all ranks. But this source of advantage and animation has to a considerable extent been withdrawn by the course taken by the railways, and, except on market days or on special occasions, there is little to enliven its streets. As a cathedral town, however, it possesses very good society, and the tenants of the numerous villas and country seats around it contribute to its respectability and well-being. Johnson said of his fellow-townsfolk that "they were the most sober, decent people in England —the genteelest in proportion to their wealth, and spoke the purest English." Boswell remarked that the two principal manufactures in his time were sailcloths and streamers for ships, but thought, on the whole, that the inhabitants of Lichfield were idle; to which Johnson magniloquently replied:—"Sir, we are a city of philosophers; we work with our heads, and make the boobies of Birmingham work for us with their hands." The name — Leichenfield, or "field of corpses"—is said to record a massacre

Route 28.—Lichfield: Cathedral.

of the Christians in the reign of Diocletian: the arms of the city, consisting of the dead bodies of three men, armed and crowned, are by some supposed to refer to this very doubtful event; whilst others say they commemorate a battle, of equally uncertain date. Johnson, in his Dictionary, under the word *Lich*, a dead carcase, adds. "*Lichfield*, the field of the dead, a city of Staffordshire, so named from murdered Christians—Salve magna Parens." Others derive the name from *Lyccidfelth*, meaning "the field of water," because the city lay near very swampy ground.

The most prominent building, and the pride of Lichfield, is of course the

CATHEDRAL, one of the most beautiful, though by no means the largest, in England, and differing from all others in being still surmounted by 3 spires. It was originally founded by Ceadd, or St. Chad, a hermit, who became Bp. of Mercia, and who dwelt, in the 7th centy., in a cell at Stowe, near to the town. The only traces of the Saxon Ch. are now worked into the foundations, as may be seen beneath a grating outside the N. aisle. There are hardly any remains of the Norman one which succeeded it (ascribed to Bishop de Limesey, 1086–1117), and there is some uncertainty respecting the erection of the existing edifice, though the following table of probable dates, as supplied by Prof. Willis, may be accepted:—

	Circ.
Lower part of three westernmost bays of choir, with the sacristy on south side	1200
South transept	1220
North transept and chapterhouse	1240
Nave	1250
West front	1275
Lady chapel	1300
Presbytery	1325

The chief portions are thus entirely E. E. and Dec. Perp. windows were inserted during the 15th and 16th cents., and the central spire, which was battered down by the Parliamentarians during the civil war, was rebuilt after the Restoration, from a design of Sir Christopher Wren. These gradual changes in Lichfield show a curious parallelism with those in York.

The W. **front** (early Dec.), flanked by two spires, rising to a height of 183 ft., is exuberantly adorned, resembling in this respect, and in the arrangement of its central porch, some of the Continental cathedrals, especially in the *exterior* sedilia, which seem better suited for the sunny climate of Southern France or Italy than to the Midlands of England.

It is divided into 3 stages, comprising in the lowest the 3 doorways; in the middle, 3 rows of arcades and the W. window, which rises also into the third. The restoration of the West Front was completed in 1884, when the base stucco mouldings and figures of 1822 were replaced according to the original design in stone—under the supervision of Mr. J. Irving, Mr. John Oldred Scott being the architect. The niches have all been filled with statues by various artists, so that the W. Front is now, in the happy phrase of the present Archbishop of Canterbury, "a very Te Deum in stone." Our Lord in glory stands high above all in the central gable between the two spires, and below Him the 4 Archangels, then comes a tier of Patriarchs, two tiers of Prophets, a tier of Saxon and Norman Kings, and at the base the 12 Apostles. On the North of the N.W. Tower are figures of St. Helena, H.M. the Queen, St. Mark and St. Luke, and at the base a remarkable statue of St. Cyprian; while on the South side are figures of the six Bishops who either built or restored the fabric of the Cathedral, Clinton holding the Norman Ch., Patteshull, the builder of the Choir, Walter Langton, who designed and bore the expense of the Lady Chapel, Hacket, who restored the central spire, Lonsdale, who held the See when the whole interior was restored, and Selwyn, under whom the work on the exterior was begun. Formerly a figure of Charles II. occupied the niche now filled by one of our Lord. It was so highly placed in consideration of the King having given timber out of the royal chases for the repair of the building after the Restoration. This figure was the work of Sir William Wilson, once a stonemason of Sutton-Coldfield It has now been removed to another part of the Cathedral. A wheel window in the centre, which was injured during the siege, was restored at the expense of James II. when Duke of York, but was replaced by a memorial window to Canon Hutchinson in 1868.

The side doors of the W. front are triply recessed with very rich mouldings. The central porch, which is also deeply recessed, shows a figure of our Lord, attended by angels, the Virgin and Infant, and four statues. viz. Mary Magdalen, Mary the mother of James, St. Peter, and St. John. The visitor should notice the original ironwork (late 13th centy.) with which the upper portions of the doors are covered.

The noble **nave** exhibits the transition from E. E. to Dec. "The view which opens from this point is, since the restoration, one of extreme richness and beauty. The details of the nave itself are unusually graceful; and beyond the light choir screen, gilt and coloured, the eye ranges to the elaborate design of the altar, a mass of precious marble and alabaster, and finally rests on the stained glass of the Lady Chapel, glowing with the splendour of jewels, between the dark lines of tracery." The nave consists of 8 bays, and is divided from the aisles by octagonal pillars, with richly foliated capitals.

The triforium consists of 2 arches in each bay, and has a general resemblance to that of Westminster Abbey. The clerestory windows are very elegant, in the shape of a spherical triangle, with curved sides, containing 3 circles within them, and the whole enclosed by dog-tooth moulding. A string-course, with the same sort of moulding, runs under the clerestory, and encircles the capitals. "Nothing can exceed this nave in beauty and gracefulness. But in sublimity it is exceeded by many—that, for instance, of Beverley Minster, which, from its actual size, fairly admits the comparison. And the reason seems to be that a bay of the Lichfield nave is clearly limited in its height. The triforium is made a principal instead of a subordinate feature, and you feel that, if by the heightening of the pier aisles it were placed at a different level from the eye, much of its beauty would be lost."—*Petit*. The windows in the aisles of the nave are 3-light geometrical, and below them is a very rich arcade, of 6 arches in each bay. Near the W. door is the font, octagonal and of Caen stone, designed by *Slater*, on which is sculptured the ark, the passage through the Red Sea, and the baptism and resurrection of our Lord. Close by is a monument to Dean Launcelot Addison, father of Joseph Addison. The old tombs in the nave were destroyed by the Puritans, and there are only two left in the S. aisle (*post*). There is also in this aisle a brass to the Earl of Lichfield (d. 1854). The N. door has been lately restored.

The **S. transept** is of the date of 1220, and has superseded a Norman one. The W. wall is adorned with an E. E. arcade, and the windows are E. E., save that over the S. door, which is Perp. In the S. window of the transept aisle is similar stained glass as that to be seen in the Lady Chapel. The monuments here are

[*Derby, &c.*]   M

162   Route 28.—Lichfield: Cathedral.

one to Anne Seward, her father and mother, the inscription on which is by Sir Walter Scott; one to Bishop Smalbrooke (d. 1749); one to the members of the 80th regiment who fell at Sobraon in 1846; and one to Adm. Sir W. Parker (d. 1866); also to Johnson and Garrick. The former was a native of Lichfield; and Garrick, though born at the Angel Inn, Hereford, Feb. 20, 1716, had his home for many years in Lichfield.

The **N. transept** is of rather later date than the S., and contains an E. E. trefoiled arcade, and a Perp. window filled with stained glass, representing the principal founders and benefactors of the cathedral. In the E. aisle of this transept is the organ. The N. doorway is very fine. Notice the carved moulding with figures. Two are supposed to represent St. Chad baptizing Prince Wulfhere.

"The work of 4 distinct periods meets in the great piers of the central tower," viz. E. E., later E. E., early Dec., and Perp. The **tower** itself rises but one square above the roof, it has on each face canopied windows, each of two lights trefoiled, with quatrefoiled heads, and is battlemented, with pinnacled turrets. The spire is hexagonal, and crocketed, and its very numerous windows give a great lightness of appearance.

The choir-screen, of wrought iron, copper, and brass, was designed by *Scott* and is the work of *Skidmore*, as are also the wrought iron gates opening to the N. and S. choir aisles. The Lichfield screen, which was the first of its work in the kingdom—that of Hereford being subsequent to it—"is remarkable for the delicate manipulation of its capitals, many of which, derived from early examples of gold and silver work, are entirely hammered from sheet copper."

The **choir**, originally Norm., has undergone several changes, and now consists of 6 bays, of the following dates:—1st 3 bays from tower, E.

E.; 2nd 3 easternmost, Dec.; the 3rd pier from the tower being half of each. There is no distinct triforium. The spandrils of the 3 western arches are ornamented by statues (restored) of St. Christopher, St. James, and St. Philip, on the S. side, and St. Peter, Mary Magdalen, and the Virgin, on the N. The original statues existed in the time of Pennant, who took exception to the fact that one of Mary Magdalen's legs was bare. Notice particularly the altar and the reredos, designed by *Scott*, and erected in 1860, the arcades of which contain exquisite carvings of the Crucifixion, emblems of the Evangelists, and angels bearing instruments of the Passion. The materials used were alabaster from Tutbury and Derbyshire marble. The pavement, by *Minton*, represents the early history of the see in the following subjects on incised slabs by *Clayton*:—

1. The consecration of St. Chad to the see of York.
2. His appointment to that of Mercia.
3. The translation of his bones to the present church.
4. Restoration after the civil war.

On the N. side of the chancel is the diocesan memorial for Bishop Lonsdale. It consists of an altar-tomb, with recumbent figure by *Watts*, under a crocketed canopy by *Sir G. G. Scott*.

The choir aisles, partly E. E. and partly Dec., contain a beautiful arcade of canopied arches, divided by slender buttresses; the windows are Dec. The monuments in the S. aisle are those of Major Hodson (of Hodson's Horse), killed at Lucknow, the subject of which is the submission of the King of Oude; of Archdeacon Hodson, on the alabaster panels of which are the Crucifixion, Ascension, Burial, and Resurrection of our Lord (both by *Street*); the tomb of Bishop Hacket, whose effigy is coloured. He was the zealous re-

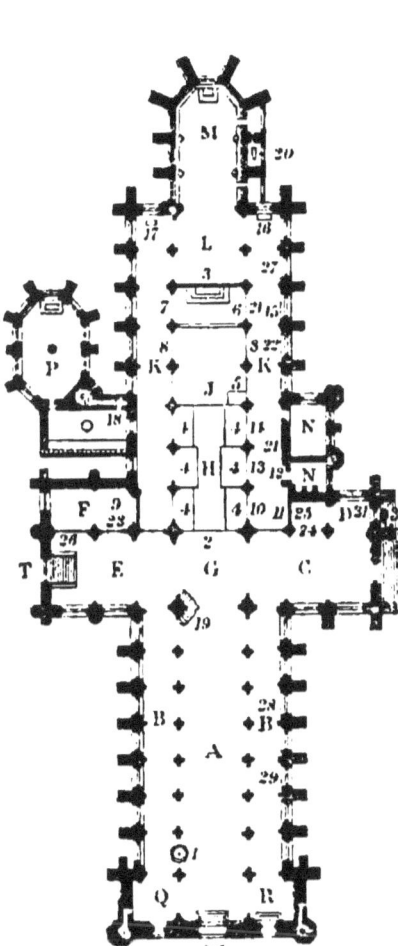

GROUND-PLAN, LICHFIELD CATHEDRAL.

Scale, 50 ft. to 1 in.

REFERENCES.
A Nave.
B B Nave-aisles.
C South Transept.
D East Aisle of ditto.
E North Transept.
F East Aisle of ditto.
G Central Tower.
H Choir.
J Presbytery.
K K Choir-aisles.
L Retro-choir.
M Lady-chapel.
N N Sacristy and Treasury.
O Vestibule to Chapter-house.
P Chapter-house.
Q North-west Tower.
R South-west Tower or Jesus Bell-steeple.
S South Porch.
T North Porch.
W West Front.

1 Font.
2 Reredos.
3 High Altar.
4 Stalls.
5 Bishop's Throne.
6 Sedilia.
7 Monument of Bishop Lonsdale.
8 Light Screen.
9 Organ.
10 Monument of Major Hodson.
11 Monument of Archd. Hodson.
12 Perp. Monument of Sir John Stanley.
13 Monument of Bp. Langton, 1321.
14 Monument of Bp. Patteshull, 1241.
15 Monument of Bp. Hacket, 1671.
16 Chantrey's Sleeping Children.
17 Chantrey's Statue of Bishop Ryder, 1836.
18 Entrance to Library.
19 Pulpit.
20 Monument of Bp. Selwyn, 1878.
21 Monument of Dean Howard, 1868.
22 Monument of Archd. Moore.
23 Organ Screen, monument to soldiers killed in the Zulu war.
24 Monument to men of 80th (Staffordshire) Regiment.
25 Westmacott's Busts of Dr. Johnson and David Garrick.
26 Monument of Dean Heywode, 1492.
27 Semi-effigy of Canon Strangeways, 14th cent.
28, 29 Semi-effigies.
30 Exterior canopied monument to an unknown deacon.
31 Monument of Admiral Sir W. Parker, 1866.

To face page 102.

storer of the cathedral after its desecration by Parliamentary soldiers, who had reduced it to such a state, that the chapter-house and the vestry only had a roof to shelter the clergy when they took possession in June, 1660 (Aubrey's Letters). The very morning after he reached his see he set his own servants and carriage horses to work to remove the rubbish, and ceased not his pious labours till the whole building was brought back to something like its original splendour, though not without the expenditure of large sums of money on his own part, and that of the chapter, aided by subscriptions from the gentry of the diocese. He held a solemn reconsecration service on Christmas-eve, 1669, and he died Oct. 28, 1670. In reference to this good cause are the mottoes round his tomb, which was erected by his son. Nor should his own well-known "posie." "Inservi Deo et lætare," be forgotten. Under the E. window of this aisle is the far-famed monument of the two children of the Rev. W. Robinson, the masterpiece of *Chantrey*, whose art has never more truthfully or exquisitely represented the tranquillity of sleep and the innocence of childhood than in this beautiful group. The design was sketched for Chantrey by Stothard. Under the E. window of the opposite aisle is another monument by Chantrey, the kneeling figure of Bishop Ryder (d. 1836). Perhaps the most remarkable monuments in the Cathedral are the three semi-effigies in the S. aisles of the nave and choir, and the Perp. monument to Sir John Stanley. One of the semi-effigies in the nave is fairly perfect, the head and feet are sculptured in the wall, a plain stone separating the two portions. Remains of colour are visible upon the drapery. The semi-effigy in the choir represents Canon Strangeways; it is mutilated. These three date from the 14th cent. The Perp.

tomb of Sir John Stanley represents a knight, bare to the waist, ready to receive flagilation at the hands of the clergy. The legs are in armour, and above them, a skirt, painted with the arms of Stanley, depends from the waist. During the siege the tomb was mutilated ; it was repaired in 1877. This monument is said to be unique. Near the door of the N. transept may be seen the emaciated figure of Dean Heywode (1492) ; it is a portion of a larger monument. There are in the S. choir aisle two ancient monuments to bishops, one supposed to represent Hugh Patteshull (1241), the other Walter de Langton (1321). There are also a memorial tomb of Archdeacon Moore, by Armstead, erected in 1879; and a very beautiful tomb of Bishop G. A. Selwyn, erected in 1881. Leading out of the S. choir aisle are the sacristy, and consistory courts, formerly the Treasure House, E.E. In an upper room are kept the documents of the Cathedral. Over the door is a gallery, which probably served as a watching-chamber.

The retrochoir formerly held the great shrine of St. Chad, which attracted pilgrims from all parts. A portion of this shrine was found during the restoration in the screen of masonry which separated the nave and the choir, and has now been worked up into the sedilia on the S. side of the sanctuary within the altar rails.

The **Lady Chapel**, commenced by Bishop Langton in 1296, is a continuation of the presbytery, and terminates in a polygonal apse. The windows were originally filled with geometrical tracery, but have been altered since the devastation at the siege. The arcade with its projecting canopy running round the lower part of the chapel is of the utmost elegance and richness. But it is chiefly remarkable for its painted windows, two of which were made

M 2

by Sir John Betton, and are filled with coats of arms of the bishops and prebends of Lichfield. The other 7 are probably the finest in this country. They were brought from the ancient dissolved abbey of Herckenrode, a Cistercian nunnery near Liége, by Sir Brooke Boothby, who handsomely transferred them to the cathedral for the price they had cost him, viz. 200*l*., not one-fiftieth part of their actual value; they are admirable specimens of the art of glass-painting and staining, as it flourished in the hands of the scholars of Van Eyck, at the beginning of the 16th centy., in the Low Countries. Mrs. Jameson attributes these designs to Lambert Lombard, the first and by far the best of the Italianized-Flemish school of the 16th centy. Two of the windows (date 1532) contain portraits of members of the families of De Lechy and Mettecoven, benefactors of the abbey, with their patron saints. One conspicuous figure in the left-hand window is the Cardinal Everard de la Marc, Archbishop of Liége (1505), on his knees, with St. Lambert behind him. In two other compartments are portraits of knights of the illustrious houses of Egmont, Flores, and Maximilian, Counts of Buren. The other 5 windows (date 1539) contain Scripture subjects, many of which may easily be identified, and exhibit in their execution all the characters of the early German and Flemish schools of painting.

The beautiful **Chapter-house** is entered from the N. aisle by a corridor, lined with a fine arcade of E. E. niches, curiously groined. The chapter-house, an excellent specimen of that style, is in plan an elongated octagon, with a central clutched pier, radiating into ribs, which support the roof. The richly carved foliage of the capitals of the piers, as also the arcade of 49 arches, deserve attention. A fresco of the Assumption of the Virgin of the 15th century has lately been discovered above the doors which lead into the chapter-house. It is very interesting in some of its details.

The original library was a detached building to the N. of the N. transept, built by Dean Heywode (1457-1493). The present **Library** is over the Chapter House, and was established about 1793, when the Duchess of Somerset bequeathed more than one thousand volumes. The library is rich in Bibles, and contains many 17th-century controversial works, and some curious tracts relating to the civil war. Here also are preserved the MS. Household Book of Prince Henry, eldest son of James I., and a MS. of Chaucer. One relic may be seen here, however, of which the interest can hardly be exaggerated. This is the volume known as the "Gospels of St. Chad," containing the Gospels of St. Matthew, St. Mark, and part of St. Luke. The style of its writing, miniatures, and profusion of scroll work may certainly be ascribed to the Hiberno-Saxon school. There is a tradition that it was written by St. Gildas, and on the margins of several of the pages are entries in Welsh, one of which states that the volume had been purchased by Gelhi, and presented to St. Teilo, the patron Saint of Llandaff. It was probably written in the 8th century. On a blank page of the MS. the Lord's Prayer according to the Vulgate version has been inserted in a writing of later date—the version of the Lord's Prayer in the MS. of St. Matthew being taken from the Vetus Itala. On this page all solemn oaths were formerly taken. The relics of St. Chad are now deposited in the Roman Catholic Cathedral at Birmingham, having been abstracted from the shrine in the retrochoir in Edward VI.'s reign by Prebendary Arthur Dudley.

The length of the cathedral within

is 375 ft., and its height is 60 ft. from the pavement to the roof. The building does not stand due E. and W., but inclines 27 degrees to the N., and the walls of the choir and the nave are not in a straight line. It stands within a tranquil and neatly kept close, laid out in grass-plots, and planted with trees. On the N. side are the Bishop's palace (built 1687 by Bp. Wood, and enlarged by Bp. Selwyn) and the Deanery, and on the S. the prebendal houses, with gardens stretching down to the Minster pool. At the N.W. angle is a remarkable timber house, at the S.W. Newton's College for the widows of the clergy, and at the S.E. angle is the Theological College. The close was walled and moated by Bishop Langton—"Lichfield's moated pile"—but the walls have in great part been demolished, except a small portion in the Palace garden, and the Eastern portion of the moat has been drained and used as a garden, whilst the southern portion is now the bright clear Minster pool, beside which runs a pleasant public walk.

At the time of the Great Rebellion, in 1643, the close was strengthened and put into a state of defence, and garrisoned for the king, and the red flag of defiance was hoisted on the central tower; the town, however, took the opposite side.

Parliament soon despatched troops to attack and dislodge the Royalists from their stronghold, and the command was given to Lord Brooke, a warm enthusiast, and in strong opposition to both the Church and the King of England, although Baxter, in his 'Saints' Rest,' enumerates him as one of the persons whom he looks forward to meeting in heaven.

On the second day of the assault, while directing his artillery, which was planted on the extremity of the causeway, now called Dam-street (leading to the Market-place), against the S.E. gate of the close, a musket-shot glanced through a side opening,

and struck Lord Brooke as he was coming out of the porch of a house. It was fired by a deaf and dumb gentleman named Dyott, posted on the central tower. This event, which dispirited the assailants, and caused them to cease their attacks for the rest of the day, gave new life to the loyal garrison, whose leaders were not slow to point it out as a visitation of Providence that Lord Brooke, who had openly vowed the extermination of episcopacy, and destruction of all cathedrals, had received his death-wound from St. Chad's Ch. upon St. Chad's day. Lord Brooke's buff-coat was preserved at Warwick Castle until it perished in the fire there in 1871, and the gun with which he was shot was in the possession of General Dyott, of Freeford, near Lichfield.

"Fanatic Brooke
The fair cathedral stormed and took;
But thanks to God and good St. Chad,
A guerdon meet the spoiler had."

Though the house in which Lord Brooke was killed is removed, the spot where he fell in Dam-street is marked by a white marble tablet in front of a modern red-brick house. The siege was renewed, after Lord Brooke's death, with great vigour by Sir John Gell, and the want of ammunition and provisions compelled the garrison of the close to send a messenger in white, who was conducted blindfold to the quarters of the Parliamentary general to treat. The close surrendered March 5th, 1643. Not many weeks after, it was regained by the Royalists, headed by Prince Rupert, and Villiers Duke of Buckingham, who both fought in the breach.

Lichfield was besieged for the third time in 1646, and yielded only when the cause of King Charles had become hopeless. The lead was on that occasion stripped from the cathedral, and, with the bells, melted to make bullets and cannon.

There is a pretty walk from the Cathedral by the side of Stowe Pool, passing the spot where Dr. Johnson's willow stood, to Stowe, or **St. Chad's Ch.**, an interesting Gothic building, at the further end of the pool. The S. aisle, and the tower with its fine Dec. window and massive buttresses, are the oldest portion, the N. aisle, chancel, clerestory, and S. porch having been restored. Here St. Chad was buried before his remains were transferred to their costly shrine in the cathedral. The saint lived here in a cell the life of a pious anchorite. The Ch. contains a monumental tablet to Lucy Porter, Johnson's stepdaughter. His favourite Molly Aston lived on Stowe Hill.

St. Chad's Well, in a garden hard by, was looked upon as holy, and was in former times dressed out with flowers on Holy Thursday, on which day the Choristers of the Cathedral still walk in procession to the well, carrying green boughs, and sing the old 100th Psalm, and the Priest Vicar reads the Holy Gospel for that day. The tree called Johnson's willow, because it was supposed to have been planted by him, was blown down in 1815. A slip, however, from it now represents the size and vigour of the former one. Johnson's father had a parchment manufactory near this spot, and was prosecuted by the Excise for some infringement of the law, which may perhaps account for the son's acrimonious definition of the word "Excise" in his Dictionary.

St. Mary's Ch., in the Market-place, which was of the poorest style of the 18th centy., had, in 1853, a lofty tower and spire added by *Street* at the W. end, and the body has since been rebuilt as a memorial to Bishop Lonsdale. Here is the Dyott family vault, where the members of this family have been for generations buried at midnight. There is a monument to one of the sons of Sir Richard Dyott.

In **St. Michael's Ch.**, which is outside the town, Johnson's father, the bookseller, was buried, opposite the pulpit. The inscription on the pavement is by his son, whose own name appears in the baptismal register. There is also a monument to Mrs. Cobb, whom Johnson considered the "most impudent" woman he had ever met with. During some alterations, a recumbent figure, supposed to be that of William de Waltone, full-length, in civil costume of the time of Richard II., was discovered and deposited in the chancel. "The chancel and aisles of this Ch. seem to have been rebuilt; the pillars and arches, the groining of the chancel, the woodwork of the ceiling in the nave and aisles, and the windows generally, filled as they are with beautiful painted glass, are notable objects."

Christ Ch. was built in 1847 and was enlarged in 1885 by the addition of two transepts. It contains a wrought-iron screen of good design at the entrance to the chancel.

St. John's Hospital, in St. John's-st., was built 1495, soon after the general introduction of chimneys, and has 8 of these appendages projecting into the street like buttresses, with small windows between them. It is a curious specimen of domestic architecture. The chapel (restored) has an open timbered roof, and windows of Perp. and Dec. date.

The **Friary**, in Bird St., once the old Franciscan establishment, is now a private house, which has built into the wall the tombstone of Richard the Merchant, its founder, together with some verses in Lombardic characters.

The **Free Library** and **Museum**, standing in well kept grounds, to which a recreation ground has recently been added, is a plain brick structure in the Italian style, and contains interesting local collections. The Guildhall in Bore St. is a modern stone building in Gothic style. There are some fine timber houses in this street. The Market Hall may also be noticed.

Lichfield has no little glory in the number of eminent men born in it, at the head of whom may be placed Samuel Johnson. The house in which he was born, 1709, is at the corner of the Market-place, partly resting on 3 stone pillars; it is now a restaurant. It is much to the credit of the corporation that they presented to him, in token of respect, the lease of this tenement, which had been built by his father, and which he held till his own death. A **Statue** of the great moralist, in a somewhat rustic style of art, was set up in the Market-place in 1838 by the Rev. Chancellor Law. The bas-reliefs are intended to represent events in his life. 1. Johson, perched on his father's shoulders, listening to a sermon from Dr. Sacheverell.† 2. Carried on the back of his schoolfellows to school. 3. Doing penance in the Market-place, Uttoxeter, for having disobeyed his father. After his marriage with a lady twice as old as himself, he attempted to establish a school at Edial Hall, a large square-built mansion, surmounted by a cupola and balustrades, about a quarter of an hour's walk from the city. Among his pupils was Garrick. Boswell records that, in visiting Lichfield with Johnson for the first time, he ascertained that oats, which Johnson had sneered at as "the food of men in Scotland," were also the food of his fellow-townsmen. Other buildings associated with him are, Lucy Porter's house in Tamworth-st., and that of Mrs. Gastrall at Stowe-

† This episode of Johnson's life has been shown by Mr. Croker ('Boswell,' p. 6) to be apocryphal, as it has been proved by the corporation records that he could only have been 9 months old when Dr. Sacheverell visited the town.

hill, which was afterwards successively occupied by the author of 'Sandford and Merton,' and Miss Edgeworth's father. Other distinguished natives are, Judge Weston, Ashmole the antiquary, Bishop Smallridge, and Bishop Newton.

The George Hotel was the scene of the 'Beau's Stratagem'; the author, Farquhar, was stationed here some time as a recruiting officer, and makes his Boniface praise the ale. The Swan is one of the oldest hotels, it was in repute in the days of Charles I.

On the Monday in Whit-week an annual fair is held in Lichfield. The morning is ushered in with bell-ringing, and towards mid-day, after breakfast at the Guildhall, the Mayor and Corporation, in state robes, preceded by the Town Crier, Constable, Mace and Sword Bearers, walk through the town to the Cathedral, and thence to Green Hill, where a "Bower" or tent, decked with branches and flowers, is erected; here cake, wine, and other refreshments are given freely to all comers during the day. The procession usually includes men in armour, men with "posies" or flower-bedecked models, representing different trades, and cars filled with men at work also represent various city guilds and fraternities of craftsmen. The pageant is, in fact, much like the Lady Godiva show at Coventry, and sometimes that famous lady's modern representative rides in the procession.

There are large Barracks on Whittington Heath about 2 m. outside the city. They are the depôt and centre for the Staffordshire regiments.

Lichfield has 2 Rly. Stations, which are connected : the South Stafford, or City Stat., near St. John's-st., and the L. & N.-W., or Trent Valley Stat., on the Burton road, 2 m. from the Cathedral.

Borrowcop Hill, ½ m. S.E. from the city, may be visited for the sake of its view; of it Johnson writes, "I believe you may find Borow or Boroughcop Hill in my dictionary, under Cop or Cob. Nobody here knows what the name imports."

The antiquary should visit **Wall**, a village with a pretty Ch., and charmingly situated on a ridge of wooded hill, about 2 m. to the S. of Lichfield. Wall was the Etocetum of the Romans, though scarcely any foundations are visible. Coins of the reigns of Nero and Domitian, as well as portions of Roman pavement, have been dug up here, and bricks, tiles, and pottery may be frequently found on the road. The Watling Street passes through it, and is here crossed by Icknield Street, which runs from Alcester by way of Birmingham and Sutton Park to Wall. "A trench, dug northwards through the foundations of the wall from which the place is named, and which formerly, in the memory of the inhabitants, existed breast-high, brought to light the base of a square apartment, with walls of strong masonry, and a floor of plaster laid on extremely hard concrete. This apartment had been plastered and coloured in red, green, yellow, and white, with well-made stripes."—*Garner*. Several of the objects found are preserved in the Museum at Lichfield.

½ m. S. of Wall is **Chesterfield**, where the Elizabethan half-timber manor house of the Allens is worth notice. Other hamlets, with names suggestive of the Roman dominion, occur in the neighbourhood, as Fossway, Streethay, &c.

In the vicinity of Lichfield are many fine seats, of which notice should be taken.

2 m. N. is **Elmhurst Hall** (G. Fox, Esq.); and 1 m. W. is **Maple Hayes** (A. O. Worthington, Esq.). 1 m. E. is **Whittington Hall**, very near which

is **Freeford** (belonging to the Dyotts), a very old seat of that family. **Swinfen Hall** (Major A. Finlay), a short distance from Freeford. It is a noble domain, with a fine sheet of water. It was the property of John Swinfen, a sturdy Parliamentarian, who fought against Charles I., he laboured hard to exclude the Duke of York from the throne, and was a warm adherent of the Prince of Orange (d. 1694); he was commonly called "Russet-coat," from his affected plainness of dress.

3 m. S of Lichfield is **Shenstone** (Stat.. Sutton Coldfield branch L. & N.-W. Rly.), which was granted by William I. to Robert d'Oiley, and has been since held by many successive Earls of Warwick. Only the tower of the old cruciform Perp. Ch. remains; a new Ch. in the Early Dec. style was built on another site in 1853. *Shenstone Lodge* (the property of Sir W. B. Parker, Bart.) is a plain house of the time of George I.; the estate was held by the Grendons in 1236.

From Lichfield the S. Stafford Rly. continues a N.E. course, crossing the L. & N.-W. (Trent Valley) line (Rte. 31), and keeping parallel with the ancient Iknield Street, which runs from Etocetum to Derventio (Little Chester, near Derby).

28 m. **Alrewas** (Stat.). The *Ch.* (founded A.D. 820), which was one of the earliest prebends of Lichfield, is mixed Dec. and Perp., and has been completely restored. It contains a Norm. door, a high-pitched chancel-roof, a good Perp. font, and some ancient carvings.

½ m. S. is **Fradley Hall**, a half-timbered house, with the arms of the Gorings over the door; it belonged to the Gilberts in the early part of the 17th centy.

About 1 m. further the Rly. crosses the Trent close to its junction with the Tame, and very soon after unites with the Midland Rly. at Wichnor Junction, and after passing **Barton** and **Walton** (Stat.) arrives at **Burton-on-Trent** (see Rte. 29).

ROUTE 29.

BIRMINGHAM TO BURTON-ON-TRENT, BY TAMWORTH.

MIDLAND RLY. 31½ m.

Leaving Birmingham from the New Street Stat. the line pursues a N.E. course (see *Handbook for Warwickshire*), and enters Staffordshire at Tamworth.

17½ m. ☿ **Tamworth** (Stat.; which also serves for the Trent Valley line of the L. & N.-W. Rly., Rte. 30) is a well-to-do midland town, having a fair number of opulent residents, and dependent partly on the surrounding rich grazing district, and partly upon its own internal trade. It is partly in Warwickshire, standing on both banks of the Tame, over which and its tributaries there are several bridges. There are two large stretches of common land, called the Warwick and the Stafford moors, upon which the inhabitants have rights of pasture. A thousand years ago the natural advantages of this place induced the Saxon kings of Mercia to select it as a residence. Deeds and charters exist dated from the Royal palace of Tamworth in the 8th and 9th centuries. "No one who looks on the district—no one who sees the extent of its woodlands, the delightful rivers that water it, enriching the spacious meadows that border them, who sees also the extensive champaign country, affording the opportunity of arable cultivation for pleasure and profit, can be surprised to find that, in the earliest times, it was the chosen seat of those who were the conquerors of the country."—*Sir R. Peel*.

In the fields W. of the town, says the legend, the combat took place between Sir Lancelot of the Hall and Sir Tarquin, knights of the Round Table; and a castle was built near the junction of the Tame and the Anker by Ethelfleda, the daughter of Alfred. The town was given by William I. to Robert Marmion, of Fontenay in Normandy, who thus became Lord of "Tamworth tower and town." From the Marmions it descended to the Frevilles and the Ferrers, and from them, with the barony, to the Marquis Townshend.

The **Castle** (occupied by T. Cooke, Esq.) occupies the site of Ethelfleda's fort, on the rt. bank of the Tame, but is mainly a Jacobean building, placed on a lofty artificial mound; its most striking feature is a multangular ivy-clad tower. The hall has an open roof of wood, springing nearly from the floor, and is curious, but very gloomy. Two chambers are panelled and decorated with armorial bearings. There is little else to see in the interior, which is fitted up as a modern residence. From the leads of the tower is a very fine view of the Vale of Trent, Drayton Manor, and Lichfield spires. During the Civil Wars the Castle was taken by the Parliamentarians, and held by Governor Waldyke Willington.

The *Ch.*, dedicated to St. Edith, the daughter of King Edgar, who is buried here, is a very fine building, of Dec. and Perp. dates, with a handsome and conspicuous tower, intended to carry a spire, of which the base only remains. The first Marmion, according to the legend, seized all the property of the Ch.. but on receiving a nocturnal visit from the saint, he not only restored the spoil but gave many additional manors, and made the Ch. collegiate, which it remained until the Dissolution. The Norm. Ch. was burnt in 1345, but some fragments remain, worked up in the present building, which was in part restored by *Butterfield*. There is a crypt filled with human bones, and, in the tower, a curious double staircase, communicating, the one with the inside, the other with the outside, both distinct though intertwining. In the chancel are several monuments of early date, presumably of the Marmions and the Frevilles, but the great monument of the last of the Ferrers has been placed under the tower. To the E. of the Ch. are some rude walls of early date, and in Church-st. is a picturesque timber house, figured in Parker's ' Dom. Architecture.'

Thomas Guy, the bookseller and founder of the noble London hospital that bears his name, represented Tamworth for 7 Parliaments; he founded some almshouses, and rebuilt the Town-hall (to which the first Sir Robert Peel made additions), which stands on the arches of an older building. In front of it is a bronze statue of Sir Robert Peel, the Minister, who took much interest in the town, and was mainly instrumental in founding its present flourishing Natural History and Antiquarian Society.

1½ m. S. of Tamworth is **Fazeley**, where in 1785 Mr. Peel established his cotton-mills, and promoted the construction of the canal by which Fazeley communicates with the northern counties.

3 m. S.W. of Tamworth is **Drayton Bassett**, and the house of Drayton Manor (Rt. Hon. Sir Robert Peel, Bart.). The manor once belonged to Hugh Lupus, Earl of Chester, and was granted by him to Richard Bassett, the son of the great justiciary of Henry I., in marriage with his granddaughter Maud. The Bassetts held it till 1390, when it passed into the hands of the Staffords, and it was forfeited on the attainder of the Duke of Buckingham. It afterwards was the residence of Lettice, countess of Essex, the mother of the favourite of Queen Elizabeth, who visited here in one of her progresses. The countess, who afterwards married Dudley, Earl of Leicester, survived her son; she died at Drayton on Christmay Day, 1634, and was buried at Warwick. After the death of her grandson, the Parliamentary general, it came to the Thynnes, and the first Marquis of Bath sold it in 1790 to Mr. Peel. H.M. the Queen visited the father of the present owner here in 1843. The old manor-house was a timbered structure, but the existing one (which is not shown to the public) is a handsome modern mansion, designed by *Smirke* in a style neither Italian nor Elizabethan, but relieved in its outline by towers and turrets. In extension of the north front of the house is the picture gallery, forming a wing 100 ft. long. The exterior, which is Elizabethan, is decorated by 4 stone statues of Rubens, Vandyck, Reynolds, and Lawrence. The portrait-gallery is very interesting, consisting of eminent statesmen and men of celebrity in literature and the arts and sciences.

The old Ch. was pulled down in 1792, and replaced by the present plain stone edifice. In it is buried Sir Robert Peel, the statesman, died July 1850, who refused a tomb in Westminster Abbey, to lie here beside his father, the first baronet. The present baronet has added a chancel, and filled the windows with stained glass.

2 m. N.W. of Drayton is **Hints**, where the Ch., rebuilt in E. E. style

in 1883, has monuments to the Floyers and the Lawleys. On Hints common a pig of lead weighing 150 lbs. was discovered in 1771, which bore the inscription " Imp. Vesp. VII. T. Imp. Cos." 1 m. N.W. is **Weeford**, the Ch. of which contains some beautiful stained glass brought from France at the time of the first Revolution.

At **Canwell**, 1 m. S. of Hints. a small Benedictine priory once existed, founded in 1142 by Geva, the daughter of Hugh Lupus. St. Modwena's well indicates the site. *Canwell Hall* (A. B. Foster, Esq.) is a handsome modern house, by *Wyatt*.

From the Tamworth Stat. the line runs northward, passing on W. the village of **Wigginton**, beyond which is *Comberford Hall* (S. Fisher, Esq.), once the seat of an old Staffordshire family of the same name. On E. of Wigginton is **Statfold**, where the little Ch. has several monuments of the Wolferstans. *Statfold Hall* (F. S. Pipe-Wolferstan, Esq.) is an Elizabethan mansion, with an octangular turret built as an observatory by Francis Wolferstan, the friend of Plot; he was a lawyer, a vehement Jacobite, and a very indifferent poet. 2 m. N.E. is **Thorpe Constantine**, the lofty spire of the Ch. being a good landmark. *Thorpe Hall* (W. F. Inge, Esq.).

23 m. **Elford** and **Haselour** (Stat.). The village of Haselour, which lies N., is very small. Almost adjoining E. is **Harlaston**, where there is an old timbered *Hall* of the Vernons, who were seated on this spot from the 12th to the 16th centy., when George Vernon of Harlaston removed into Derbyshire, where he became so popular that he was commonly known as " the King of the Peak." 2 m. E. is **Clifton Campville**, where the handsome Ch. has a spire 160 ft. high. It contains a *brass* for some unknown lady (c. 1360), half effigy on a bracket, a fine alabaster table-tomb for Sir John Vernon and his wife Ellen, 1545, and monuments by *Rysbrack* to Sir Charles (1721) and Sir Richard Pye (1724). *Clifton Hall* (H. J. Pye, Esq.) was begun in 1708 by Sir Charles Pye, who built the wings before the centre, and was unable to finish it according to the plans.

1 m. W. of the stat. is **Elford**, on the river Tame, said to derive its name from the number of eels formerly found in the river. Elford Hall (the Hon. Eleanor Bagot) is the successor of a mansion at which it is said Henry VII. slept the night before the battle of Bosworth Field. The Dec. Ch., which has been most carefully restored, has much historic interest in its well preserved tombs, dating from 1400. The most remarkable are those of Sir Thos. Arderne and wife (c. 1400), in rich costume, he wearing the collar of SS., while around are statuettes of mourners; Sir John Stanley, in armour (d. 1447); a grandson of Sir John Stanley, who was killed when a child by a tennis-ball. It represents a youth in a long garment and curled hair, with a ball in one hand and pointing to his ear with the other, with the motto of " Ubi dolor, ibi digitus ; " and a fine altar - tomb to Sir Wm. Smyth (1526), between his 2 wives, one of whom was Isabella Neville, the niece of the King-maker. To the S. of the village, near a point where the river is crossed by a bridge to Fisherwick (Rte. 31), there are two tumuli or " lows," called Robin Hood's Butts, near which there must have been a British or Roman road, as a farm adjacent bears the name of the Portway. A remarkable oak - tree, which is mentioned in Domesday Book, still stands in the parish, though now dead.

24¾ m. **Croxall** (Stat.). The Ch. on the banks of the Mease (in Derbyshire), contains numerous monuments of the Curzons, who settled at Croxall Hall (T. Levett-Prinsep, Esq.), about 1200 A.D., and of the Hortons of Catton Hall (Mrs. Anson-Horton); also, with its manor, in this parish. Mary Curzon, the heiress of Croxall, early in the 17th century married the Earl of Dorset, who fought for Charles I. in his wars with the Parliament, and the Dorsets became lords of Croxall. Queen Henrietta Maria, after the battle of Bradford Bridge in 1643 A.D., slept at Croxall Hall when moving to Walsall with 3000 troops. The fifth Earl of Dorset was the patron and friend of Dryden, after his deprivation of the poet laureateship, under William III., and had him at Croxall Hall from time to time. The bridge, along which a foot road extends to Catton Hall, is still known as Dryden's favourite walk. S. of Croxall is the manor of *Oakley*, formerly belonging to Sir John Stanley, where Edward IV. used to stay when hunting in the neighbourhood.

A little beyond Croxall, near the junction of the Trent and the Tame, the rly. crosses the former river, by a low viaduct ¼ m. long, resting on piles driven 15 ft. below the bed of the river. At the junction of the two rivers the stream is augmented by that of the Mease, a small brook that takes its rise in Leicestershire, and here divides the counties.

On the N. bank of the Trent is Wichnor Junction (Rte. 28), where the South Staffordshire line falls in. **Wichnor** Ch. is small, with a square tower. There was formerly a moated Hall, which has given place to a plain brick Lodge (Col. T. J. Levett), built on a spot further removed from the river floods. The manor, like several neighbouring ones, was granted by John of Gaunt to Sir Philip Somerville on the tenure that the holder should always (except in Lent) keep a flitch of bacon, and other provisions, to be given to any man who had been married a year and a day and would thus swear, "Hear ye, Sir Philip de Somerville, Lord of Wichenor, mayn-tennor and gyver of this baconne; I, A B, sithe I wedded my wife, and sithe I had her in my kepyng and at my wylle by a year and day after our marriage, I would not have changed for none other, fairer ne fouler, richer ne poorer, &c. And if the said B were sole and I sole, I would take her to be my wyfe before all the wymen of the world. So help me God and his saints, and all fleshes!" The condition of the claimant having been ascertained by the oath of two witnesses, he received, if a freeman, half a quarter of wheat and a cheese, but if a villein, only half a quarter of rye, in addition to the bacon. The happy pair were then escorted on horseback to the boundary of the manor by the tenants with music and rejoicing: and the sub-tenant of the manor of Rudlowe (for a long time of the name of Knightly) had to furnish carriage, "that is to say, a horse and a saddle, a sack and a pryle," to convey the gift a day's journey out of the county if necessary. He was to be paid for this by the holder of Wichnor, and if he refused to perform the service he was liable to a fine of 100 shillings. The custom is amusingly detailed in the 'Spectator,' but more accurately in Blount's 'Jocular Tenures,' where it is said that the bacon was also claimable by any ecclesiastic if non-repentant of his profession. The custom has long fallen into disuse, but, as a memorial, a wooden flitch hangs in the kitchen of the Lodge.

On the rt. or Derbyshire bank of the Trent is Calton Hall, whence a prettily wooded ridge skirts the river to

27½ m. **Barton** and **Walton** (Stat.).

Barton-under-Needwood is on the confines of the forest (Rte. 30). The Perp. Ch., enlarged and restored in 1861 and 1885, was built about 1530 by John Taylor, D.D., Master of the Rolls to Henry VII. Dr. Taylor was one of three sons, born at one birth. His father lived in a cottage on the spot where the Ch. now stands, and being a poor man, was much distressed at this great increase of his family. Henry VII., being out upon a hunting expedition in the Forest of Needwood, happened to pass through the village and to hear of the birth of the boys and the father's distress. The King whereupon undertook to make provision for their maintenance and education, and all three entered learned professions. The coat-of-arms of the Doctor, three boys' heads, and a white and a red rose, are cut upon various walls of the Ch., and there is a latin inscripton, setting forth his various titles. The east end of the chancel is peculiar, being a half hexagonal apse. 3 m. N. is **Tatenhill**, in which, according to Erdeswick, "there is nothing worth noting, except a man should account it for a beauty, whereof I never heard any man make any great account except Thomas Leeson (1539), a poor priest that was parson of Packington, in Leicestershire, and was born here. who, commending, in a sort, his birthplace, left these verses upon his monument in Packington Ch. :—

Me Tatenell genuit, ast Asbbi devia nutrix; Packington tumulus, sic mea fata ferunt."

Erdeswick, however, must have been but an indifferent judge of architecture, or he would have had a word of commendation for Tatenhill Ch., which is a large and handsome 12th-centy. building, with Perp. windows, and has been well restored. It contains a curious monument of the Griffiths family, of 1585. At Rangemoor, a part of the parish verging on the forest, is Rangemoor Hall (Lord Burton), a modern Italian structure in a good park. There is also a district Ch. and School, built by the late Mr. Bass.

31½ m. ☧ **Burton-on-Trent** (Stat.) is a rapidly increasing town situated on both banks of the Trent, which here forms the boundary between Staffordshire and Derbyshire, it has recently become a municipal borough, and its boundaries have been enlarged to include the villages of Winshill, Stapenhill, and Hornington. The municipal buildings were presented by Lord Burton to the town. The houses are mostly built of red brick, and the streets are regular and monotonous. The Derbyshire bank of the river is well wooded and laid out in walks and terraces as a recreation ground for the inhabitants.

Burton is renowned all the world over for its ale and bitter beer, to supply the demands for which no less than 25 firms of brewers have erected enormous establishments. These occupy about 300 acres of land, and are "solid, bold, capacious buildings, neither deficient nor conspicuous in architectural detail, but well and studiously arranged and systematically connected by chains of railways—which, as sanctioned by Parliament in 1860, cross the streets on the level—the goods stations with the malting offices, and these with the breweries, the cooperages, the stores, and the yards." These private lines are more than 20 miles long.

The principal firms are Bass & Co., Allsopp and Sons, Salt & Co., Worthington & Co., Peter Walker & Co., and the Burton Brewery Co. Four large London firms, Ind. Coope & Co., Truman, Hanbury & Co., Mann and Crossman, and Charrington & Co., have branch establishments here, and the other Burton breweries are on a scale which would be considered very large elsewhere. Amongst them they employ either directly or indirectly almost the entire population. On application at the counting-house permission is readily granted to inspect any of these works, and any visitor to the town would do well to avail himself of it.

The premises of Messrs. Bass & Co. occupy more than 140 acres of land, the quantity of malt brewed in the season amounts to not less than 300,000 quarters, taking more than 60,000 acres to grow the requisite quantity of barley, more than 2000 workmen are employed in Burton alone, 600,000 casks are in use, and more than 12 miles of private railways belong to the firm. The traffic in and out being worked by 10 locomotive engines and about 100 horses. The amount of coal and coke consumed is about 50,000 tons per annum. The brewers employ spring water in preference to that from the Trent, and the brewings generally commence in October, when the weather cools. "The ale of Burton has been celebrated from an antiquity too remote to trace with certainty; but its consumption was principally local, not extending much beyond Derby until 1623, when it was first introduced into London under the name of Derby ale." Camden remarks on the celebrity of Derby ale and its exceeding wholesomeness; although, he says, all persons did not share in his opinion, for Henry d'Avranches, poet laureate to Henry III., wrote—

"Of this strange drink, so like the Stygian lake
(Men call it ale), I know not what to make."

The ale brewed down to the close of the last century was a very strong drink, and was almost entirely supplied to the English ships that traded to Northern climates; but in 1822 one Hodgson, a London brewer who had settled at Burton, brewed something like the present bitter ale, which he accomplished in a teapot in his counting-house, and called it "Bombay beer." A retired East India captain, named Chapman, improved on this, and "Burton ale" soon attained the celebrity that has made the names of Bass and Allsopp "household words" all over the world (Molyneux, 'Burton and its Breweries').

A great part of the town belongs to the Marquis of Anglesey, this and other manors having been bestowed on his ancestor Sir William, 1st Lord Paget, by Henry VIII.

Burton may fairly be said to owe its origin to the fact that the site of the present town was visited in the 7th centy. by the Irish saint Modwena, who built a mission church, dedicated to St. Andrew, on the island opposite the present parish ch.-yard. On this island, which still bears the name of Andresey, she died and was buried, the epitaph on her tomb being recorded by Camden. Upwards of 300 years after her death a Benedictine Monastery was founded (1002) by Wulfric Spot, a Mercian Earl, who was mortally wounded at Ruymire near Ipswich in a battle with the Danes, and was buried at Burton. His original will, written in Saxon, is in the possession of the Marquis of Anglesey. Only few remains of the Abbey still exist, consisting of a fine Perp. doorway in the grounds of the house, now known as the Abbey, but formerly the Abbot's residence, and some Dec. windows, concealed by the new stonework of the house itself. A portion of the porter's lodge and entrance-gate to the Abbey still remains fronting the High-street. Readers of 'Ivanhoe' will remember that the Baron Front de Bœuf speaks of Burton Abbey as "a howlet's nest worth the harrying." The Abbey Ch., a magnificent structure with three large towers, was slightly injured in the civil war, and was pulled down in 1720 to make room for the present Palladian building which contains little of interest beyond the 15th-centy. font and a good altar-piece of white marble. In the register, which commences in 1538, is an entry of the baptism, on Dec. 28, 1572, of William, the son of the 3rd Lord Paget, to whom Lord Burleigh was godfather.

Though but a slight remove from the High-street the churchyard is a pretty retired spot, sloping down to the Trent, and commanding a fine view of the opposite hills.

The Burton 'Annals' are one of the chief sources for the history of the reigns of Richard I. and John, and contain much important information to be gathered from no other source.

Sincy Park, the name borne by the high ground to the W. of the town, was a grange farm belonging to the Abbey. The 15th-centy. house is still standing, though rapidly falling into decay. But until 1867 the most remarkable antiquity of Burton was its *Bridge*, which certainly existed in the reign of Henry II., and was supposed to date from the Norman era. It consisted of 36 arches, scarce any two of which were alike either in size or style, and it stretched across the river in a curved line. A severe engagement took place on it in 1322, between the Royal forces under Edward II., and those under the Earl of Lancaster, who was defeated with much loss, and put to flight. He was soon after taken, carried to his own castle at Pontefract, and beheaded. A chapel was erected on the bridge for priests to pray for the souls of the slain. The bridge, from its length and narrowness, was a very defensible position, and Sir Thomas Tyldesley, in the civil war, made six ineffectual attacks before he could force his way over it. The Midland Rly. Company have built a handsome stone bridge in its stead, which is continued as a viaduct over the many lines of rly. that occupy the l. bank of the river, and serve as "ale docks" for the different brewing firms.

Of the 8 churches of Burton only two are of old foundation. The parish Ch., dedicated to St. Modwena, and St. Peter's in Stapenhill; the latter was rebuilt in 1882. Of the modern churches the best worthy of notice are St. Paul's, a fine cruciform building, erected in 1874 by the late Mr. M. T. Bass, and situated near the Rly. Stat.; and Holy Trinity Ch., near the bridge, built in 1882 from designs of Mr. J. Oldrid Scott, to which Sir Hy. Allsopp was the principal contributor.

An extension of the ferry bridge has been opened. It was built by Lord Burton and presented to the borough at the cost of about 10,000*l*. The two portions of the borough are now united.

2 m. to the S. of the town on the Derbyshire side of the Trent is Drakelow Hall, the property of the Gresley family, which is described in Domesday Book as being held by Nigel de Stafford by the service of providing a bow without a string, a quiver and 12 arrows.

ROUTE 30.

WALSALL TO RUGELEY, BY CANNOCK. [NEEDWOOD FOREST.]

L. & N.-W. RLY. 15 m.

This, the Cannock and Rugeley branch, serves both as a colliery rly. from the coal districts of Cannock Chase, and as a connecting link between mid-Staffordshire and the manufacturing districts of the North. Soon after leaving Walsall it approaches the high grounds of Cannock Chase.

1½ m. **Birchhills** (Stat.), an outskirt of Walsall, with ironworks, and some collieries.

2½ m. **Bloxwich** (Stat.). This is a considerable manufacturing district, the inhabitants of which are almost entirely employed in the making of stirrups, bits, saddlers' needles, and awl-blades, the latter being a speciality of Bloxwich, as are locks at Willenhall. The Ch. was built early in the 18th centy.; it was extensively restored, and reconsecrated in 1877 by the name of All Saints. A rude pillar, apparently the shaft of a cross, stands in the ch.-yard. Notice the inscription to Sam. Wilks (d. 1764), a village Hampden. Hence the line ascends an elevated country to

6½ m. Wyrley and Church Bridge (Stat.). Great Wyrley is a mining and agricultural village, with a good modern Ch. It stands on the Watling Street, and the river Penk rises in its neighbourhood. Tradition ascribes to the waters of an old well here the quality of giving sight to the blind. About 2 m. to the N., in the hamlet of Little Wyrley, midway between Wyrley and Brownhills, E., is **Wyrley Grove**, a curious mansion of the 17th centy., which was formerly in the possession of the Fowkes of Brewood (Rte. 27), but latterly in that of the family of Hussey. Among the Harleian MSS. is a letter from Christopher King, dated 1694, in which he says "he is so charmed with his good and learned friend Dr. Fowke [the translator of 'Plutarch's Lives'], as to stay at Wyrley much longer than he intended, where he enjoys all the pleasures of study and retirement." At Church Bridge are large Edge Tool Works (Messrs. Gilpin & Co.).

8 m. ☦ Cannock (Stat.). This, the chief place of the moorland district of Cannock Chase, is an ancient town, where King Henry I. once had a house, now occupied by a blacksmith. It has revived in consequence of the extensive coal workings opened in its neighbourhood of late years. There are good Public Rooms, and a very pleasant-looking bowling green, with an avenue of lime-trees, a somewhat unusual feature in the district. The Ch. (enlarged), of which the well-known Dr. Sacheverell was once curate, has a Perp. nave and a square embattled tower. The chancel has been rebuilt in Dec. style.

About ¾ m. to the S.E. is *Rumour Hill*, which was famous many years ago for its springs, to which all the fashion of the county resorted.

The name Cannock (pronounced Cank) is probably derived from Knut's Wood (Canute's Wood), the site of a battle between the Danes and Saxons, close to which are the ruins of a British camp. Although there are now little or no remains of the forest save the name of Chase, history records that an extensive forest and a favourite hunting locality of the then monarchs existed during the Mercian era. The Chase covers an extent of 36,000 acres, very little of which has as yet been reclaimed, though the formation of a great Central Arsenal there has been suggested; but, though unproductive on the surface, it contains vast riches underneath in the shape of coal-beds. These are principally worked by the Cannock and Rugeley Colliery Co., whose works are on a very large scale. There are also the collieries of the East Cannock and Leacroft Companies.

The Rly. pursues its course in a northerly direction into the very heart of the Chase, to

10 m. ☦ Hednesford (Stat.), a place once only known from the training ground for horses afforded by the neighbouring hills. It is now, owing to the collieries in the parish, a busy market town, with a modern Ch., built on a site given by the Marquis of Anglesey, whose seat of Hednesford Hall is now an hotel. About equi-distant from this Stat. and that of Armitage is **Beaudesert**, the beautiful park of the Marquis of Anglesey (Rte. 31). Leaving Hednesford the scenery becomes wooded and picturesque as the line descends from the uplands of the Chase towards Rugeley.

15 m. ⚹ **Rugeley** (Stat.), a prettily situated and busy little town notwithstanding the unpleasant associations with which its name was associated in the minds of some people as the residence of Palmer, and the scene of his wholesale poisonings, now almost forgotten. Rugeley was a possession of the see of Lichfield, but was granted to Sir William Paget by Henry VIII. The parish Ch. is modern but the chancel and W. tower, a good specimen of 14th-centy. work, of the old Ch. are still in existence. The former has been restored, and now used for divine service; it contains the tombstone of John Weston, an ecclesiastic of the 16th centy. The Public Buildings opened in 1879 contain a Market Hall, an Assembly Room, and Municipal Offices. Adjoining the town is *Hagley Hall* (the property of the Marquis of Anglesey), a fine old mansion, in a park.

The line passes E. of the town, and across the river to the Rugeley Stat. of the Trent Valley Branch (Rte. 31).

From Rugeley an interesting *Excursion* may be made to the pleasant district of **Needwood Forest**, returning through **Abbot's Bromley**.

Proceed along the Armitage road, and cross the Trent by the one-arched iron bridge, 140 ft. wide, near the Armitage Stat. (Rte. 31) to the hamlet of **Hansacre** (3 m.). Notice the old Manor-house, with the moat. At a short distance N. are the 3 villages called the **Ridwares**. The nearest, **Mavesyn Ridware**, is so called from the Norm. family of Malvoisin, corrupted into Mavesyn. Of the last member of this family [*Derby, &c.*]

Erdeswick says, " Well might he be called Malvoisin—for (as the report of the country is), going towards the battle of Shrewsbury, he met with his neighbour Sir William Handsacre going also into the said battle, either of them being well accompanied by their servants and tenants: and upon some former malice, it might seem, or else knowing the other to be backed by the contrary party, they encountered each other, and fought as it were a skirmish, or little battle, when Mavesyn had the victory, and, having slain his adversary, went on to the battle, and was there slain himself." The *Ch.*, which has been restored, contains the monument of this warlike Sir Robert, an armed figure, with sword and dagger; also monuments and a stained glass window to the Chadwicks, who were lineally descended from the Malvoisins. **Pipe Ridware** lies to the N., and beyond it is **Hamstall Ridware**, situated on the little stream of Blyth, which joins the Trent at King's Bromley. In the village of Hamstall Ridware is an Elizabethan manor-house, now occupied as a farmhouse. The Ch. has a nave, aisles, and clerestory, and contains some carved oak stalls and a screen, together with some good old painted glass. In the Ch.-yard is the shaft of a cross. 1 m. to the N.W. of Hamstall Ridware is **Blithbury**, the site of a priory founded in the reign of Stephen by Hugh Mavesyn, of which the memory is preserved by the name of the Priory Farm.

About 2½ m. to the E. of Armitage, at the confluence of the Blythe with the Trent, is **King's Bromley**, the manor of which was in possession of the Crown for 2 centuries after the Norm. Conquest, but was by Henry II. granted to the Corbetts. The Perp. Ch. has a good square tower, and some handsome windows. *King's Bromley Manor* is the seat of J. H. Lane, Esq., who is a descendant

N

of the Lanes of Bentley, so conspicuous for their devotion to Charles II. (Rte. 27). A celebrity of King's Bromley is mentioned in Plot, one Mary Cooper, an old woman who saw 5 generations of her descendants before she died, all of whom were alive at the same time, so that she could say, "Rise, daughter, go to thy daughter, for thy daughter's daughter hath got a daughter."

2 m. N. is **Yoxall**, a village on the border of Needwood Forest. The *Ch.*, Norm. Dec. and Perp., was restored in 1868 (the late Lord Palmerston being a contributor), and contains a very fine altar-tomb for Humphrey Welles and Mary his wife, of Hoarcross (d. 1565, 1584), also a *brass* for Thomas and Joan Welles (1509). Their moated manor-house has been replaced by a modern building, Hoarcross Hall (Mrs. Meynell-Ingram). *Longcroft Hall* (Holland Franklyn, Esq.), an ancient mansion which, with the park, was granted by charter to Roger de Yoxhall in 1216; and was in the possession of the Arden family for full 3 centuries afterwards.

The whole of the district between Yoxall, Burton-on-Trent, and the river Dove, is occupied more or less by the **Forest of Needwood**, "which was chiefly enclosed about the beginning of the present centy., leaving a portion belonging to the Crown and one lodge. It had formerly 4 wards and 4 keepers, with a handsome lodge to each, but is now in the hands of different private gentlemen. In Queen Elizabeth's time it was 24 miles in circumference, and in 1658 it contained 47,150 trees and 10,000 cords of hollies and underwood, valued at 30,710*l*. It and Bagot's Park, formerly part of it, still contain some of the largest oaks and hollies in England."—*Harwood*. Near the centre of the forest, a Ch. called Christ Church in Needwood,

was erected in 1820, and there is another in the village of **Newborough**, 2 m. N. On the E. skirt of the forest is a spot styled **Callingwood**, being a corruption of Challengewood ("Boscum calumniatum"), referring to the legend that Robert de Ferrers at the battle of the Standard, to animate his men promised a grant of land in Needwood to the one who showed the most valour. One Ralph had the prize adjudged to him. By far the most picturesque portion of Needwood is on the north, where the land declines into the valley of the Dove, with abrupt and beautifully wooded hills. The soil is rich and good, and is thus described, together with its opposite, Cannock Chase, by Drayton :—

"But two of all the rest
That Staffordshire calls hers, these both of high account,
The eld'st of which is Cank; though Needwood here surmount
In excellence of soil, by being richly placed
'Twixt Trent and batt'ning Dove."

3 m. W. from Newborough is the decayed market town of ₰**Abbot's Bromley**, once the property of the abbots of Burton, whence the name. The *Ch.*, originally an E. E. structure, has been restored in Perp. style. It has a good E. window with seven lights. In the tower are preserved some deer's heads, still used annually with the hobbyhorse at the "Wakes" on the Monday after the Sunday nearest to Sept. 4th, notwithstanding that the county historians speak of it as a matter of the past. "There was here a custom, now discontinued, similar also to one long observed at Stafford and at Seighford, but it was continued here till the civil war, and Sir Simon Degge often saw it. A person carried between his legs the figure of a horse made of thin wood, and in his hand a bow and arrow, which, passing through a hole in the bow and stopping on a shoulder of it, makes a snapping noise as he drew it to and fro, keep-

ing time with the music. With this 10 or 12 others danced, carrying on their shoulders as many reindeer's heads, some of them painted white and some red, with the arms of the families of Paget, Bagot, and Welles, to whom the chief property of the town belonged, painted on the palms of them with which they danced. To this hobbyhorse dance there also belonged a pot, which was kept by turns by four or five of the chief of the town, whom they called Reeves, who provided cakes and ale to put into this pot, and collected pence for that purpose."—*Harwood*. Another old custom still practised here is the tolling of the curfew from Michaelmas to Shrove Tuesday.

The Manor House Farm was the Abbot's Country House. An underground passage from the cellars, now bricked up, is said to go in direction of the Ch. A room in the house has some fine old tapestry, and a pane of glass is preserved in this room on which is inscribed with a diamond a Latin inscription saying that Mary Queen of Scots passed through this town, Sept. 21, 1586. This was on her way from Chartley to Fotheringhay, where she was beheaded, Feb., 1587.

There is an old Market Cross in the Marketplace, with a wooden roof supported by wooden pillars, said to be quite 400 years old

1½ m. to the north of the town is **Bagot's Park**, a remnant of Needwood, detached from the rest in early days, the old inheritance of the Bagot family, who had a moated manor-house here. The park is of 1000 acres in extent. Here may be seen 18,000 oaks of unusual size and age. There are two very fine ones, known as the Beggar's oak and the King's oak, and a third, the Squitch oak, is 61 ft. high and 23 ft. in girth. " The noblest oaks in England, and, I suppose, therefore, in the world."— *Saml. Wilberforce.* Near the park is

an obelisk erected in 1811 to commemorate the migration of the Bagot family to the neighbouring house of *Blithfield* (Lord Bagot), which is about halfway between Abbot's Bromley and Colwich. It contains a fine oak staircase, and a collection of family portraits, some by Sir Joshua Reynolds.

Blithfield is near the river Blythe. The Ch., dedicated to St. Leonard, contains some interesting monuments to members of the Bagot family, specially two bronze recumbent figures of Richard Bagot and his wife (1596), and two incised alabaster slabs of the first half of the 16th centy. The glass of the side windows of the chancel is of the 14th centy., and the W. window, containing figures of the two wives of Sir Lewis Bagot, is of the time of Henry VIII. There is a 13th centy. tomb of Henry de Blithfield in the S. outside wall of the chancel. In the Ch.-yard is a cross, the base of which is very old.

If the tourist should not wish to return to Rugeley or Colwich from Abbot's Bromley (the distance is about 4¼ m. by fields to either), he can make his way through a pleasant country to either Uttoxeter (6 m.) or Sudbury (7 m.). both Stats. on the North Staffordshire Rly. (Rte. 33). Or he may proceed to the Grindley Stat. (4 m.) on the Stafford and Uttoxeter Rly. (Rte. 32).

ROUTE 31.

TAMWORTH TO NEWPORT, BY RUGELEY, COLWICH, AND STAFFORD.

L. AND N.-W. RLY. 34¼ m.

The Trent Valley Rly., which forms a direct connection between Rugby and Stafford, was designed by George Stephenson to abridge the distance between London and the north, the trains formerly having to run through Birmingham. Now the latter line is devoted to the local traffic, while the Trent Valley accommodates all the through and express trains. It enters the county of Stafford at Tamworth (Rte. 29), taking thence a north-westerly direction, and passing over the Staffordshire Moor, where, in the presence of many thousand spectators, the late Sir Robert Peel cut the first sod of the line in Nov. 1845. It soon after crosses the Tame, having on rt. Comberford Hill, and on l. the rising ground and woods of Hopwas, which fringe the left bank of the river.

At the back of the woods is *Packington Hall* (R. T. K. Levett, Esq.), a handsome house built in 1760, by the father of James Wyatt, who thus brought himself into notice. It was once the residence of Sir Wm. Stamford, a crown lawyer in the 16th centy., from whom it descended to the Babingtons, a branch of the Derbyshire family of that name. Further on, at 4 m. the rly. skirts the meadows of *Fisherwick Park*, now only farming ground, but formerly the site of two noble mansions. The first, a Jacobean edifice, was built by the first Lord Chichester, and is figured in Plot; this was pulled down in 1766, and replaced by a classic pile by Lancelot Brown, which, however, was never finished, and was itself demolished in 1810. On the southern side of the line is Whittington Heath, the property of the War Department, where the Lichfield Races are held. The pile of buildings on the eminence—the Depôt of the N. and S. Staffordshire Regts.—accommodates a population of nearly 1200, including the permanent staff of four Militia battalions. The Ch. has a lofty spire of ancient date, but the body is modern.

The graceful spires of Lichfield are shortly seen; and at 6½ m. the Rly. passes under the S. Staffordshire line and reaches the Trent Valley Stat., which, however, is nearly 2 m. from the Cathedral (Rte. 28).

11 m. **Armitage** (Stat.). The country, which has been gradually becoming more broken, is here exceedingly varied and picturesque. On W. are the abrupt and wooded knolls that fringe the northern border of Cannock Chase; on E. are the high grounds of Needwood Forest, whilst in the foreground the Trent glides with placid stream. Armitage Ch. occupies a romantic position overlooking the river. It was partly rebuilt in 1844, but still retains its Norm. tower and doorway, surrounded by a series of grotesque faces. The antiquity of Armitage is proved by ancient deeds, in which it is spoken of as the "Hermitage of Hondeshakere;" and there is a tradition that a hermit dwelt here, possibly St. Chad. In the immediate neighbourhood are some fine seats, as *Hawksyard Park* (J. Spode, Esq.) and *Armitage Lodge* (T. J. Birch, Esq.). In the former house, a modern Gothic edifice, is preserved an old helmet that once hung in the Ch. and is believed to have belonged to a former owner of the estate, Sir Simeon Rugeley, who was a colonel in the Parliamentary army, and was charged with the demolition of Stafford Castle.

About 3 m. to the W. of Armitage is **Beaudesert**, the property of the Marquis of Anglesey, situated in a charmingly picturesque and varied park. The house (the E. front of which is engraved in Plot) is of the date of Elizabeth and, as was then not unusual, is built in the form of the letter ⊔; it was honoured by a visit from the Prince Regent in 1815. The house, which formerly belonged to the Bishops of Chester, was rebuilt by Thomas Lord Paget in the 16th centy., and has since been enlarged and modernised. The great sources of attraction, however, are the woods and hills that constitute the broken ground of Beaudesert Old Park, and especially the Castle Hill, which commands a very extensive view, and is surmounted by a large British camp. At **Radmore**, a short distance S.W., are some vestiges of a Cistercian abbey, the brethren of which were removed to Stoneleigh in Warwickshire, temp. Hen. II., on their complaint that they could no longer endure the outrages of the neighbouring foresters. On the return to the stat. the archæologist may make a détour of about 3 m. to two interesting churches, Farwell and Longdon.

At **Farwell**, or Farewell, was a priory founded by Roger Bp. of Lichfield, in 1140, for Regular Canons, but afterwards suppressed in 1527 for the benefit of the choir of the cathedral. There are only few remains of the ancient religious house, but the chancel of the Ch. contains some good early windows and some oak stalls. **Longdon** Ch. is of Norm. date, as may be seen by the chancel arch, and possesses an aisle called the Haunch or Stonywell chapel. It contains the tomb of John Stanywell, a Benedictine monk, abbot of Pershore, and suffragan bishop "Poletensis," who was buried here in 1553, with the punning motto, "Educit aquam de petrâ;" also some monuments to the ancient family of Arblaster.

Lysways Hall (Sir Charles Forster, Bart.) belonged to the Arblasters, a Leicestershire family, from the time of Edward III, to the civil war. *Haunch Hall* (S. Stokes, Esq.) was the property of the Ormes, who suffered greatly for their loyalty.

Following the valley of the Trent, the line reaches

At **14 m. Rugeley** (Junct. Stat.). The town lies ¼ m. S.W., and has a stat. on the Cannock branch (Rte. 30). Between this and Colwich the line passes on the E. *Bellamour Hall*, which has superseded an older one, built by Herbert Aston in the 17th centy., and so named by him, because his friends helped him to furnish it; and **Colton** Ch., rebuilt from designs by Street. It contains some sedilia and a curious leaden font. Next is passed the handsome seat of *Bishton Hall* (Mrs. Harland), close to the bridge across the Trent, and

At **17 m.** is **Colwich** (Junct. Stat.). (Hence the N. Staffordshire line runs off, on N. to the Potteries, &c., Rte. 33.) Colwich *Ch.*, which is Dec. and has been well restored, has a fine tower, and in the interior a tomb and effigy of Sir William Wolseley, who was drowned in his coach in a flood, 1728; also tombs of the Ansons, one of them, Lord Anson, the circumnavigator, and one by *Westmacott* to Thomas, Viscount Anson (d. 1818). There are a number of beautiful seats in the neighbourhood of Colwich, both river and railway passing through a succession of lovely parks and woods. To the S. of the village is a romantic and broken region, forming the northern escarpment of Cannock Chase, a spot much resorted to by picnic and pleasure parties. **Wolseley Hall** (Sir C. M. Wolseley, Bart.) was the seat of that family prior to the Norm. Conquest, Edric de Wholseley being described in Domesday Book as holding large possessions previous to the survey. It has a deer-park, and possesses the *chartered* right of a deer-leap from Cannock Chase, the only instance of the kind in England.

Adjoining Wolseley is *Oakedge*, where once upon a time "lived Mrs. Whitby, known by the name of the 'Widow of the Wood,' who was married at midnight in the Ch. of Colwich to Sir William Wolseley, which marriage was set aside, she having previously married another gentleman."

Very soon after leaving Colwich Stat. the train passes through the beautifully wooded park of **Shugborough**, the seat of the Earl of Lichfield, spoken of by Leland as "Shokesborrow Haywood, because it standeth by it." The old house, which was the birthplace of Lord Anson, was purchased by his great-grandfather, Thomas Anson, in the reign of Elizabeth. The present mansion, which is of Italian character, is not seen from the Rly., but is on the rt., situated at the angle where the Sow runs into the Trent. In its course through the park the rly. enters a long tunnel and emerges on the bank of the Sow.

Across the river is **Tixall**, with a small modern Ch., built on very old foundations. **Tixall Park** is the property of the Earl of Shrewsbury, having been purchased by his father, Earl Talbot. The park was contiguous to that of Ingestre, and is united to it (Rte. 32). The present house was built in 1750, in the place of a noble Elizabethan edifice, in which Mary Queen of Scots was confined for a short time, and of which only the gateway, of Jacobean date, remains. This is a curious mixture of styles, embracing in its 3 stories the orders of Doric, Ionic, and Corinthian architecture. The stables are noticeable as being in the form of a crescent. The Astons were formerly possessed of Shugborough, but removed to Tixall in the time of Henry VIII. The house was built in 1580 by Sir Walter Aston; his grandson, of the same name, was the patron of Drayton, the author of 'Poly-Olbion,' who thus mentions the place:

"To Trent by Tixall grac'd, the Astons'
ancient seat,
Which oft the Muse hath found her safe
and sweet retreat."

On *Tixall Heath* are two tumuli, called King's Low and Queen's Low. About a century and a half ago two urns, supposed to be Roman workmanship, were found near them. It was the scene of a tragedy in Henry VII.'s time, when Sir William Chetwynd, one of the ushers to the king, was attacked by Sir Humphrey Stanley (who was jealous of his influence) and a body of 20 retainers, and there and then assassinated.

Drawing near to Stafford, after passing Milford and Brockton (Stat.), is seen on the W. the little Ch. of **Baswich** (formerly Berkleswick), on the bank of the Penk, near where that stream falls into the Sow. In this parish is the hamlet of **Weeping Cross**, ½ m. S. of Baswich, once the place of public execution, but now the site of several handsome residences, including *Weeping Cross* (T. Salt, Esq.).

At **23 m.** the line joins the loop line from Birmingham, and at 23½ m. is **Stafford** (Junct. Stat.) (Rte. 27).

The main line continues N. to Crewe (Rte. 27), a branch to the E. to Uttoxeter, &c. (Rte. 33), whilst the remainder of this route is performed by another branch of the L. & N.-W. Rly. known as the Shropshire Union Rly. It leaves Stafford in a direction due W., passing N. of the wooded knoll on which Stafford Castle is placed, and arrives at

27½ m. Haughton (Stat.). The Ch. has a fine alabaster incised slab, with figure of Nicholas Cranmer, in eucharistic vestments, holding a chalice (d. 1520). He was rector, and built the handsome Perp. tower and St. Katharine's Chapel. The Ch. dates from the 13th centy. It was completely restored, and partly rebuilt, under J. L. Pearson, R.A., in 1887, in memory of the late rector. 3 m. N. is **Ranton**, where an Augustinian priory was founded by Robert Fitz-Noel, temp. Hen. I. The site is occupied by the modern house of Ranton Abbey (the property of the Earl of Lichfield), but some portions of the old priory Ch. are left, consisting of an early Perp. tower, with

Route 32.—Colwich to Stoke-on-Trent. 183

a fine 5-light window, and 2 headless figures below it. In the garden are preserved several carved capitals and bosses, from the ruins. The old vicarage is now a farmhouse; in it is a panelled room of great interest. 2 m. further N. is the pretty village of **Ellenhall**, once the seat of the Noels.

29½ m. Gnosall (Stat.). The *Ch.* (restored in 1888) is a large and fine edifice, ranging from Norm. to Perp. in its architecture, and with a handsome tower in which hang 6 bells brought from Ranton Abbey. The W. front, however, has been miserably disfigured. In the chancel is an altar-tomb, with a figure in armour, probably of the 13th centy.

3 m. N.W. is **Norbury**, a rather remote village, but worth a visit for the sake of the Skrymsher monuments in the Ch., which is of Dec. date, except the modern tower of red brick. One of the effigies, lying under a rich canopy, is a cross-legged figure; there are 3 figures of knights and 2 of ladies. 14th cent.; a *brass* for Halys Boteler, and some 17th and 18th cent. monuments, the latest bearing date 1718. The Manor-house of the Skrymshers, engraved by Plot, was a gabled and moated structure; the site is now occupied by a farm, but the moat can be traced. **High Offley** Ch., 2 m. to the N., also contains monuments to the Skrymshers, as does that of **Forton**, nearer Newport. Tradition says the family sprang from a certain "Hugh the Skirmisher," a mercenary brought into the country by King John in his wars with the barons. They had great possessions in these parts, and Plot tells a story of the lapwings, or pewits, who were "so wholly addicted to this family," that they would build and breed nowhere else but on its lands (Plot, 'Staffordshire,' p. 231). The country around abounds in sheets of water,

the larger called meres, and the smaller pools, and the Pewit pool beside the road to Eccleshall is a well-known spot.

From Gnosall the line runs S.W. through a very pleasant country. At **33 m., 1 m. N.**, are the fine grounds of *Aqualate Hall* (Sir T. F. Boughey, Bart.). The old house, engraved by Plot, was a gabled structure, with a noble gatehouse, and the railing surmounted by busts. Behind the house stretches the largest sheet of water in the county called Aqualate Mere; it is more than a mile in length, and upwards of a third of a mile in breadth. The Shropshire border is now crossed, and at **34½ m.** is ☆**Newport** (Stat.). (See *Handbook for Shropshire*.)

ROUTE 32.

COLWICH TO STOKE-ON-TRENT, BY SANDON, STONE, AND TRENTHAM [CHARTLEY].

NORTH STAFFORDSHIRE RLY.
18¾ m.

Quitting Colwich (Rte. 31). the line ascends the valley of the Trent, having Shugborough Park (Rte. 31) on the W., and on the E. the village of **Great Haywood** (Stat.), where some remains of the old religious house are to be seen, worked up in the modern *Haywood Abbey* (Mrs. Woodroffe); it reaches, at **3 m. Hixon** (Stat.). On W. are the saltworks of Shirleywich and the parks of Tixall (Rte. 31) and **Ingestre**. The latter, the property of the Earl of Shrewsbury, was originally the seat of the Chetwynd family, from whom it passed by marriage in the last centy. to Earl Talbot (a cadet of the Shrewsbury line), whose descendant, the present Earl of Shrewsbury's grandfather, established in 1858 his right to the premier earldom. The most famous of the family was Walter Chetwynd, an antiquary in the 17th centy. The façade of the house is a graceful example of the Jacobean style, with domed turrets and very ornamental bays. The garden front was built by *Nash* for the late Earl Talbot, in good imitation of the old part. The whole building was almost entirely destroyed by fire in 1882, but has since been restored to its original character. A handsome bridge crosses the Trent, affording access from Ingestre to Weston. Adjoining the Hall is Ingestre *Ch.*, a small but handsome building in the Italian style, with balustraded square tower and an altar-screen of carved oak. The old Ch. having suffered much in the civil war, the present edifice was built in 1676 by that doughty Churchman and royalist, Walter Chetwynd. A curious narrative of its consecration is given in Plot. Care was taken, on the day, to have the celebration of every rite of the Church, including a baptism, a marriage, and a burial. The nave contains a handsome monument to Lady Victoria Talbot, sister of the late earl (d. 1856); and in the chancel are several mural tablets to the memory of the Chetwynd family, besides recumbent figures of Charles Chetwynd, second Earl Talbot (d. 1849), and of Henry John Chetwynd, 18th Earl of Shrewsbury and 3rd Earl Talbot (d. 1868).

4½ m. **Weston** (Stat.). The Ch., restored in 1872, is E. E., with good tower and spire, and several painted windows.

[At Weston the N. Stafford line is crossed by the Stafford and Uttoxeter branch of the G. N. Rly., and which may be here described. Starting from Stafford (Rte. 27), which is 6 m. S.W. (4 m. only by road), the rly. at 4 m. reaches **Salt** (Stat.), and then crosses **Hopton Heath**, the scene of a battle, March 19, 1643, when the Parliamentarians were defeated, but the Earl of Northampton, the Royalist commander, was killed. The registers of both Sandon (*post*) and Weston churches contain entries of burials of soldiers who were killed at Hopton.

At 5½ m. is **Ingestre** (Stat.) (*ante*), and at 8 m. is **Chartley** (Stat.). Near to the Stat. is the village of **Stowe**. The *Ch.* is of various dates, with square embattled tower, and has a good Norm. chancel-arch. It contains a canopied tomb for Walter Devereux, first Viscount Hereford (d. 1558) and his 2 wives; he was the grandfather of Elizabeth's favourite, Essex; and a *brass* to Sir Thomas Newport, Essex's steward of the household (1587). There is also a tomb for one of the Ferrers of Chartley. A stone reredos, representing the Last Supper, after Leonardo da Vinci, has recently been added.

At a short distance N., and well seen from the line, standing out boldly from a hill-side, are the ruins of **Chartley Castle**, consisting of a stretch of wall and 2 round towers, all clad with ivy, and almost hidden by aged yews. It was built in 1220 by Ranulph Blundeville, Earl of Chester, on his return from the Holy Land. At a short distance is *Chartley Hall* (Earl Ferrers), an old timber building, still surrounded by a moat, but otherwise differing considerably from its representation in Plot. Elizabeth visited it in 1575, on her way to Stafford, and Mary Queen of Scots was confined in it for a considerable time. Her room is still in existence, and escaped both the conflagrations which twice destroyed the rest of the building.

The park skirts the road to Uttoxeter, and comprises upwards of 1000 acres of heathery, uncultivated land, well stocked with red and fallow deer.

Route 32.—Grindley—Sandon.

There is also a breed of wild cattle, similar to those at Chillingham in Northumberland. " They are cream-coloured rather than pure white, and have black muzzles and ears, with the tips of their horns black also. They are very shy, so that it is not easy to approach them, but they are not dangerous unless wautouly disturbed."—*Garner*. The lovers of old houses will find, a little beyond Chartley Castle, a good specimen in Chartley Manor, gable ended, with broad lattice windows and central porch. Chartley Moss beside the Rly. is a place of interest, especially to entomologists.

10 m. **Grindley** (Stat.) is a hamlet of Stowe, on the little river Blythe. in the midst of a rich grazing district. At 12½ m. the line falls into the Churnet Valley Rly., and at 15 m. Uttoxeter is reached (Rte. 33).]

Returning to the main line, and proceeding towards Sandon, at **6 m.**, and at about 1 m. on E.. is the Ch. of **Gayton**, well restored in 1870. It is of various styles, Trans.-Norm. to Dec., has a very early font, ancient encaustic tiles with the arms of the Ferrers, and a recumbent figure of one of that family, which, when the building was "churchwardenized" a century ago, was banished to the Ch.-yard, the S. aisle where it stood being then pulled down; it is now placed in the chancel.

6½ m. ♂**Sandon** (Stat.). From early times Sandon has been a place of some importance. Originally one of the 5 forests of Staffordshire, it was in possession of William de Malbank at the time of the Conquest, from whom it descended to the Vernons, and then by marriage to the family of Stafford. But in 1339 Margaret Stafford married Thomas Erdeswicke, ancestor of Samson Erdeswicke, the Staffordshire antiquary (d. 1603). Richard Erdeswicke, only son of the antiquary, sold the estate to his half-brother, George Digby, whose daughter Jane (to whom Plot's engraving is dedicated) married Lord Gerard of Bromley. To them succeeded their son, Digby Lord Gerard, whose daughter was wife of the Duke of Hamilton, and brought the estate into that family. This was the Duke slain in the duel in Hyde Park with Lord Mohun (who also died an hour after of his wound) in 1712. Lord Mohun had married a relation of the Duchess, and the quarrel arose out of a lawsuit about the Sandon property. In "Esmond" Thackeray introduces these characters and the duel. Ultimately by purchase it became the property of the noble family of Ryder about 1776.

Sandon Hall (Earl of Harrowby) is a very handsome Jacobean building, from designs by Burn, and has replaced an older Hall, built by the Hamiltons, which was burnt down in 1848. In the park near the Ch. is the site of a yet earlier Hall, surrounded by a moat, and approached by an avenue of trees. It was a half timbered house, with a stone domed gatehouse, as engraved by Plot. But the glory of Sandon is in the grounds, which, both by nature and art, are of the most charming description, the beauties of which the public is liberally admitted to share. The principal objects of interest are the orchard and aquatic houses, and the conservatory, which contains a fine collection of exotics; the Pitt Monument, after Trajan's Pillar (75 ft. high), and erected to the memory of that statesman by Dudley Lord Harrowby; Perceval's Seat, a Gothic temple, in memory of Spencer Perceval, who was assassinated in 1812 in the lobby of the House of Commons; and the Reservoir, which is a copy of the tomb of Helen, daughter of Lysias. The woodland walks, and views from the summit of the park, are lovely in the extreme, embracing the Wrekin, the Clent Hills, Tittensor Heath, Chartley, Lichfield, Cannock Chase, Beaudesert, with a foreground of the woods of Shugborough, Ingestre, Tixall and Wolseley—in fact, a most characteristic and pleasing English landscape.

The *Ch.*, which stands on a hill bordering on the park, consists of a nave with S. aisle, chancel, a N. chapel, and a W. tower; the aisle is separated from the nave by E. E. pillars. It contains a portion of the old roodscreen, and a very curious monument erected by Samson Erdeswicke, the antiquary, a portion of which is said to have been actually made by himself. It is of great height, and of a Corinthian style of architecture, built of freestone, painted to resemble marble. The upper portion is resplendent with blue and gold. Recumbent on the tomb is Erdeswicke himself, in full costume, in which the visitor should notice particularly the painting in imitation of needlework at the edges of the sleeves. The motto on the ledge of the tomb is that of the Vernons, his ancestors, "Ver non semper viret." Above are two arches, each containing a kneeling effigy; these represent his wives, Elizabeth Dikeswell and Maria Neale, by a former marriage wife of Everard Digby, and mother of Sir Everard Digby, the Gunpowder Plot conspirator; the inscription is surrounded by 38 shields of arms. In the chancel are 4 other altar-tombs to members of the same family, male and female, the earliest bearing the date of 1473. In the chancel window is some good ancient stained glass, with shields of the families of Ferrers and Malbank; the latter were probably the founders of the Ch. There are handsome brass and marble monuments in the N. chapel to the 1st and 2nd Earls of Harrowby and their countesses.

11½ m. ☥STONE (Junct. Stat.) is a well-built busy town, in the angle formed by two branches of the N.

Staffordshire Rly. The chief occupation is shoemaking, but malting and brewing are also largely carried on. A house of secular canons was founded here in the 7th centy. by Wulfhere, of Mercia, of which the Ch. existed until 1749, when it fell down, and the present building was erected. Only a few fragments of wall remain, above ground, of the monastic buildings. The parish *Ch.* is dedicated to St. Michael, and has a picture of Michael binding Satan, by *Beechey*, presented by Earl St. Vincent; also a bust by Chantrey of the earl, who is buried in the Ch.-yard. where is also the vault of the Granville family, and a fine altar-tomb, with the effigies, of Sir Thomas Crompton and his wife, saved from the old Ch. On *Stonefield*, a suburb to the N.W., the Duke of Cumberland drew up his army in 1745, while waiting an engagement with the Pretender's forces. The neighbourhood of Stone is varied and pretty, particularly to the N., at **Darlaston**, which is sheltered by a range of hills and the woods of Darlaston Hall (Mrs. Meakin). At **Oulton**, 1 m. E. of Stone, is a modern Abbey, in the chapel of which are some fine painted windows. Near by is *Meaford Hall* (Lady Forester), the birthplace of Earl St. Vincent. On the hill above is *Bury Bank*, an oval British camp, surrounded by a fosse, which is traditionally supposed to have been the site of the ancient Mercian capital. Excavations have been made, but no interments were found—in fact, nothing but some stones and charcoal. A similar mound is to be seen at Saxon Low, on Tittensor Heath, a little further on.

14¼ m. **Barlaston** (Stat.). The *Ch.* has a stone tower, of early date, but the body was rebuilt 1888 as a memorial to the eminent divine, Rev. Prof. J. J. Blunt, author of 'Undesigned Coincidences in the Bible,' who is buried in the Ch.-yard. *Barlaston Hall* (the property of H. J.

Route 32.—Trentham: Church.

Boughton-Adderley, Esq.) is finely placed, and commands an excellent view of Trentham and Tittensor Hills and Obelisk.

16 m. Trentham (Stat.). The magnificent seat of ⚭ **TRENTHAM HALL** (Duke of Sutherland) is about 1 m. to the W. Though so modern-looking, from the lavish display of art and luxury, the Hall is in reality a very old place, a nunnery having existed here in Alfred's time, which rose to some importance in the reign of Henry I., when Ranulf Earl of Chester enlarged it, and made it a priory for Augustinian Canons. The buildings, after the Dissolution, were occupied by the family of Leveson, and doubtless formed the nucleus of the old Hall, which was an Elizabethan mansion, erected by Sir Richard Leveson. An engraving of it is given in Plot, representing the garden-wall and balustrades, which formed the open-work inscription:—

" Carolo Brittanniæ rege, Ricardus Leveson
Eques Balnei ædes hasce hic fieri voluit."

But about the commencement of the last century it was taken down, and a portion of the present building substituted; and at different times it has been enlarged and beautified so as to make it what it now is, one of the most superb mansions in England. Many of the most important alterations were made by the late Duke, in whose time the whole of the front was reconstructed, and the belvedere tower added under the inspection of *Sir Charles Barry.* As it now stands, Trentham has a fine Italian frontage, from the centre of which rises a campanile tower 100 ft. high, which relieves what would otherwise have a somewhat formal appearance; while from the centre project the dining-room on the E., and the conservatory on the W., connected by a gay terrace-garden. The situation of the Hall unfortunately is low. The park is liberally thrown open to the public, by whom (and especially those of the neighbouring Pottery towns) the boon is greatly appreciated. The gardens are of great extent, and have the advantage of a fine sheet of water, fed by a source irrespective of the Trent, which is here polluted by the drainage of the neighbouring Pottery towns. From its banks the ground rises on all sides, fringed with beautiful shrubs and noble timber, until the setting of the picture is completed by the Tittensor and Barlaston hills. The principal features of the gardens are the Terrace garden, the Parterre, the Italian gardens, the Trellis Walk, the Nursery, and the Rainbow Walk. Indeed, look which way one will, it is obvious that landscape gardening has here been carried to the highest pitch, and every advantage that wood and water can give has been used as accessory to the scene. The rhododendron flourishes in the park with immense vigour, but it is a curious fact that neither the laurustinus, Irish arbutus, nor common laurel, will grow at Trentham.

The *Ch.* adjoins the N. side of the Hall, and serves as a private chapel. It is an E. E. edifice, and was completely restored in 1844 by the 2nd Duke of Sutherland, when care was taken not to displace the ancient Norm. piers, which were supposed to have been built by Ranulf, Earl of Chester. The nave and aisles are divided from the chancel by a beautifully carved Jacobean oak screen, containing goats' heads and the arms of the Levesons (three laurel-leaves). There are several monuments and brasses to members of the same family, and a beautiful monument to Harriet, Duchess of Sutherland, with an inscription by Mr. Gladstone. The burial-ground is at some distance on the high road, and contains a stately mausoleum erected in 1807 by the Marquis of Stafford, who in 1833 was created Duke of Sutherland.

The tourist should not omit to extend his excursion to Tittensor Heath, which at its S. end contains some interesting "lows," such as Saxon Low and Bury Bank (*ante*). Even if antiquarian relics have no charm for him, he can at all events enjoy the magnificent view from the Monument Hill, on which is a colossal statue of the late duke. The prospect embraces a large extent of country, from the Shropshire Wrekin to the North Staffordshire hills, more or less dotted with thriving Pottery towns, such as Longton, Stoke, Shelton, Hanley, and Burslem (Rte. 33), backed in the distance by Mow Cop and the hills near Macclesfield.

The traveller, leaving Trentham Stat., soon bids adieu to green fields and hedges as he nears the smoky Pottery district.

17 m. on E. are **Blurton** and **Dresden**, both busy places, and the latter remarkable for its brick Ch., designed by *Scott*, which has a bell-turret of Minton's ornamental tiles.

18¾ m. **Stoke - on - Trent** (Stat.) (Rte. 33).

ROUTE 33.

CREWE TO BURTON-ON-TRENT, BY STOKE-ON-TRENT, UTTOXETER, AND TUTBURY [THE POTTERIES].

N. STAFFORDSHIRE RLY. (LOOP LINE). 47 m.

For the country from Crewe to Harecastle Junction for Kidsgrove, see *Handbook for Cheshire*.

8½ m. **Harecastle** (Junct. Stat.), where the line from Crewe on W. unites with that on E. from Maccles-field. Just before reaching the stat. the line passes on E. **Linley Wood** (the Misses Marsh Caldwell). At a short distance W. is the colliery village of **Talke**, commonly known as **Talke-o'-th'-Hill**, as it stands on very high ground, from which, it is asserted, that even Snowdon is sometimes to be seen. The place has gained a mournful celebrity from a colliery explosion in the year 1866, by which 91 lives were lost, and another in 1875 in the Bunker's Hill coalpits, in which 42 men were killed. The village of **Kidsgrove** is a place of modern growth, mainly dependant on the great colliery and iron-works of Clough Hall. Clough Hall is now a public pleasure resort.

The traveller, if he has perforce to wait for a train at Harecastle, can pleasantly pass the time by inspecting the canal-works at the tunnel, which in its day was considered the *chef-d'œuvre* of Brindley, the great Staffordshire engineer. The *Grand Trunk Canal*, which connects the Trent and the Mersey, and in fact is the great waterway for all the English midland counties, is unquestionably one of the most important works of the kind ever executed. "The Harecastle tunnel, which is 2880 yards long, was constructed only 9 ft. wide and 12 ft. high. The most extensive ridge of country to be penetrated was at Harecastle, involving by far the most difficult work in the whole undertaking. This ridge is but a continuation of the high ground forming the backbone of England. The flat county of Chester, which looks almost as level as a bowling-green when viewed from the high ground near New Chapel, seems to form a deep bay in the land, its innermost point being immediately under the village of Harecastle. That Brindley was correct in determining to form his tunnel at this point has since been confirmed by the survey of Telford, who there constructed his parallel tunnel for the same canal, and still more recently by the engineers of the North Staffordshire Rly., who have also formed their railway tunnel nearly parallel with the line of both canals."—*Smiles*. So great did the traffic become on the canal that there was one perpetual block at this tunnel, which from its low and narrow size could only be traversed by the laborious process of " legging," viz. by the propulsion of the barge by means of the boatmen's legs against the roof of the tunnel; and as bargees were then, as now, not of the most patient or refined habits, terrible rows took place. It was determined therefore to make another tunnel, which Telford did, of a size sufficiently large to enable horses to work the traffic. The scene at the mouth of the tunnel, with Kidsgrove Ch. at the back, is exceedingly wild and picturesque; in fact, the whole of this part of the district is old-world and quaint, and must have been charming before the establishment of ironworks and collieries.

About 2 m. E. of Harecastle is **New Chapel**, where Brindley, who did so much for this country, lies buried; and where, according to tradition, lived the Harmonious Blacksmith, whose quick and regular strokes on the anvil attracted the attention of Handel, then staying at Turnhurst, a neighbouring mansion afterwards occupied by Brindley, and where he died, Sept. 27, 1772.

The Rly. goes through several deep cuttings before it enters the Pottery district, and after passing Goldenhill (Stat.) and Pitts Hill (Stat.), arrives at

10½ m. ♂**Tunstall** (Stat.), a busy market-town, of modern growth. The inhabitants are almost entirely occupied in the manufacture of earthenware and in the iron trade. the Goldendale ironworks employing a large number of hands. The churches are modern, and have arisen with the necessities of the town, which is, on the whole, well built, and contains a fair amount of public buildings. The Town Hall, erected in 1883, is a handsome structure in the Dutch Renaissance style, and comprises capacious assembly and court rooms. The Victoria Institute, erected to commemorate the Jubilee of the Queen, includes a Free Library and Schools of Science and Art.

12¼ m. ♂**Burslem** (Stat.). This town has increased very rapidly within the last few years. But it must not be thought that Burslem is a modern town, for it was known in the 'Domesday Book' as Barcardeslim; and in subsequent years was the earliest place in the district to give signs of its pre-eminence in its present trade. In the time of the Stuarts it was called the Butter Pottery, owing to the fact that there was a small establishment for the manufacture of butter-pots.

Plot writes in 1686: " The greatest pottery they have in this county is carried on at Burslem, near Newcastle-under-Lyme, where for making several sorts of pots they have as many different sorts of clay which they dig round about the town all within half a mile's distance, the best being found near the coal, and are distinguished by their colours and uses." At the end of the 17th centy. the trade of Burslem included the manufacture of dishes, tygs, and other articles, all coloured, the white clay not being introduced till later on, when it was found in Cornwall and brought to Staffordshire. In the years 1710-15 Burslem contained 43 manufactories. These were no doubt merely small places carried on by families, they gradually became extinct and larger factories succeeded them. In 1759 Josiah Wedgwood, a native of the place (b. 1730; d. 1795), began his first pottery in a small manufactory called Ivy House Works; and though he afterwards removed his works to Etruria (*post*), the town has continued to prosper. At present it is a flourishing place, dependent, more or less, on some 60 earthenware and pottery establishments, dotted about the town and the suburbs of Cobridge and Longport. The mounds of broken pottery give a squalid appearance, but Burslem is well built and well arranged. It contains a handsome Town-hall, in Italian architecture, together with the "Wedgwood Memorial," an Italian Gothic building, by Edgar, a pupil of Scott, designed so as to present an example of constructive ceramic architecture, of which the first stone was laid by Mr. Gladstone in 1863. It contains a Free Library, School of Science and Art, and a Museum. A steam tramway connects the town with Hanley, Stoke, and Longton. A short distance E. of Burslem was the Cistercian Abbey of Hulton, founded in 1223 by Henry de Audley; but no remains exist.

After passing **Cobridge** (Stat.), the line reaches

At **14 m.** ↯**Hanley** (Stat.), a municipal and County Borough, which including the township of Shelton and the villages of Etruria and Northwood, is the largest and most populous pottery town. It is placed on a hill which commands an extensive tract of country; but the picturesque is sadly interfered with by the smoke from ironworks, collieries, and potteries. The Town Hall, formerly the Queen's Hotel, is a spacious building, and at the rear of it is a fine Assembly Room, called the Victoria Hall, erected in 1887. The Mechanics Institute has been converted into a Free Library and Museum. There is a good School of Art adjoining them.

Shelton is to a considerable extent dependent on the enormous bar-ironworks of Lord Granville. It has a fine Ch., remarkable for its tower.

At Old Shelton Hall, almost destroyed by fire in 1853, was born Elijah Fenton, the Staffordshire poet, 1683, who had a share in the translation of Pope's Homer.

15 m. Etruria (Stat.). This pottery village, founded by Wedgwood, is a part of the municipal borough of Hanley. No one in the district was so inventive as he, of new mixtures and wares. To him the trade is indebted for terra-cotta resembling granite or porphyry; basaltes, or black porcelain biscuit; white porcelain biscuit; jasper, which is like the last, but possesses the property of receiving colour through its substance. Wedgwood's greatest discovery, however, was his "Queen's ware," composed of the whitest clays mixed with a due proportion of flint, and celebrated for its extreme purity and durability. For this he obtained the appellation of the "Queen's Potter." Finding the works at Burslem too limited for his business, he purchased the Ridge-house estate, on the bank of the Grand Trunk Canal, which he had greatly contributed to form, and there he, in 1769, began the establishment of a large work and village, which he called Etruria, after the Etruscan district of that name. He also built *Etruria Hall*, a fine large brick mansion to the W. of the loop line and E. of the main line of the Rly. The house contains the cellars in which Wedgwood mixed his materials in solitude, so as to preserve his valuable trade secrets. The pottery establishment of Etruria is still in the hands of the Wedgwood family, but, although beautiful productions are still turned out from it, the manufactory has not, in these days of competition, the same prestige as formerly.

1½ m. W. of Etruria, and occupying a magnificent position on the hill-side, is **Wolstanton** Ch., one of the oldest in the county, and formerly possessed by the Earls of Lancaster, from whom it descended to John of Gaunt. Having fallen into decay, it was very carefully restored in 1862. As it now stands it consists of nave, aisles, and chancel, with a massive W. tower, from which rises a lofty tapering spire. The base of the spire has pinnacles at 3 of the angles, and a stair turret is carried up to serve as a 4th. The interior of the Ch. contains some beautiful piers and arches of the 13th centy., and in the chancel are sedilia and a piscina. There are also some Elizabethan and other monuments to the family of Sneyd, who have been proprietors in this parish for many generations. There is a very fine view from the Ch.-yard, extending all over the Pottery district.

The direct line after leaving Harecastle passes **Chatterley** (Stat.) and **Longport** (Stat. for Wolstanton), and joins the loop line at Etruria. After crossing the Stoke and Market Drayton Branch (Rte. 37), it soon arrives at

17 m. ⚑ STOKE-ON-TRENT (Junct. Stat.). The Stat. and offices of the North Staffordshire Rly. are of red brick, in the Elizabethan style. Opposite is the hotel, occupying one side of Winton Square, in the centre of which is a fine bronze statue of Wedgwood, by Davis, erected by public subscription in 1863.

Stoke lies almost entirely to the south of the Rly., and consists more of a long straggling series of townlets than of one distinct and compact town. There are, however, several good streets, and some handsome public buildings, as the Town-hall, the School of Science and Art, which is a Memorial to the late Herbert Minton, and a Free Library and Museum adjoining. *St. Peter's Ch.* is a very good specimen of modern E. E.: it was built in 1830, and has a handsome pinnacled tower. The chancel is larger than was then usual, and has been well arranged. In it is a mural monument to Wedgwood, with a bronze bust by *Flaxman*, which served as a model for the statue in the square. Opposite are the monuments of the elder and younger Spodes (d. 1827 and 1829), and in the body of the Ch. a *brass* to T. Minton (d. 1836). The slabs of earthenware, arranged diamond fashion round the church, with the names of the deceased, are particularly neat. The ch.-yard, in which is an epitaph to the father of Elijah Fenton, the poet, occupies one side of a square; on the other is the Townhall. The Market-hall is a large and commodious building.

Stoke is generally considered the show-place of the Pottery district, mainly owing to the beautiful collections of ceramic art formed by the Copelands and the Mintons, who are celebrated throughout the world for their exquisite productions. The factory of the latter was established in 1789 by Thomas Minton, of Caughley, and is of great celebrity.

A very beautiful Gothic *Ch.* (Sir G. G. Scott, architect) was erected at **Hartshill**, on a commanding site 1 m. N. of Stoke, by Mr. H. Minton, 1843. Not far from it is the range of buildings of the North Staffordshire Infirmary. The Rom. Cath. Ch. and convent, a picturesque pile of Gothic buildings, is prominent from the Rly. on the woody hill joining Stoke to Hartshill.

18½ m. Fenton (Stat.), a township of extensive area on the outskirt of Stoke. It has a rapidly increasing population, and numerous earthenware manufactories.

19½ m. Longton (Stat.), the last of the Pottery towns. It has 3 churches, and a handsome Town-hall, the lower part serving as a covered market, and one of the wings accommodating the

Athenæum. The business of the place is principally cheap china and earthenware, but brewing and brick-making are also largely carried on.

The traveller will notice that the district known as the Potteries is curiously concentrated and limited, embracing an area of only about 10 m. in length by 2 in width. But every available yard in this ground is densely populated, and occupied by the staple trade, which includes not only earthenware-factories proper, but also colour-mills and flint-mills, together with collieries and ironworks as accessories. The whole manufacture exhibits a singular instance of the concentration of trade; for, with the exception of coal, and the coarse clay used to make the "saggars" (? safe-guards) or large pans in which the earthenware is burnt, almost everything is brought from afar—the china-clay from Cornwall, and the flints from the south coast of England, and from France. The clay comes by sea from the Cornish coast to Runcorn, whence it is brought in enormous quantities by barge along the Grand Trunk Canal. The condition of the population of this district can vie with any other in order and regularity, as well as the intelligence of the artizans. Indeed, the very nature of the art or trade in which they are engaged requires a high standard of cultivation, and the means for this are liberally supplied by Free Libraries and Schools of Art in almost every town.

Leaving Longton the line passes through a tunnel, and emerges into the country. No manufactures are in sight, and the contrast between the dirt and smoke of the towns and the green fields is very marked.

22¾ m. **Blyth Bridge** (Stat.). This is a hamlet of Dilhorne, and a pleasant village. *Dilhorne Hall* (Sir M. E. Buller, Bart.). 1½ m. N. of the Stat. is **Caverswall**, where the Ch., restored in 1880, has a monument by *Chantrey* to Lady St. Vincent, and another to Sir William de Caverswall, the builder of the castle, temp. Edw. I. (1275), which is styled by Leland " the prati pile of Carswell." The Castle seems to have fallen into ruin, and in 1643 Matthew Cradock erected the present building on the same site. " It is of plain character, with a massive tower in good imitation of a mediæval castle, with a moat and wall of enceinte, with buttresses and corner turrets" (Parker's 'Dom. Arch.'). It was for some time occupied by a community of nuns, and there is a Rom. Cath. Ch. in the grounds. The tomb of the founder bears the following inscription:—

" Castri structor eram, domibus fossisque
   cemento
Vivis dans operam, nunc claudor in hoc
   monumento."

To which an English version succeeds, of later date :—

" William of Carswall here lye I,
That built this castle and pooles herebye;
William of Carswall, here thou mayst lye,
But thy castle is down, and thy pooles are
   drye."

Cheadle is 4 m. N.E. (Rte. 35).

24½ m. **Cresswell** (Stat.). ½ m. N. is **Draycott-in-the-Moors**, where is a fine Dec. *Ch.*; the chancel, which has been rebuilt, contains a cross-legged effigy, and several later tombs, all ascribed to the Draycott family. One of them is to Anthony Draycott, archdeacon of Huntingdon and prebend of Lichfield, who was deprived of his preferments and imprisoned in the Fleet in 1560; he died in 1571. Their seat was at Painsley Hall, where the moated site is now occupied by a farmhouse.

27¾ m. **Leigh** (Stat.). The river Blythe is here crossed. The *Ch.* stands finely on a hill to the E. It is cruciform, with a massive central tower which stands on four

Route 33.—Bramshall—Uttoxeter.

fine 14th-century arches, and has the unusual feature of projecting battlements. The nave with its aisles was exactly restored in 1845, but the features of the transepts were only partially retained, and the chancel almost entirely altered. The date of the Ch. then existing was about 1370, and the work, chiefly Dec., had a few Perp. additions as well as some Transition remains. From remains which have been dug up in the Ch.-yard, it is probable that the former building was of Norm. date. There is some interesting old glass in the most eastern of the N. and S. windows of the chancel. In the S. transept is a stately tomb with recumbent figures of a banneret of the Field of Spurs, Sir John Aston and his wife Dame Joan, granddaughter of Sir T. Littleton, bearing the date 1523, and probably of Italian workmanship.

About 1½ m. N.E. is the Ch. of **Checkley**, dating from 1190 with later additions. The base of the tower is Norm. The windows of the large E.E. chancel contain some stained glass of the 13th cent. representing among other subjects the murder of Thomas à Becket and the penance of Henry II., and having a border of fleur-de-lis and castles, the cognizance of Eleanor, Queen of Edward I. There are also numerous coats of arms of a later date, and some small glass medallions, said to have been in the old Rectory house, emblematic of the months, February, netting, March, pruning, April, planting, May, flowers, July, mowing, October, swine feeding, and others. There are an alabaster tomb of the 16th cent. with recumbent effigies of Godfrey and Margaret Foljambe, an alabaster slab said to cover the remains of Thomas Chawner, last Abbot of Croxden, and another, with a curious inscription, of Rev. James Whitehall. The carved font is Norm., and some old oak seats have the arms of

[*Derby, &c.*]

the Draycots. In the Ch.-yard are three upright stones, two of them with interlaced ornamentation. They are Saxon, but of uncertain date and origin, probably "praying stones" set up by the missionaries before the first church was built.

30¾ m. **Bramshall.** The Ch. is a plain edifice, rebuilt in 1835 by Lord Willoughby de Broke, in whose family (Verney) the manor, and the greater part of the parish has been vested from a very remote period. 1 m. S., in the parish of Uttoxeter, is *Loxley Hall.* The house is partly modern, but a recollection of the old mansion is preserved in panels on the wall of the fine entrance hall: these are figures of the Apostles and Evangelists, and the armorial bearings of James I. and his sons, together with those of many Staffordshire families; the date is 1607, and is said to commemorate a royal visit. About the time of Edward III. Loxley passed into the family of Kynnersley by marriage of John de Kynnersley with Joanna, daughter and heiress of Thomas de Ferrers of Loxley. Since that time the manor and estate of Loxley descended, in regular succession, from father to son, to Clement Kynnersley, who died in 1815 without male issue, and bequeathed his estates to his nephew, Thomas Sneyd, on condition of his assuming the name and arms of Kynnersley in addition to those of Sneyd, in which family it still remains. According to tradition, Loxley was the birthplace of Robin Hood, and an ancient horn preserved at the hall goes by his name; it bears the arms of the Ferrers.

At a short distance beyond Bramshall, the Stafford and Uttoxeter line (Rte. 32) falls in, and the Rly. arrives at

33½ m. ₰**Uttoxeter** (Bridge-st. Stat. There is also a stat. at Dove Bank, on the Burton and Maccles-

O

field Line (Rte. 34). Locally Utcheter, Uxeter, Utceter, or sometimes Toxeter. This is a well-built little town, pleasantly placed on elevated ground near the river Dove. Some Roman remains have been found in its neighbourhood. Camden considered it to represent the Etocetum of Antoninus, but this has been disproved. At Stramshall, 1½ m. N.W., are tracts of early earthworks. Uttoxeter was a part of the honour of Tutbury, and Robert de Ferrers made it a free borough, in the time of Stephen. Afterwards it passed to the Dukes of Lancaster, and John of Gaunt bestowed a part of the forest of Needwood on its burgesses. Its chief trade is in the dairy produce of the rich pastures around, but recently a manufactory of agricultural implements and a factory for corset-making employ many hands. In the centre of the town is the Market-place, where Michael Johnson exposed his books for sale, and where his son 50 years after underwent his self-imposed penance; a representation of the occurrence taken from his statue at Lichfield is inserted in the conduit. The body of the Ch. was rebuilt in Dec. style in 1828, but the fine original tower and spire, 180 ft. high, remain. There are 2 altar-tombs preserved, belonging to the Kynnersleys of Loxley, and another, with the figure of a nun, presumably of the same family; other monuments, to the Mynors, hereditary stewards of Tutbury, which existed in the time of Shaw (1794), have perished. There is a long black-letter inscription for the Rev. Thos. Lightfoot (the father of the celebrated Hebrew scholar), who was incumbent of the Ch. for 36 years. Thomas Allen, the mathematician, Sir Simon Degge, the Staffordshire antiquary, Admiral Lord Gardner, and Mary Howitt, the authoress, were all born at Uttoxeter. Alleyn founded the Grammar School in 1558; he was patronised by Leicester, and, like Dr. Dee, he lay under the stigma of practising magic arts for his service.

At 34½ m. the line joins the Churnet Valley Rly. which runs N. (Rte. 35). On the opposite, or Derbyshire side, of the Dove, are **Doveridge** village and Hall, the property of Lord Waterpark. For the remainder of the distance the Rly. keeps close to the side of the Dove, alternating between the counties of Stafford and Derby.

36¼ m. Marchington (Stat.). The Ch. is a modern brick building, but contains a fine altar-tomb for Sir Walter Vernon (d. 1592). The country at the back of the village is beautifully wooded and broken, being in fact the northern escarpment of Needham Forest.

38 m. Sudbury (Stat.). Across the river, in Derbyshire, is *Sudbury Hall* (Lord Vernon), a fine Elizabethan house, in which the late Queen Adelaide resided for some years. In the course of drainage operations here, human and animal remains, apparently belonging to a very remote period, were discovered. A memorial window was placed in the Ch. in 1853 by the Queen and Prince Consort to Mr. G. E. Anson, keeper of the privy purse, who was a native of Sudbury. There are also two 13th cent. monuments, and a fine reredos erected in memory of the late Lord Vernon.

In **Somersall** Ch. (2½ m.) there is a fine Norm. font. The old Hall, belonging to the Fitzherbert family, is a picturesque half-timbered building. At **Marston Montgomery**, 2 m. further N., the Ch. has a Saxon chancel arch.

2½ m. S.E. of the stat. on the high ground of Needwood, is **Hanbury**, a very pleasant village. The Ch. (restored 1883) owes its origin to St.

Werburgh, daughter of Wulfere, king of Mercia, and the niece of King Ethelbert, who here founded a nunnery, in which she was buried; but owing to the ravages of the Danes in the 10th cent., her remains were removed to Chester. It was restored in 1849, when fragments of several incised slabs of the 14th cent. were discovered, used as bonding stones; they are now preserved in the nave. There are a cross-legged effigy of Sir John de Hanbury; some curious figures of the Agards, the husband in a cloak and frill, and the wife and daughter with ruffs and broad-brimmed hats (d. 1608, 1628); and a recumbent figure of Charles Egerton, ranger of Needwood in the civil war (d. 1662). Burton, the antiquary, is also buried in the Ch.; and there is a memorial window to the Prince Consort, much of the parish belonging to the Duchy of Lancaster. The tourist should ascend the Ch. tower, for the sake of the view, which is varied and beautiful, and extends as far as Belvoir on the E., at least 40 m. distant, and the Wrekin on the W.

A short distance E. of Sudbury the line crosses the Dove, which frequently overflows its banks, rendering them so fertile that it is a local saying

"In April Dove's flood
Is worth a king's good."

On N. is **Scropton**, a Derbyshire village with a handsome Ch., and on S. *Fauld Hall* (now a farmhouse), where the family of Burton the antiquary was settled for several generations, and where he died in 1645. Nearing Tutbury, the ruins of the castle have a very imposing appearance on their height above the Dove.

41½ m. ₰**Tutbury** (Stat. on the Derbyshire side of the river) was a stronghold of the Mercian kings, and in the 11th cent. it belonged to Ulfric Spot, the founder of Burton Abbey (Rte. 29). By William I. it was bestowed on Henry de Ferrers, and the honour of Tutbury, a tract of country of very large extent, remained in his family until forfeited by Robert de Ferrers, Earl of Derby, in 1266. It was by Henry III. given to his son Edmund Earl of Lancaster, and it still forms part of the duchy.

The Castle was built by Henry de Ferrers, but was in after times greatly added to by John of Gaunt, who often made it his residence. In 1569 Mary Queen of Scots was removed from Bolton Castle, in Yorkshire, to Tutbury, under custody of George Earl of Shrewsbury, and, with one or two changes, remained there till 1572. The castle was a considerable royal garrison in the civil war, and was one of the last to surrender; it was dismantled and pulled down after its capture by the Parliamentary General Brereton in 1646. The existing gateway and part of the northern front (afterwards occupied by Mary Queen of Scots) were built by John of Gaunt, but strengthened with massive bastions in the time of Charles I. The circuit of the walls includes an area of 3 acres, known as the Tilt-yard; within is a conical mound, once crowned by the keep, which has disappeared, and has been replaced by an artificial ruin called Julius' Tower. "There seems little difference of date and style between the great gateway of the castle and some of the buildings on the opposite side of the court, both being originally of rich Perp. architecture. At the latter side remain the walls of two fine halls, with windows at each end, their fireplaces having jambs adorned with animals: the two rooms below these halls were groined."

Thomas 2nd Earl of Lancaster, the chief of the barons who opposed Edward II. and his favourite in 1322, was driven out of Tutbury Castle by the royal' forces. In crossing the Dove a little below Tutbury, his military chest containing a large sum of money was dropped and lost. In 1831 a considerable quantity of gravel being removed from the bed of the river, several pieces of silver coin were found by workmen about 60 yards below the bridge, and on another occasion some thousands. On advancing up the river, the grand deposit was reached, 150 coming up on a single shovel. The coins were mostly of Henry III., Edward I. and II., but Scotch and foreign pieces also occurred, the whole number being estimated at 100,000. A portion was claimed as treasure-trove by the Crown, and these are now preserved in the British Museum.

The Ch., which is the nave of De Ferrers' foundation, with subsequent additions, is a large and handsome edifice, at a short distance W. of the castle. The nave is Norm., with a very rich W. doorway; the S. aisle is E. E., and the N. aisle a modern imitation of the same style. There is also a square embattled tower. In 1863-68 the church was restored by Sir Oswald Mosley, when an upsidal chancel (E. E.) was added by *Street*.

Tutbury was formerly celebrated for its sport of bull-running:

" The battle was fought near to Titbury town
Where the bagpiper baited the bull,"

which John of Gaunt is said to have instituted, also the Wichnor and other jocular tenures (Rte. 29) for the amusement of his Spanish bride. The town acquired some notoriety from the tricks of one Anne Moore, the "fasting woman," who dwelt there in 1817, and so plausibly acted her part as to induce people to imagine that she could live without food.

1 m. beyond Tutbury is **Marston-on-the-Dove**; the E. E. Ch. has a good spire, and a Norm. font. In the hamlet of **Hilton**, ½ m. E., is a timbered mansion, gabled and quaintly ornamented, called Wakelyn, which is worth seeing. Near Marston a branch line goes off E. to join the Midland Rly. at Willington (Rte. 1), but the main line crosses the Dove.

At **43 m.** it passes on W. **Rolleston Hall** (Sir Oswald Mosley), with the Ch. adjoining. The Hall, which was greatly damaged by fire in 1871, was rebuilt, and is a very handsome modern building, on a site that was occupied by the Rollestons from the 13th to the 17th centy. The estate was bought in the time of James I. by Sir Edward Mosley, Attorney-General for the Duchy of Lancaster. The *Ch.*, which has a good spire, is mainly Dec., but has a Norm. door. There are an effigy of an ecclesiastic, and monuments of the Rolleston and Mosley families. 1 m. E. is Dovecliff House (W. J. Smith, Esq.). At **45 m.** **Stretton** is passed, where are extensive ironworks, and the line runs into the Midland Rly. about ¾ m. before reaching at

47 m. Burton-on-Trent (Rte. 29).

ROUTE 34.

UTTOXETER TO BUXTON, BY ASHBOURNE AND HARTINGTON [DOVEDALE].

N. STAFF. RLY. AND ROAD. 31 m.

This very picturesque route is on the border of the two counties of Stafford and Derby, and frequently crosses the Dove, which divides them. The rly. is only available to Ashbourne (11 m.).

For **Uttoxeter**, see Rte. 33.

Leaving the town by the Churnet Valley line, the Rly. keeps near the Dove for the whole distance. On E. (in Derbyshire) is the village of **Doveridge**, the lofty spire of the Ch. showing well on the hill, and the grounds of Doveridge Hall (property of Lord Waterpark) extending to the river. At 1 m. on E., but in Staffordshire, is Crakemarsh Hall (C. T. Cavendish, Esq.); the village is mentioned in Domesday as a possession of Earl Algar of Mercia.

4 m. Rocester (Junct. Stat.). Hence the Churnet Valley Line runs N. to Alton, Leek, &c. (Rte. 35), but the Ashbourne branch proceeds N.E. to

6 m. Norbury (Stat.). The Ch. is a fine structure, mainly Perp., with a Dec. chancel. It has some good early glass, and several tombs and brasses of the Fitzherberts. The monument of Sir Anthony Fitzherbert, the judge of Henry VIII.'s time (d. 1538), in full judicial costume, with his wife in a heraldic mantle, should be noticed.

1 m. W. is **Ellastone**, a very extensive parish, and is the reputed scene of 'Adam Bede.' by George Eliot. The Perp. Ch. has an embattled tower, and contains the altar-tomb of Sir Richard Fleetwood of Calwich (temp. Charles II.). N. of Ellastone is the limestone range of Weever, where, at *Moat in Ribden*, is a quadrangular hillock within a trench, supposed to be a British barrow. In Ellastone parish are several fine seats, as *Wootton Park* (Mrs. Cathcart), with an old mansion in the style of Inigo Jones, the grounds of which are romantic and beautiful; and *Wootton Hall* (Sir H. Hope-Edwardes, Bart.), where Jean Jacques Rousseau resided for more than a year. Also in the parish is *Stanton*, the birthplace of Gilbert Sheldon, Archbishop of Canterbury,

on whom Bishop Hacket wrote the following lines:—

" Sheldonus ille Præsulum primus pater
Hos inter ortus aspicit lucem Lares;
O ter beatam Stantonis villæ casam!
Cui cuncta possum invidere marmora."

They still hang in a bedroom in the farmhouse where Sheldon was born.

Nearer to the river Dove is *Calwich Abbey* (A. C. Duncombe, Esq.), a modern mansion, built in 1848. It stands near the site of a cell founded in the time of Stephen by Nicholas Fitz-Nigel, and bestowed on the Abbey of Rocester. At the Dissolution the property was purchased by one of the Fleetwoods, and came afterwards to the Granvilles, who built a house (now pulled down) that was often visited by Handel, and where he is said to have composed a large portion of his "Messiah."

8 m. On E. **Snelston**, with a Perp. Ch. with low square tower. Snelston Hall (John Harrison, Esq.). On the W. side of the river is the village of **Church Mayfield**, where Moore wrote his ' Lalla Rookh.' The solitary cottage still stands in High Mayfield in which the poet lived, and where he was visited by Rogers. Mayfield Ch. contains many interesting Norm. details, and particularly a Norm. door in the S. porch, the margin of the arch being cut into lozenge-like cavities, with trefoils between.

10 m. Clifton (Stat.). The *Ch.* is a small modern E. E. edifice.

11 m. ☥Ashbourne (Stat.), anciently spelt Esseburne, is a very prettily-situated town, situated on the Henmore or Scholebrooke. It was said by Cotton to be famous for the best malt and the worst ale in England. This place is frequently selected as the headquarters whence to explore the lovely scenery of Dovedale. It consists mainly of one long street, at the foot of which, opposite the Stat., is the *Ch.* placed under the brow of a hill overlooking the valley of the Dove, from which, however, it is distant a full 1½ m. The Ch., approached through an avenue of limes, is a very fine cruciform building, principally E. E., with later additions, and noticeable for possessing a S. aisle only. From the centre rises a tower and fine octagonal spire, 212 ft. in height, called in the district the Pride of the Peak. The E. window of the chancel is a 7-light Perp. window, and there are in the Cokayne chapel some particularly beautiful triple lancets. The nave is E. Dec. In the vestry is a marble tablet, containing an inscription, on brass, to the effect that the Ch. was dedicated to St. Oswald by Hugh de Pateshull, Bishop of Coventry and Lichfield, in 1241.

In the chancel are monuments to the Bainbrigges, Knivetons, and Erringtons; also in the N. transept several to the Cokayne family who flourished from the 14th to the 17th centy. One of them, Sir Thomas Cokayne, according to the epitaph :—

"was a knight so worshipfull,
So virtuous, wyse, and pitifull;
His dedes deserve that his good name
Lyve here in everlasting fame."

Of the Boothby monuments, notice the sculptured figure, by *Banks*, of Penelope, only child of Sir Brooke Boothby (d. 1791), and the melancholy inscription (with others in Latin, French, and Italian):—

"She was in form and intellect most exquisite. The unfortunate parents ventured their all on this frail bark, and the wreck was total."

In the N. transept is an Elizabethan alabaster altar-tomb to Sir Humphrey Bradburne and his wife.

The Grammar-school is a picturesque 16th-centy. building, and the Almshouses of Christopher Pegg, founded 1669, are worthy of notice. Opposite the school is the house where the Rev. Dr. Taylor, the intimate friend of Johnson, lived for many years.

Ashbourne Hall (Mrs. Frank), through the grounds of which the Henmore Brook flows, was the seat of the Cokayne family, from the time of Stephen, but was sold by Sir Aston Cokayne, the author of several poems and plays, shortly before his death in 1683, to the Boothby family, in whose possession it remained till the present century. Sir Aston was the last male heir of the elder line of his family. His great grandfather, Sir Thomas Cokayne, was also an author, having published, in 1591, "A short treatise of Hunting," embellished with woodcuts, and now of extreme rarity. The Hall was occupied by Prince Charles during his visit to Derbyshire in 1745, and one of the doors still shows the name of the officer to whom the room was appropriated. Other seats in the neighbourhood are—*Osmaston Manor* (Sir A. B. Walker, Bart.), a curious pile, with a single tower-like chimney, on the Derby road, and *Okeover Hall* (H. C. Okeover, Esq.), in Staffordshire (*post*).

The high road from Ashbourne to Buxton runs in its southern part parallel with Dovedale, but on the wrong side of the hill to allow the tourist to see its beauties.

At **13 m.** is **Fenny Bentley**, where are some remains of an old castle of the Beresfords, now a farmhouse. The *Ch.* has been enlarged, but fortunately the very fine Perp. screen has been preserved. In the chancel are several monuments of the Beresfords, the most noticeable of which is a high tomb, obviously remade in the 17th cent., but bearing the effigy of Sir Thomas Beresford, who fought at Agincourt, and who lived to send a troop of his own sons and retainers to the wars of the Roses. *Bentley Brook*, which runs into the

Dove below Ashbourne, is celebrated in 'The Complete Angler' as "full of very good trout and grayling, but so encumbered with wood in many places as to be troublesome to an angler."

15 m. Tissington. The *Hall* (Sir W. Fitz-Herbert, Bart.) is an Elizabethan mansion of stone, approached by an avenue. In the oak-panelled dining-room is a noble chimney-piece of Hopton stone reaching to the ceiling. There are some fine paintings by Murillo, Rubens, Cuyp, Sir Joshua Reynolds, and Gainsborough, and amongst the family portraits two by Angelica Kauffman, and one of Mrs. Meynell, of whom Dr. Johnson said that she possessed the best understanding he had ever met with in any human being. The Rev. Richard Greaves, author of the 'Spiritual Quixote,' once resided at the Hall, and has introduced in that work, written here, many allusions to persons and things in the vicinity. In the Ch., which has some Norm. portions, are monuments of the Fitz-Herberts, who have possessed the estate from the time of Henry IV. Judge Fitzherbert, author of the 'Natura Brevium,' was born here in 1458; he is buried at Norbury (*ante*).

An ancient and curious custom of dressing the 5 springs, which well up out of the ground in this village, with flowers on Holy Thursday is still kept up, and is known as "*Well-dressing*." A wooden framework in the shape of the pattern to be followed is formed and covered with clay, into which the flowers are stuck, forming a sort of floral mosaic; this is placed over the water, which appears to issue out of the flowers. The Hall Well, under the hill on which the Ch. stands, is most carefully ornamented; sentences from the Bible, in letters formed of flowers, encircle its basin. Service is performed at the Ch., after which the inhabitants walk in procession to each of the wells and repeat the psalms and collects of the day. The custom, once a general one, had come to be confined to Tissington, but has been lately revived at Matlock, Wirksworth, and other places. "The origin of the well-dressing was doubtless from a pious feeling of thankfulness for the bountiful supply of pure water; and in towns like Buxton and Wirksworth, which were badly off for it, the revival dates from the period when public wells and taps were opened."

Near Tissington a flat barrow, called Sharp Low, was opened by Mr. Bateman, who found the skeleton of a young person, without the usual protection of a cist; it was lying, however, on the l. side, a proof that it dated from Celtic times. Near Thorpe Cloud he opened another barrow, containing a man's skeleton, and an immense number of water-rats' bones.

About 3 m. E. of Tissington is **Bradbourne.** In the Ch.-yd. are the fragments of a fine ancient cross, rudely carved with scriptural subjects and interlacing foliage similar to that on the cross at Bakewell.

[Dovedale may be reached by turning off W. opposite the park gates of Tissington. Carriages must proceed through ⑤**Thorpe**, but the pedestrian can make his way by a footpath across the fields, and materially shorten his journey.]

From Tissington a long ascent through a bleak and monotonous country succeeds, offering a striking contrast to the beautiful parallel valley which lies so close on the left.

17 m. Alsop, a village with a small Norm. Ch. (restored). Here Becon the Reformer found shelter during the Marian persecution, and here he wrote his 'News out of Heaven both Pleasant and Joyful,' as a new year's gift to his patron, Sir George Pierrepont. The Allsopp family (Lord

Hindlip) trace their origin from this place. 2 m. E. is **Parwich**, where a Roman camp may be traced.

20 m. **Biggin**, a village with a modern Ch. In the high road is the *Newhaven House* inn, built by the 5th Duke of Devonshire. The surroundings are pleasant, but the country beyond is wild; it is, however, a convenient place for visiting the singular circle of Arborlow (Rte. 5). Hartington is 2 m. W., whence there is easy access to Beresford Dale (*post*). At **22 m.** the High Peak Rly. is crossed, and a Roman road runs parallel with the turnpike-road, falling into it at Hen Moor.

24 m. Monyash is 1½ m. E. In Domesday it is called *Maneis*. Here a barmote court is held twice a year for the settlement of mining disputes. The Ch.-yd. has a fine grove of lime-trees, planted by the unfortunate Mr. Lomas (see Parson's Tor, Rte. 6). In the neighbourhood is One Ash Grange, the site of a place of confinement for refractory monks from Roche Abbey. At *Benty Grange*, near Monyash. on opening a barrow, beside the skeleton were found several Saxon antiquities. They included the silver edging and ornaments of a leather cup, together with some personal ornaments, enamels, and beads. The vale of Lathkill (Rte. 6) may be well visited from here.

26 m. Church (or **Earl**) **Sterndale**. This is a part of the extensive parish of Hartington. It has a plain modern Ch. The neighbouring hills have many tumuli, in some of which, as at Cronkstone hill, the horns of deer have been found along with human remains (*post*).

31 m. Buxton (Rte. 7).

DOVEDALE.

The name Dovedale in strictness only belongs to a space of about 3 m. between Ilam and Mill Dale, but in a more extended sense it includes Mill Dale, Hall Dale, and Beresford Dale, thus really taking in all the border district of Derby and Stafford between Ashbourne and Hartington, a distance of about 14 m. It is in this wider sense that the term is here used.

There is a choice of roads from Ashbourne into Dovedale. The Buxton road may be taken as far as Sandybrook. There a signpost on the left indicates Thorpe and Dovedale; or the Leek turnpike road may be followed for 1½ m. ; after crossing the Dove at Hanging Bridge the road bears to the right through Okeover Park (**3 m.**), and then through Blore (*post*). Or a shorter way may be taken passing The Cottage (Lady Waterpark) and through **Mappleton**, where the temperance inn (Okeover Arms) is a good fishing station. The Ch., the mother Ch. of Ashbourne, is a singular-looking edifice, having a dome surmounted by an urn. A road, a short distance N., leads to a bridge across the Dove, here a broad, placid stream, and just beyond is *Okeover Hall* (H. C. Okeover, Esq.), which has been the property of the Okeovers from Saxon times. Mr. Plumer Ward. the author of 'Tremaine,' and stepfather of the present Mr. Okeover, resided here for some years. The old gabled house, engraved in Plot. contains a few good pictures, and among them a Holy Family by Raphael, a replica of one at Madrid. The Perp. Ch. contains several monuments of the Okeovers, and was elaborately restored by *Scott*. A valuable old brass which had been stolen many years ago has recently been found and brought back.

Pedestrians will find a pathway leading from Ashbourne to Dovedale almost entirely through fields — a beautiful 4 m. walk over two ridges and along the E. bank of the stream. Lovers of scenery should notice the

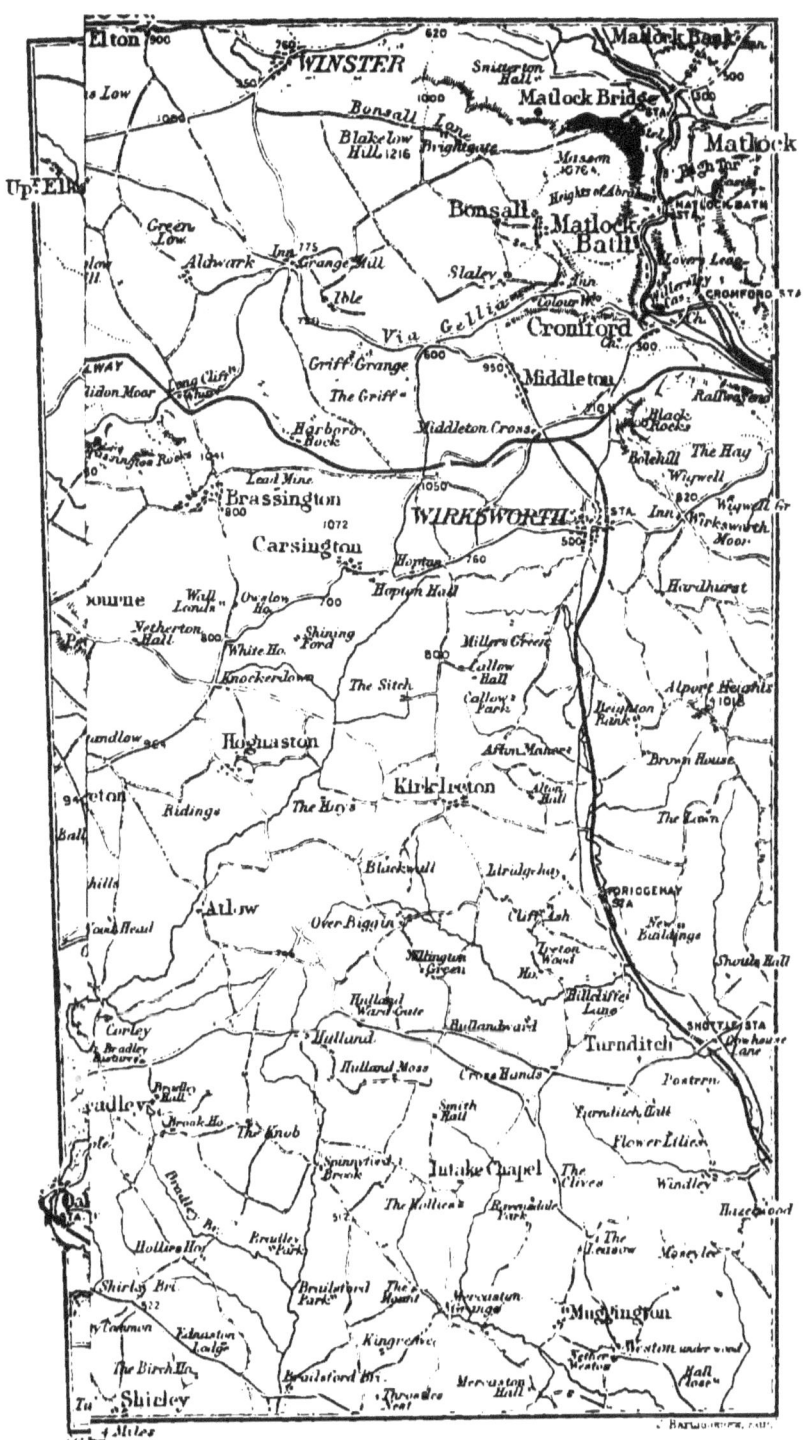

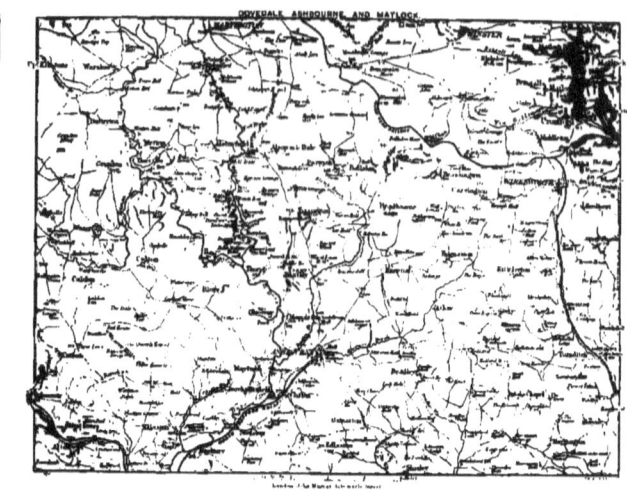

Route 34.—Blore—Ilam.

fine view from Okeover Bridge with Thorpe village in the distant foreground, with Thorpe Cloud, a conical hill, immediately behind it.

4 m. On W. is the village of **Blore**, with a small Ch., dedicated to St. Bartholomew, containing a remnant of early stained glass, some 15th-centy. brasses and a fine altar-tomb of the Bassets, formerly of Blore Hall, a mansion long since converted into a farmhouse, but still interesting with its grand old kitchen fireplace and panelled oak room.

The present Duke of Portland is the direct representative through the female line of the younger branch of the Basset family, who up to the 16th centy. were the owners of Blore. In the neighbourhood are many interesting Lows or pre-historic burial places.

As the traveller proceeds up the vale the most conspicuous objects are the two great sentinel heights of Thorpe Cloud (E.) and Bunster (W.), which flank the entrance of Dovedale proper.

At 5 m. is ☧ **Ilam**. The *Hall* (Robert William Hanbury, Esq.), a beautiful place on the Manifold, which here emerges out of a rock, as does also the Hamps, within a few yards of it, each river having pursued an underground course for several miles, and uniting at Ilam in a copious stream, which soon falls into the Dove. Of these rivers Drayton sings in his 'Poly-Olbion:'—

> " Hanse, that this while suppos'd him quite out of her sight,
> No sooner thrusts his head into the cheerful light,
> But Manifold, that still the runaway doth watch,
> Him, ere he was aware, about the neck doth catch;
> And as the angry Hanse would from her hold remove,
> They, struggling, tumble down into their lord, the Dove."

The house, built by its late owner in a style of mixed Tudor and Elizabethan, with a Norm. tower, is a rather imposing mass. In the grounds stands the *Ch.* (with a W. saddleback tower), which was sumptuously restored by Scott. In the S. chancel aisle is a curious E. E. shrine of a saint (St. Bertholin or Bertram of Stafford). But the most noticeable feature is an octagonal Gothic mausoleum, built from the designs of *Chantrey*, to contain a monumental group by him to the memory of Mr. D. Pike Watts. He is represented in a reclining attitude, giving his parting blessing to his daughter and her three children. The building will not stand criticism in its details, but it is grandiose, and, opening as it does into the Ch., gives effect to the whole structure. In the Ch. may be observed some funeral garlands, of modern date, a revival of the old custom. (See Ashford, Rte. 6.)

The scenery in the grounds is beautiful, and traditionally it is said to have suggested to Dr. Johnson his description of the "happy valley" in 'Rasselas.' Here is the grotto where Congreve composed his 'Old Bachelor.' Ilam Hall is only a short walk from the Izaak Walton Inn (*post*), where permission can generally be procured to see it.

The village is a charmingly picturesque collection of cottages, with a well cared-for school-house. Near the bridge over the Manifold is a Dec. Gothic Eleanor cross erected to the memory of Mrs. Watts-Russell, the base of which serves as a well and fountain for the use of the villagers, with the following pretty inscription:—

> " Free as for all these crystal waters flow,
> Her gentle eyes would weep for others' woe.
> Dried is that fount; but long may this endure,
> To be a well of comfort to the poor."

[At Ilam the tourist should for a while leave Dovedale to the E., and follow the Manifold (wholly in Staffordshire) up its, for a considerable distance, dry bed. This river has a

Route 34.—Grindon—Dovedale.

course generally parallel to that of the Dove, rising somewhat to the S.W. of that stream, and running all the way through the gritstone district, while the most romantic glens of the Dove, such as Dove, Mill, and Beresford Dales, are in the limestone—a fact that explains the difference of the scenery of the two rivers.

Not far from Ilam on W. is *Throwley Hall*, belonging to Earl Cathcart, a very picturesque Tudor mansion, now a farmhouse. The upper valley of the Manifold possesses much sylvan beauty, but at this lower part the hills attain great height, with awe-inspiring forms. To the W. is **Grindon** (5 m. from Ilam), picturesquely situated on a steep bank, with the sharp spire of its modern Gothic Ch., conspicuous for miles. To the E., high up on the hillside, which rises as a bare rock in the upper part to the height of 350 ft., is *Thor's Cave*, thought by some to be so called from its having been dedicated to Thor. It is more probable, however, that this is a mere corruption, the "tor" or hill in which it is situated, being really meant. In 1864 much of the dirt that had accumulated for generations was cleared, and some interesting Romano-Britannic relics discovered.

A little to the N. of the cave the tourist comes from the N.E. round the flank of the bold *Ecton Hill*, noticeable for its copper-mine, which yielded the revenues out of which the 5th Duke of Devonshire built the Crescent at Buxton (Rte. 7). After a long period of neglect, a company resumed the working, but with diminished success. Near this is *Wetton Bridge*, where the Manifold sinks into the ground. From Thor's Cave, through Wetton and Alstonefield, it is about 3 m. to the head of Mill Dale (*post*).

From excavations made in 1848 and subsequent years at a spot called the *Borough* (Burgh) *Holes* near Wetton, it was ascertained that this was the site of a Romano-British village. Not only skeletons and bones of animals, but weapons and articles of domestic use, were discovered, together with pavements and Roman coins.]

The tourist will now enter Dovedale, but he must be informed that by far the greater part can only be traversed by the pedestrian, and that the fallen stones under foot, and the rough stone walls that occur every few hundred yards, will make his progress very slow. The stream is crossed by numerous weirs, and by a small bridge of the rudest description. Fishing is strictly preserved. Tickets, however, at 2s. 6d. a-day, giving a range of 2 or 3 m., may be obtained at the Izaak Walton hotel, Ilam, and for the upper part of the stream, at the Charles Cotton, at Hartington (*post*).

At the foot of Bunster, in Staffordshire, and adjoining Ilam, is the *Izaak Walton Hotel*, 5 m. from Ashbourne, a comfortable little inn, and the paradise of fishers, who are now approaching the region sacred to anglers by the labours of Walton and his friend Chas. Cotton, who thus apostrophises his favourite river:—

"The rapid Garronne and the winding Seine
    Are both too mean,
Beloved Dove, with thee
    To vie priority:
Nay, Tame and Isis, when conjoin'd submit,
And lay their trophies at thy silver feet."

The Dove rises in Axe Edge, and throughout its course furnishes a boundary between the counties of Derby and Stafford, and joins the Trent below Burton (Rte. 1). Of the many vales through which it flows, that called, par excellence, the **Dovedale**, extending for about 3 miles, from Ilam to Mill Dale, presents in its course scenes of unparalleled beauty. It is "a secluded valley or glen, through which flows a clear and rapid stream, with green banks and shelving slopes, hemmed in by bold and lofty hills, mantled with thick scrub and brushwood, through which protrude grey weather-beaten crags and walls of naked limestone rock."— Croston.

The first cluster of isolated rocks is that on the Staffordshire side, called the Twelve Apostles. Then follow, on the Derby shore, the conical group of Tissington Spires; opposite which is a high castellated mass styled the Church Rock. Reynard's Cave, or Hall, is a cavern on the right, a lofty domed archway, near the summit of the cliff. A rope is placed here to assist tourists in their ascent. In July, 1761, Dean Langton of Clogher, who was on a visit to Ashbourne, attempted to ride to the top of one of the slopes near Reynard's Hall with a young lady seated behind him. When near the summit, the horse slipped and rolled down, killing the Dean and much injuring the lady; her life was saved by her being caught by the hair in a thorn bush.

The dale higher up contracts suddenly, at the *Strait*, leaving but a narrow passage for the river, and an indifferent footpath. Emerging from this defile, and passing on the rt. the rock called the Lion's Head, the most remarkable group in the dale is reached, the Pickering Tors, isolated conical peaks, with the Ilam Stone opposite. The Doveholes, just opposite the entrance to Mill Dale, are the usual termination of most of the excursions to the Dale, but the tourist will not regret continuing his exploration as far as Hartington, or even to Earl's Sterndale. Dr. Johnson in his tour visited Dovedale, of which he says: "I certainly expected a large river, where I found only a quiet, clear brook. I believe I had imaged a valley enclosed by rocks, and terminated by a broad expanse of water. He that has seen Dovedale has no need to visit the Highlands."

The *Gramnitis ceterach* grows in the clefts of the high rocks in Dovedale, and the *Osmunda regalis* is met with near Ashbourne.

9 m. **Mill Dale**, a picturesque little hamlet, in which the houses seem fitted into their respective niches in the hillside, where Cotton's Viator found "the sign of a bridge which a mouse could hardly go over," and asked, "Do you use to travel with wheelbarrows in this country?" The bridge is still standing, but somewhat dilapidated. A road leads W. to Alstonefield and Wetton, **Alstonefield Ch.**, partially restored in 1880, contains some specimens of Norm., E. E., Dec. and Perp.; but the feature in it, which will most interest the ecclesiologist, is a very early specimen, at the E. end of the nave and just N. of the small Norm. chancel arch, of the combined pulpit and reading desk, bearing date 1637-1639, and covered with inscriptions and Renaissance carving. In the N. aisle is the Beresford Hall carved pew, erected at the same time. It was painted and gilded at the beginning of the present century. The scenery around Alstonefield is very picturesque.

At 10 m. is **Load Mill**. This is, generally speaking, the extreme N. point of those who only think of "doing" Dovedale. The reach of the river above it is of a stern, bare character, the banks on either side closing upon the stream, varied only by a grey face of rock or a stunted tree. The lofty height of Wolf's-cote overhangs it on the Derbyshire side, and opposite it, on the Staffordshire side, the hills turn suddenly away to the W., but with a short intervening space of flat meadow, forming, with the Derbyshire heights, the northernmost of the four glens which may collectively be termed Dovedale.

This is **Beresford Dale**, noticeable both as the cradle of the well-known family of that name, and as the seat of Charles Cotton, and the locale of the fishing-excursion (more than equivalent to a modern journey to Norway) of the Stafford-born but London-bred Walton, celebrated in Cotton's 2nd part of the 'Complete Angler.' Beresford Hall, whose pleasure-ground is formed by this dale, seems to have been from Saxon times the residence of a stock who lived at the Bear's ford, branching off to Fenny Bentley and other neighbouring places. A cadet of the family settled in Ireland at the time of James I.'s plantation of Ulster, and his descendant in the last century, intermarrying with the heiress of De La Poer of Curraghmore in the county of Waterford, was the ancestor of the noble families of Waterford and Decies. Eventually Beresford passed early in the 17th centy. to the family of Stanhope of Elvaston, whose daughter and heiress eloped with Cotton's father. The Cottons were a thriftless race, and the property passed away in the time of the angler's son, until, after successive changes and deteriorations, it was purchased in 1825 by Marshal Lord Beresford, the victor of Albuera, and bequeathed by him to his kinsman, the late Mr. Beresford-Hope. The house (in Staffordshire), a picturesque gabled structure of the 16th and 17th cents., becoming ruinous, was pulled down, and a new building erected by the late Rt. Hon. A. J. B. Beresford-Hope.

Beresford Dale, about ½ m. long, is a scene of singular beauty, from the combination which it offers of mountain stream, grey rock, grass-slope, and well-grown timber picturesquely disposed. At its side is a small natural cave in which Cotton was wont to hide from his creditors,† while the height above is crowned by

† "Oh! my beloved Caves, from Dogstar's heat,
And all anxieties, my safe retreat,
What safety, privacy, what true delight,
In the artificial night
Your gloomy entrails make,
Have I taken, do I take."
COTTON's *Retirement*.

the ruins of a tower, in which, as he commemorates in one of his poems, his 2nd wife the Countess of Ardglass used to light a beacon to guide him home. His bowling-green can, according to some, be traced close by, whilst others believe that it was close to the Fishing-house (see below). But the chief feature of the dale is the *Pike Pool* and *Rock*—" a rock springing up in the middle of the river. This is one of the oddest sights that ever I saw." So says Viator in Cotton's 'Angler,' and he does not exaggerate. This natural obelisk of grey stone is the more beautiful from being set against a background of luxuriant foliage almost dipping into the Dove.

At the head of the dale the glen ceases, the Derbyshire range of hills indeed continuing, but falling back from the river, while the continuity of the Staffordshire range is rather interrupted. Where the meadows begin to contract stands the famous Fishing-House built by Cotton, with the inscription " Piscatoribus sacrum, 1674," and the interlaced initials I. W. and C. C., the symbol of the strange friendship between men so unlike as the saintly Walton and the pleasure-loving Cotton. It is a small square building, with a high pyramidal roof and a fireplace, but Cotton's " fine wainscot " has gone, and a round " marble table " replaces the square one which he set up; otherwise it is *in statu quo*. A pleasant walk of about ⅜ m. through meadows leads us to

14 m. ⚵ **Hartington**, a small Derbyshire market-town, nestling between the hills, and an admirable station for the angler, the tourist, or the archæologist, who desires to explore the numerous tumuli and " lows " in the neighbourhood between it and Winster, such as Gib Hill, Kenslow, and Arborlow. The parish is of enormous size, divided into Upper, Middle, Nether, and

Town Quarters, and extending almost to Buxton; it also touches Hope and Bakewell. The Ch. is of mixed styles, cruciform, and with W. tower; the N. transept is small, but the S. one has a W. aisle, recently enriched by a painted window. Notice a memorial window to the Sleighs, some quaint paintings of the emblems of the 12 tribes in the N. transept, and a square altar-table carved with the names of the four wardens of the Quarters, a Puritan relic. Beside the vicar, the Ch. has a dean, whose office is neither very onerous nor very lucrative. *Hartington Hall*, now a farmhouse, the ancient seat of the Batemans, is a very picturesque gabled house. The town gives the second title to the Duke of Devonshire.

The universal greenness of all this upland region is very striking, and dairy farming is the general occupation. Such hay as is made has in rainy seasons to remain uncut till late in the autumn, while wheat is virtually unknown, and the only cultivation practised is that of oats, with the risk of their sometimes not ripening. The oat-cake, which is the general diet of farmers and labourers, is not the sweet crisp edible which is obtained in Scotland, but a sour, flabby substance. Such as it is, however, it is much relished.

From Hartington it is better to follow the road up the Staffordshire side, crossing the Dove at Hartington Mill. The way leads with occasional dips along a plateau boldly scarping to the E. upon the Dove, and to the W. sloping down to the Manifold. The scenery, with the millstone-grit hills of Staffordshire on the W. rising up to the moorland summit of Morridge, and the limestone hills of Derbyshire on the E., is very fine.

About 2 m. from Hartington, on the plateau, is the tree-embosomed village of **Sheen**, a little parish wedged in between the enormous ones of Alstonefield and Hartington.

The *Ch.*, rebuilt early in the present centy. in the conventual style, was recast by the late Mr. Beresford-Hope in 1852, the original structure serving as nave, while a chancel has been added with a stone-ribbed roof copied from the side chapels of Scarborough Ch. The fittings are those which stood in Margaret Street Chapel, London, prior to its demolition to make way for All Saints Ch. A pretty parsonage by *Butterfield* adjoins. From the summit of Sheen hill, a little to the N.W., a beautiful panoramic view of the country is to be obtained. On the N., in Derbyshire, is High Wheeldon, a hill which, under certain aspects, looks like a regular pyramid. The traveller may enter Derbyshire under this hill at the little hamlet of Crowdecote, but he is advised rather to push on to **Longnor**, 3 m. N.W. of Sheen, on the plateau between the Dove and the Manifold (at which point the valley bends considerably to the W.), from which by a steep descent he will cross the Dove at Glutton Bridge, and enter the striking pass of Glutton Dale, near the village of **Church** (or **Earl's**) **Sterndale** (*ante*). The scenery above Glutton Bridge towards Axe Edge is fine, including in particular the rocky height of Park Hill, and the still loftier one of Chrome Tor, veritable mountains in miniature. The labour of the ascent of Chrome Tor is amply repaid by the beauty of the view from the summit. It is best made from a meadow adjacent to the farmhouse of Dowel. A short stiff climb places the walker upon the sharp, serrated hog's-back, from which the hill slopes on stone buttresses to the W. and a steep grass bank to the E. He should notice a curious natural arch in the limestone of the topmost ridge. The huge mass of Axe Edge bounds the view to N., over the stony line of hills called the Frith. To S. Park Hill lies low beneath, and beyond it the panorama of the Dove and Manifold valleys spread out. The adjacent hill (of gritstone) to W. is Hollins, famous for a whimsical panic in 1806, which drove the inhabitants of the district to encamp upon its summit for three weeks, under the conviction that there they would be safest from the invading hosts of Bonaparte. At the head of the narrow glen to the E. running up from Dowel is a deep orifice in the ground resembling the once famous Eldon Hole.

On the eminence of *Hitter Hill*, near the village of Earl's Sterndale, a large barrow was opened in 1862, when several skeletons and funeral urns were discovered; while in Hindlow were found more skeletons, with Saxon implements and ornaments. From Earl's Sterndale it is 5 m. to Buxton (Rte. 7).

ROUTE 35.

UTTOXETER TO MACCLESFIELD, BY ALTON TOWERS AND LEEK [CHEADLE].

N. STAFFORDSHIRE RLY. 32 m.

For the first few miles the Rly. follows the course of the Dove, passing rt. (in Derbyshire) Doveridge village and Hall, the seat of Lord Waterpark, and, a little further, Crakemarsh Hall (C. T. Cavendish, Esq.) (Rte. 34).

4 m. Rocester (Junct. Stat.). Hence a branch goes off on E. to Ashbourne (Rte. 34). Just before reaching the stat. Woodseat (J. F. Campbell, Esq.) is seen on W., and in the space between the two lines, Barrow Hill (Capt. Dawson) and Dove Leys (Sir Thos. P. Heywood, Bart.). Rocester, which was a Roman station, had a house of Black Canons founded by Richard Bacon about 1146, some foundations of which remain in a field S. of the Ch. The Ch. was rebuilt, with the exception of the tower, and a spire added, in 1872; in the Ch.-yard is the shaft of a cross, with interlaced work, and 3 sculptured sepulchral slabs.

2 m. W. of Rocester is **Croxden**, which contained a famous **Abbey**, founded for Cistercians by Bertram de Verdon in 1176; his widow Rocsia was the foundress of Grace Dieu, in Charnwood (Rte. 24). In it were buried a number of the descendants of that family, together with the heart of King John, whose physician was Abbot of Croxden. His name was Thomas Shepeshed, and his Chronicle is extant in the British Museum.

The remains of the abbey, which are incorporated with the farm-buildings, are of considerable extent. They consist principally of the ivy-clad W. front, lighted by 3 lofty E. Eng. windows deeply splayed. The W. door is a very fine example, and is deeply recessed. The S. wall of the nave still stands, as also the S. transept lighted by E. Eng. windows, and containing a round-headed doorway and some piers with plain capitals. This doorway probably led into the sacristy, now used as a carthouse. To the S. of this transept are the walls of the monastic buildings, of which the great hall and the refectory are the best preserved, and offer some beautiful details. Several stone coffins, and an effigy (probably of one of the Verdons), will be noticed. The situation of the abbey is delightful, and the walk from it to Alton or Rocester (each about 2 m. distant) abounds with varied country scenery. Croxden Ch. was rebuilt in 1885 by the Earl of Macclesfield.

The line now proceeds up the valley of the Churnet, which joins the Dove 1 m. below Rocester, and presently enters the defiles of a broken and romantic district, which extends several miles in a N.W. direction, and has on E. the Moorlands (*post*).

5½ m. **Denstone** (Stat.), where a very beautiful Ch. has been built by Sir Percival Heywood from designs by *Street*; it has painted windows, and is profusely ornamented with Derbyshire marble. Near the Ch. is *St. Chad's College*, for middle-class education in connection with St. Nicholas' College, Lancing, on a site given by Sir Percival Heywood. The ground-plan of the building is in the shape of the letter H: architects, Slater and Carpenter. Centrally seated as this institution is for the great towns of the Black Country, the Potteries, Lancashire, and Birmingham, the site is admirably chosen.

7½ m. ⚜**Alton** (Stat.). The stat. occupies a most picturesque position in a valley, on one side of which rises a lofty cliff crowned by a modern nunnery and some slight remains of the old castle of Alton (*post*), and on the other is the very striking modern pile styled

⚜**ALTON TOWERS** (Earl of Shrewsbury and Talbot). The estate was an ancient property of the Talbot family, and their lands were entailed by the famous Duke of Shrewsbury, who obtained an Act for the purpose at the beginning of the 18th centy. Lower Heythorp, Oxfordshire (*see Handbook for Oxford*), was their ordinary residence, till the attention of Charles, 15th Earl of Shrewsbury (from 1787 to 1827), was directed to this beautiful spot. He erected a moderate house, and turned his energies to landscape-gardening, commencing in 1814. His nephew and successor John, "the good Earl," while improving the gardens, specially devoted himself to architecture, and took the house in hand, converting it into a vast, dreamy, ill-connected series of galleries and towers—picturesque at a distance, uncomfortable to inhabit — and thoroughly incorrect in style and detail. The name Alton Towers was his invention. Later in his life, and after he had become intimate with Pugin, he began remodelling the building on sounder principles. Unhappily the deaths of both architect and owner have left the noble pile unfinished. Pugin when he ceased work was engaged in fitting-up and decorating the bed-chambers. Earl John died in 1856, leaving no issue, and on the death of his successor Earl Bertram, shortly after his majority, the senior line of the Talbots failed, and the title and estates were claimed by the late Earl Talbot of Ingestre, who established his right to the earldom in 1858, and was in 1860 adjudged in the Court of Exchequer to be the owner of Alton and the remaining entailed estates.

From motives of convenience, approach to Alton Towers is usually made from the S., when a castellated gateway will be seen at a short distance E. of the Stat., but by far the most striking view is obtained from the opposite quarter (or from the Stat. at Oakamoor, *post*), where, from the abundance of bare rock, and the abruptness of the tree-clad banks, the scenery is almost of mountainous character. In fact, Alton Towers stands on the southern extremity of those high lands which, commencing in Staffordshire and Derbyshire, culminate, as far as England is concerned, at the Northumberland borderland. The house is built on an elevated plateau near the valley of the Churnet, up which the Rly. runs, and at the head of a subsidiary valley in which the famous flower-garden is situated. In front is a sheet of water, and beyond this the stables, poor in themselves, but masked by an imposing screen wall of baronial architecture. Alton Towers is a picturesque building, but there is a want of composition in it. Its towers do not combine into a whole, and thus do not produce the impression of its real extent. The grand entrance is through a lofty tower, approached by a flight of steps guarded by the family supporters, two tall rampant Talbot dogs, each holding a gilt banner, with the motto, "Prest d'accomplir." In the days of Earl John a blind Welsh harper was seated in the vestibule to maintain the baronial illusion. Crossing beneath a narrow tower, open to the roof, the Armoury is reached. It is a long narrow gallery, and once contained a valuable collection of arms, 50 suits being ranged round the walls, with weapons of war and the chase. Under the oak roof, in the Tudor style, hang numerous banners, including that of Ireland, which is borne before the Earl, as hereditary high steward. At the end, a glazed screen formed of spears and halberts leads into a continuation called the Picture Gallery, contents of which were sold and dispersed on the death of Earl Bertram. the last Roman Catholic Lord Shrewsbury.

Beyond these two galleries is the Octagon, a spacious apartment, in imitation of the chapter-house of a cathedral. With better details it would be a fine feature, but the imitation groining of the roof is both of plaster and of a depressed and ungraceful outline. The lancet windows are filled with portraits of bishops and archbishops of the Talbot family in stained glass. To this, 4th in order of the apartments, succeeds the Talbot Gallery, decorated by *Pugin*; the upper part of the wall is divided into compartments filled with shields bearing the quarterings of the Talbots, and showing their descent from the Conqueror.

The Conservatory, which forms the entrance to the private apartments, branches from the Octagon to the right. The iron framework is partially Gothic in form. In addition to rare and beautiful plants, trees, and flowers, filling the air with their fragrance, through the windows a view is gained of the little *recherché* flower-garden of the lady of the castle, encircled by its buildings.

Next comes the Transept Gallery, so called because it runs across the suite of rooms. The corridors, panelled with black oak, once contained a museum of antiquities.

The Chapel, in the Tudor style, was one of the early rooms, but taken in hand by *Pugin* as far as the decoration of the altar went. The reredos, which is highly coloured and gilt, contains statues of St. Augustine, St. Thomas of Canterbury, Edward the Confessor, and St Chad, first Bishop of Lichfield. Since the accession of the present line it has been devoted to the service of the Church of England.

The Great Dining Hall, rebuilt by *Pugin* on the site of the previous dining-room, is a really beautiful specimen of a baronial hall in Perpendicular architecture, with open oaken roof.

The **Gardens**, formed out of a bare rocky glen, the sides of which are boldly planted, on which Earl John lavished his attention, are alike remarkable for their natural beauty, and the questionable taste of many of the artificial decorations. A small Gothic temple incloses a bust of Earl John, with the inscription, "He made the desert smile."

The grounds and woodlands are very grand, while from the abundance of conifers and rhododendra they are full of verdure even in winter, and the trees, though none of them are old, have attained a satisfactory growth. On a projecting knoll of sandstone rises a tower, about 90 ft. high, a reproduction of the choragic monument of Lysicrates at Athens, which commands a view extending to the Welsh border, though, strangely enough, it is not placed on the highest point of the estate. That is occupied by a large reservoir, which abounds in fish, and also supplies the fountains with water. These are whimsical in their construction: the War fountain is so named from the numerous jets crossing each other like spears; the Screw fountain is a short pillar with deeply-grooved sides, in which the water flashes like bands of silver; and the Chinese fountain, where a jet of water streams like a flag from the gilt pinnacle of a pagoda.

The house is very seldom shown, but the gardens and grounds are open to the public on certain days in summer, and are visited by excursionists in thousands.

Across the narrow valley of the Churnet (up which the rail winds) is the village of Alton, with some slight remains of its old Castle, commanding the junction of Alton Glen with the Vale of Churnet. It was a stronghold of the De Verdons and Furnivals, ancestors of the Talbots. Close by stands the pretty Rom. Cath. chapel of St. John by Pugin, but the chief feature is the pile by the same architect, half castellated, half ecclesiastical in aspect, overhanging the rock, with its lofty apsidal chapel, like some castle of Rhineland It was intended as an asylum for aged priests, but remains unfinished; by the side of it is a convent, occupied by the Sisters of Mercy. In the chapel and cloisters are monuments and brasses to the last Rom. Cath. Earls of Shrewsbury; Charles (d. 1827), John (d. 1852) and his countess; and Bertram (d. 1856).

Alton Ch., originally Norm., has been restored; it retains a good E. E. doorway at the W. end.

From Alton the line continues through the same broken and romantic valley to

9 m. Oakamoor (Stat.). This is a [*Derby, &c.*]

hamlet of Cheadle, with a modern Ch. Here are the works of Messrs. Bolton & Sons for making telegraph wire; there are also extensive brass and copper works. 3 m. S.W is Cheadle, the road lying through a pleasantly-wooded country.

[♂ Cheadle is a small market-town. It lies at the base of a slight eminence, in the centre of a basin, surrounded by a belt of high land, which was an open moor half a century ago, but has now been brought into cultivation. A small river, the Tean brook, which drains this basin, has an excellent reputation as a trout stream. The Ch., which stands on high ground, was rebuilt about 1840 in Perp. style; it contains some stained glass, and the chancel is ornamented by good oak carving, the production of a local workman. But by far the most noticeable object in Cheadle is the Rom. Cath. Ch. of *St. Giles*, a rich Dec. Ch. of red sandstone by *Pugin*, built chiefly at the expense of John Earl of Shrewsbury in 1846. It consists of a nave with aisles, chancel chapels, and a sacristy. It has a very lofty and graceful spire, which, although the Ch. stands in a low situation, forms a conspicuous feature in the landscape for miles. The interior contains some beautiful stained glass, and is elaborately decorated. Notice the triptych altar-piece of gilded oak in the Lady Chapel, carved by Flemish artists, and representing the Passion; the chancel arch painted by Hauser of Rome, subject, the Last Judgment; the elaborate brass screen in front of the Chapel of the Holy Sacrament; the reredos and sedilia; the great E. window representing the tree of Jesse; and the W. door, each leaf of which displays the lion rampant of the Talbots in brass, of large dimensions. Around the Ch. is a spacious enclosure, which contains a priest's house, a guest-hall, and schools. The whole is said to have cost

P

120,000*l.* Cheadle is apparently in the centre of a small coalfield. There are several small collieries in the neighbourhood, but they cannot be developed for want of railway communication. In the town, and at Tean in the neighbourhood, are the tape mills of Messrs. J. & N. Philips & Co. Various old customs are observed here. The curfew rings at 8 o'clock in the winter; on the first Friday in the year is the *gayboys* (pronounced *gawbys*) fair, a reminiscence of the old hiring fairs, and the *wake fair* takes place in the week after St. Giles' day (Sept. 1st).

1½ m. E. is *Hales Hall* (Mrs. Whieldon), with a noble yew avenue. The property once belonged to Sir Matthew Hale, but the present house was built by his grand-daughter. Near is *Woodhead Hall* (W. S. Allen, Esq.). 2½ m. S., at *Upper Tean*, the old Hall, part timber, part brick (1615), serves as the office and residence of the manager of Philips' tape mills; the interior is worth seeing.]

12 m. **Froghall** (Stat.). This is a busy place, where the rich earthy hæmatite iron-ore is found in the neighbourhood and conveyed to the North Staffordshire iron-works. There is a steep tramway, 3 m. long, by which lime is brought from the quarries at Cauldon Low. 2½ m. N. is **Ipstones**, most picturesquely placed beneath Ipstones Edge, where are extensive quarries of gritstone. *Belmont* was built by one of the Sneyds, who planted 10,000 larch trees in its neighbourhood. On the W. side of the line is **Wetley**, standing under a bold ridge of limestone, called Wetley Rocks. Wetley Abbey (Josiah Hardman, Esq.) is a large modern edifice in the Dec. style. It was the birthplace of George Mason, A.R.A., the painter, and Wetley Moor supplied the landscapes for his well-known pictures. Consall Hall (Captain H. S. Smith) stands between Wetley Rocks and the Rly., and is bounded on E. by the Cauldon Canal, which traverses a deep and most picturesque glen on its way to Cheddleton and Norton. Close to the Rly. is Basford Hall, the modern seat of J. W. Sneyd, Esq.

16 m. Cheddleton (Stat.). The Churnet valley here widens considerably, and affords a good extent of rich pasture. The *Ch.*, mainly Dec., but with late Perp. tower, was restored by *Scott*; it has a piscina, sedilia, and a modern font of alabaster. There is a Ch.-yard cross, and a handsome lichgate. Ashcombe Hall (Dryden H. Sneyd, Esq.) stands in a fine deer park, on the site of Bothams, an Elizabethan house; and Westwood Manor (W. Meakin, Esq.), the old seat of the Powys family, is a modern stone edifice.

[At 17 m. a *branch line* goes off on W. to Stoke (Rte. 33). It follows the course of the Cauldon Canal, and has stats. at Endon (3½ m.), Milton (7 m.), and Bucknall (10 m.). **Endon** is very prettily situated, and has a large number of good houses occupied by the thriving business men of the Pottery district; the Ch. has been restored. The Derbyshire custom of well-dressing has been introduced, but the festival is held on " Restoration-day ; " it is accompanied by a Ch. service. Milton and Bucknall are in reality suburbs of Burslem and Hanley.]

18½ m. ♂ **Leek** (Stat.) stands on high ground, 640 ft., near the head of the valley of the Churnet, and is a busy place, where the traveller will observe his approach to the silk districts of Macclesfield in the general engagement of the population in the manufacture of sewing silk, there being upwards of 50 mills in the town and its vicinity. Leek belonged to Algar of Mercia, and was at the Conquest given to Hugh Lupus, the 1st Earl of Chester. Ralph, the 6th Earl, gave it to Dieulacresse Abbey, which he founded in the 13th centy. Button-making was a trade very early practised here, but it has been superseded by the silk trade introduced by the French Protestant refugees.

The old *Ch.*, dedicated to St. Edward the Confessor, stands on high ground in the centre of the town. A former Ch. was burnt in 1297, and the present edifice must have been built soon after, its main features being Dec.; it is remarkable for its fine pinnacled tower, and for the richness of its fittings, including chancel screen, stalls, and painted windows. In the N. aisle is a very beautiful rose window. The chancel was rebuilt by *Street*, and a reredos, pulpit, and font, all of highly ornamental character, were added. There are but few monuments, but the small *brass* of John Ashenhurst (d. 1597) may be noticed; it represents himself, his 4 wives and 10 children. In the Ch.-yard is a monument to Wm. Trafford of Swithamley, d. 1697, æt. 93, who in the time of the civil war refused to answer any questions, or indeed to give any answer, but "Now thus," whereupon they set him down as an idiot, and left him. On the stone is depicted a man threshing corn, and the words "Now thus," with the date 1697. There is also a remarkable Danish pillar, about 10 ft. high, with a carved capital and sides. The view from the Ch.-yard, looking N., is exceedingly fine. To the W. is the *Cloud Hill* (1190 ft.), behind which, for a few days in summer-time, the sun appears to set twice, reappearing on its northern side after sinking out of sight.

St. Luke's Ch., on the Buxton road, is a modern edifice (1848), l Dec., with a good tower, copied from that of Brislington, Somerset (see *Handbook for Somerset*).

The Ch. of All Saints was built by Norman Shaw, R.A., in 1887.

The *Nicholson Institute*, containing a Free Library, an Art Gallery and School of Art, was built and given to the town by the late Mr. Joshua Nicholson.

Lord Chancellor Macclesfield (b. 1666) was the son of an attorney at Leek, and the grandson of General Venables, the conqueror of Jamaica. He founded the Grammar School, and his descendant, the Earl of Macclesfield, is now lord of the manor.

Westwood Hall (J. Robinson, Esq.), a short distance from Leek, occupies the site of a picturesque gabled house of the Trenthams, to which a ghostly legend was attached. The Lady Trentham of the time of James I. being accidentally killed in leaping a gate, was, by her unsympathizing husband, buried in the cellar. Her ghost, resenting such usage, haunted the Hall, and when the neighbouring clergy were summoned to exorcise her, she pleaded so powerfully with them that they ordered the body to be removed to the Ch., after which the spirit was seen no more.

About 1 m. N. of the town are some remains of **Dieulacresse Abbey**, founded in 1214 for the Cistercians by Ralph de Blondeville, Earl of Chester. He was a renowned Crusader, and was also very liberal to the monastic orders. The Chronicle of Dieulacresse tells a wild legend, how, after death, the evil one was baffled in keeping possession of his soul, by the great white mastiffs (Molossi) of Dieulacresse and other abbeys howling to such a pitch as to disturb the very depths of hell itself. At the suppression the abbey was valued at 243*l.* per annum. It was granted by Edward VI. to Sir Ralph Bagenal, when the whole building was pulled down, and the existing farm-house was erected, but additions have since been made, and portions of sculptured stone worked up in a gateway, with the date of 1667; detached corbels also are to be seen every here and there in the walls, and a cowhouse has the upper part of a handsome 14th-centy. window. In another place is seen an incised sepulchral slab, with a cross ragulée and a sword.

2 m. beyond Dieulacresse is the village of **Meerbrook**, where a small Ch. built circa 1562 by Sir Ralph Bagenal, the grantee, was replaced in 1870 by one in early 14th century style by R. N. Shaw, R.A. The village underlies the wild tract of the **Roaches**, a moor with bold and picturesque gritstone rocks, shooting up into varied aiguilles, reaching to a height of 1670 ft. The most conspicuous features are two parallel serrated ridges (of which the least elevated, but not the least grand, overhangs the Buxton and Leek road, from which it may in a few minutes be mounted) and an isolated hill standing out like an advance-guard, called Hen-Cloud (1000 ft.). The loftier ridge is known as the Back Forest. On its remote verge towards the N.E., adjacent to Swythamley and to the beautiful wooded glen of Gradbach, is to be seen one of the most wonderful sights in all this romantic region, worthy to be classed with the seven wonders of the Peak, viz. the rock crevasse of *Lud Church*. From the moor nothing is seen but the tops of a few scrubby trees forming an irregular line, and the entrance has to be closely looked for. It will be found by following a footpath leading S. under a cluster of rocks called Castle Cliffs. A flight of rough steps will be seen, descending which the tourist will find himself in a chasm bounded by perpendicular rock-walls, rich with the ferns and plants that nestle in the clefts, of a width never exceeding a few feet, and of a variable height according to the levels of the footway, but averaging 30 feet. The whole length, reckoning the turns and angles, is nearly 300 yards. A flight of steps leads out of the chasm on the S., but the chasm itself continues some distance further, and ends in a cavern, in which a subterranean stream is heard, but cannot be reached. The Gradbach glen joins at Quarnford that of the Dane, of which the opposite bank is in Cheshire.

[The high road from Leek to Buxton (12 m.) passes near the S. foot of the Roaches (leaving Meerbrook to the W.), and thence over the very wild and rough country on the borders of Stafford and Derby.

To the E. stretch the Moorlands, with the heights of Morridge rising to 1500 ft., and with the Black Meer or Blake Meer, of which Plot tells marvellous tales. A small moorland inn, the Mermaid, near this, stands midway between it and the source of the Hamps, which will be found not far from a farm called the Lumb. Further E. lies Butterton Moor, above which rises Ecton Hill; to the S. is the ridge of Weaver (1154 ft.). Looking northward, the open moors of Fawfield and Heathy Lee are seen, with a few scattered farmhouses and single dwellings. To the W. the Roaches occupy a considerable space, and they are succeeded by Goldsitch Moss, flanked by a tributary of the Dane, and some remains of Macclesfield Forest. Coal of poor quality is found in the district.

On the high road, at 3 m. from Leek, is Upper Hulme, where there is a large flax-mill, and where a tributary of the Churnet runs through a most picturesque glen far below the bridge.

At 7 m. is an inn which bears the name of the *Royal Cottage*, from the tradition that Charles I. once passed a night there. On the verge of the county is the village of **Flash**, with an inn, called the Travellers' Rest, much visited from Buxton. Flash is now a neat, quiet-looking little place, with a small Ch.; but, like the whole surrounding district, it was formerly of evil repute, the resort of coiners, and also gave its name to the "badgers," or hawkers, who "squatted on the waste lands and commons in the district, and were notorious for their wild, half-barbarous manners and brutal pastimes. Travelling about from fair to fair, and using a cant or slang dialect, they became generally known as 'Flash-men.'"— *Smiles*. Badgers' Croft, near Flash Bottom, preserves the remembrance of their earlier appellation. A good though steep road leads down S.W. from Flash to Quarnford and Gradbach, and forms the easiest access from Buxton to the wonders of Lud's Church. On the other side the steep byeway from Flash to Longnor (Rte. 34) affords fine prospects of the hills about the heads of the Dove and Manifold. For the remainder of the road to Buxton (4 m.), see Rte. 7.

A good hill-walk may be taken from Buxton to Leek by the following route:—Buxton over Axe Edge (1750 ft.) to Cat and Fiddle (4 m.); passing down Dane Bower by Gradbach to Lud's Church (3 m.); thence to Leek by Swithamley Hall (5 m.).]

20½ m. ♂ **Rudyard** (Stat.). This is a hamlet, consisting only of a few farmhouses, but it is a pleasant resort, on account of the picturesque reservoir of 2 m. in length, called *Rudyard Lake*, and made for the purpose of supplying the Cauldon Canal. Rudyard Hall (now a farmhouse) was the residence of Sir Benjamin Rudyard, an eminent member of the Long Parliament. He was one of the most accomplished men of his time; a scholar, a poet, and a distinguished orator. Ben Jonson addressed three epigrams to him. At a short distance is **Horton**, where the Ch. has been restored. It contains some stained glass, and monuments to the Crompton, Fowler, and Wedgwood families. Part of the reservoir is in this parish, the banks are steep and well fringed with wood, and here is Cliff Park Hall (Rev. E. D. Boothman).

23½ m. **Rushton** (Stat.). There are 3 small townships known as the Rushtons. At Rushton Spencer (once a possession of the Despensers) is a small ancient Ch. styled the "chapel of the wilderness"; it is almost wholly of wood, and was built temp. Henry III. "The situation of this humble but highly picturesque little chapel is eminently striking, perched as it is on the summit of a steep elevation apart from the village, and screened by noble old black firs and yew trees." — (*Sleigh's History of Leek*.) The date 1630 over the E. window probably marks the time when some portions of the wooden structure were replaced by stone, but the very massive font is believed to be coeval with the original building. In the ch.-yard is a gravestone with the singular inscription. "Thomas, son of Thomas and Mary Meaykin, interred July 16, 1781, aged 21 years. As a man falleth before wicked men, so fell I. Βια θανατος." This has reference to a tragic story of a youth who dared to make love to his master's daughter, and was supposed to have been drugged and buried alive at Stone. His friends had his coffin opened, when the body was found on its face; they then removed it to Rushton, his native place, and erected the above memorial.

The line enters Cheshire soon after quitting Rushton, and reaches at

32 m. **Macclesfield** (Stat.). See *Handbook for Cheshire*.

ROUTE 36.

STOKE-ON-TRENT TO CONGLETON, BY BIDDULPH.

N. STAFFORDSHIRE RLY. 14 m.

The line on leaving Stoke (Rte. 33) runs S. for some distance; then, sweeping round to the N.E., it at 2¼ m. reaches **Bucknall** (Stat.), a suburb of Hanley. At 4 m. the branch to Leek is given off (Rte. 35), and at 5¼ m. is Ford Green (Stat.), where are the ironworks of the Messrs. Heath. In the immediate neighbourhood are the populous places of Norton-in-the-Moors, Brown Edge, Milton, and Smallthorne, all engaged in either the coal or the iron trade. The line ascends the valley of the infant Trent, having on E. the high ground of Norton, and on W. the smoky district of Tunstall, with the large Union House of the Parishes of Wolstanton and Burslem.

At 7¾ m. is **Black Bull** (Stat.), from which New Chapel, where Brindley is buried, is about 1½ m. W. (Rte. 33). The ground now becomes very broken, and romantic as the Rly. runs under the eastern base of the millstone-grit ridge of *Mow-Cop*, or Congleton Edge, which rises to a considerable height, and constitutes the boundary between Staffordshire and Cheshire.

10 m. **Gillow Heath** (Stat.). To the E. are the townships of **Biddulph**, Biddulph Moor, Knypersley, Bradley Green, and Brindley Ford, all except the first comparatively recent places, and all seats of collieries, quarries, and ironworks. Biddulph is mentioned in Domesday, and it had a Ch. at a very early period: but the existing building is modern Gothic. It contains stained glass windows from Belgium, a richly carved stone altar, and an altar-tomb to the Bowyers of Knypersley, also their pew in good carved woodwork. The glass represents the Virgin and Child, the Wise Men of the East, Abraham offering Isaac, &c. In the Ch.-yard is a mortuary cross of Dec. date. On being removed seven incised slabs were found at its basement.

Not far from the Ch. is the noble seat of **Biddulph Grange** (Robert Heath, Esq.), formerly the residence of Mr. Jas. Bateman, who, some 50 years ago, created out of an old farmhouse and a swampy moor a series of the most perfect gardens in England, celebrated alike for the beauty and rarity of their contents, and for the choice and ingenious examples of landscape gardening, all rendered the more surprising from occurring in such a lofty and inhospitable region. A great feature in these gardens is the exquisite taste with which groupings of shrubs, such as Irish yews, aucubas, tree-ivy, &c., have been arranged. There are also an orangery, camellia and rhododendron houses, the latter filled with some of the most splendid specimens in England, such as R. Windsori and R. Nuttaliæ.

The house itself is a long irregular Italian building, and contains a very interesting geological gallery, and a model of a Roman tomb, in which is arranged a collection of cinerary urns and sarcophagi.

Among the many curiosities in the horticultural way may be mentioned the Egyptian Court, characterised by yew obelisks and pyramids; the Pinetum, devoted to pines, araucarias, and deodars; the Ravine, filled with ferns; the Arboretum, partly paved with stones brought from the Appian Way; the Wellingtonia Avenue; the Obelisk Walk, the gradients of which are so treated as to deceive the eye into the impression that what is really a path is an obelisk; the Rainbow, planted with rows of different coloured rhododendrons and azaleas; an Italian Garden, beyond which is a small sheet of water with a picturesque island; the Chinese Garden, which is approached by two mysterious paths through tunnels. At one of the entrances to which is the Glen, a romantic rocky hollow with a small lake hemmed in by masses of rocks, which are decorated by Chinese joss-houses, temples, bridges, dragons, and other Chinese monstrosities, such as bulls and frogs, which startle the visitor by their unusual and unexpected apparition. A tiny fort mounting two cannons commands the whole place. The pyracanths, junipers, barberries, &c., in this garden are extraordinarily fine. At the eastern end is the "Stumpery," which serves for a collection of Greenland roots and trailing plants. In fact, the whole of these unequalled grounds are cultivated and ornamented in every particle—not an inch is lost or wasted, and not a single opportunity is missed of a beautiful vista, a quaint decoration, or a surprise almost verging on the sensational. Immediately in front of the house are the cherry orchard, and what is called the Dahlia Walk, a splendid vista of colour when those flowers are blooming, but which is so arranged that it may be altogether avoided when they are out of flower. The whole excites a feeling of surprise and admiration that endures long after one has emerged again from this fairy-land into the moorland and rough country of North Staffordshire.

Visitors are admitted to the grounds with the guidance of a gardener. A waiting room is provided for their accommodation. The extensive fruit and vegetable gardens are at *Knypersley Hall*, which lies to the S., an old seat of the Bateman family. The glasshouses are most complete, including orchard houses for forcing full-grown trees. Prior to the Batemans it belonged to the Bowyers, and before them to the Knypersleys, in the time of Henry III. Sir John Bowyer was an active Parliamentarian, and Sir W. Dugdale records in his Diary, that he removed the Bowyer achievements from Biddulph Ch.

Adjoining the Grange are the ruins of Biddulph Hall, a noble specimen of Elizabethan manor-house (date 1588), built by Francis Biddulph, and destroyed in the time of his grandson, who was a devoted royalist. The siege took place in 1643, under Sir Wm. Brereton, the garrison being commanded by his nephew, Lord Brereton. But the Hall was very difficult to destroy, so they sent to Stafford for a famous cannon called "Roaring Meg," by the help of which the siege was successful. A modern house of the same name occupies a part of the old site (Robert Bateman, Esq.).

In the parish of Biddulph, in the opening between Cloud and Woof Lowe, stood the *Bridestones*, now destroyed, a fine early circle of 8 upright stones. Biddulph Moor, on which the Trent rises, was formerly inhabited by the "Biddlemoor men," a fierce, half-gipsy race, traditionally said to be descended from a Saracen, whom one of the early lords of Biddulph brought from the Holy Land, and made bailiff of this wild spot.

About 2 m. beyond Biddulph the line enters Cheshire, and reaches at

14 m. ♂ Congleton (Stat.). See *Handbook for Cheshire*.

ROUTE 37.

STOKE - ON - TRENT TO MARKET DRAYTON, BY NEWCASTLE-UNDER-LYME.

N. STAFFORDSHIRE RLY. 17½ m.

Leaving Stoke, the line passes the suburb of Hartshill, where are the new Ch., the Rom. Cath. convent, and the N. Stafford Infirmary, all buildings of considerable architectural merit (Rte. 33).

2 m. ♂ Newcastle-under-Lyme

Route 37.—Silverdale—Keele.

(Stat.). The town stands on a hill by the Lyme brook, but retains no trace of the New Castle, built about 1180 by Ranulph, Earl of Chester, whence it had its name. This was founded in the place of a Saxon stronghold at Chesterton, 2 m. N., but the town itself is of earlier origin, as is shown by the Norm. W. door of the Ch. Newcastle received a charter from Henry III. in 1235, and was possessed by Simon de Montfort, John of Gaunt, and other historic characters, but is not known as the scene of any important event. The waste lands around were inclosed in 1816, and a part of them has been laid out in public walks; other improvements have since been effected, but still the appearance of the place is quaint and old fashioned, without possessing any object of striking interest. The tower of the *Ch.* is lofty and well-proportioned, Norm. in the lower part and Dec. above. The body of the Ch., which was rebuilt in 1720, has been replaced by a structure more in agreement with the tower. The Educational Endowments are important, and include a High School and a Middle School for boys, and a High School for girls.

Newcastle was once a place of great business in hat-making, but it is now more occupied with brewing and paper-making; there are also ironworks and collieries in the neighbourhood. It was the birthplace of Sir Ralph Bagenal, a courtier and soldier of the time of Henry VIII. and the three succeeding reigns. Of him it is recorded that he alone, of all the Parliament, refused to be reconciled to Rome by Cardinal Pole, saying that he was sworn to the contrary to his old master. Harrison the regicide was also a native of the town, and Serjeant Bradshaw was its recorder. New Municipal Buildings, erected in 1890, in the Flemish style, provide an Assembly Hall and accommodation for the Free Library and School of Art.

5 m. **Silverdale** (Stat.), a colliery village, with a handsome modern Ch. with tower and spire. The geologist will find it to his account to examine the shale-heaps from the pits at Silverdale, which have yielded an extraordinary number of coal fishes. They have been figured by Sir Philip Egerton. There are also very extensive ironworks. From Silverdale a branch line goes off on N. to Harecastle (Rte. 33).

6¼ m. **Keele** (Stat.). Here also is a handsome modern Ch., in Dec. style, which has replaced the old structure. *Keele Hall* (R. Sneyd, Esq.) has been the seat of the family of Sneyd from the time of Edward III. The picturesque gabled structure, built by Ralph Sneyd in the 16th centy., having fallen into decay, his namesake re-erected it from Mr. Salvin's designs (1855). The new house, of red sandstone like the older one, follows its general features, but is much enlarged and enriched, and is one of the most successful of modern-antique mansions, while it is full of costly works of art. The gardens and grounds are very beautiful, command fine views, and have been much improved by the present proprietor. The hemlock spruce flourishes, and there is an avenue of deodars; but the chief lion is a clipped holly-hedge, 100 years old, measuring 612 ft. in length, 23 in height, and 24 thick at the base, and tapering upwards. There are other notable holly-hedges, but none so large.

9 m. **Madeley Road** (Stat.). For the village of Madeley, which lies 1 m. N. (Rte. 27).

At 11 m. the line passes into Shropshire.

11½ m. Pipe Gate (Stat.).
14¾ m. Norton-in-Hales (Stat.).

17½ m. **Market Drayton** (Stat.). See *Handbook for Shropshire*.

INDEX AND DIRECTORY, 1904.

Note.—While every effort has been made to render the information in the Index and Directory accurate up to the date of issue, travellers should, nevertheless, verify locally, and, in regard to conveyances, consult the current time-tables.
Mr. Edward Stanford, 12, 13, and 14, Long Acre, London, W.C., will be grateful for any corrections relating to these pages which travellers may be kind enough to address to him.

A.

ABBOTT'S BROMLEY, 178.
  Inns: *Dolphin; Bagot Arms; Goat's Head.*
  Pop.: 1318.
ABBOTT'S OAK, 127.
ABNEY MOOR, 56.
ACTON TRUSSELL, 147.
ALBION, 142.
ALBRIGHTON, 142.
ALDERWASLEY, 26.
ALDRIDGE, 158.
ALFRETON, 15.
  Inn: *George.*
  Pop.: 17,505.
ALLESTREE, 16.
ALREWAS, 168.
ALSOP, 199.
ALSTONEFIELD, 203.

ALTON, 207.
  Inns: *Shrewsbury H.; Talbot.*

ALTON TOWERS, 207.
  Stat.: Alton, N. Staff. Rly.
  Gardens and grounds are open to the public on Monday, Tuesday, Wednesday, and Saturday in summer. Admission 1s. House seldom shown.
AMBER RIVER, 20.

AMBERGATE JUNCTION, 20.
  Inn: *Hurt Arms.*
ANCHOR CHURCH, 3.
ANDLE STONE, 31.
ANNESLEY HALL, 87.
Antiquities, [25].
APEWOOD CASTLE, 157.
AQUALATE HALL, 183.
ARBORLOWS, 32.
Arkwright, Sir Richard, 27.

[*Derby, &c.*—vi. '04.]

ARLEY CASTLE, 154.
ARMITAGE, 180.
ARNSBY, 130.
ASFORDBY, 117.

ASHBOURNE, 197.
  Inn: *Green Man.*
  Pop.: 4039.
  Distances: Derby, 13 m.; Burton, 25 m.; Uttoxeter, 11 m.; Alton Towers, 9 m.

ASHBY - DE - LA - ZOUCH, 122.
  Inns: *Royal H.; Queen's Head H.*
  Pop.: 4726.
ASHCOMBE HALL, 210.

ASHFORD, 43.
  Inns: *Devonshire Arms; Bull's Head.*
ASHLEY, 150.
ASHOP RIVER, 57.

ASHOPTON, 58.
  Inn recommended.
  Distances: Hathersage, 6 m.; Mytham Bridge, 3 m.; Hope, 4 m.; Derwent Chapel, 1¼ m.; Glossop, 13 m.; Sheffield, 11 m.

ASHOVER, 21.
  Inn: *Red Lion.*
  Hydropathic Establishments: *Ashover; Prospect House.*
ASHWOOD DALE, 44.
ASLACTON, 80.
ASTON HALL, 143.
ASTON JUNCTION, 143.
ATTENBOROUGH, 66.
AUDLEY, 152.
AULDLEY'S CROSS, 100.
AULT HUCKNALL, 90.
AVERHAM, 76.
AXE EDGE, 49.
AYLESTONE, 108.

B.

BACH TOR, 53.
BACK FOREST, 212.
BADGERS' CROFT, 213.
BAGOT'S PARK, 179.
BAGSHAW'S CAVE, 56.
BAGWORTH, 121.

BAKEWELL, 33.
  Inns: *Rutland Arms H.* (tickets for fishing in the Wye can be obtained at the hotel); *Red Lion; Queen's Arms.*
  Pop.: 2850.
  Distances: Buxton, by road 12 m., by rail 11½ m.; Matlock, 9 m.; Ashbourne, 16 m.; Stony Middleton, 5 m.; Castleton, 14 m.; and by Middleton, 16 m.; Chatsworth, 4 m., by Edensor, 3 m.; Haddon, 2 m.
BALDERTON, 78.
BAMFORD, 58.
BARDON HILL, 122.
BARLASTON, 186.
BARLBOROUGH, 24.
BARMOOR CLOUGH, 50.
BARMOTE COURTS, 18.
BARNBY MOOR, 103.
BARNSTON, 121.
BARR BEACON, 144.
BARROW-ON-SOAR, 132.
Barrows, [26].
BARTON IN FABIS, 66.
BARTON - UNDER - NEEDWOOD, 173.
BASFORD, 83.

BASLOW, 62.
  Inns: *Peacock; Wheatsheaf; Rutland Arms; Devonshire Arms; Royal;* also a large Hydropathic Establishment.

Q

BASWICH, 182.
BATHAM ROAD, 59.

BAWTRY, 104.
Inn: *Crown.*
BEACON HILL, 131.
BEAUCHIEF ABBEY, 25.
BEAUDESERT, 180.
BEAUMANOR, 131.
BEAUMOND CROSS, 77.
BEAUMONT LEYS, 109.
BEAUVALE ABBEY, 83.
BEE LOW, 32.
BEELEY, 31.
BEESTHORPE HALL, 99.
BEESTON, 67.
BELGRAVE, 131.
BELLAMOUR HALL, 181.
BELMONT, 210.

BELPER, 19.
Inn: *Lion H.*
Pop.: 10,934.
BELTON, 126.

BELVOIR CASTLE, 81.
Stats.: Bottesford (G. N. Rly.) and Redmile (G. N. and L. & N. W. Joint Rly.). The Castle is open free daily (Sundays excepted), from 11 A.M. to 5 P.M. Tickets of admission, 3d. each, may be obtained at the Stations.
BENTLEY BROOK, 198.
BENTLEY HALL, 145.
BENTY GRANGE, 200.
BERESFORD DALE, 203.
BERESFORD HALL, 204.
BERRY HILL, 151.
BERTH, THE, 151.
BESCOT, 144.
BESCOT HALL, 144.
BESTWOOD COLLIERY, 83.
BESTWOOD LODGE, 74.
BETLEY, 152.
BETLEY ROAD, 152.
BIDDULPH, 214.
BIDDULPH GRANGE, 214.
BIDDULPH HALL, 215.
BIDDULPH MOOR, 214.
BIGGIN, 200.
BILHAUGH, 96.
BILLESDON, 119.
BILSTON, 137.

BINGHAM, 79.
Inn: *Chesterfield Arms.*
BINGHAM ROAD, 121.
BIRCHILLS, 175.
BIRD'S NEST, 129.
BIRKLAND FOREST, 96.
BIRSTALL, 131.
BLABY, 116.
BLACK BULL, 214.
BLACKLANDS, 154.
BLACK MERE, 212.
BLACK ROCKS, THE, 27.
BLACKWELL, 16.
BLAKE LOW, 45.
BLAKOW HILL, 103.
BLASTON, 107.
BLEASBY, 75.
BLITHBURY, 177.
BLITHFIELD, 179.
BLORE, 150, 201.
BLOXWICH, 175.
BLUE JOHN MINE, 55.
BLURTON, 188.
BLYMHILL, 147.
BLYTH, 104.
BLYTH BRIDGE, 192.
BOBBINGTON, 154.
Bobbin-net, [21].

BOLSOVER, 91; The Castle, 91.
Visitors are allowed to walk in the grounds, but the interior is private except on special application.
Inn: *Swan.*
Pop.: 6844.
BONSALL, 29.
BOOTH'S EDGE, 60.
BOROUGH HOLES, 202.
BORROWASH, 65.
BORROWCOP HILL, 167.
BOSWORTH FIELD, 114.
BOTHAMS, 210.

BOTTESFORD, 80.
Inn: *Rutland Arms.*
BOW CROSS, 37.
BRADBOURNE, 199.
BRADFORD RIVER, 32, 43.
BRADGATE PARK, 127.
BRADLEY, 137.
BRADLEY GREEN, 214.
BRADLEY HALL, 155.
BRADSHAW HALL, 51.
BRADWELL, 56.

BRAMCOTE, 14.
BRAMPTON, 23.
BRAMSHALL, 193.
BRAND, THE, 131.
BREADSALL, 16.
BREASTON, 66.
BREEDON, 12.
BREEDON BULWARKS, 12.
BRENT'S HILL, 66.
BRETBY PARK, 124.
BRETTELL LANE, 155.
BREWOOD, 146.
BREWOOD HALL, 146.
BRIDESTONES, 215.
BRIERLEY HILL, 155.
BRINDLEY FORD, 214.
BROCKTON, 182.
BROMLEY HALL, 150.
BROOKHILL HALL, 15.
BROOKSBY, 117.
BROUGH (DERBY), 59.
BROUGH (NOTTS.), 78.
BROUGHTON, 150.
BROUGHTON-ASTLEY, 130.
BROWN EDGE, 214.
BROWNHILLS, 159.
BRUSHFIELD HOUGH, 44.
BUCKMINSTER, 119.
BUCKNALL, 214.
BUDBY, 100.
BUGSWORTH, 51.
BULWELL, 83.
BULWELL FOREST, 83.
BUNKER'S HILL, 32.
BUNSTER, 201.
BURBAGE, 49.
BURNTWOOD, 159.
BURROW, 120.

BURSLEM, 189.
Inn: *Leopard.*
Pop.: 38,766.
BURTON CLOSES,
BURTON HALL, 133.
BURTON JOYCE, 74.
BURTON LAZARS, 118.
BURTON OVERY, 108.

BURTON-ON-TRENT, 173.
Inns: *Queen's; George; White Hart.*
Pop.: 50,386.
Distances: London, 122¼ m.; Derby, 11 m.; Tutbury, 5 m.; Tamworth, 13 m.; Swannington, 13¼ m.; Ashby-de-la-Zouch, 9¼ m.;

INDEX AND DIRECTORY. 219

Lichfield, 12 m.; Wolverhampton, 28 m.; Rugby, 52 m; Birmingham, 33¼ m.
BURY BANK, 186.
BURY RING, 147.
BUSHBURY, 145.
BUTLER'S HILL, 83.
BUTTERLEY HALL, 15.
BUTTERLEY IRON COMPANY, 17.
BUTTERTON HALL, 151.
BUTTERTON MOOR, 212.

BUXTON, 46.
  Inns: *Palace H.*, near the Stat.; *Empire H.*; *St. Anne's H.*; *Crescent H.*; *Old Hall H.*, in the Crescent; *Lee Wood H.*; *George H.*; *Shakespere H.*; *Grove H.*; *Eagle H.*; *King's Head H.*; *Midland H.*
  Hydropathic Establishments: Clarendon (Corber Hill); Haddon Hall; Buxton Hydro.
  Pop.; 10,181.
  Distances: Bakewell, 12 m.; Chatsworth, 14 m.; Haddon Hall, 14 m.; Miller's Dale, 5 m.; Tideswell, 7 m.; Ashford, 10½ m.; Dove Holes, 3 m.; Castleton, 12 m.; Chapel-en-le-Frith, 6 m.; Leek, 12 m.; Longnor, 6½ m.; Axe Edge, 3½ m.; Macclesfield, 12 m.; Whaley Bridge (by rail), 9 m.
BYRCHOVER, 31.
Byron, Lord, 28, 84, 87, 94.

C.

CAKES OF BREAD, 58.
CALKE ABBEY, 12.
CALLINGWOOD, 178.
CALVER, 62.
CALVERTON, 75.
CALWICH ABBEY, 197.
CAMP HILL, 151.

CANNOCK, 176.
  Inn: *Crown.*
  Pop.: 23,974.
CANWELL, 171.
CARBURTON, 101.
CARCLIFF TOR, 32.

CARCOLSTON, 80.
CARL'S WARK, 60.
CARLTON, 74.
CARLTON-CURLIEU, 107.
CARLTON-IN-LINDRICK, 104.
CARLTON-ON-TRENT, 101.
CASTLECHURCH, 149.
CASTLE CLIFFS, 212.
CASTLE DONINGTON, 13.
CASTLE OLD FORT, 159.

CASTLETON, 53.
  Inns: *Castle* (comfortable); *Nag's Head; Bull's Head.*
  Pop.: 547.
CAT AND FIDDLE INN, 50, 213.
CAULDON CANAL, 210.
CAULDON LOW, 210.
CAUNTON, 99.
CAVE DALE, 56.
CAVERSWALL, 192.
CHADDESDEN, 64.

CHAPEL-EN-LE-FRITH, 51.
  Inn: *King's Arms.*
CHARLESWORTH, 63.
CHARLEY HALL, 127.
CHARNWOOD FOREST, [17], 133.
CHARTLEY, 184.
CHASE TOWN, 159.

CHATSWORTH, 37.
  Inn: See EDENSOR.
  Stats.: Rowsley, Bakewell, and Hassop (Midland Rly.).
  Conveyances from Bakewell and Buxton.
  Admittance to Chatsworth House and grounds is liberally given to all persons every day in the week (except Sunday), between the hours of 11 A.M. and 4 P.M., except on Saturdays, when no one is admitted after 1 P.M. The park is open on Sundays.
CHATTERLEY, 191.

CHEADLE, 209.
  Inns: *Wheatsheaf; Royal Oak.*
  Pop.: 5186.
CHEBSEY, 149.
CHECKLEY, 193.
CHEDDLETON, 210.
CHEE TOR, 46, 49.

CHELLASTON, 10.
CHELMORTON, 44.

CHESTERFIELD, 22.
  Inns: *Angel H.; Station H.*
  Pop.: 27,185.
  Distances: Sheffield, by road, 12 m.; Bolsover, 6 m.
CHESTERFIELD (STAFFS.), 168.
CHILLINGTON HALL, 141.
CHILWELL, 66.
CHINLEY CHURN, 51.
  The Rly. between Chinley and Dore was opened in 1894.
CHROME TOR, 205.
CHUNAL, 63.
CHURCH BRIDGE, 176.
CHURCH GRESLEY, 124.
CHURCH MAYFIELD, 197.
CHURCH ROCK, 203.
CHURCH STERNDALE, 200.
CLAREBOROUGH, 102.
CLAYBROOKE, 129.

CLAY CROSS JUNCTION. 16, 22.
CLAYWORTH, 103.
CLIFTON (DERBY), 197.
CLIFTON (NOTTS.), 67.
CLIFTON CAMPVILLE, 171.
CLIFSTONE, 95.
CLOUD HILL, 211.
CLOWN, 24.
CLUDD'S OAK, 94.

CLUMBER PARK, 100.
  Stats.: Worksop and Mansfield (G. C. Rly.).
  Conveyances to be obtained at the Hotels, where permission to drive through the park may be obtained. The house may be shown during the absence of the family if previous application is made.
Coal-fields, [4], [8], [10], [13], [14], [23].
COALVILLE, 122.
COBRIDGE, 190.
COLNOR PARK, 15, 17.
CODSALL, 141.
COLEORTON, 124.
COLLINGHAM, 78.
COLTON, 181.
COLWICH, 181.
COLWICK HALL, 74.

Q 2

COMBERFORD HALL, 171.
COMB'S MOSS, 50.
Communications, [16].
CONEYGREE, 78.
[CONGLETON], 215.
   Inns: *Swan; Bull*.
   Pop.: 10,707.
COPLOW, THE, 120.
COP MERE, 150.
COPT OAK, 127.
CORTLINGSTOCK, or COSTOCK, 134.
COSKLEY, 143.
COTHAM, 121.
COUNTESTHORPE, 130.
COXBENCH, 16.
COXE'S ROUGH, 142.
COXMOOR, 87.
CRADLEY, 151.
CRAKEMARSH, 197, 206.
CRANOE, 108.
CRESSBROOK DALE, 44, 45.
CRESSWELL, 192.
CRESWELL, 24, 96.
CRESWELL CRAGS, 25, 96.
CRESWELL HALL, 149.
CREWE, 152.
CRICH, 26.
CRICH HILL, 26.
CROFT, 116.

CROMFORD, 26.
   Inn: *Greyhound*.
CROMFORD MOOR, 27.
CROMFORD SOUGH, 19, 27.
CROMWELL, 101.
CRONKSTONE HILL, 200.
CROWDECOTE, 205.
CROXALL, 171.
CROXDEN ABBEY, 206.
CROXTON, 150.
CROXTON KYRIEL, 120.
CROXTON PARK, 120.
CUCKLET CHURCH, 61.
CUCKNEY HILL, 96.
CUCKOO BUSH, 67.

D.

DADLINGTON, 115.
DALBURY, 4.
DALE ABBEY, 64.
DANES' BALK, 24.

DARLASTON, 145, 186.
DARLEY, 30.
DARLEY ABBEY, 16.
DARLEY DALE, 31.
DARNALL, 25.
DAYBROOK, 82.
DEAN HALL, 99.
DEEPFIELDS, 143.
DENBY, 17.
DENSTONE, 207.
DEPTH O' LUMB, 20.

DERBY, 4.
   Inns: *Midland H.* (close to the Stat.); *Royal H.*; *Bell H.*; *St. James's H.* (in the town).
   Pop.: 105,912.
   Railways: Midland Rly. chief Stat., Midland Road, also Nottingham Road Stat.; Great Northern Rly. Stat. in Friargate; London and N.-W. Rly., and North Staffordshire Rly. at Midland Stat.
   Distances: London, 127 m.; Birmingham, 42¼ m.; Leicester, 29¼ m.; Nottingham, 15¾ m.; Manchester, 59 m.; Lichfield, 23¼ m.; Chesterfield, 24 m.; Trent Junction, 8 m.; Ashbourne, 13 m.

DERWENT CHAPEL, 58.
DERWENT HALL, 58.
DERWENT RIVER, 58.
DESFORD, 121.
DETHICK, 29.
DEVON RIVER, [9], 76.
DIAMOND HILL, 49.
DICKON'S NOOK, 115.
DIEULACRESSE ABBEY, 211.
DILHORNE, 192.
DINTING VIADUCT, 63.
DISHLEY GRANGE, 132.
DOE HILL, 16.
DONCASTER, 104.
DONINGTON PARK, 13.
DONNINGTON-ON-THE-HEATH, 122.
DORE, 25.
   The Rly. between Dore and Chinley was opened in 1894.
DOVECLIFF HOUSE, 196.

DOVEDALE, 200.
   For Inns, see THORPE and ILAM.

DOVE HOLES, 50.
DOVEHOLES, 203.
DOVERIDGE, 194, 197.
DOVE RIVER, 195.
DOWEL, 205.
DRAKELOW HALL, 124, 175.
DRAYCOTT (DERBY), 66.
DRAYCOTT-IN-THE-MOORS, 192.
DRAYTON BASSETT, 170.
DRESDEN, 188.

DRONFIELD, 25.
   Inn: *Blue Posts*.
   Pop.: 3809.

[DUDLEY], 155.
   Inn: *Dudley Arms H*.
   Pop.: 48,733.
DUDLEY PORT JUNCTION, 142, 157.
DUFFIELD, 17.
DUKE'S DRIVE, 48.
DUKE'S FOLLY, 95.
DUKERIES, THE, 95.
DUNFORD BRIDGE, 64.
DUNGEON TOR, 28.
DYMPUS, 51.

E.

EAKRING, 99.
EARL SHILTON, 116.
EARL STERNDALE, 200.
EAST LEAKE, 133.
EAST MARKHAM, 102.
EAST MOOR, 23.
   Inn: *Robin Hood*.
EAST NORTON, 119.
EAST RETFORD, 102.
EAST STOKE, 75.
EASTWOOD, 15.
ECCLESALL, 25.
ECCLESBOURN, VALLEY OF THE, 17.

ECCLESHALL, 149.
   Inns: *Royal Oak; King's Arms*.
ECKINGTON, 24.
ECTON HILL, 202, 212.
EDALE, 57.

EDENSOR, 37.
   Inn: *Chatsworth H.*, first

INDEX AND DIRECTORY. 221

class and very moderate.
Tickets for fishing may be
procured at the hotel, and an
omnibus meets the trains at
the Rowsley Stat.
EDGBASTON, 142.
EDINGLEY, 94.
EDWALTON, 119.

EDWINSTOWE, 96.
   Inn: *Royal Oak H.*
EGGINTON, 2.
ELDON HOLE, 52.
ELFORD, 171.
ELLASTONE, 197.
ELLENHALL, 183.
ELMESTHORPE, 116.
ELMTON, 24, 96.
ELTON, 80.
ELVASTON, 65.
ELVASTON CASTLE, 65.
ENDON, 210.

ENVILLE, 154.
   Inn: *Stamford Arms H.*
EREWASH VALLEY, 13.
ERRWOOD HALL, 50.
ESSINGTON, 145.
ETHEROW RIVER, 63.
ETOCETUM, 159, 168.
ETRURIA, 190.
ETTINGSHALL ROAD, 138, 141.
ETWALL, 3.

EYAM, 61.
   Inn: *Bull's Head.*
EYAM MOOR, 60.

F.

FAIRBROOK NAZE, 57.
FAIRFIELD, 49.
FARNSFIELD, 94.
FARWELL, 181.
FAULD HALL, 195.
FAWFIELD, 212.
FAZELEY, 170.
FENNY BENTLEY, 198.
FENTON, 191.
FERNILEE, 50.
FERNS, THE, 12.
FILLYFORD BRIDGE, 43.

FIN COP, 44.
FINDERN, 4.
FISHERWICK PARK, 180.
FISKERTON, 75.
FLASH, 213.
FLASH BOTTOM, 213.
FLAWFORTH, 67.
FLOOD DYKE, 95.
FORD GREEN, 214.
FOREMARK HALL, 3.
FORTON, 183.
FOSSE WAY, [32], 66, 129.
FOUNTAIN DALE, 87.
FOUR ASHES, 146.
FOUR CROSSES, 146.
FOXTON, 108.
FOX TOR, 43.
FRADLEY HALL, 168.
FRISBY, 117.
FRITH, THE, 205.
FROGHALL, 210.
FROLESWORTH, 130.
FULWOOD'S CASTLE, 32.

G.

GARENDON PARK, 132.
GAYTON, 185.
GEDLING, 74.
Geology, [7].
GIB HILL, 32, 204.
GILLOW HEATH, 214.
GLAPWELL, 90.
GLENFIELD, 121, 129.
GLEN MAGNA, 108.
GLEN PARVA, 116.

GLOSSOP, 63.
   Inn: *Howard Arms.*
   Pop.: 21,526.
GLUTTON BRIDGE, 205.
GLUTTON DALE, 205.
GNOSALL, 183.
GOADBY MARWOOD, 120.
GOLDSITCH MOSS, 212.
GONALSTON, 75.
GOPSALL HALL, 116.
GORNAL, 141.
GOSPEL HILLOCK, 44.

GOTHAM, 66.
GOYT RIVER, 50.
GRACE DIEU MANOR, 125.
GRADBACH, 212.
GRAND JUNCTION RAILWAY, 143.
GRAND TRUNK CANAL, 186.
GRANED TOR, 32.

GRANTHAM, 82.
   Inn: *Angel H.*
GREASLEY, 15.
GREAT BARR, 144.
GREAT BRIDGE, 157.
GREAT BRIDGEFORD, 149.
GREAT DALBY, 120.
GREAT HAYWOOD, 183.
GREAT MADELEY, 151.
GREAT WIGSTON, 108.
GREENDALE OAK, 96.
GRESLEY, 124.
GRESLEY CASTLE, 83.
Grey, Lady Jane, 127.
GRIMSTON, 119.
GRINDLEFORD BRIDGE, 60.
GRINDLEY, 185.
GRINDON, 202.
GRINGLEY, 103.
GRINLOW, 49.
GROBY CASTLE, 128.
GROBY POOL, 129.
GUMLEY, 107.

H.

HADDON HALL, 34.
   Stats.: Rowsley and
   Bakewell (Midl. Rly.).
   Conveyances from Row-
   sley, Bakewell, and Buxton.
HAGLEY HALL, 177.
HALES, 151.
HALES HALL, 210.
HALLAMSHIRE HOUNDS, 60.
HALLATON, 119.
HALLOUGHTON, 94.
HAMBLETON HILL, 88.
HAMMERWICH, 159.
HAMPS RIVER, 212.
HAMSTALL RIDWARE, 177.

HAMSTEAD HALL, 144.
HANBURY, 194.
HANDSWORTH, 135.
HANGING BRIDGE, 200.

HANLEY, 190.
Inn: *Saracen's Head*.
Pop.: 61,599.
HANSACRE, 177.
HARBORNE, 136.
HARBY, 121.

HARDWICK HALL, 89.
Stat.: Rowthorn and Hardwick (Midl. Rly.).
Conveyances from Chesterfield and Mansfield.
Open to the public daily from 10 A.M. till 4 P.M.
HARECASTLE, 188.
HARLASTON, 171.

HARTINGTON, 204.
Inn: *Charles Cotton*.
Distances: Winster, 7½ m.; Ashbourne, turough Tissington, 10 m.; Bakewell, 9 m.; Arborlow, 4 m.; Kenslow, 3½ m.; Youlgreave, 6 m.; Longnor, 5 m.
HARTSHILL, 191, 215.
HASELOUR, 171.
HASSOP, 45.
HATHERN, 133.

HATHERSAGE, 59.
Inns: *Ordnance Arms; George*.
HATHERTON HALL, 146.
HAUGHTON, 182.
HAWKSYARD PARK, 180.
HAWTON, 78.

HAYFIELD, 61.
Inns: *Royal; George*.
Pop.: 2614.
HAY TOP, 45.
HAYWOOD ABBEY, 183.
HAZLEWOOD, 17.
HEANOR, 14.
HEATHFIELD, 135.
HEATHY LEE, 212.

HEDNESFORD, 176.
Inn: *Anglesey H*.
HEELEY, 25.
HEIGHTS OF ABRAHAM, 29.
HEMINGTON, 134.
HEMLOCK STONE, 14.

HEN CLOUD, 212.
HEN MOOR, 200.
HENGRAVE, 94.
HIGGAR TOR, 60.
HIGH CROSS, 129.
HIGHLOW, 60.
HIGH OFFLEY, 183.
HIGH PEAK RAILWAY, 27, 49, 200.
HIGH TOR, 28.
HIGH WHEELDON, 205.
HILTON, 196.
HILTON PARK, 145.
HIMLEY HALL, 157.

HINCKLEY, 114.
Inn: *George*
Pop.: 11,304.
HINDLOW, 206.
HINTS, 170.
HITTER HILL, 206.
HIXON, 183.
HOARCROSS HALL, 178.
HOBY, 117.
HOCKLEY, 134.
HODSOCK PRIORY, 104.
HOLBEACH HOUSE, 157.
HOLBROOKE, 16.
HOLBROOKE HALL, 17.
HOLLINS, 206.
HOLME, 101.
HOLME PIERREPONT, 79.
HOPE, 58.
HOPTON HALL, 19.
HOPTON HEATH, 184.
HORSLEY, 17.
HORTON, 213.
HOVERINGHAM, 75.
HOWBANK HILL, 119.
HUCKNALL TORKARD, 83.
HUGGLESCOTE, 122.
HULTON ABBEY, 190.
HUMBERSTONE, 120.
HURST HILL, 143.

I.

IBSTOCK, 121.
Icknield Street, [14].
IDRIDGEHAY, 17.

ILAM, 201.
Inn: *Izaak Walton H*.
ILAM STONE, 203.

ILKESTON, 14.
Inn: *Rutland H*.
Pop.: 25,384.
Industrial Resources, [19].
INGARSBY, 120.
INGESTRE, 183.
INGLEBY, 3.
IPSTONES, 210.
IPSTONES EDGE, 210.
Iron Manufacture, [23].
IRONVILLE, 15.
IZAAK WALTON HOTEL, 202.

J.

JAMES BRIDGE, 145.
JOHN O'GAUNT, 120.
Johnson, Dr. Samuel, 116, 167.
JORDAN CASTLE, 99.

K.

KEDLESTON, 10.
KEDLESTON HALL, 8.
KEELE, 216.
KEELE HALL, 216.
KEGWORTH, 133.
KELHAM, 99.
KELHAM HALL, 76.
KENSLOW, 32, 204.
KETTLEBY, 117.
KIBWORTH, 107.
KIDSGROVE, 188.
KILBURN, 17.
KIMBERLEY, 15.
KINDER, 61.
KINDERSCOUT, 51, 63.
KING JOHN'S PALACE, 95.
KING RICHARD'S WELL, 115.

KING'S BROMLEY, 177.
KINGSHAUGH, 102.
KING'S LOW, 182.
KING'S NEWTON, 11.
KING'S STERNDALE, 44.
KING'S SWINFORD, 155.
KINGSTON HALL, 133.
KINGSTON-ON-SOAR, 133.
KINLET, 154.
KINVASTON, 146.
KINVER, 154.
KIRBY BELLARS, 117.
KIRBY MUXLOE, 121.
KIRKBY FOREST, 87.
KIRKBY JUNCTION, 15, 87.
KIRKLINGTON, 94.
KNAVE'S CASTLE, 159.
KNEETON, 75.
KNESALL, 99.
KNOWL HILLS, 12.
KNYPERSLEY, 214.
KNYPERSLEY HALL, 215.

L.

Lace Manufacture, [21].
LAIDMAN'S LOW, 49.
LAMBLEY, 75.
LANGAR, 80.
LANGFORD, 66.
LANGLEY MILL, 14.
LANGTONS, THE, 107.
LANGWITH, 24, 96.
LAPLEY, 147.
LATHKILL, VALE OF, 43.
LAUND ABBEY, 120.
LEA, 29.
LEA HURST, 26.
Lead mines, [20].

LEEK, 210.
  Inns: *George; Red Lion; Roebuck.*
  Pop.: 15,484.
LEEN RIVER, 68.

LEICESTER, 108.
  Inns: *Bell H.; Wellington H.*
  Pop.: 211,579.

Railways: Midland and L. & N.-W. Rlys. Joint Stat., Campbell St.; G. N. Rly. Stat., Belgrave Rd; Midland Rly. to Coalville, Stat. West Bridge; G. C. Rly. Central Stat.
  Distances: Lutterworth, 13 m.; Syston, 4¼ m.; Mount Sorrel, 7 m.; Loughborough, 12 m.; Bosworth Field, 14 m.; Bradgate Park, 6 m.; Newtown Linford, 5¼ m. Groby, 4 m.; Ulverscroft Priory, 7 m.; Charnwood Forest, 10 m.; Belvoir Castle, *via* Melton, 27 m.

LEICESTER HEADLAND, 124.
LEIGH, 192.
LENTON, 82.

LICHFIELD, 159; CATHEDRAL, 160.
  Inns: *George H.; Swan H.*
  Pop.: 7902.
LINBY, 83.
LION'S HEAD, THE, 203.
LITTLE ASTON HALL, 158.
LITTLE EATON, 16.
LITTLE HUCKLOW, 46.
LOAD MILL, 203.
LOCKINGTON, 134.
LOCKO PARK, 64.
LODDINGTON HALL, 119.
LOMBERDALE, 32.
LONG CLAWSON, 121.
LONGCROFT HALL, 178.
LONGDON, 181.
LONG EATON, 13.
LONGNOR, 205.
LONGPORT, 190, 191.
LONGSTONE EDGE, 44.
LONGSTONE, GREAT AND LITTLE, 45.
LONGTON, 191.
LORD'S SEAT, 60.
LOSEBY HALL, 120.
LOSE HILL, 53, 57.

LOUGHBOROUGH, 132.
  Inns: *King's Head; Bull's Head.*
  Pop.: 21,508.
  Rly. Stat.: G. C. Rly.
LOVER'S LEAP, 45, 48, 62.
LOVERS' WALK, 28.
LOWDHAM, 75.
LOW HARDWICK, 88.

LOW HILL, 145.
LOXLEY HALL, 193.
LUBBESTHORPE ABBEY, 108.
LUD CHURCH, 212.
LUMB, THE, 212.

LUTTERWORTH, 129.
  Inns: *Denbigh Arms; Hind.*
  Rly. Stat.: G. C. Rly.
LYE, THE, 153.
LYME HALL, 50.

M.

MACCLESFIELD, 213.
MADELEY, 151.
MADELEY MANOR, 152.
MADELEY ROAD, 216.
MADWOMAN'S STONES, 57.
MAER, 151.
MAJOR OAK, 96.
MAM TOR, 52, 56.
MANIFOLD RIVER, 201.

MANSFIELD, 88.
  Inns: *Swan; Midland.*
  Pop.: 21,445.
MANSFIELD WOODHOUSE, 95.
MAPLEBECK, 99.
MAPLEWELL, 131.
MAPPLETON, 200.
MARCHINGTON, 194.
MAREFIELD, 120.
MARKET BOSWORTH, 115.
MARKET DRAYTON, 151, 216.

MARKET HARBOROUGH, 106.
  Inns: *Three Swans; Angel.*
  Pop.: 7735.
MARKFIELD, 127.
MARKHAM MOOR, 102.
MARKLAND GRIPS, 24.
MARSTON MONTGOMERY, 194.
MARSTON-ON-THE-DOVE, 196.
Mary Queen of Scots, 8, 21, 38, 46, 47, 90, 104, 122, 184, 195.
MASSON, 29.

INDEX AND DIRECTORY.

MATLOCK BANK, 30.
Hydropathic Establishments : Smedley's ; Matlock House ; Rock Side House.

MATLOCK BATH, 27.
Inns: *New Bath H.; Royal H.; Temple; Bath Terrace H.*
Pop. (including Scarthin Nick and Matlock): 7798.
Swimming Baths: Fountain Baths ; and at the New Bath and Royal Hotels.
Distances: Rowsley, 5; m. ; Haddon Hall, 7¼ m. ; Bakewell, 10 m. ; Chatsworth, 10 m. ; Wingfield Manor, 9 m. ; Hardwick, 17 m. ; Alton Towers, 22 m. ; Buxton, 22 m.
One-horse carriage for 15 m. cost 25s., and a pair horse carriage, 35s.
There are omnibuses in the season to Chatsworth, Haddon Hall, and other places.

MATLOCK BRIDGE, 29.
Inns: *Old English H ; The Crown ; Queen's Head.*
MATLOCK CAVES, 28.
MATLOCK DALE, 27.
MATTERSEY, 103.
MAVESYN RIDWARE, 177.
MAYFIELD, 197.
MEAFORD HALL, 186.
MEDBOURNE, 106.
MEERBROOK, 212.

MELBOURNE, 11.
Inn: *Melbourne H.*
MELLOR, 51.

MELTON MOWBRAY, 117.
Inns: *Bell H.; George H.*
Pop. : 7454.
METCULEY, 136.
MICKLEOVER, 4.
MIDDLETON, 29.
MIDDLETON DALE, 62.
MIDDLETON HALL, 62.
MILFORD (DERBY), 19.
MILFORD (STAFFS.), 183.
MILL DALE, 203.
MILLER'S DALE, 44, 45.
MILTON, 210, 214.
MOAT IN RIBDEN, 197.
MOCK BEGGARS' HALL, 32.

MOIRA, 123.
Mompesson, Rev. W., 61.
MONMORE GREEN, 143.
MONSAL DALE, 44.
Montague, Lady Mary Wortley, 100.
MONTASH, 200.
MOORHOUSE, 102.
MOORLANDS, THE, [11], 212.
MORLEY, 16.
MORRIDGE, THE, [14], 205.
MOSELEY OLD HALL, 145.
MOUNT ST. BERNARD ABBEY, 126.

MOUNT SORREL, 130.
Inn: *White Swan.*
MOW COP, 214.
MOWSLEY, 108.
MOXLEY, 137.
MUCKLESTONE, 151.
MUSKHAM BRIDGE, 101.
MYTHAM BRIDGE, 57, 59.

N.

NARBOROUGH, 116.
NEEDWOOD FOREST, 177, 178.
NELSON'S PILLAR, 23.
NETHER SEAL, 124.
NETHERTHORPE, 24.
NETHERTON, 155.
NEVILL HOLT, 106.

NEWARK-ON-TRENT, 76 ;
THE CASTLE, 76.
Inns: *Clinton Arms H. ; Ram H. ; Saracen's Head ; Ossington Coffee Palace.*
Pop. : 14,992.
NEWBOLD VERDON, 121.
NEWBOROUGH, 178.

NEWCASTLE - UNDER - LYME, 215.
Inn: *Castle.*
Pop. : 19,914.
NEW CHAPEL, 189.
NEWHAVEN HOUSE INN, 200.
NEW MILLS, 51.

NEWPORT, 183.
Inns: *Shakespeare; Victoria.*
NEWSTEAD, 83.

NEWSTEAD ABBEY, 83.
Stats. : Newstead on Midl. and G. N. Rlys.
Admission to view the Abbey and grounds is granted on Tuesdays, Wednesdays, and Fridays by tickets only, which are obtainable by visitors to the *George H.*, Nottingham, *Swan H.*, Mansfield, and *Newstead Stat. H.*, to which a limited number of tickets are issued under certain conditions. The Abbey is always closed in Easter and Whitsun weeks.
NEWTHORPE, 15.
NEWTON ROAD, 144.
NEWTON SOLNEY, 2.
NEWTOWN LINFORD, 127.
NEW VILLAGE, 143.
Nightingale, Miss Florence, 26.
NINE LADIES, 31.
NORBURY (DERBY), 197.
NORBURY (STAFFS.), 183.
NORMANTON, 4, 81.
NORMANTON-ON-SOAR, 133.
NORTH LEES, 59.
NORTH MUSKHAM, 101.
NORTH WINGFIELD, 22.
NORTON, 25.
NORTON BRIDGE JUNCTION, 149.
NORTON-IN-HALFS, 216.
NORTON-IN-THE-MOORS, 214.
NORWOOD, 94.
NOSELEY, 108.

NOTTINGHAM, 67 ; THE CASTLE, 68 ; STANDARD HILL, 69.
Inns: *George H. ; Clarendon H. ; Flying Horse H. ; Wellington ; Victoria ; Maypole ; Grosvenor H.*, at Carrington.
Pop. : 239,743.
Railways : Midland Rly. Stat. in Station Street ; G. N. Rly , London Road ; Great Central and G. N. R., Mansfield Road.
Distances : Derby, 15½ m. ; Mansfield, 14 m. ; Sheffield, 80 m. ; Newark, 17½

m.; Lincoln, 33½ m.; Leicester, 27¼ m.; Birmingham, 58¼ m.; Peterborough, 52 m.; Grantham, 23 m.; Boston, 55 m.
NUTHALL, 83.
NUTHALL TEMPLE, 83.

O.

OADBY, 108.
OAKAMOOR, 209.
OAKEDGE, 181.
OAKENGATES, 142.
OAKHAM, 119
OAKLEY, 172.
OAKS, 127.
OCKBROOK, 65.
OCKER HILL, 143.
ODIN MINE, 56.
OGLEY HAY, 159.
OGSTON HALL, 21.
OKEOVER HALL, 200.
OKER HILL, 30.
OLDBURY, 142.
OLD DALBY, 119.
OLD HARDWICK HALL, 90.
OLD JOHN HILL, 128.
OLD SHELTON HALL, 190.

OLLERTON, 100.
   Inn: *Hop Pole*.
   Pop. 1 690.
ONE ASH GRANGE, 200.
ORDSALL, 102.
ORSTON, 80.
OSBERTON, 98.
OSCOTT, 144.
OSMASTON HALL, 4.
OSSINGTON, 101.
OULTON, 186.
OVER HADDON, 43.
OVER SEAL, 123.
OVER STONNALL, 159.
OVERTON HALL, 21.
OXTON, 75.
OWTHORPE, 80.

P.

PACKINGTON HALL, 180.
PADLEY, 60.
PALTERTON, 24.
PAPPLEWICK HALL, 87.
PARCELLY HAY BARROW, 32.
PARK HILL, 205.
PARLIAMENT OAK, 95.
PARSON'S TOR, 43.
PARWICH, 200.
PATSHULL, 142.
PATTINGHAM, 142.

PEAK, THE, 57.
PEAK CASTLE, 53.
PEAK CAVERN, 54.
PEAK FOREST, 50. 52.
PELSALL, 158.
PENDERFORD, 143.
PENKRIDGE, 147.
PENNOCRUCIUM, 146.
PERLETHORPE, 100.
PERRY BARR, 144.
PERRYFOOT, 52.
PERRY HALL, 144.
PERSHALL PARK, 150.
PEWIT POOL, 183.
Physical Features, [1].
PICKERING TORS, 203.
PIKE POOL, 204.
PIKE ROCK, 204.
PILATON HALL, 147.
PILGRIM'S OAK, 83.
PILSLEY, 62.
PINXTON, 15.
PIPE GATE, 216.
PIPE RIDWARE, 177.
PLEASLEY, 16, 88.
PLUMTREE, 119.
POOLE'S CAVERN, 49.
PORTOBELLO TOWER, 145.
PORTWAY, 171.
POTTER'S HILL, 78.
Pottery, [24].
POTTERY DISTRICT, 191, 192.
PRESTWOLD, 133.
PRESTWOOD, 153.

PRIESTFIELD JUNCTION, 138.
PRINCE'S END, 143.
PULPIT ROCK, 61.
PYE BRIDGE, 15.
PYE HILL, 15.

Q.

QUARNFORD, 212.
QUEEN'S LOW, 182.
QUENBY HALL, 120.
QUENIBOROUGH, 117.
QUORNDON, 132.

R.

RADBOURNE, 4.
RADCLIFFE, 78.
RADFORD (NOTTINGHAM), 83.
RADFORD (WORKSOP), 98.
RADMORE, 181.
RAGDALE, 117.
RAINWORTH, 94.
RANSKILL, 103.
RANTON ABBEY, 182.
RATBY, 121, 128.
RATCLIFFE-ON-SOAR, 134.
RATCLIFFE-ON-THE-WREAK, 117.
REARSBY, 117.
REDMILE, 121.
REDMIRES, 60.
RENISHAW, 24.
REPTON, 2.
RESERVOIRS AT GLOSSOP, 63.

RETFORD, 102.
  Inn: *White Hart*, in East Retford.
REYNARD'S HALL, 203.
RIBER CASTLE, 30.
Richard III., 115, 116.
RIDDINGS, 15.
RIDGEWAY, THE, 60.
RIDWARES, THE, 177.
RILEY STONES, 61.

RIPLEY, 17.
  Pop.: 10,111.
RISLEY HALL, 14.
RIVELIN RIVER, 58.
ROACHES, THE, 212.
Robin Hood, [30].
ROBIN HOOD'S BUTTS, 171.
ROBIN HOOD'S CAVE, 58, 87.
ROBIN HOOD'S CHAIR, 87.
ROBIN HOOD'S HILL, 87.
ROBIN HOOD'S INN, 94.
ROBIN HOOD'S LARDER, 96.
ROBIN HOOD'S STRIDE, 32.
ROCESTER, 206.
ROCESTER JUNCTION, 197, 206.
ROCHE ABBEY, 105.
ROECLIFFE HALL, 131.
ROGER RAIN'S HOUSE, 55.
ROLLESTON HALL, 196.
ROLLESTON JUNCTION, 75, 92.
ROOSDYCH, 51.
ROTHERBY, 117.
ROTHLEY, 131.
ROTHLEY TEMPLE, 131.
ROUNDOAK, 155.
ROWLEY, 153.

ROWSLEY, 31.
  Inn: *Peacock*.
  Omnibuses to Haddon and Chatsworth.
ROWTHORN, 24.
ROWTOR ROCKS, 31.
ROYAL COTTAGE, 213.
RUDDINGTON, 67.

RUDYARD, 213.
  Inn: *Rudyard*; Station.
RUDYARD HALL, 213.
RUDYARD LAKE, 213.
RUFFORD ABBEY, 99.

RUGELEY, 177, 181.
  Inn: *Shrewsbury Arms*.
  Pop.: 4447.

RUMOUR HILL, 176.
Runic Cross, 62.
RUSHALL, 158.
RUSHTON SPENCER, 213.
RUSHTONS, THE, 213.
RUSHUP EDGE, 52.

S.

SADDINGTON, 108.
SALTBY HEATH, 120.
SALT CELLAR, 58.
SANDIACRE, 14.

SANDON, 185.
  Inn: *Dog and Doublet*.
SANDWELL PARK, 137.
SANDYBROOK, 200.
SAWLEY, 66.
SAXBY, 119.
SAXONDALE, 79.
SAXON LOW, 186.
SCALFORD, 120.
SCARCLIFFE, 91.
SCARTHIN NICK, 27.
SCREVETON, 80.
SCROOBY, 103.
SCROPTON, 195.
SEAL EDGE, 57.
SEDGBROOK, 82.
SEDGLEY, 143.
SEIGHFORD, 149.
SEISDON, 157.
SELSTON, 15.
SERLBY HALL, 103.
SHACKERSTON, 116.
SHARDLOW HALL, 66.
SHARESHILL, 146.
SHARP LOW, 199.
SHEEN, 205.
SHEEPBRIDGE, 25.
SHEEPSHEAD, 133.
SHELFORD, 79.
SHELTON, 190.

SHENSTONE, 168.
SHENTON HALL, 115.
SHERIFF HALES, 147.
SHERWOOD FOREST, 87.
SHIFFNAL, 142.
SHIPLEY GATE, 14.
SHIPLEY HILL, 117.
SHIREBROOK, 24, 96.
SHIREOAKS, 98.
SHIRLAND, 21.
SHIVERING MOUNTAIN, 56.
Shrewsbury, Countess of, "*Bess of Hardwicke*," 89, 91.
SHOTTLE, 17.
SHUGBOROUGH, 182.
SHYNING CLIFF, 26.
SIBTHORP, 80.
SILEBY, 130.
SILVERDALE, 216.
SIMMONDLY, 63.
SIR WILLIAM HILL, 61.
Skeleton Tours, [36].
SMALLTHORNE, 214.
SMETHWICK, 135.
SMETHWICK JUNCTION, 135.
Smite River, [7].
SNAKE INN, 58.
SNEINTON HERMITAGE, 70.
SNELSTON, 197.
SNOW HILL, 134.
SOHO, 134, 142.
SOMERSALL, 194.
SOOKHOLME, 96.
SOUTH MUSKHAM, 101.
SOUTH SCARLE, 78.

SOUTHWELL, 92; THE MINSTER, 93.
  Inn: *Saracen's Head*.
SOUTH WINGFIELD, 20.
SPARROW PIT, 52.
SPEEDWELL CAVERN, 55.
SPINK HILL, 24.
SPONDON, 64.
SPON LANE, 142.
SPREAD EAGLE, 146.
STADDON MOOR, 50.

STAFFORD, 147.
  Inns: *North Western H.*; *Swan*.
  Pop.: 20,895.
  Distances: London, 132 m.; Birmingham, 29 m.; Crewe, 24½ m.; Derby, 39 m.;

Lichfield, 16 m.; Manchester, 56 m.; Shrewsbury, 29 m.; Tamworth, 23 m.
STAFFORD CASTLE, 149.
STANAGE EDGE, 58.
STANCLIFFE HALL, 30.
STANDON BRIDGE, 151.
STANFORD PARK, 133.
STANTON, 197.
STANTON-BY-BRIDGE, 11.
STANTON GATE, 14.
STANTON-IN-THE-PEAK, 31.
STANTON MOOR, 31.
STAPENHILL, 124.
STAPLEFORD, 14.
STAPLEFORD HALL, 119.
STATFOLD, 171.
STATHERN, 121.
STAUNTON, 80.
STAUNTON HAROLD, 12.
STAVELEY, 24.
STEETLEY, 25.
Stephenson, George, 23.
STEWPONEY, 153.
Stocking-trade, [23].
STOKE GOLDING, 114.

STOKE-ON-TRENT, 191.
Inn: *North Staffordshire H.* (first class).
Pop.: 30,458.

STONE, 186.
Inn: *Crown*.
Pop.: 5680.
STONEFIELD, 186.
STONEY MIDDLETON, 62.
STONNIS, 27.

STOURBRIDGE, 152.
Inn: *Talbot*.
Pop.: 9800.
STOURTON CASTLE, 153.
STOUR VALLEY LINE, 142.
STOWE, 184.
STRAIT, THE, 20].
STRAMSHALL, 194.
STRETTON (BREWOOD), 146.
STRETTON (BURTON), 196.
STRETTON (DERBY), 21.
STRINES, 51.
SUDBURY, 194.
SUGARLOAF, 151.
SUGNALL HALL, 150.
SUMMIT BRIDGE, 136.
SURLSLOW, 52.

SUTTON, 103.
SUTTON CHENEY, 115.
SUTTON IN ASHFIELD, 87.
SWANNINGTON, 122.
SWAN VILLAGE, 137.
SWARKESTONE, 10.
Swift River, [9].
SWINFEN HALL, 168.
SWITHLAND, 131.
SWYNNERTON, 151.
SWYTHAMLEY, 212.
SYSTON, 116, 130.

T.

TADDINGTON, 44.
TALKE, 188.

TAMWORTH, 169.
Inn: *Castle H.*
Pop.: 7271.
Distances: Birmingham, 17¼ m.; Burton-on-Trent, 13 m.; Lichfield, 7 m.; Stafford, 23 m.; Rugby, 27 m.
TAPTON HOUSE, 23.
TATENHILL, 173.
TAXAL, 50.
TEDDESLEY PARK, 147.
TETTENHALL, 141.
TEVERSALL, 16, 89.

THORESBY PARK, 100.
Stats.: Worksop and Mansfield, G. C. Rly.
Conveyances can be obtained at the Hotels.
THOROTON, 80.

THORPE, 199.
Inns: *Peveril of the Peak H.*; *Dovedale H.*; *Dog and Partridge*.

THORPE ARNOLD, 119.
THORPE CLOUD, 199.
THORPE CONSTANTINE, 171.
THORPE LANGTON, 107.
THOR'S CAVE, 202.
THROWLEY HALL, 202.
THRUMPTON HALL, 66.
THURCASTON, 130.
THURGARTON, 75.
THURMASTON, 130.
THURNBY, 120.
TINSHELF, 16.
TICKHILL, 105.
TICKNALL, 13.

TIDESWELL, 45.
Inn: *George*.
TILTON, 119.
TIPTON, 143.
TISSINGTON, 199.
TISSINGTON SPIRES, 203.
TITTENSOR HEATH, 186.
TIVIDALE, 142.
TIXALL, 182.
TOADHOLES, 31.
TONGE, 12.
TONGUE END, 45.
TOTLEY, 25.
TOTLEY MOOR, 52.
TRENT COLLEGE, 13.
TRENTHAM, 187.

TRENTHAM HALL, 187.
Inn: *Trentham H.*
Admission: The park open to the public. The gardens, a small fee charged, which is devoted to local charities.
TRENT JUNCTION, 13 66.
Trent River, [16].
TROWELL, 14.
TRYSULL, 157.

TUNSTALL, 189.
Inn: *Sneyd Arms*.
Pop.: 19,492.
TUNSTALL HALL, 140, 151.
TUNSTEAD, 51.
TUR LANGTON, 107.
TURNER'S HILL, 153.
TURNHURST, 189.

TUTBURY, 195.
Inn: *Castle*.

TUXFORD, 102.
Inns: *Newcastle Arms;
The Hotel.*
TWELVE APOSTLES, 20].
TWYFORD, 120.

U.

ULLESTHORPE, 129.
ULVERSCROFT PRIORY, 127.
UNSTON, 25.
UPPER ARLEY, 154.
UPPER BROUGHTON, 119.
UPPER HULME, 212.
UPPER TEAN, 210.
UPTON, 92.

UTTOXETER, 193.
Inn: *White Hart.*
Pop.: 5133.

V.

VAUXHALL, 143.
VENNONS, 129.
VERNOMETUM, 79.
Vernon Sir John, " King of the Peak," 33.
VIA GELLIA, 29.

W.

WAKELIN, 196.
WALL, 168.

WALSALL, 158.
Inns: *George H.; Stork H.*
Pop.: 86,430.
Distances: Birmingham, 8 m.; Wolverhampton,

6 m.; Lichfield, 11 m.; Dudley, 6¼ m.; Willenhall, 3 m.
WALTHAM ON THE WOLDS, 120.
WALTON, 172.
WANLIP, 130.
WARSOP, 96.
WARTNABY HALL, 117.
WATER SWALLOWS, 49.
WATLING STREET, [34], 159.
WEAVER HILLS, 212.
Wedgwood Pottery, 190.

WEDNESBURY, 137, 157.
Inns: *Anchor H.; White Horse H.*
Pop.: 26,554.
WEDNESFIELD, 145.
WEEFORD, 171.
WEEPING CROSS, 182.

WELBECK ABBEY, 96.
Stats.: Elmton and Creswell (2¼ m.), also Mansfield and Worksop, G. C. Rly.
Conveyances to be obtained at the Hotels.
Admission: A fee of 1s. is charged to visitors, the proceeds are divided by the noble owner amongst Hospitals and other charities.
WELL DRESSING, 199.
WELLINGTON, 142.
WELLOW, 99.

WEST BROMWICH, 136.
Inn: *Dartmouth H.*
Pop.: 65,175.
WEST HALLAM, 64.
WESTHOUSES, 16.
WEST LEAKE, 133.
WEST MARKHAM, 102.
WESTON, 184.
WESTON-ON-TRENT, 13.
WESTON PARK, 142.
WEST RETFORD, 102.
WESTWOOD HALL, 211.
WESTWOOD MANOR, 210.
WETLEY, 210.
WETTON BRIDGE, 202.
WHALEY BRIDGE, 50, 52.

WHATSTANDWELL, 26.
Inn: *Bull's Head* (Crich).
WHATTON, 80.
WHESTON, 46.
WHISSENDINE, 119.

WHITFIELD, 63.
WHITMORE, 151.
WHITTINGTON HEATH, 167, 180.
WHITTINGTON JUNCTION, 24.
WHITWELL, 25.
WHITWICK, 125.
WICHNOR, 172.
WIDMERPOOL, 119, 134.
WIGGINGTON, 171.
WIGSTON JUNCTION, 108.
WIGWELL GRANGE, 26.
WILD CAT TOR, 27.
WILFORD, 67.
WILLENHALL, 145.
WILLERSLEY, 27.
WILLINGTON, 2, 196.
WILLINGSWORTH HALL, 137.
WILLOUGHBY-ON-THE-WOLDS, 119.
WILNE, 66.
WINDY GAP, 50.
WINGERWORTH HALL, 22.
WINGFIELD, 20.
WINGFIELD MANOR, 20.
WIN HILL, 53, 57.
WINNATS, 53.

WINSTER, 31.
Inns: *Angel; Crown.*
Hydropathic Institution: Bank House.
WINTHORPE HALL, 78.

WIRKSWORTH, 18.
Inns: *George; Red Lion.*
Pop.:, 3807.
WISTOW, 108.
WITHCOT HALL, 120.
WOLF'S COTE, 203.
WOLLATON, 74.
WOLLATON HALL, 73.
WOLSELEY HALL, 181.
Wolsey, Cardinal, 113.
WOLSTANTON, 190.

WOLVERHAMPTON, 138.
Inns: *Star and Garter H.; Victoria H.; Swan and Peacock H.; Coach and Horses.*
Pop.: 94,187.
Railways: L. and N.-W. Rly., and Midland Rly. High Level Stat.; G. W. Rly. Low Level Stat.
Distances: Birmingham, 13 m.; Shrewsbury, 29¼ m.;

Stafford, 16 m.; London, 125 m.; Dudley, 6 m.; Worcester, 32 m.; Oxford, 79 m.; Kidderminster, 17 m.; Crewe, 41 m.; Wellington, 19 m.
WOMBOURNE, 157.
WOODBOROUGH, 75.
WOODEND, 16.
WOOD GREEN, 145.
WOODHEAD RESERVOIR, 63.
WOODHOUSE, 131.
WOODHOUSE EAVES, 131.
WOODHOUSE JUNCTION, 25.
WOODLANDS, 58.

WOOTTON HALL, 197.
WOOTTON PARK, 197.
WORKSOP, 98.
  Inn: *Lion H.*
  Pop.: 16,112.
WORKSOP MANOR, 97.
WORMHILL, 49.
WORTHINGTON, 12.
WREN'S NEST, THE, 157.
WROTTESLEY HALL, 141.
WYMESWOLD, 133.
WYMONDHAM, 119.
WYRLEY, 176.
WYSALL, 133.

Y.

YOULGREAVE, 32.
  Inn: *Bull's Head.*
YOXALL, 178.

www.ingramcontent.com/pod-product-compliance
Lightning Source LLC
Chambersburg PA
CBHW032046230426
43672CB00009B/1486